Computer-Assisted Career
Decision Making
The Guide in the Machine

Computer-Assisted Career Decision Making
The Guide in the Machine

Martin R. Katz
Educational Testing Service

LEA LAWRENCE ERLBAUM ASSOCIATES, PUBLISHERS
1993   Hillsdale, New Jersey   Hove and London

Lawrence Erlbaum Associates, Inc., Publishers
365 Broadway
Hillsdale, New Jersey 07642

Library of Congress Cataloging-in-Publication Data:

  Katz, Martin R.
    Computer-assisted career decision making: the guide in the machine
  / by Martin R. Katz.
      p.   cm.
    Includes bibliographical references and index.
    ISBN 0-8058-1262-8 (cloth)   ISBN 0-8058-1328-4 (paper)
    1. SIGI PLUS.   2. Vocational guidance--Computer programs.
  3. Vocational guidance.   I. Title.
  HF5381.K369 1992
  331.7'02'02854 – dc20   92-13749
                                                                     CIP

Printed in the United States of America
10 9 8 7 6 5 4 3 2 1

This book is dedicated to the band of colleagues and friends who worked with me for varying periods over the last 25 years in the Guidance Research Group at ETS—and particularly to Lila Norris and Laurence Shatkin, who carry on research and development in guidance and continue to uphold the standards and spirit of that group.

Contents

INTRODUCTION

When a man knows he is to be hanged in a fortnight, it concentrates his mind wonderfully.

— Samuel Johnson

Dr. Johnson's apothegm implies that a compression of time future – a literal deadline – forecloses freedom to dream and speculate on boundless possibilities in this life. It forces focus on immediate decisions, ranging perhaps from disposition of belongings and the menu for a final dinner to matters of eschatology. Decisions about a career are not among these topics. The necessary conditions for career decision making include a sense of freedom and of future.

Freedom to make career decisions, however, is not an unmixed blessing. Career decisions shape lives. They offer prospects of satisfaction and success; but on the horizon with these bright prospects loom risks of unhappiness and failure. Freedom entails responsibility for making career decisions and for dealing with the consequences. Despite the importance of these decisions, people often feel a lack of competence in career decision making and do not know how to concentrate their minds on them.

This book, completed at the gateway to the 1990s, is about career decision making, career guidance, a computerized system of career guidance, and the interplay among them.

Career decision making (CDM) describes the way people sort themselves, or are sorted, into educational and occupational options. The options represent the content of CDM, and the sorting represents the process. The sequence of decisions may extend over a lifetime, but several crucial choice-points tend to occur at predictable stages in a career.

Career guidance is a professional intervention in CDM. "Professional" implies that practitioners hew to a standard of ethics, knowledge, and competence beyond what may be offered by other intervenors. Guidance is partly an art, but it is also partly a science—at least an application of science, based on a synthesis of logic and evidence derived from research.

The computerized *System of Interactive Guidance and Information* (SIGI™) is a designated guidance "treatment," clearly defined and specified. It was developed according to an explicit model, derived from a particular rationale for guidance. It uses modern technology to amplify the practice of career guidance. At this writing, the current version called SIGI PLUS™[1] is being used at more than 1,000 colleges and universities, as well as at secondary schools, libraries, corporations, community-based organizations, and counseling agencies in the United States. It has also been adapted for use in Australia by the Australian Council for Educational Research.

FROM THEORY TO PRACTICE – AND BACK

These three interdependent topics are treated in a progression: from a theory of CDM to a rationale and a model for guidance to the design and development of a system. But direction can be reversed, as practice contributes to theory. Major decisions in the development of a system require adjudication between competing principles and propositions. Explaining how such issues are resolved invokes research and evokes theory. So this book weaves together theory (principles, propositions, rationales, models), research, and development. The product of that development, SIGI, helps to define theory, to exemplify it, and also to test it. This is in keeping with C. S. Peirce's dictum that the meaning of a concept is nothing more than the observable actions and consequences that flow from it.

Developing a computerized career guidance system is different in many respects from playing the lead in a hanging. But there is a similarity in the extent to which it "concentrates the mind." A computer program requires clear and explicit instructions. It provides little tolerance for vagueness or waffling. Developers should know where they are coming from—what theory and rationale their system is based on—and must know where they are going; that is, the treatment represented by the system must be specified.

---

[1]SIGI and SIGI PLUS are trademarks of Educational Testing Service, registered in the United States and many other countries.

Theories of CDM and guidance are usually offered as a basis for practice by human counselors; but the reflection of such theories in practice is often blurred. Counselors who espouse different theoretical frameworks (ranging perhaps from "behaviorist" to "existential") sometimes behave in similar ways, while practitioners who profess allegiance to the same school of thought may vary in what they do. Indeed, a counselor may be inconsistent from one occasion to another. Thus, the actual "treatment" in a private dyadic context is hard to observe and classify, and counselors are seldom held to account for their theories and rationales.

A computerized system, on the other hand, is more visible and easier to hold accountable; it is a more *public* treatment. "Public" does not imply lack of privacy for individual users. Rather it signifies that the treatment is explicitly specified, is open to examination, is consistent across occasions, and is available for use by large numbers of people. Although the system is responsive to individual differences, the distinctive responses emerge from a constant content and structure. "System" itself implies coherent and integrated functions, an orderly attempt to accomplish specified purposes. These purposes, content, structures, functions, and all their components are accessible to scrutiny. They objectify and operation ally define the treatment to which outcomes may be related. Reaching many more people than any counselor, computerized systems are capable of widespread help or harm and should be held to the highest standards of accountability. The decisions that go into developing a particular public treatment (and the products of those decisions), therefore, provide a clear field and focus for observation, evaluation, and research, and consequently for the examination of theoretical issues in CDM and guidance.

More specifically, because SIGI/SIGI PLUS has been providing career guidance to millions of people, it should not be regarded as a black box. To open it to public scrutiny, this book first places it in the context of CDM and guidance and then discusses its derivation, development, and evaluation. It treats such questions as: What kinds of career decisions do people make? Why do they need help? What stakes are held by other players in CDM, such as government, educational institutions, and corporations? What rationales underlie different approaches to guidance? How can one adjudicate between them? What principles have governed the development and revisions of SIGI/SIGI PLUS? What reasoning and evidence support its design and content? What does it accomplish?

GODS AND GUIDES

This emphasis on openness of a computerized system may run counter to widely held stereotypes of computers as working in obscure and perhaps magical ways. In classical drama, problems were often solved by a god transported to the stage by a machine – hence the term *deus ex machina* (the god from the machine). Over the centuries, the term came to refer more broadly to external interventions in problem solving. When machines (i.e., computers) came into use about 1970 for career guidance and planning systems, they tended to evoke the notion of a *deus ex machina:* the expectation in the popular mind that some superhuman element in the mechanism would, in its omniscience, provide correct answers to all career decision-making problems.

At that time, computers were known to have solved other difficult "guidance" problems; for example, travel in space required fast and accurate computerized "guidance systems." Of course, guidance in this sense referred to solving problems in navigation to a destination that had already been chosen. In career guidance, the choice of the destination (out of the many options available) must precede setting a course to reach it. Still, it is not surprising that people expected the computer to reveal the "right choice." This expectation was consistent with the trait-and-factor theory and practices that had dominated guidance at least into the 1950s. Such theory and practices emerged in the context of a Newtonian world view, in which everything is considered ultimately predictable if only one has data enough and knows how to process them. The notion that career trajectories may more closely resemble "chaotic" phenomena (Gleick, 1987), and may be as unpredictable as long-term weather patterns, economic cycles, and other "turbulent" systems, had not occurred to members of the guidance profession or to their clients.

Many people who come to use a computerized career guidance system, therefore, anticipate that it will tell them what occupation they should enter and how they should enter it. Although similar blind faith in other manifestations of the godhead (e.g., astrology, phrenology, counselors, tests) has been debunked for most people, the computer is generally perceived as more powerful and comprehensive than such preceding objects of faith. Indeed, reputable practitioners of counseling and testing have often emphasized the limits on the help they can offer in CDM. They can provide useful information and other assistance but insist that they cannot (and should not) determine "the right choice" of an occupation. While these disclaimers have not registered in the minds of all prospective clients (and even astrology, discredited as it has been, still retains its believers), most people are quite willing to accept the fallibility of counselors and test scores as determinants of "the right choice." But computers are held in greater awe. They are seen to have solved extraordinarily complex and otherwise intractable problems – from moon landings to medical diagnoses. So why not career decisions? Cannot the god in the machine, having wrought so many other wonders, tell each person the right thing to do?

But of course there is no such god in the machine. Instead, there may be a "guide" in the machine (never, Latinists, to be called *dux in machina*). That is, developers with uncommon expertise in career guidance may have put some of their knowledge and wisdom into the machine in the form of data bases, structures, and scripts, with which the client can interact. Thus, computerized career guidance systems typically contain a great deal of information; some of it meets high standards of accuracy and currency. Also visible in the systems are coherent structures–ways of organizing, expressing, and retrieving information, sometimes quite usefully. There are also, occasionally, ideas in them–the authors' ideas about the CDM process and about ways of developing users' competence in CDM; these ideas are manifested in scripts or scenarios that engage users in a dialogue and guide them through the complexities of data bases, structures, re-trievals, printouts, and interactions with the system. In the best systems, users are helped not only to *make* career decisions but also to learn a *process* of informed and rational CDM by engaging in it: They progress from novices to initiates to masters of the system–and of the process; that is, they gain competence in CDM.

Underlying the data bases, structures, and scripts are theories of CDM, rationales for guidance, and models for system development. CDM can be said to exist only when some variety of options is available, and individuals are free to make choices. (A primitive society, in which there is little or no differentiation of occupations for individuals, or a society in which there is no mobility–for example, where people are restricted to the occupations of their parents–does not bring CDM into play.) So the study of CDM comprises both social and psychological events, involving a transaction between the individual and the environment. It includes both content and process. Content–the timing of choice-points and the options available at each point–raises questions of social arrangements and contexts. Pro-cess–the way in which each person arrives at a decision–raises questions of individual competence in taking responsibility, in acquiring information, and in exercising reason. Career guidance–a professional intervention in the process–deals with effective ways of enhancing such competence.

CHAPTERS OF THE BOOK

Six major chapters follow this introduction. The first chapter starts by analyzing career decision making, with initial emphasis on context and content, plus some introductory attention to process. Useful concepts, issues, and definitions are introduced, along with some brief historical background. The content of CDM is seen to vary from one occasion to another in a person's career (while much remains constant in the process of CDM). At certain times, our society requires or expects people to make specific choices for immediate action and encourages them to make tentative choices for the more distant future. The options are embedded in such contexts as work, occupations, jobs, positions, education, and training (each of which is defined). Unaided, most people tend to make these decisions unaware of many of the options available, with a paucity of information (or with misinformation) about the options they do perceive, with little sense of the interactions between immediate and long-range decisions, with inchoate knowledge of themselves, and with scant or erroneous notions of how to relate knowledge of themselves to information about options. These conditions – the discrepancy between people's actual state of knowledge or wisdom and the necessary or desirable state for competence in decision making – imply a need for help in CDM. That is where guidance comes in.

The second chapter deals more extensively with the needs for guidance. It spells out the common and distinctive needs of different groups of clients (students and the general adult population). It also considers the needs of other parties to CDM. For example, national needs may to some extent overlap with individual needs but may often be a source of conflict and tension; thus, an important comparison is made between manpower models and guidance models of CDM. A resolution of this conflict emphasizes common themes in the processes by which national policy decisions in a democracy and individual decisions in a guidance model are ideally made. The needs of colleges are also analyzed. Fragmented by the centrifugal forces of increased specialization, colleges can find in a coherent guidance model not only satisfaction of certain pragmatic needs but also unifying principles that complement and support the liberal arts in providing a centripetal force. Attention is also given to the needs of corporations. Finally, an analysis of the needs of guidance system developers summarizes common concerns and describes distinctions between various systems, while providing some unique historical notes on system development.

Turning more explicitly to the process of CDM, the third chapter examines rationales and models of career guidance. It describes those underlying SIGI and compares them with counter propositions represented in three other approaches to guidance.

The fourth chapter focuses in some detail on four major functions in guidance generally and in SIGI and SIGI PLUS particularly: self-appraisal, structured search for occupations and direct access to occupational information, closure on choice of an occupation, and planning for action. It analyzes the issues involved in each function, summarizes and interprets relevant research, explains in some particularity the decisions that went into the design of SIGI, and explicitly counters arguments for alternatives. Topics include the domains of self-understanding, the dimensions of values, the structure of interests, the role of aptitudes and chances of success, the structure of skills, the accuracy and currency of occupational information, a strategy for decision making, and translating decisions into actions. This chapter invokes theory and feeds back into theory, as the particular "concentrates the mind" on the general.

The fifth chapter, on evaluation of guidance, describes the dilemma of wanting to ask big questions ("the fool's question") that cannot be answered and settling for answers to small questions that are not worth asking. It attempts to resolve the dilemma in terms of three major facets of validity: strength, accuracy, and efficacy. The use of these three facets is illustrated by application to the evaluations of SIGI and SIGI PLUS. Special attention is given to the criterion problem in defining evidence related to efficacy.

As for the concluding chapter, it somehow seems inappropriate to talk about conclusions in the introduction. Samuel Johnson said, "There are two things which I am confident I can do very well: One is an introduction to any literary work stating what it is to contain, and how it should be executed in the most perfect manner; the other is a conclusion, showing from various causes why the execution has not been equal to what the author promised to himself and to the public." But such a dismal view of a conclusion might make it preferable to close with the introduction. So perhaps, as I. A. Richards (1968) suggested in his essay on "The Secret of 'Feedforward,' " the beginning will become the end. But that remains to be seen.

★   ★   ★

PERSONAL NOTE

A person who develops a career guidance system and writes about it is not, on that account, likely to be *hanged*—not, at least, if the system proves successful. But it also concentrates the mind to know that one's work is to be *hung*, like an artist's painting, for close scrutiny and possible criticism. When artists, authors, and other developers are "wrapped up" in their work, it is not just the work that is hung; it is some element of themselves, their persona, their ego, that is on display. No matter how objective they may try to appear, no one is fooled. They are "involved." Some may question whether such persons can avoid partiality.

But there is no reason for a pretense of complete objectivity. Usually, knowledge of any field is highly correlated with activity in it. Most people competent to write about career guidance have been engaged in specific career guidance activities. Having chosen and shaped their particular projects rather than some others, they are not expected to be perfectly impartial. As long as they acknowledge their own involvement and support their judgments with evidence and logic in the open marketplace of ideas, there is no reason to fault them. They need not apologize for knowing the field "from the inside." Their knowledge as avowed participant observers is likely to be more intensive and penetrating than that of "outside" observers—a good trade-off for more superficial, albeit less overtly partial, knowledge.

So I write openly as a person who is involved in the work, not distanced from it. In keeping with this commitment to openness, I generally avoid impersonal and passive dictions and speak unabashedly in my own voice.

Martin R. Katz

1

Career Decision Making

Blessed is he who has found his work; let him ask no other blessedness. He has a work, a life-purpose; he has found it, and will follow it.

— Carlyle *(Past and Present)*

Work is the curse of the drinking classes.

— Anonymous

In the annals of humankind, work has been variously described as blessing and as curse, ego involving and ego denying, fulfilling and frustrating. It first appears as a curse in the expulsion from Eden: "In the sweat of thy face shalt thou eat bread." In our own time, it has been viewed, on the one hand, as a major source of gratification of psychosocial needs, implementing self-concepts and providing an abundance of rewards and satisfactions, and, on the other hand, as a source of alienation—monotonous, dreary, and demeaning—and sometimes of stress and consequent illness.

In any case, within our culture it has been widely assumed that work, for better or for worse, plays a crucial part in the passage from adolescence to adulthood. Indeed, adolescence itself may be regarded as a modern invention, dating to delayed entry of youth into the labor market. Typically, the adolescent's role is seen to be mainly that of student. Work is incidental to this role. Adults, however, are often likely to be identified by the *kind* of work they do (i.e., their *occupation*). Adolescents are instructed in this sign of passage when they are confronted with that awkward favorite of adults' conversational gambits: "What are you going to be?" Being, in this context, always refers to occupation. Any other response is nothingness. A

1

large part of the life space of many adults is taken up by occupation. Lynd and Lynd (1937) called occupation "the most nearly dominant single influence in a man's life" (presumably, had they been writing more recently they would have included women) and "the watershed down which the rest of one's life tends to flow."

The shift in terminology here from "work" to "occupation" is no accident. Work–regardless of occupation–usually provides the basic means for livelihood and consumes the largest portion of one's waking hours. It can be distinguished only from leisure and other forms of nonwork. Occupations represent the different kinds of work. The fourth edition of the *Dictionary of Occupational Titles* (DOT) and its *Supplement* (United States Department of Labor, 1977, 1986) define thousands of occupations. These occupations can be characterized and classified in many ways–according to kinds of activity, entry requirements, wage or salary levels, working conditions and environments, opportunities for various satisfactions, and the like. This differentiation of work into occupations exercises a major influence on the lifestyles of many adults–involving such elements of identity as socioeconomic status, self-esteem, network of friends and acquaintances, place of residence, opinions, attitudes, and so on. The influence is not one way: Some of these elements of identity affect choice of occupation.

Differences between *people* have also been characterized and classified in such terms as abilities, interests, values, skills, temperaments, amount or kind of education, sex, ethnic affiliation, socioeconomic level, and so on. These attributes seem relevant to the process by which people sort themselves or get sorted into the different occupations that are available at a given time. Selection and placement (e.g., by educational institutions and employers) are part of this process. They often impose constraints but sometimes provide special opportunities. At any rate, within the elastic bounds of these external "reality factors," individuals can generally exercise considerable freedom of choice.

Indeed, a *career* usually involves a sequence of choices, particularly visible at regular transition points imposed by the educational, legal, or economic system. But there is more to a career than choices. There is, for example, a set of outcomes for each choice. Having chosen, a person acts to gain a certain position. If rejected, he or she may loop back to another option. If accepted, he or she performs well or poorly, enjoys satisfaction or suffers discontent. The effects of such outcomes may be felt in subsequent choices. That is to say, one can learn from experience. So the notion of a sequence suggests that any single choice bears some relationship both to antecedent and to subsequent choices.

The nature of this relationship has been described as a "means–ends chain." Because people both remember and imagine, they can evaluate their past experience and anticipate their future performance and satisfaction. Each of these evaluations and anticipations represents a self-appraisal; a number of such self-appraisals may be integrated to constitute a self-concept. Self-concept is thus engaged reciprocally with career decisions: The concept of self shapes the individual's choices and is shaped by them.

COMPONENTS OF CAREER DECISION MAKING

These interactions among *options, persons, environments, processes*, and *outcomes* introduce major components of the career decision-making drama in which people act as they enter or pass through adulthood.

Options. First, there are the dilemmas, which provide the major content of career decision making (CDM) and get the plot moving. They define the domains of the decisions (what it is people decide about) and identify the options in each. A few examples: to work or not to work, to enroll in one educational program or another, to make a commitment to one occupation or another, to accept or reject a job offer, to remain in a position or apply for another.

Persons. Second, there is the protagonist, the person facing the dilemma and making the choices, who develops and entertains a certain self-concept, who obtains and processes information about options, who devises plans, takes actions, evaluates outcomes, and recycles through the whole procedure—or who drifts or flounders or withdraws. What dimensions of individual differences are relevant and how do they operate?

Environments. Third, there is the setting. The culture exercises great powers over the first two components. It may determine the nature of the choices to be made, restrict the options, govern the schedule. Different environments may grant vastly different resources to people and impose vastly different constraints on them. Events—such as war, depression, and invention—have potent effects, as do other conditions of time and place, of custom and legislation, of demography and Zeitgeist.

Processes. Fourth, there is the dramaturgy, the state of the art of decision making itself. A variety of approaches to CDM are extant. For example, there are different ways—at different levels of sophistication—of getting and processing information. In addition, an extensive apparatus for professional intervention has become a presence in the drama: Sometimes it plays a supporting role; sometimes it acts like a *deus ex machina;*

sometimes it is the *raisonneur;* sometimes it merely carries a spear; but it is almost always *there,* even if only waiting in the wings for a cue.

Outcomes. Finally, there is the denouement of all the complications of CDM. How does it come out? Does the protagonist get what he or she chooses? Does he or she live happily ever after? To the betterment or detriment of society? What are the outcomes in terms of success and satisfaction, efficiency and productivity, discontent or harmony?

This chapter focuses mainly on issues in the *content* of CDM. (Later chapters emphasize persons, environments, processes, and outcomes.) But even in this chapter the other topics are not ignored. Like the drama critic who may discuss plot, characterization, theme, setting, and so on sequentially, we know that these components have no independent existence. They are useful for critical analysis simply because it is easier to talk about one category at a time than everything at once. We recognize, however, that the components overlap and interact and also that each component comprises some diversity of elements. We cannot discuss options without taking into account decision makers, settings, information processing, and outcomes. Identifying and labeling the components does not allow us to cut CDM into separate slices that can be buttered and eaten one at a time. Rather, each slice is a different plane through a common center. Thus, there is no slice that does not contain some part of all the others: When we have finished the content of choice, we will find a bite taken out of individual differences, environments, processes (including professional interventions), and social and individual consequences.

Content of Choice: Dilemmas, Domains, and Options

What are the decisions in CDM made about? What are the options for each choice? What are the linkages between domains? A few illustrations indicate the range of the domains. There are decisions about *education:* which course or curriculum or major to elect; whether to undertake postsecondary education, graduate education, "continuing" education, nontraditional or experiential education; which school to apply to or attend; whether to return to formal education after an absence; whether to attend a school full time or part time; whether to seek an apprenticeship or other on-the-job training. There are decisions about the centrality of *work* or commitment to work: behaviorally, whether to work overtime, full time, part time, or not at all. There are decisions about volunteer activities: whether to engage in them, what kind, for how much time. There are decisions about *occupations:* which occupation to prefer, plan for, prepare for, attempt to enter, or eliminate from consideration. There are decisions about *jobs:* which organization, industries, or companies to apply to or accept an offer from. There are decisions about *positions:* to remain in a given position or apply for another.

These types of decisions are usually interconnected. Nevertheless, as perceived by the decision maker at a given time, each choice may be made discretely. It may be responsive to a pressing need or want, providing immediate relief from such pressure or early gratification of such wants. Examples: A high school student elects to take Algebra 2 because she likes algebra. A high school graduate applies for a job in a local factory because he needs the paycheck. A junior executive changes jobs to move to a better climate. In many cases, however, a longer view is in evidence: A high school student elects Algebra 2 because she wants to become an engineer, and algebra is one step in preparing for that occupation. A high school graduate applies for a local factory job because it will put him in line for a toolmaker training program in that plant. A junior executive makes a lateral move across companies because he sees a better chance to get on a fast track for promotion.

To the decision makers in the second set of instances, the longer view evokes not just discrete choices but a sense of continuity. Not only an option at one point but an entire sequence of options is being chosen. Entire scenarios are envisioned. There is an awareness of possible and probable career *paths* and *linkages* involving each successive choice in the domains of education, occupation, job, and position.

Thus, *career* must be added to the domains for decisions. One of the alternatives is to take the long view, to make choices that take into account cumulative returns over a large portion of a career. The other, the short view, focuses on an immediate payoff. It is not entirely clear to what extent this decision is consciously made or is dependent on differences in temperament. The veridicality of information is not the issue here: The *belief* that a path or linkage exists need not be verified for career to serve as a domain for decision.

Definitions

Before elaborating on the dilemmas and options in some of the domains that have been mentioned, it may be appropriate to pause for some explicit definitions. A number of terms—such as *work, career, occupation, job, position*—have been used so far in contexts that might be expected to establish their meaning inductively. Although these terms have often been used loosely and interchangeably in the literature, there is an advantage to be gained from defining them precisely and distinctively. For the most part, the glossary given here is consistent with Shartle (1952) and Super (1976). The latter is the more extensive and warrants particular attention for two reasons: First, it was preceded by an analysis of usage in five "major works" from each of seven fields of behavioral and social science – labor economics, industrial sociology and anthropology, personality and social psychology, industrial psychology, counseling psychology, school counseling, and career education. Second, a considerable degree of consensus was reached by a panel of 15 prominent career psychologists.

Work, as used here, is both more comprehensive and more primitive in meaning than the other terms. It includes what people do in positions, jobs, occupations, and careers. It denotes activities involving economic gain, the expenditure of physical or mental energy, presumably productive – that is, intended to accomplish something of value. Thus, as a noun it evokes its homonymous verb. More basic and less differentiated than the other terms, work can stand in for them collectively. It rings of atavism: It represents what the species has done for survival.

Position is used to designate the group of tasks to be performed by one person at work. Thus, the Carl S. Gode Chair of Social Psychology at Cavern University would be a position; another position would be held by the barber who ministers to the occupant of the third chair from the window at Sal's Hairstyling Salon, and another (to make clear that a chair is not the inevitable appurtenance of a position) by the sales representative who covers a certain territory for the Whitehead Brewery. Of course, one person could hold those positions successively or even (conceivably) concurrently: The number of positions would still be three.

Positions are nested within *job*, a group of similar positions in a single organization. All members of the Social Psychology faculty at Cavern would have the same job. Social psychologists at Cloud University would have another job. All the barbers at Sal's would represent one job, and all the Whitehead sales representatives another.

Jobs are nested within *occupation:* Social psychologist, barber, and sales representative (malt liquors) are occupational titles for respectively similar jobs across all organizations (and include also similar work done by people who may be unaffiliated with any organization).

"Similar" in this definition requires some sharp judgments in order to "carve at the joints." How many specialties should be identified in psychology, in wholesale sales, and so on? Various techniques have been used for clustering and differentiating occupations: It has been convenient for many people to accept the titles embodied in the fourth edition of the *Dictionary of Occupational Titles* and its *Supplement* (United States Department of Labor, 1977, 1986) as representing the universe of occupations. (But the *Dictionary*, as is explained later, has its shortcomings.)

Career, as indicated previously, represents the sequence of positions held by a person over a lifetime. It is extended, however, to include not just work but also work-related roles such as student or retiree.

DECISIONS ABOUT WORK[1]

Falstaff: Why, Hal, 'tis my vocation, Hal; 'tis no sin for a man to labor in his vocation. (*Henry IV, Part I*, I, ii)

The options for *work* are indicated by such questions as whether to work, when, how hard, how long. There are choices between work and schooling, work and leisure, work and retirement. There are also choices involving the degree of commitment to work, which indeed may underlie many of the other choices.

Mention has already been made of the spectrum of attitudes toward work–ranging from dedication to alienation. One pole is represented by "vocation," which retains its earlier religious connotation: a calling to the service of God, usually in some activity of a spiritual nature. Thus, the paradox in Falstaff's oily rationalization swings on the transition from religious to secular meaning: If man is called to his work, and the call comes from God, clearly " 'tis no sin" to heed the call (even if the vocation to which he has been called and has dedicated his talents happens to be "purse-taking"). "Vocation" prejudges the case for commitment, and it is interesting to note its diminishing use as a synonym for work or occupation. ("Vocation" survives in the name of at least one professional organization, the American Vocational Association; but another organization that was founded early in the century by humanitarian reformers imbued with egalitarian zeal and the conviction that *everyone* should seek self-fulfillment through work changed its name in 1987 from the National Vocational Guidance Association to the National Career Development Association.)

Historically, this attitude toward work as vocation appears during the Renaissance and particularly after the Reformation. Other attitudes have prevailed at various times in various cultures. As has been previously noted, *after* the beginning there was *work*. Adam's sentence to hard labor had many echoes throughout ancient times. Work was often seen as a necessary evil, as in this couplet from Pope's translation of the *Iliad:* "To labor is the lot of man below; And when Jove gave us life, he gave us woe." The Greeks of classical times saw no dignity in menial tasks. Slaves worked. Aside from soldiery, achievements deemed worthwhile by the Greeks required leisure. Their most notable contributions–in art, drama, philosophy, politics, and so forth–were the product of a leisure class supported by slave labor. The modern notion that the dramatist or philosopher or athlete works at his profession would have been incompre-

---

[1]Historical highlights here draw on earlier work (Katz, 1973).

hensible to the Greeks, whose most competent "old pros" never lost their amateur status.

In the days of the Roman republic, a folk hero was Cincinnatus, who left his plow to defend the state and then returned to the plow when victory had been won. But by the time of the Caesars, the practical Romans had managed to translate their distaste for work into a 6-hour work day, and about half the days of the year were designated as holidays.

The early Hebrews, too, as Wilensky (1964) pointed out, "conceived of work as dismal drudgery," but accepted it as "an expiation. . . . Rabbinical literature held that no labor, however lowly, is as offensive as idleness." Still, neither they nor the early Christians saw work as partaking of "vocation." The Christians came to differentiate "work" from "vocation" but did not differentiate one kind of work from another.

It was not until the Reformation that work came to be identified as a major way of serving God. Luther emphasized the equal spiritual value of all kinds of work and regarded excellence of performance as a high duty. According to Weber's (1930) famous treatise, the "Protestant Ethic" assisted in the rise of capitalism by giving powerful religious approval to hard work, worldly achievement, and high profits.

Regardless of the validity of Weber's thesis, it is clear that the prevailing attitude toward work had undergone a change (at least among intellectuals). It had taken on a connotation of religious endorsement in the spirit of the Italian proverb, "Working at your calling is half praying." The merchant, the farmer, the craftsman all served God well by doing their work well. The differentiation, then, was between successful work (work that God prospered) and unsuccessful work. Even the Industrial Revolution, which stretched so many workers on the rack of the machine, did not dampen the glorification of work. To the hard-working Carlyle, whose own energies and productivity seldom flagged, man's heroic stature was not diminished by the kind of work he did—as long as he worked: "All work," he wrote in *Past and Present*, "even cotton-spinning, is noble; work is alone noble."

Gradually there had emerged, from the concept of work as a spiritual calling, the concept of work as a secular calling. Work was extolled not just for the glory of God but for the self-fulfillment of man. Thus, Carlyle wrote the secular benediction quoted as an epigraph for this chapter; and the 19th-century social reformist, Ruskin, kept one foot on the spiritual dock as he too stepped into the secular boat: "God intends no man to live in the world without work; but it seems to me no less evident that He intends every man to be happy in his work." Thus, we see that Carlyle and Ruskin were concerned not just with success but with happiness. A similar concern for individual success, satisfaction and fulfillment, along with a similar humanitarian and reform spirit, appears in the origins of the vocational guidance movement in the United States at the turn of the century (Brewer, 1942; Parsons, 1909; Rockwell & Rothney, 1961; Stephens, 1970).

This concept of self-fulfillment in work was entirely compatible with the ambitions of achievement-oriented, upward-striving America at that time. The opportunity to rise economically, to earn a better living, helped to glorify hard work. Where barriers to economic and social mobility were relatively high, work continued to be regarded as debasing and ignominious. But the Horatio Alger ideal prevailed elsewhere. Man's worth was assessed in terms of his productivity. Of course, many failed to rise, even though they were hard working and conscientious. But the ideal of work as a means for upward mobility was substantiated often enough to remain credible and acceptable. It may be said to have formed a major tenet of the American ethic.

Furthermore, the pressures of humanitarianism and reform–to say nothing of the labor movement–began to improve the lot of the "working classes." Thus, there began to materialize in some measure the promise that hard work and productivity would be rewarded not only by a laborer's rise *through* the strata of classes, but also or alternatively by his rise *with* the laboring class. Success–or productivity–in work was expected to raise the level of economic rewards for *all* classes to the extent that all persons would feel pride of accomplishment and satisfaction.

This expectation led to the belief that satisfaction was largely a function of success; so individuals would find their greatest satisfaction in the work that they could perform most successfully. This suggested the crucial importance of *choice* of work. While all work grew increasingly acceptable, *vocation* came to mean the kind of work a person could do best.

Elsewhere (Katz, 1973), I have traced further developments and changes in prevalent attitudes toward work. Highlights reflecting the compulsion to attribute themes to decades (a form of intellectual decadence) include the yearning for security of any kind during the Depression years; the shakeup during the postwar boom, when the venturesome spirit of people who had survived the war sought–more than subsistence–work that promised high fulfillment of ambitions, enhancement of self-esteem, and satisfaction of psychosocial needs; the more noncommittal attitudes toward work that appeared among youth in the 1950s; the explosive mixtures of anger, resentment, apathy, withdrawal, and disorientation that characterized youthful attitudes toward work–and especially toward middle-class values of work–during the 1960s, when nonwork gained greater recognition as a way of life for young people. (Many children of the middle-aged middle class rejected their parents' commitment to work and began to drop out at a rate that caused alarm and bewilderment in their elders.) During the 1970s and 1980s, however, a new generation of youth (sometimes called the "me" generation) have seemed to vie for the "fast track" to high income, economic security, job advancement, and consumer power. Applying some of the tenets of capitalistic self-interest unabashedly, they are accused of being less committed to the intrinsic satisfactions and more to the extrinsic rewards of occupations. For example, fewer of them have tended to prepare for the helping professions, like health and education, and more have flocked to business schools in accordance with perceived market rewards. Thus, according to *Medical Education in the United States, 1987-1988* (1988), from 1974 to 1988 the number of people applying to medical schools decreased from 42,624 to 28,123, with the sharpest decline occurring in the middle to latter 1980s. Similarly, in 1970 to 1977, 25% of all degrees conferred were in education; in 1984-1985, this percentage was only about half that, while the percentage of degrees conferred in business, almost the mirror image of education, increased from 13% to 23% in those same years. Of the more than one million students who took the Scholastic Aptitude Test in 1989, business and commerce were, by far, the most popular intended college majors (*College Board News*, 1989).

It is interesting that by the 1980s most of the earlier dropouts of the 1960s seemed unable or unwilling to sustain their withdrawal from work. They reported, in a number of cases, that work–even work to which they felt no strong commitment–restored a balance to their lives that they were missing.

One wonders whether the total deletion of regular work from an individual's life space may not, in our culture, upset the delicate ecology of human happiness. Then such otherwise desirable elements as relaxation, leisure, and freedom become too gross and insupportable. This has been the experience often reported by retirees, whose withdrawal from work suffers from no lack of social approval. It was also evident in the responses of a national sample of employed men who were asked whether they would go on working even if they inherited enough money to live comfortably without working (Morse & Weiss, 1955): 80% said they would. Their reasons? Almost 40% gave reasons having to do with fear and uncertainty: They "would feel lost, would go crazy, wouldn't know what to do with the time." Over 30% more expressed similar concerns in more positive terms: "to keep occupied." In a more recent survey, 76% of a national sample of men 18 to 49 years old said they would continue to work even if guaranteed an adequate income without working (Harris & Associates, 1979). Still more recently (Kohut & DeStefano, 1989), in a Gallup Organization survey, 70% of a national sample of full-time workers said they "would continue to work even if they did not have to."

More generally, a review of studies on the "Meaning of Working" (MOW) in a variety of countries (MOW International Research Team, 1987) showed 65% to 95% in national labor force samples (i.e., people already working or seeking work) would continue to work even if they had enough money to live comfortably without working. Of course, the percentages vary by country and time. In the MOW study of eight countries in the 1980s, Japan represented by far the highest level of "work centrality"; Yugoslavia and Israel were moderately high; the United States and Belgium were at the average level; the Netherlands and West Germany were moderately low; and Great Britain was the lowest. The mean for Japan was about three quarters of a standard deviation higher than the mean for Britain. Although there were differences by occupation and, to a lesser extent, age and educational level (and very slight differences by gender) within each country, country accounted for about one-and-one-half times as much of the total variance as did occupation. On a "Centrality of Work Index" individuals in every country were at every score level from lowest to highest (except Japan, where no one scored at the lowest level!), but in general over the eight countries about two out of three people indicated a strong commitment to working, leaving about one out of three with a relatively weak commitment.

Relevant to this international study, the Gallup Poll survey (Kohut & DeStefano, 1989) reported that 57% of a sample of full-time workers in the United States got a "sense of identity" from their job, while 40% said their job was "just what they do for a living." (Interestingly, a sharp age difference was reported in these attitudes: Workers under 50 were less likely to get a "sense of identity" from their job, and this difference was not a function of greater job seniority or higher income of those over 50.)

Thus, there seems to be a strong attachment to work in a large majority; no other activity can replace it. (But this attachment to work does not necessarily apply to current occupation: Most of the men in the earlier study [Morse & Weiss, 1955] would have preferred to continue work in a different occupation, usually one with higher status and autonomy. In the Gallup Poll, "only 39% would continue at their current job.")

Choices remain, nevertheless, both about whether to work, especially at a given time in one's life, and about the degree of commitment to work. There are various culturally approved opportunities for nonwork, such as having a baby (substituting labor for work), going to school, taking a sabbatical, or electing early retirement. (Homemaking for one's own family used to be regarded as an alternative to work. Such homemakers are not counted in the labor force or listed in the *Dictionary of Occupational Titles* as an occupation; but to list it here as an alternative to work rather than a kind of work would court distracting controversy.) Furthermore, welfare programs and unemployment insurance have softened somewhat the raw requirement of work for survival. Nevertheless, there is no question that some young people have more options than others.

Often, nonwork is not a matter of choice. In the 1960s, 1970s and early 1980s, the level of unemployment in some segments of the adult population was high–as high as about 30% for Black teenagers. Despite recent improvements, unemployment rates for Blacks and teenagers have continued to be multiples of those for White adults. For example, Department of Labor figures show that even during the low unemployment of the first 9 months of 1988, the unemployment rate among Blacks was more than double that among Whites (11.8% to 5.4%). In addition, periodic employment has been prevalent. For example, between 1966 and 1971, among young men who were out of school, about half the Whites and two thirds of the Blacks experienced at least one spell of unemployment (Kohen, Grasso, Myers, & Shields, 1977). In these circumstances, it is obvious that many people cannot regard their work as commitment to a "vocation."

Options for degree of commitment include a region between the poles of "vocation" and nonwork. Call it *employment*. The "employed" do not live to work but work to live. Their work contributes in some way to society, they know, but the connections between work and product are not a major source of satisfaction. The rewards tend to be extrinsic. Employment fills only a small portion of the vessel of career. There are time and energy to emphasize other things–family, hobbies, leisure, avocations. This detachment from work may tend to encourage a hedonistic trade-off: Employment represents an exchange of time at work for the wherewithal to pursue intrinsically rewarding activities in the time away from work. The "employed," then, find little intrinsic satisfaction or ego involvement in their work. They are likely to adhere to Omar Khayyam's dictum to "take the cash and let the credit go." This description is confirmed by the MOW findings that individuals with high work centrality scores tend to give high weight to such intrinsic values as autonomy, variety, and responsibility and tend to put relatively low weight on pay, whereas people with low work centrality scores show the opposite pattern.

"Employment" is by no means always an involuntary status for those who have no alternative. Particularly during the late 1960s, there was a well-publicized tendency for many youths of high ability, who had attended selective colleges, who had almost unlimited options, to seek out employment that was unchallenging (e.g., Reinhold, 1971). Apparently, they felt such jobs provided the necessary remuneration (enough to buy a "stereo and wheels"), without encroaching on the nonwork identities, avocational activities, and lifestyles they cherished. "Employment," they believed, gave them more freedom to follow their "calling" than would "vocation."

This illustration is not intended to suggest that "vocation" and "employment" necessarily reflect occupational level. Although some association is inevitable, the crucial element is not the level or the actual conditions of

work but the attitude of the individual toward work: the depth of commitment to work and degree of fulfillment sought in it. This attitude may vary
across workers at any level; it may also vary in a person over time. Indeed,
the complaint is often made that there is insufficient commitment at *any*
level. This disillusionment is not philosophical but practical: "Nothing
works any more because no one cares any more." Neglect of work and lack
of commitment are seen among physicians, medical technologists and
hospital orderlies; engineers, draftsmen, and inspectors; architects,
plumbers, and laborers. But low levels of commitment seem less likely to
survive long periods of preparation for the higher level occupations. Thus,
most people who enter professional and managerial occupations are apt to
be motivated by some sense of "vocation"–an expectation of gaining
powerful intrinsic satisfactions from the work. Lower level occupations,
however, to the extent that they are composed of people unwilling to
tolerate delayed entry and earnings, are likely to contain a higher proportion of workers who seek "employment" rather than "vocation."

There are other explanations for preferring "employment" to "vocation."
Much work is so specialized or fragmented that products and outcomes of
work are invisible to the workers (O'Toole, 1973). These products and
outcomes are often regarded as trivial in any case, not really worthy of
wholehearted commitment of self. There is also the expectation that many
workers will have to change occupations, usually several times in the
course of a career, because of changes in technology, the economy, or other
forces beyond their control. Understandably, people may be unwilling to
make commitments to occupations that may vanish: They find it difficult to
maintain a sense of identification with work when the nature of the work
changes with some frequency. If they cannot possess an occupation, they
may refuse to be possessed by it. Furthermore, modest expectations of
fulfillment in work can prevent disillusion, bitterness, and alienation.

Data to substantiate one facet of this proposition can be found in a STUDY
follow-up study 5 years after high school of a panel of 2,213 males who had
entered Grade 10 in 1966 (Bachman, O'Malley, & Johnston, 1978). While
61% were "very satisfied" or "quite satisfied" with their jobs, the point
here is that job satisfaction was not related to amount of education. Two
interactive forces in the relationship appeared to counterbalance each
other. To the extent that high education led to a high-status job, satisfaction was likely to ensue. But high education was also associated with high
aspirations, which made satisfaction more difficult. Thus, for any given
level of educational attainment, a high-status job was positively related to
job satisfaction ($r = .28$). But for any given level of job status, amount of
education (or ability) showed a slight tendency to be inversely related to
job satisfaction. The size of the "mismatch" group might be expected to
increase if the ratio of highly educated people to high-status jobs increases.

In a similar way, aspiration for high satisfaction, as for high status, incurs what may be an increasing risk.

Such conjecture aside, what is the prevalence in the young adult population of inclination toward "vocation" or "employment"–of intrinsic and extrinsic work values? In the National Assessment of Educational Progress (NAEP) of 1973–1974, national samples of 17-year-olds and of young adults (ages 26–35) were asked to "list ten different things that a person should think about in choosing a job or career." ("Job" and "career" were used loosely in the NAEP exercises and often included "work" or "occupation," as defined in this chapter.) Nine out of 10 in each age group mentioned extrinsic values at least once, in the form of money, benefits, or working conditions. What appeared to be intrinsic values, classified under the rubric "Personal Satisfaction, Interest, Desires or Goals," were also mentioned at least once by 71% of the adults and 84% of the 17-year-olds (Katz, 1978a).

In interpreting these responses, frequency of a category should not be confused with importance. A category like working conditions includes many highly visible characteristics of jobs (location, hours, and so on), which generate a large number of responses. In fact, such extrinsic factors were named two or more times by 75% of the adults (and 69% of the 17-year-olds). But there was a sharp drop in the percentages of respondents listing more than one aspect of intrinsic satisfaction: Among adults, two or more such items were mentioned by 21% and three or more by only 4% (with slightly higher percentages for 17-year-olds). Some global or holistic concept of intrinsic work satisfaction, often vaguely expressed, appeared to come to mind right off the bat in response to the question; it was promptly mentioned, and that subject was exhausted. On the other hand, respondents were able to think of many specific items that had to do with extrinsic values, such as income and working conditions.

Other categories of response–even some other extrinsic values–do not seem to occur to people so readily. For example, security might be considered particularly important to many, especially during periods of high unemployment. Yet there were virtually no mentions of tenure, invulnerability to seasonal, technological or economic change, favorable outlook for demand and supply, and the like (1% of the adults and none of the 17-year-olds). But other studies have shown that, when security is included in an array of specified categories, each clearly defined, and young adults are asked to assign weights to the categories to indicate the relative importance of each one, security tends to outweigh working conditions (Chapman, Katz, Norris, & Pears, 1977; Harris & Associates, 1979; Norris & Katz, 1970; Norris, Katz, & Chapman, 1978; Quinn, Staines, & McCullough, 1974).

This theme of significant discrepancies between examined and unexamined values has been substantiated in structured interviews and simulated occupational choice (Katz, Norris, & Kirsh, 1969; Katz, Norris, & Pears, 1976, 1978). The things that pop into people's heads when they have not subjected their values to close scrutiny, but are only responding to a survey, are often less important to them than the things they emphasize when they have thoroughly explored or examined their values, as in a more systematic process of career decision making.

The point here is that both intrinsic and extrinsic values are prominent in the ways that people construe work, even though free responses pertaining to the latter are more frequent, detailed, and specific. A similar pattern of responses was evident when questions were asked in NAEP about things liked and things disliked in a current (or recent) job. Of the categories used to describe things liked, "Interpersonal Relations" was mentioned by nearly 50% of the respondents in both age groups. Responses categorized under "Good Working Conditions, Hours, Location, Fringe Benefits" were made at least once by about a third of each group, and "Good Pay" by about a fourth. All these responses seem clearly to reflect extrinsic values. Intrinsic values were not so popular: About 20% of the adults and 17% of the 17-year-olds mentioned specific duties and requirements of the job; 13% of the adults and 5% of the 17-year-olds mentioned the opportunity for independent work; 13% and 3%, respectively, indicated that the job was interesting or fun to do; and the same percentages indicated that the job provided a challenge and a sense of responsibility. (The converse of the last category, *lack* of responsibility, appealed to 4% of the adults and 11% of the 17-year-olds.) Nevertheless, the responses tallied here – plus a scattering of others grouped under such rubrics as "Job Is Worthwhile, of Help to Mankind" and "Ability to Produce a High Quality Product" – showed about two thirds of the adults mentioning *some* intrinsic value. Clearly, this is more than would be in professional or managerial occupations.

When it came to things disliked, the combined Don't Know and No Response categories accounted for about 50% of each age group. (This finding is compatible with the many studies of job satisfaction that indicate most people are satisfied with their jobs – see, e.g., Quinn et al., 1974, for a review of job satisfaction studies covering a period of 40 years.) Although there are some differences in rank order of categories between the "likes" and the "dislikes," the most frequently "disliked things" fit in the same four categories as the most frequently "liked things." Thus, similar constructs were elicited regardless of whether the question was phrased in positive or negative terms. This finding tends to contradict theories (Herzberg, Mausner, & Snyderman, 1959) that the dimensions of job satisfaction are different from the dimensions of job dissatisfaction. Instead, the dimensions along which most people evaluate their job likes and dislikes appear to be bipolar (e.g., "good pay" vs. "low pay").

Responses to the question, "Is there anything in your work that gives you a sense of satisfaction or that is particularly worthwhile about your job?" found 90% of the adults and 50% of the 17-year-olds saying yes. When asked to specify, 39% of the adults and 14% of the teenagers made at least one response that was collected under the somewhat cumbersome category, "Ability to Produce a Quality Product or Just Doing the Best He or She Can." About 22% and 11%, respectively, mentioned interpersonal relations. "Worthwhile (Societal Sense)" accounted for 18% and 6%, respectively, and "Pay" was a source of satisfaction to 10% and 13%. Here, the wording of the question obviously called for intrinsic values and, for the most part, generated some considerable expression of them, vague and inchoate though it might be. (For a fuller analysis of the NAEP data on career and occupational development, see Tiedeman, Katz, Miller-Tiedeman, & Osipow, 1978.)

A survey of a national probability sample of U.S. workers in 1969 and 1970 (Quinn et al., 1974) obtained importance ratings of 23 "job facets." Intrinsic values—such as those pertaining to interest, autonomy, and availability of resources for work—were rated very important by a substantial majority. So were such extrinsic values as pay, security, and friendly co-workers; but other extrinsic values, like convenient travel, physical surroundings, and "not being asked to do excessive amounts of work" were rated very important by only a minority. The most striking differences between white-collar and blue-collar workers' responses were in the items grouped under the factor named Financial Rewards: A majority of each group, but notably larger numbers of blue-collar workers, rated these as very important, with the difference reaching about 15 percentage points. When a national sample of men ages 18 to 49 (Harris & Associates, 1979) were asked about 27 aspects of their jobs, 79% rated "a chance to use your mind and abilities" and 70% rated "job security" as "very important." But the rank order changed when the task was to "name the four or five most important to you." Only 34% named the former and 50% the latter; "a good salary" rose from sixth to first rank, chosen by 56%. Thus, extrinsic rewards tended to get higher priorities than intrinsic when comparative judgments were made.

In short, it seems clear that both intrinsic and extrinsic values are reflected in most people's attitudes toward work. "Vocation" and "employment," while useful constructs, appear to be part of a continuum in attitudes toward work centrality that may approximate a normal distribution, with perhaps some negative skew. Thus, a plurality of young adults seek a balanced mix of intrinsic satisfactions and extrinsic rewards, while diminishing numbers incline more toward one extreme or the other, with "workaholics" and nonworkers at the tails.

Here the question must be raised as to whether attitudes toward work represented by points on this continuum are really options for choice, correlates of choice, or consequences of choices. Probably all three. But what may be unchosen and unanticipated consequences (as events prey on decisions) for some people become options as successive cohorts of decision makers perceive them as possible outcomes of decisions. For example, gender differences in attitudes toward work have long been noted. A review of research on gender roles (Lipman-Blumen & Tickamyer, 1975) indicates that women had been socialized to receive their total gratification through family roles, whereas men could seek fulfillment in both work and family roles. But these traditional roles have been changing (Lipman-Blumen, 1976; Mason, Czajka, & Arber, 1976). Thus, many female high school and college students now entertain work and occupational values that are quite similar to males', and the variance of weights assigned to each value dimension by any group (males, females, minorities, people of various ages) appears to be quite high, with virtually rectangular distributions (Norris et al., 1978; Tittle, 1981). This is not to say that exposure to the workplace has been fulfilling for all women. In a series of Roper studies, the percentage of women who preferred staying at home to working decreased from 60 in 1974 to 45 in 1985 (but rose to 51 in 1990, perhaps in response to financial pressure). To the extent that women have become liberated from traditional gender roles and have become aware of some variety of role models, they have extended their options for career choices. (See *Comparisons of Males and Females in CDM*, chapter 5, this volume.)

In other words, attitudes toward work can be chosen, either directly or indirectly. If chosen directly and consciously, as explicit work values, they may readily be seen to subsume congruent occupational and job values and thus to exercise some effect on the nature of occupations, jobs, positions, and education considered. In short, work values may govern the quality of career aspirations.

DECISIONS ABOUT OCCUPATIONS AND JOBS

Once the choice has been made to work, a propensity toward "vocation" or "employment" may shift the balance perceptibly in the relative importance of occupation and job. For those who aspire to "vocation," the choice of an occupation will be the primary concern. Choice of occupation has been the focus of a vast amount of formal study. In many respects, occupational characteristics are relatively stable, as social phenomena go. For example, the prestige or status of occupations has been perceived with remarkable consistency by many samples of respondents over a period of at least 50 years (Centers, 1949; Siegel, Hodge, & Rossi, 1974).

Of course, new occupations are born and obsolescent ones fade away.

(The fourth edition of the *Dictionary of Occupational Titles*, compared with the third, added about 2,100 new occupational definitions and deleted about 3,500). Salaries and wages of occupations change, and the balance between supply and demand for a given occupation may fluctuate over time. Education, training, and other requirements for entry tend to show a generally ascending curve, with an occasional downward squiggle in periods when the labor market is tight. But over the years, the opportunities offered by various occupations to satisfy members' interests and values have remained rather constant. For example, Strong Vocational Interest Blank profiles of comparable samples of various occupations tested about three decades apart were remarkably similar (Strong, revised by Campbell, 1966).

Thus, it appears that the quest for self-fulfillment in work implied by "vocation" must focus on occupational choice: Which occupations offer the opportunities for a level of intrinsic satisfactions that is worthy of strong commitment and identification? The search for "employment," on the other hand, may emphasize extrinsic rewards and concomitant conditions of work–features such as convenience of hours and access, pleasant surroundings, fringe benefits, vacation time, and congenial co-workers, which are more likely to be functions of jobs than of occupations.

Making the point in this way overstates it, because obviously occupations and jobs may vary in both intrinsic and extrinsic returns. But the tendency toward categorical difference is perceptible enough to be worth noting. It helps to explain why either occupational values or job values may be in the subjective foreground for an individual's decision making: It is often a question of more basic work values that tilt toward "vocation" or "employment." Thus, although an occupational title is the most commonly expected answer to a question about work choices, a not uncommon answer might be the name of a local industry, company, or other organization ("work at the Yonder Aircraft Corporation," "civil service," or "Umbrella Insurance Company"). Incidentally, it may be interesting to note that such an answer would be the most frequent one in Japan: Students there typically hope to enter the most prestigious company that will hire them, without regard to occupation. Specific job training is then provided by the company. Thus, in Japan CDM is fundamentally different from CDM in most Western industrialized countries, and there has been scant recognized need or explicit provision for career guidance.

Number of Occupational Options

For those who are choosing occupations, the identification and definition in the *Dictionary of Occupational Titles (DOT)* of thousands of occupational titles would seem to present a bewildering multitude of options. The first question that might occur is how the number considered by any one person is reduced to manageable proportions. The answer is, mainly by ignorance.

Most people find it difficult even to name a large number of occupations. Data from the National Assessment of Educational Progress illustrate the general paucity of occupations considered: When a national sample of 17-year-olds were asked to name five occupations they had considered, 86% were able to name one and 75% named a second, but only 56% a third, 29% a fourth, and 15% a fifth (Katz, 1978a). Nor do college students appear to consider any greater number of occupations. Samples of students at six colleges, ranging widely in location, size, characteristics of student body, and other variables, were asked: "How many occupations have you explored as possibilities for yourself?" (Chapman et al., 1977). Distributions of responses tended to be quite consistent across schools, with a median of 5% indicating they had considered *no* occupations, 51% one or two occupations, 33% three or four, and only 12.5% more than four. (One of the effects of intervention–use of the computerized System of Interactive Guidance and Information [SIGI]–was a very significant increase in the number of occupations considered by students at each of these six colleges.)

Of course, ignorance has not been regarded as the best way to reduce the number of occupations to more manageable proportions. Enlightenment has also been tried. One approach is exemplified by the widely distributed *Occupational Outlook Handbook* (OOH; U.S. Department of Labor, 1988), which "describes in detail about 225 occupations–comprising about 80% of all jobs in the economy," focusing particularly on those that "require lengthy education or training." It also provides "summary information on about 125 occupations–accounting for about 10% of all jobs in the economy." The *OOH* (issued biennially) provides information about "nature of the work; working conditions; employment; training, other qualifications, and advancement; job outlook; earnings; related occupations; and sources of additional information."

Occupational Clusters

But the *OOH* by itself is essentially passive. It does not direct attention to any occupation or set of occupations for any given reader. It is a reference book. Another approach is more active, seeking to group or cluster occupations according to some specified characteristics. This procedure aims to reduce the options for decision to more manageable proportions, such as "families" of occupations, with the idea that eliminating large groups or clusters permits more focused and detailed attention to the remainder. But how should occupations be clustered for such sequential CDM procedures?

A number of salient classification features have been used. For example, occupations have been classified according to "levels" of general ability (such as "IQ" or "G") observed in their members (Roe, 1956; Stewart, 1947; U.S. Department of Labor, 1965). Such ordering of occupations by "level" offers no direct prediction or probability data to career decision makers, although a number of studies (e.g., Project TALENT and a review and reanalysis of various longitudinal studies by Jencks and his associates) have shown that there is—as would be expected—a positive relationship between ability measured in adolescence and adult attainment of member-ship in occupations ranked at certain "levels" (American Institute for Research, 1976; Jencks et al., 1979). The Jencks study concluded that the effects of ability on occupational status are exercised primarily through educational attainment. There is no doubt that general ability is related to attainment of *credentials* required for entry to certain occupations. The extent to which it is related to *competence* required for successful perfor-mance in such occupations is not so clear. However, Thorndike (1985) and Schmidt, Hunter, and Northrop (1983), in meta analyses of many validity studies, have found consistent relationships between general cognitive level (as indicated by standardized test scores) and successful performance in many occupations.

Other systems for classifying both individuals and occupations have focused on interests (D'Costa, Winefordner, Odgers, & Koors, 1969; Hol-land, 1973; Kuder, 1960; Roe, 1956; Strong, 1948; U.S. Department of Labor, 1979). Interests are probably the most widely studied of the "psychological" variables that are presumed to relate individual to occupa-tional differentiation. Considerable attention has also been given to the domain of specific aptitudes (assembled in test batteries) as predictors of success or membership in an occupation (Flanagan, Tiedeman, Willis, & McLaughlin, 1973; Ghiselli, 1966; Thorndike & Hagen, 1959; U.S. Employ-ment Service, 1958). As Thorndike (1985) and Schmidt et al. (1983) demon-strated, however, the role of specific aptitudes seems to be overridden by the general factor ("g" or general cognitive level). Needs of individuals and reinforcement patterns of occupations have been at the core of one extensive research program (Borgen et al., 1968). Individual values and occupational rewards and satisfactions have played a central role in another (Katz, 1963, 1974). A research program on cognitive styles moved to incorporate some data on occupational choice (Witkin et al., 1977). These different approaches and emphases imply different assumptions about the *process* of CDM, as is elucidated later.

Meanwhile, it is apparent that each of the domains mentioned—general ability, specific aptitudes, interests, needs, values, cognitive styles—taken singly provides only a fragmentary approach to self-appraisal, to occupa-tional differentiation, and to decision-making processes. Furthermore, measurement or appraisal of individual differences in these domains is sparsely linked by research to comprehensive occupational data bases.

On the other hand, a number of comprehensive clustering and classification systems of occupations have provided a framework for extensive programs of data collection, storage, and publication. Most of these systems were not designed to differentiate occupations in ways that are useful for CDM. For example, several of them serve a variety of purposes of federal agencies such as the Census (U.S. Bureau of the Census, 1970), the Standard Industrial Classification (Executive Office of the President, Office of Management and Budget, 1972), the Office of Education (U.S. Department of Health, Education, and Welfare, n.d.), and the *Dictionary of Occupational Titles (DOT)* nine-digit code (U.S. Department of Labor, 1977). In addition, the Standard Occupational Classification (U.S. Department of Commerce, 1977), which took 10 years to develop, was supposed to replace census categories and all other systems used by federal agencies to gather data. Thus, although the various systems were not designed to be compatible, attempts have been made to cross-reference them: Each Standard Occupational Classification (SOC) group includes a listing of *DOT* titles, and the biennial *Occupational Outlook Handbook* lists *DOT* and SOC numbers for each occupation. People working with occupational information have also recognized that, even though the *systems* are generally not useful for CDM, the *data* (particularly as published in statistical series such as the census) often are: hence such developments as a census–*DOT* cross-reference tape (Temme, 1975). Nevertheless, a basic problem has persisted: The domain of occupational information represented by such systems is not isomorphic with the domain of individual differences defined and measured through psychological research.

Linking Occupational to Individual Attributes

A Department of Labor publication, *Guide for Occupational Exploration*, was developed specifically to mediate between these two domains (U.S. Department of Labor, 1979). It partitions the universe of occupations first into 12 "interest areas," then subdivides them into 66 groups based on "capabilities and adaptabilities," and further classifies them into 348 subgroups determined by a mix of criteria (such as materials and products involved, or handwork vs. machines). The simplifying notion is that the user can start with interests (measured by an inventory or checklist with scales presumed to represent the same 12 "interest areas") and then narrow consideration down successively to smaller groupings or "families" of occupations on the basis of other traits and characteristics embodied in the classification and associated measurement systems.

Unfortunately, this rigid classification system does not lend itself to use in CDM. For example, the *Guide* assigns each occupation to only one "interest area." Therefore, an occupation that involves activities appealing to two or more kinds of interests is not retrieved from each area. For instance, engineering occupations, including research engineers, appear in the "Mechanical" but not in the "Scientific" area. So a person with "Scientific" interests would not be prompted to consider engineering occupations. Thus, the sequential procedure prevents occupations classified in different "interest areas" (as defined by the *Guide*) from being considered in the same cluster. Yet occupations classified by the *Guide* in different interest fields can resemble one another not only in interests but in a variety of other characteristics that may indeed be more important for some decision makers than "interest area" (Chapman et al., 1977; Norris et al., 1978; Tittle, 1981).

An alternative procedure, operational in the computerized System of Interactive Guidance and Information (Katz, 1975), is to screen occupations simultaneously on a number of variables selected flexibly according to their importance to the individual decision maker. The model for this approach is described later. But mention of alternative clustering procedures raises again the question (at the heart of occupational choice): What constitutes an occupation? along with the closely related question: In what respects can occupations be classified as similar or different?

People who hold the same occupational title often have varying opportunities to shape their own work. There is evidently more elasticity in some occupations than in others. For example, in some occupations there is a tendency toward "budding," the creation of new occupations. Occupations are not so stable over time as are biological species. Thus, Psychologist has proliferated (in the fourth edition of the *DOT*) into nine defined titles and Crown Pouncer into three. It is noteworthy that the Psychologist titles in the *Guide for Occupational Exploration* (U.S. Department of Labor, 1979) are split between the "interest area" designated "Humanitarian" (for Clinical, Counseling, and School Psychologists) and the one labeled "Leading–Influencing" (for Comparative–Experimental–Physiological, Developmental, Educational, Social, Engineering, and Industrial–Organizational–Personnel Psychologists).

The rubrics for the "interest areas" suggest some of the questions raised by the definition of the interest domain that is fundamental to the *GOE*. Many of the labels seem to pertain to the *object* of activities (e.g., "Plants and Animals"), to the *purpose* of activities (e.g., "Protective, Humanitarian"), and to the *setting* of activities (e.g., "Industrial") rather than to distinctions that might reside in the nature of the activities themselves. This problem is highlighted by the definition of the interest factor called "Leading–Influencing": "Interest in leading and influencing others through activities involving high-level verbal or numerical abilities." Logically and semantically, this definition seems to identify two kinds of activity interests, one verbal and the other numerical. These might be applied to a variety of purposes—protective, humanitarian, and leading–influencing presumably being among them. Although this is not the place to examine critically the procedures by which the interest domain was defined and the factors identified, suffice it to say that they do not seem sound enough to warrant use as a primary basis for partitioning the universe of occupations.

It was suggested earlier that the domains of individual differences are not isomorphic with the domains of occupational information. This point warrants some clarification. For example, the term, *interests*, is often used loosely (as in the *GOE* described earlier), as if it characterized occupations. More strictly speaking, interests are not a property of occupations but of persons. *Activities* characterize occupations. Thus, the activities involved in an occupation provide *opportunities* (greater or less) for satisfaction of one or more of an individual's interests. But simple trait matching— "square pegs in square holes"—does not work. Many occupations require some variety of activities. While people in these occupations may be able to emphasize some activities more than others, in keeping with their own preferences, they are rarely able to limit themselves only to the activities that appeal to them. At the same time, and conversely, people usually have a "surplus" of interests beyond those that correspond to occupational activities. Furthermore, some occupations require activities that hold very low intrinsic interest for most people; activities in others may tend to be quite popular. It is clear that—even when corresponding dimensions are identified—the distribution of interests in the population is far from identical with the distribution of corresponding activities in the world of work. Part of the *process* of choice, then, is first to decide how important it is to satisfy some major interest and second, only if it is important, to identify occupations (part of the *content* of choice) in which a large share of the activities meet that interest.

In a similar sense, other traits of people are far from a perfect match with characteristics of occupations. Workers' abilities and aptitudes are often much broader than the requirements of their work; credentials as well as competencies may also be broader than those required. Corollary to this observation is the concept of *multipotentiality*. Although some occupations require highly differentiated skills and talents, many others can be handled successfully by most of the work force. (That the full range of individual differences in interests and aptitudes is not reflected in the range of occupational activities and requirements need not be a source of frustration, as long as one's work requires distinctly human interests and abilities. To be human is to be sharply differentiated from other species. Insofar as human work was invented by human beings, it tends to be related to their capabilities and their predilections.)

Analogous to the problem of linking individual interests to occupational activities, and abilities to requirements, is the problem of finding appropriate connections between people's values and the opportunities for rewards and satisfactions offered by occupations. As with interests and abilities, people have more values than work can fulfill; they can get some satisfactions and rewards from virtually any occupation, but (usually) none will provide complete satisfaction. So again there is almost always a need for compromise. Only the naivete of a Candide would expect perfect compatibility between what a person wants and the opportunities for gratification offered by occupations and jobs. The solution again is to identify and define appropriate dimensions that link values to occupational characteristics. Given that some values are more important than others to any person, which occupations tend to provide opportunities for relevant rewards and satisfactions, and to what degree? Developing a structure of occupational information that permits such linkages to a corresponding structure of individual characteristics is a major contribution to the content of CDM.

What Is an Occupation?

Thus, the occupational universe can be conceptualized in a multiple-domained, multidimensional space. The domains might include nature of work activities – construed along dimensions that might correspond, in part, to various interest factors; requirements and opportunities for entry – with dimensions linked, in part, to amount and kind of education or training, aptitudes, abilities, and skills; and returns or instrumentalities, the opportunities offered by occupations for various kinds of rewards and satisfactions – with dimensions relevant, in part, to occupational values. (Work environment and conditions, as indicated before, may be properties not so much of occupations as of jobs.) In any given case, it is important to note that the interface between sets of individual characteristics and occupational attributes tends to involve only selected facets from each domain – not like the hackneyed square peg in a square hole, but more like the fit of a person to a favorite chair.

Each occupation represents some set of central tendencies on such attributes (i.e., *activities*, *requirements*, *returns*). Around the centroid are distributions on each dimension of each attribute, representing variations within an occupation. Obviously, a given pair of occupations may overlap in one or more attributes and differ in others. That is why no singular or hierarchic system for classifying occupations is satisfactory. Rather, the decision maker needs to be able to select some reasonable number of dimensions that are important to him or her. Given a multivariate classification system, the universe of occupations can be screened on a selected set of specifications simultaneously; a residual list of occupations can be retrieved that are – at some reasonable confidence level – similar in the respects specified. The list will change as specifications are changed.

In answering the question of what an occupation is, then, it is necessary to recognize that *occupations are generalizations or abstractions from observed phenomena.* They cannot be defined or described without the benefit of generalizations about such attributes as activities, requirements, and returns. As always in generalizations, some information is lost. This loss is outweighed by a gain in summary power. Granted, some jobs and positions within an occupation are out at the fringes of the generalizations. These deviations from the centroid come into focus when one chooses jobs or positions. But the centroid itself (say, the mean plus or minus one standard deviation on each dimension) is what one chooses when one chooses an occupation.

This is fortunate for long-range decisions and plans, because the central tendencies represented by an occupation are more stable than the individual jobs that it comprehends. Shifts and change in the latter may even out: For example, in one occupation, within a year, training requirements for a job in the sun belt might be lowered, while requirements for a job in the snow belt are raised. But the center (the occupation) will hold. Thus, a student deciding now to enter that occupation some years hence can plan with more confidence than he or she can for a particular job.

Job Attributes

Still, there are consistencies in some types of jobs, or employment settings, just as there are in occupations. As Bisconti and Gomberg (1976) concluded from a 1971 follow-up of large samples of two cohorts of college graduates who had matriculated in 1961 and 1966: "Men and women who enter a particular occupation tend to concur in their reasons for [their career] choice. . . . Likewise, men and women who enter a particular employment setting tend to concur in their reasons for their long-run career choice." For example, whereas business administrators (compared with people in other occupations) tended to seek high earnings, those employed in private companies were more inclined than those in government, education, and other public settings to cite high earnings; the latter, on the other hand, were more likely to cite altruism. In more general terms, independently of occupation, men and women with jobs in private companies were more likely than others to indicate that high earnings and leadership opportunities were important; those in other settings were more likely to emphasize autonomy and altruism. As the authors hastened to add, these differences were found in responses made *after* entry into occupations and jobs. It would be interesting to know whether the differences hold for values expressed prior to entry.

Thus, *job* choices fall into two categories. They may follow occupational choice or be made quite independently of it. In the first case, an occupation having been chosen, one job may be preferred to another in that occupation because of the discrepancies between them in attributes that are usually associated with occupations – that is, variations from the centroid in activities, requirements, returns. These attributes will usually be weighed along with *job* attributes, such as climate, ease of access from one's home, pleasant work conditions, convenient hours of work, attractive fringe benefits, proximity to friends, dress codes or their absence – all of which may be summarized as organizational environment. In the second case, as indicated previously, the primary choice may be a job in one organization or establishment rather than another, without regard for occupation. In such instances, when the returns from work environment loom larger than characteristic occupational rewards and satisfactions, job values can be said to outweigh occupational values (the normal case in Japan). With occupational choice subordinated to job choice, there is also usually less long-range planning to meet specific entry requirements, and there is relative indifference to satisfying interests through one array of activities rather than another. Of course, attitudes toward choice of job rather than occupation can change over time. Work experience may lead to development or explicit recognition of occupational competencies, interests, and values; then primary job affiliation may be superseded by focus on an occupational identification and choice.

DECISIONS ABOUT CAREER EDUCATION AND TRAINING

> If you start with an electron in this state at a certain time and you want to see whether it will be in some other state at another time, you just add together contributions from all of the possible histories of the electron that take it from this state to the other. (Freeman Dyson, *Disturbing the Universe*, 1979)

Attempts to describe the connections between education and training on the one hand and entry into occupations or jobs on the other do not permit easy generalizations. In some instances, singular, direct, clearly marked pathways are quite well known. In many others, there are multiple routes, sometimes quite complex and obscure. Empirical data, "sums over histories," can be gathered from two perspectives: One is *prospective:* What proportion of those who choose a certain state of education or training, say at Point A, are later found in a given occupational state, say at Point X? The other is *retrospective:* What proportion of people in a given occupational state at X previously chose a certain state of education or training at A?

Working from either direction, one must define the transition states between A and X and determine analogous proportions from point to point. Such career trees traced prospectively and retrospectively are likely to be useful to career decision makers in somewhat different ways. Thus, high school students who have made rather early specification of an occupational goal (e.g., physician) that is distinguished by a singular, well-defined route, with a number of sequential selection points, will look first at the retrospective career tree: Noting that essentially all physicians have come from medical schools via premedical college programs via a secondary school curriculum that includes sciences, they will elect courses in the sciences. Then, looking at the tree prospectively, they may note that relatively small proportions of high school students taking science courses go on to premedical programs in college, and a small proportion of those go on to medical school. In anticipation of the possibility of opting out or being screened out at some transition point, they can consider the alternative branches at each such node. This prospective tree is also of primary interest to those who do not specify an occupational goal early, either because they want to keep their options open as long as possible or because they prefer to focus on educational goals without regard to occupational implications.

Education and training can be closely connected, as in the preceding example, or virtually independent. In the latter case, a training program may be entered with only scant regard for education. For example, an occupational training program may include as enrollees both recent high school dropouts and PhD's in a field with little demand. When viewed retrospectively, successive decisions about amount and kind of education, types of training and timing of entry, and where to obtain desired education or training often appear to have formed an inevitable sequence for a given occupation or job. Yet viewed prospectively the run of such decisions may seem more consequential for directions they exclude than for goals they lead to.

Choices about amount or kind of education can be viewed as ends in themselves in terms of the intrinsic worth of each option – that is, interest in the activities associated with a particular educational program and value placed on the opportunities for satisfaction offered by it. In the context of CDM, however, an educational choice is not usually an end but primarily a means to other ends. The career education movement, which probably reached its apogee in the 1970s (Hoyt, 1974; Marland, 1974), has particularly addressed the acquisition of knowledge, skills, and attitudes useful in work or in making decisions that lead to work.

In this context, education can be differentiated from training as being broader in scope, encouraging exploration, emphasizing competencies that are universal or at least common to many kinds of work, and covering development over a considerable span of time. Training tends to be focused on preparation for a specific kind of work, usually over a relatively short period of time just before or after entering a given occupation, job, or position. Typically, there is a progression from general education (a common core of knowledge and skills), perhaps to more specialized education (in a given discipline or subject area), then perhaps to training.

Of course, these distinctions are not unequivocal. For example, as is well known, physicians go through a relatively long period of training. Nor is the progression invariant. Many people never enter training, and some students who enter occupational "training" programs in high school plan to go on to "general education" as freshmen in 4-year colleges (Grasso & Shea, 1979). But often the investment in training is such as to discourage doubling back to general education unless the training fails to result in an appropriate placement. Then the investment in training must usually be written off as a loss. Training, by its specificity, tends to have little transfer value for other occupations, jobs, or training programs. Thus, in one sense, it appears to narrow or limit options. In another sense, it may "create" an option by making it attainable. If a training program is to be chosen, then, paramount importance must be attached to the likelihood that it will result in getting a desired job that would not otherwise have been obtained.

Efficacy of Training

The variety among training programs is so great that generalizations about their efficacy in this mission are perhaps unfair if not impossible. Occupational training is offered in secondary schools, public and private agencies, business and industry, public and proprietary noncollege postsecondary programs, correspondence courses, many colleges, graduate and professional schools, and apprenticeships. Apprentice training by its nature and long history would be expected to produce excellent results, but such programs have only small enrollments (most of them in construction crafts). Interestingly, according to Freedman and Dutka (1980), over many years apprenticeships have tended to be cancelled at about the same rate as they are completed: Apprentices tend to be laid off in a loose labor market and to get regular jobs before completion of apprenticed training in a tight labor market. Freedman and Dutka (1980) concluded: "There is no standard American way of becoming a craft worker." (In contrast with

the United States, Germany has developed an apprenticeship system that
in 1990 enrolled more than 60% of the people between 16 and 18 years of
age. Apprentices serve for 3 years, attending school 1 or 2 days a week; the
other days are spent learning on jobs in clerical, administrative, sales,
manual, and technical occupations. Increasing emphasis is being given to a
wide range of academic and job skills leading to further education or
training for advancement to more demanding jobs.)

If youth unemployment were attributable mainly to "structural" problems (i.e., a bad fit between the requirements of available jobs and the
competencies of youth available to fill them), good training programs
would appear to be an appropriate prescription. However, many training
programs – both proprietary and public – have been severely criticized for
offering programs that are not related to the job market, for deceptive
advertising, and for failure to place graduates (Freedman & Dutka, 1980).
The tenor of much of the criticism of proprietary schools is summarized in
the title of a well-known book by Ivan Berg (1970), *Education and Jobs:
The Great Training Robbery*. Granted, many of their clients have been
hard to place. For example, following up a random sample of welfare
clients who had enrolled in government-financed training at private trade
schools (for occupations with high current demand, such as beautician,
secretary, computer programmer), the New York City Human Resources
Administration found that only 4% had been placed in jobs (Berger, 1989).
Public school vocational training courses have often been criticized for a
failure to use labor market information. Drewes and Katz (1975) stated:
"The prevailing philosophy seems to be that as long as students continue to
enroll in a program, the program will be offered."

Grasso and Shea (1979) used data from the National Longitudinal
Surveys of Labor Market Experience to study the effects of high school
occupational training programs. Controlling for such variables as highest
year of school completed, scholastic aptitude, socioeconomic level, and
type of community, they found (for those with exactly 12 years of school)
that job differences by curriculum were minor; there was mixed evidence
on unemployment rates for males by curriculum (depending on the criterion of unemployment), but among females less unemployment for those
who had taken a "business and office" curriculum. (*Post*secondary training
appeared to pay off in earnings slightly better for students who had taken
an occupational rather than a "general" curriculum in high school.)

The Job Training Partnership Act (JTPA), which took effect in 1983, was
designed to train and place in jobs those regarded as most in need of help,
mainly people lacking a high school education. But in 1986, over half the
trainees were high school graduates. Although most of the trainees found
jobs, the contractors, who were paid mostly in proportion to placements,
were accused of "creaming" – enrolling people who could have got jobs

without JTPA. According to Donahue (1989), there is no "evidence that the Job Training Partnership Act system . . . makes much difference for the employment, earnings, and productive capacity of American workers." In 1989, the U.S. Department of Labor indicated it would require contractors to focus more on high school dropouts, welfare recipients, and those lacking basic skills.

Ideally, one might expect that training programs could be most efficiently conducted by employers, either individually or in association, with enrollments geared to openings. But even with government support of training, as in JTPA, employers have often found it cheaper to bid for already trained workers, as needed, rather than incur or share the cost of training. As Freedman and Dutka (1980) put it, business and industry prefer to "recruit the educated" rather than "educate the recruited." A recent study by the MIT Commission on Industrial Productivity (Berger, Dertouzos, Lester, Solow, & Thurow, 1989) concluded that industry offers only "limited training, . . . typically . . . watching a colleague at work . . . [to learn] specific narrow skills for immediate application." Although many companies offer in-house training programs (75% according to a survey by Lusterman, 1977, of companies with over 500 employees), these are mainly for upgrading or updating skills of established employees. Emphasis in many companies on promotion from within makes some positions tantamount to training programs for others. Again, it makes a difference whether one looks at the retrospective or the prospective career tree. As Spilerman (1977) pointed out, the transition from assembly-line worker to foreman may hold for a high proportion of foremen but a low proportion of assembly-line workers.

In short, as documented by Freedman and Dutka (1980), training for nonprofessional occupations and jobs appears to have been largely catch-as-catch-can from the point of view of the prospective trainee. Most truck-driving schools are characterized as "rip-offs," but they note one that has had success in placing its clients because of the proprietor's close union connections. Although many industry-operated training programs result in few placements, an exemplary program called Training and Technology has been conducted by the Oak Ridge Associated Universities in eastern Tennessee, at a government-owned nuclear plant operated by Union Carbide. This program selects carefully from a pool of applicants averaging about 10 for every place in the program. In the 14 years from 1966 through 1979, about 4,000 people were trained in a factory setting for such occupations as welding, pipefitting, drafting, and metal-machining, with training tailored to specifications of major employers in the southeast. Freedman and Dutka (1980) pointed out that this program shows "what *can* be done," but also emphasized "the unusual conditions for its success."

In the aggregate, many training programs are quite likely to result in loss of investment by trainees. In loose labor markets, training credentials are often required; yet they offer at best necessary but not sufficient conditions for employment. The applicant has no guarantee of placement with such credentials but is at a competitive disadvantage without them. Thus, while aggregate payoffs are low, individuals may often find they have no better options. Then it is important to know both the market, present and projected, for the occupation considered and the placement record of the training agency. (It is often even more important to "know someone" or be in the right place at the right time.) In tight labor markets, however, large employers are likely to feel more pressed to develop their own training programs.

Economic Returns to Education

One of the alternatives to nonprofessional training is extended education. Extended general education and specialized education also represent substantial investments. Quite aside from their intrinsic worth, is it possible to account for the career payoffs on these investments as means to other ends?

Clearly, for any educational choice or sequence of choices one must debit direct costs, plus the loss of earnings and of other benefits from early entry into work. Much attention has been paid by economists and other social scientists to the net dollar value of a college degree. For example, Freeman (1976) concluded that, in general, whenever the supply of college graduates has exceeded the demand, the additional cumulative income projected from a college degree has been less than the cost of obtaining the degree. (He derived these conclusions from data obtained during the 1970s, but his methods have been keenly criticized by Levin, 1977.) Jencks et al. (1979), on the other hand, reanalyzing data from a number of longitudinal studies of males, concluded that a large "bonus" in earnings accrued to a college degree, even when background and ability variables were controlled. Although these data apply to an earlier period than the data for Freeman's inferences, the argument is offered that the relative economic return for a college degree will be maintained, if only because college graduates have a competitive advantage over high school graduates for initial appointments (as requirements for educational credentials are raised) and for promotions. This argument holds better for a loose labor market, in which the supply of applicants greatly exceeds the demand for workers, than a tight one, in which supply and demand are closely balanced. Indeed, the argument is supported by data from the National Longitudinal Survey of Labor Force Experience (Sproat, 1979), showing that the decline in real wages of college graduates after 1969 paralleled a similar decline for high school graduates, and that college graduates had lower unemployment rates.

Of course, in the debate over *average* economic returns to education, differential effects for various persons, programs, and occupations are not taken into account. Aggregating the dollar values of college degrees in this way provides little useful information to individuals making career decisions. Spilerman (1977) pointed out: "Education gets converted into . . . earnings not in some vague random manner but in relation to career lines." For example, Levy (1989) found that the advantage in favor of male college graduates over high school graduates had increased from 1973 to 1986: The average income of 30-year-old college graduates was 16% higher than that of 30-year-old high school graduates in 1973, 50% higher in 1986. This increase was due mainly to a decline in real wages of the high school graduates. The decline did not hold for women, however, whose jobs, according to Levy (1989), "were concentrated in the service sector and so more shielded from import competition."

In passing, it is important to note that the economic return to education need not be the sole criterion, nor does augmenting it with its correlate, occupational status or prestige (the sociologists' favorite), exhaust the criteria of concern in CDM. Job satisfaction does not seem to correlate high with those factors per se (Smith, 1979), although the correlation would undoubtedly be substantial for a sample of persons who set a comparatively high value on income and prestige. The correlation in the general population is reduced by those who attach greater importance to other values. Such other values widely cherished by many people include intrinsic interest, security, leadership, variety, independence, altruism, and leisure (Norris et al., 1978). Thus, occupational satisfaction (viewed as a return to education) involves a complex calculus of profits and losses, of rewards and sacrifices, of pleasures and pains.

Labor Market Information and Educational Decisions

A further complicating factor for decisions about education is the time lag between such decisions and occupational entry. Labor market information even for short-term training programs may, as we have seen, be ignored, but it is at least available. Demand and supply can be tracked regularly through "job banks," especially for a state or metropolitan district. But job markets for occupations that are generally entered only after a considerable period of education tend to be national in scope and must be projected over an appreciable span of time. Students about to enter the long educational pipeline for these occupations, however, respond to recent information about the market rather than to projections for the coming decade. Once they have entered the pipeline, demand and supply for such occupations may change to reflect technologic, economic, demographic, and other factors. But there is a considerable lag before the new outlook, reflecting these changes, reaches new cohorts of students entering the pipeline. Meanwhile, their educational decisions continue to affect the supply side of the outlook equation. This lag in communication of outlook information often contributes to oscillations in the demand–supply ratio for many occupations.

Suppose, for example, at a given time, there is a big increase in the demand for college graduates who have majored in engineering. Salaries in engineering occupations are bid up; information and publicity ensue; perhaps 2 to 4 years after the fact, word filters down to high school students who prepare and apply for appropriate college engineering programs; about 6 years later, an increased number of people with degrees in these fields come out of the educational pipeline – a total elapsed time of 8 to 10 years after the shortage has been recognized. Other things being stable, because these are not permeable occupations (not easily entered without substantial preparation), more years will go by before the market for them comes into balance. Of course, "other things" are often not stable: Sharp decreases in demand may occur – say, as a result of cutbacks in defense spending. Again there is a lag before new projections replace earlier ones and word of the changed outlook gets back to students. Meanwhile, people with engineering degrees continue to spew out of the pipeline in large numbers to face diminished demand, while older members of engineering occupations struggle to convert to other occupations. This kind of oscillation (or "cobwebbing," as economists call it) is of course most frequently found in impermeable occupations with relatively long pipelines that are also sensitive to rapid technologic and economic change.

Can such oscillations be damped by better and quicker information? To the extent that the job market is subject to change, long-term projections are bound to be shaky. Evaluations of Bureau of Labor Statistics (BLS) projections in the past (Personick & Sylvester, 1976; Swerdloff, 1969) have shown them to be fairly accurate at a high level of aggregation (i.e., for industries or broad occupational categories) but likely to be quite far off for specific occupations. However, Bishop and Carter (1990) showed that BLS growth projections have not been borne out even at a high level of aggregation. Kelley, Chirikos, and Finn (1975) concluded that "complex predictions are little more than best guesses," because of unforeseen events, government decisions, technological change, and the absence of manpower considerations in formulation of public policy.

It must be noted, on the other hand, that BLS offers "projections," not "predictions"; that assumptions about events – including absence of major war or depression – are clearly stated; and that biennial corrections and adjustments help to mitigate the effects of errors. It should also be noted that errors on the demand side have not generally been the major problem. Demand consists of two main components: growth and replacement.

Projections of growth (positive or negative) in a given occupation are often prone to error. They are derived, first, from projections of growth by industry and then allocated according to the distribution of occupations among the industries. Thus, in the past, mistaken projections for entire industries, such as construction and communications, have thrown off growth projections for many occupations. _Replacement_ rates for occupations, however, can be projected quite well on an actuarial basis (e.g., death and retirement rates are usually predictable from age distributions, and numbers transferring from most occupations can be reliably estimated). Because replacement is a far more important factor than growth, forecasts of demand are generally well anchored.

The supply side of the equation is where most of the trouble comes. Hard data scarcely go beyond numbers of people in each age cohort and the proportions expected to attain various educational levels, which are then regarded as the supply "pool" for various occupations. Useful "structural" supply models (U.S. Department of Labor, 1974) have not been developed. For permeable occupations, the supply is quite elastic and fluctuates rapidly in response to market forces. But, as indicated before, the lag in information about the market for impermeable occupations that require prolonged education causes oscillations and severe displacements.

It will be interesting to see whether the recent and continuing proliferation of computer-based occupational information systems (Katz & Shatkin, 1980), which make current outlook information much more widely accessible, especially to secondary school and college students, will tend to damp the oscillations. Although these systems often do not contain appreciably better information about demand than is now available in Department of Labor publications, they are likely to improve greatly the speed of communication of such information to students who are making educational decisions, plans, and commitments. Because occupational outlook is often an important factor in educational decisions, the supply side of the equation may in time be affected by greatly reducing the lag in information. It seems likely that outlook will then be influenced by the speed with which it is observed and communicated. Mediating this impact of faster communication on supply and therefore on outlook will be more timely changes in trend lines of educational choices.

Factors in Decisions about Education and Training

In brief, then, what are the properties of career education and training options of concern to the decision maker? A major consideration is _time_, ranging from short-term preparation for early occupational entry to long-term programs extending over several years. Obviously, time involves big differences in _investment_, although costs may vary also within programs of a given duration. *Target specificity* is an important differentiating characteristic: Some programs are aimed at one given occupation or job; others may be directed toward a number of occupations or a field of work, although progressive narrowing along the way is likely to be the rule. A closely related but not identical factor is *transferability* of education or training from one program to other programs at well-defined transition points without serious loss of investment. The inverse characteristic is *permeability*, the ease with which a program can be entered at various points. The degree of *selectivity* is also likely to affect supply and consequent placement rates. Crucial characteristics are the intrinsic *gratifications* and *pains* likely to be experienced by a given person in a program, particularly one of long duration; then checkpoints and milestones may offer symbolic reinforcement along the way: Progress can be evaluated, the occupational market can be reassessed, and goals can be confirmed, modified, or replaced. Finally, the *probability of successful completion* of the program and *entry* into a target occupation—or one related to it—is of paramount importance.

The *time* dimension is pervasive in decisions about education and training. Early in this chapter, career choices were described as a "means-ends chain." The metaphor can be extended to suggest that, as the chain lengthens, the individual tends to become increasingly fettered by it. Freedom of maneuver is progressively restricted by the succession of choices already made—and their outcomes. Although a person can still choose freely from the available options, the array of options is likely to get more narrowly circumscribed. Among the costs of a given choice are loss functions for the options foreclosed, regrets for the roads not taken.

Still, in various circumstances, people do swallow such losses, do reconsider, do double back throughout their careers, although the incidence of mid-career change may have been exaggerated (Arbeiter, 1979). Career trajectories can be idealized from a *retrospective* vantage point: Getting from there to here looks like a relatively simple problem in ballistics, when *here* is the target destination and *there* is any identified starting point. All other launch and navigation decisions appear to be subsidiary, perhaps involving only minor corrections along the way. But the *prospective* view of real career histories (getting from here to there when *here* is the starting point and *there* is the target) does not seem to follow the smooth curve of a ballistic missile flight. Rather, it traces paths full of zigs and zags, wiggles and wobbles, ups and downs, starts and stops, hops, skips, and jumps.

Summary and Transition

As this consideration of education and training illustrates, then, career decision making is not a one-shot episode, not just one major determining choice of occupation followed by a few subsidiary decisions for adjustments along the way. Instead, decision making is a recurrent activity. At each stage, new options are confronted, and new information generally becomes available for processing. This information pertains to both means and ends. Feedback mechanisms suggest course corrections for a given destination; they may also suggest changes in destinations. So the content of career decisions varies from time to time. At each choice-point, decisions about goals can be reiterated or modified in response to the information and insights gained from experience and development, and these decisions can interact with decisions about immediate options. But as the *content* of decisions changes from one set of options to another (options embedded in such contexts as education, training, occupations, jobs, and positions), much remains constant in the *process* of career decision making.

In this chapter a number of issues in the content, concepts, and context of CDM have been identified, defined, and examined. Included have been such topics as assumptions about the sorting of people into occupations; the components of CDM; dilemmas, domains, and options in CDM; definitions of work, position, job, occupation, and career; degrees of work centrality and commitment; the relative prominence of intrinsic and extrinsic values; distinctions between "vocation" and "employment"; problems in classifying or "clustering" occupations; similarities and differences in choice of occupation or job; linkages between individual characteristics and occupational attributes; the roles of education and training in CDM; the effects of labor market information on decisions; and factors in decisions about education and training.

We have noted that, unaided, many people make their choices unaware of most of the options available, with a paucity of information about the options and themselves, and with little sense of linkages between the domains of self and options. These conditions suggest a need for help. Later chapters emphasize the process of CDM as embodied in professional interventions—that is, guidance in general and SIGI in particular. To prepare the way, the next chapter introduces the process by examining needs for guidance—the needs of individuals, groups, society, educational institutions, corporations, system developers—and the possible tensions and synergies between these players in the CDM process. From this examination of needs, the argument progresses in chapter 3 to rationales and models for career guidance, including an analysis of major approaches to guidance. This in turn leads to a focus in chapter 4 on issues involved in virtually every component of career guidance; on an analysis of each issue; and on the resolution chosen for a particular guidance treatment, SIGI. Then there is an attempt in chapter 5 to show the relevance of conceptual frameworks, rationales, models, and functions of career guidance systems to the evaluation of such systems, and to illustrate by dealing specifically with the "validity" of SIGI and its offspring, SIGI PLUS.

2

The Needs for Guidance

*. . . be able to choose the line of greatest advantage instead of
yielding in the path of least resistance.*
                    −G. B. Shaw (preface to *Man and Superman*)

The needs for guidance emerge, in part, from intricacies in the *content* of
CDM, effects of the societal *setting* in which CDM takes place, individual
differences in the *people* making career decisions, and complexities in the
process of CDM.

The previous chapter emphasized the content of CDM. It described and
analyzed some of the concepts, issues, and complications in the choices that
people make about their work, occupations, jobs, education, and training.
It also recognized interactions of content with settings, persons, and
process.

For example, *content* may be determined largely by cultural, social, and
economic forces included in *setting*. The calendar of the educational system, with built-in transitions and discontinuities, may designate the
timing of choice-points. Demographic trends and economic boom or bust
may make occupational opportunities generally plentiful or scarce. The
rise and decline of industries may increase opportunities in some occupations and subtract them in others. There may be different opportunities
available to different segments of the population (say, by age, gender, or
ethnic background), and public policy may−with varying degrees of suc-
cess−be cast to compensate for inequities in opportunities or resources
available to various subgroups. A given culture may tend to approve and
reinforce choice of some options more than others. Options in a complex

industrial or information economy may not be readily visible to most people.

All these cultural, social, and economic forces included in setting are inextricably linked to the needs for guidance. People have to know how to schedule their career decisions; how to get information on the options at each choice-point; how the choices at different points are interrelated; how to get information on the outlook for the job market in general and in specific occupations. Members of a particular subgroup should know what special assistance or opportunities are available.

To help people pose and answer such questions, to help them get information, and to help them cope with the CDM problems that confront them, society (which has contributed to the need) has also provided institutions, agencies, and other apparatus to meet the need – that is, to offer guidance. Still, there are tensions between the societal stake and the individual stake in career guidance – a topic discussed later in this chapter.

The *persons* who have to make the decisions differ from one another. They come from some variety of environments and may be subject to different "sociological" influences. They also differ in such "psychological" characteristics as perceptions, needs, values, abilities, interests, preferences, development rates, knowledge, competencies, and strategies. As a consequence of these "sociological" and "psychological" differences, they may differ in their modes of approach to CDM – for example, active or passive, rigid or flexible, impulsive or planful, seeking long-range goals, seeking short-range goals, or non goal-seeking. Their need is for guidance that will help them examine and understand themselves as well as their options, in such a way as to engage in rational as well as informed CDM.

A natural history of the *process* of CDM must take into account the interaction between the content of choices, social forces, and psychological elements. To the extent that it is influenced by guidance, the process of CDM in our society also involves some variety of career guidance models and practices that may be available.

Thus, the _needs_ for guidance are implied, in part, by the nature and difficulty of the choices to be made; by the problems, obstacles, and opportunities that reside in a society and its institutions; by individual differences; and also by the state of knowledge or wisdom required for informed and rational CDM, and by the discrepancies between such an ideal and the actual state of individuals who are about to make career decisions.

The intervention known as career guidance has been made available (usually at schools, colleges, community agencies, and corporations) through counselors, publications, audiovisual materials, direct observation and experience, simulations, tests and inventories, and computerized career guidance systems. All these forms of intervention are intended to meet needs for guidance as perceived by many parties that have a stake in CDM and guidance. Thus, development of a career guidance system must recognize the needs of such parties as students, the general adult population, "society as a whole," educational institutions, corporations, counselors, and the developers themselves.

So before undertaking further study of process and models for guidance in the following chapter, we focus here on the analyses of needs that led to the development of a particular guidance intervention (SIGI). This approach is in keeping with the method described in the Introduction – to shuttle between the particular and the general, connecting theory and practice, and using each to illuminate the other. As indicated before, this chapter is concerned not only with the needs of clients, the prospective users of the system, but also with the needs of institutions and agencies that will house the system and make it available to clients; the needs of society as a whole; and, in all honesty, the needs of the developers. Two levels of needs identification are considered: those needs that are readily apparent from surveys and have been stated in general terms as a need for guidance; and those that have been defined and specified in more penetrating analyses of the functions that such guidance should fulfill. The first order of business is to look at the need for guidance as it has been universally recognized in the survey literature.

GENERAL RECOGNITION OF STUDENTS' NEEDS FOR GUIDANCE

SIGI, the forerunner of SIGI PLUS, was designed to help (mainly) college or college-bound students in their career decision making. The study of "universally recognized" needs for that system reviewed a body of research that followed two major lines: (a) surveys showed that students consistently perceived better career guidance as a foremost need; they rated it very important, they wanted it, and they did not believe they were getting sufficient help from the colleges; (b) extensive evaluations of career guidance services painted a dismal picture. For example, the report of a committee sponsored by the Carnegie Corporation bluntly characterized student personnel programs as "woefully inadequate.... Almost none of the institutions provided career information with any effectiveness." (This report prompted me to direct a proposal to Carnegie to support development of SIGI to improve the career guidance services at colleges.)

Cognizant of these shortcomings, colleges expressed a commitment to improving career guidance services as an increasingly important benefit to students and as an aid to their own recruitment and retention efforts. A long anticipated decrease in secondary school cohorts led colleges to compete more energetically for enrollments not only of current high school graduates but also of adults who had been out of school for some years. They also recognized that successful efforts to increase retention would be even more cost effective than a comparable investment in recruiting. Yet it was not feasible to attempt a significant increase in the size of professional guidance staffs.

In short, studies establishing the need for better career guidance in colleges made clear that there was little likelihood, for reasons of costs, logistics, and capabilities, that traditional resources such as counseling and publications could be expanded and improved to meet the recognized needs of students and institutions. An interactive computer-based guidance system was, therefore, designed to extend and amplify the power of the best guidance services that could be provided. An analytic specification of the needs it was intended to meet will follow a summary of needs recognized for the development of career guidance for adults.

Recognition of Adults' Needs for Guidance

Like many offspring, SIGI PLUS has outgrown its parent. SIGI PLUS inherited characteristics suitable for meeting the recognized needs of college students for career guidance, but its development for use by the general adult population required additional justification to establish the special and more varied needs of that clientele.

Briefly, a review of literature to establish the needs of adults led me first to discard an obsolescent belief in *universal stages* of career development. According to conventional theory, occupational choice was associated with the search for identity in adolescence and youth; maturity was regarded as the period for establishment, advancement, and maintenance in a chosen occupation; and old age led inexorably to decline and retirement (Beilin, 1955; Buehler, 1933; Erikson, 1963, 1968; Ginzberg, Ginsburg, Axelrod, & Herma, 1951; Havighurst, 1953; Miller & Form, 1951; Super, 1953, 1957). By the tenets of this widely accepted theory of universal stages in career development, reopening questions of occupational choice in middle or old age was not regarded as a common event and indeed might have been considered an occasion for embarrassment, going against the grain of perceived biological and psychological development.

More recently, however, this belief in age-linked stages of career development has been countered by a recognition of the prevalence of mid-career change, along with attention to the need of adults for assistance in this process. For example, Arbeiter, Schmerbeck, Aslanian, and Brickell (1976) indicated that 40 million adult Americans were in "career transitions." A report to the California legislature by Peterson and Hefferlin

(1975) emphasized that "Many adults at one time or another need help in thinking through their educational and occupational plans and relating them to their broader life goals." Cross (1978), writing about the "missing link" between adult learners and learning resources (in a synthesis of findings from surveys), called counseling about future plans "the most immediate and widespread of all learning needs."

Among the factors contributing to these conclusions has been rapid social and economic change. The aging of the population has focused more attention on the problems of older people, including career problems. Interruptions of formal education have become more commonplace, and widespread provisions have been made for "continuing" education; so the college population has also aged (*Digest of Educational Statistics*, 1987). Recognition given to independent study, experience, and other nontraditional methods of learning has provided new opportunities and has stimulated many adults to seek help in structuring their plans to prepare for career advancement or change. According to Thomas (1979), in a society that sanctions career change among adults, people feel freer to initiate new plans to find "more meaningful work," or to get a "better fit between their values and work." For example, one national survey found about 1.7 million workers (over 4% of all employed persons over 24) were searching for new jobs at a given time (Barton, 1978). Many old occupations and jobs have been wiped out by new technologies or have been exported to other countries. Dislocations in employment for such reasons, as well as for reasons of individual inefficiency or incompatibility, have made quick access to career guidance for adults valuable for sustaining morale as well as for offering practical assistance. (Decision making, planning, and acting to seek out new employment require wholehearted constructive involvement by the persons displaced; such activities can help them channel their energies productively rather than dissipate them in grief, brooding, and loss of self-esteem.) Finally, more adult women have been entering the work force or have been seeking occupational advancement. Various agencies have reported that the number of females asking for career information and assistance far exceeds the number of males.

Existing resources, institutions, and agencies were found to be inadequate to meet adults' needs for career guidance. Most college career planning and placement centers emphasize placement more than planning; the latter is often the province of faculty advisers, who focus on selection of courses within the advisers' fields and are ill prepared to cope with nonacademic choices (Ironside & Jacobs, 1977; Peterson, 1979). Resources in high schools vary enormously but in any case are rarely accessible to adults (Beder, 1977; Mezirow, Darkenwald, & Knox, 1975). Cross (1978) said that educational brokering agencies, preoccupied with day-to-day advocacy and educational assistance to clients, have had "little opportunity to think broadly about the linking functions." Career counseling in industry is limited and does not usually go beyond opportunities within the company. Libraries, unions, and community agencies provide little in the way of organized career guidance services. The State Employment Services, emphasizing placement rather than counseling, have been unable to attract or serve a large clientele for career guidance (Employment and Training Report of the President, 1977; Hitchcock, 1978). Private counseling agencies differ greatly in quality and tend to be too expensive and too few to serve large numbers of people.

Despite their limitations, a significant number of these institutions and agencies have been concerned with providing career guidance for adults. Many colleges – especially community colleges – have made use of SIGI available to the community at large. Libraries in New York State, a Delaware Valley "Compact" for continuing education, and a smattering of private counseling agencies have also offered use of SIGI to adults. Industry has also begun to provide career guidance services to employees, and several large corporations plan to use SIGI PLUS for this purpose.

It seems clear that the need for "guidance" has been recognized by prospective clients and providers, but the reviews and surveys cited do not define and specify the nature of the needs in a way that can lead to the design of an appropriate treatment. The rest of this chapter specifies the needs of each group mentioned – individuals, society as a whole, colleges, corporations, and developers – and relates these needs to the development of SIGI and SIGI PLUS.

Has yet to explain SIGI

SPECIFICATION OF INDIVIDUALS' NEEDS
FOR CAREER GUIDANCE

An early step in the specification of needs for the development of SIGI and SIGI PLUS was study of the "natural history" of career decision making. This study of the *process* of CDM started with a review of the literature and proceeded with some studies of our own, asking the question: How are people making their decisions in the absence of the treatment we propose to develop?

The process of CDM is difficult to observe directly. It is not surprising, then, that the most common approach found in the literature is, in the tradition of the social sciences, formulating and testing hypotheses about relationships between variables designated as independent and dependent. For example, from relationships found between certain categories of occupations chosen and certain antecedent conditions or circumstances, processes of CDM are inferred. Thus, economists have related investments of human capital to the pecuniary returns of occupations entered:

Labor market conditions have been seen as the mediating force. Sociologists have added the criterion of attained status or prestige to earnings and have studied the direct and indirect effects of background and environmental variables, such as parental socioeconomic level: Education has usually been found to intervene between "occupational inheritance" and "occupational mobility." Psychologists have linked occupational "level" to individual differences in measured aptitude and ability, and occupational "field" to such variables as interests and cognitive style: The respective sorting mechanisms have been presumed to be selection and choice based on predicted success and/or resemblance to occupational memberships. Studies of this kind pay little attention to what is going on in the individual, who appears to be regarded as passive or, at most, merely responsive to market forces, background characteristics, educational effects, and patterns of relationships. Clearly, these do play a part in the process of CDM: They represent constraints or opportunities. But important also are the ways in which these constraints or opportunities are perceived by each person and incorporated into that person's thoughts, intentions, and actions. Relatively scant space has been allocated to the role of individual perceptions and what these perceptions signify. A given choice may be made for different needs or "reasons," and different choices may meet the same perceived needs. Thus, it is often more appropriate, in analyzing the process of CDM, to classify modes of choosing rather than the things chosen.

Modes of Choosing

One such observational-taxonomic classification of modes of choosing is consistent with the antithesis between active choice of advantage and passive yielding to expediency stated by G. B. Shaw in the epigraph used at the beginning of this chapter: "to be able to choose the line of greatest advantage instead of yielding in the path of least resistance." This phrase was quoted by Freud in contrasting his "reality principle" with his "pleasure principle." Freud's reality principle represents an emphasis on cumulative benefits over the long run as opposed to immediate gratification.

Time perspective is indeed one of the dimensions along which decision-making processes appear to vary. Katz (1954) referred to "long-range versus short-range goal-seeking," Super and Overstreet (1960) to "planfulness," Jepsen (1975) to the "long view." In each case, the findings (from interviews and questionnaires) refer to people who at some relatively early point are oriented toward a distant goal. The goal may be more or less specific (e.g., "research pathologist" or "something in the social sciences"). In some cases, they may pursue it single-mindedly and rigidly, with no provision for contingencies. In other cases, the goal may be regarded as tentative, with outcomes of steps along the way formulated as hypotheses subject to testing. On the basis of these intervening experiences, they may confirm, modify, or replace goals, reiterating the process at periodic intervals. The point is not whether they stick with a designated goal, but that they continue to designate long-range goals as a basis for immediate decisions. Some of these long-range goal-seekers may abort the process, perhaps in the shock of disappointment or failure, and fix solely on short-term goals or even become passive; but, in general, the long-term time perspective seems to be fairly stable.

It is far from prevalent, however. Some decision makers focus only on proximate goals, basing each next decision on its own immediate appeal, leaving later options to be considered in their turn. As is noted later in this chapter, a substantial portion of the population appears not to engage in an explicit process of decision making at all, drifting "in the path of least resistance," or floundering, or acting on impulse.

These differences in modes of choosing indicate different needs and therefore suggest that varied and flexible kinds of treatment are appropriate.

Developmental Stages

The prolonged and iterative nature of CDM has led to classification by genetic or developmental stages. That is, CDM processes are said to change over time as a function of maturation (Beilin, 1955; Buehler, 1933; Ginzberg et al., 1951; Havighurst, 1953, 1964; Miller & Form, 1951; Super, 1953; Super et al., 1957). Vocational behavior has also been integrated into Erikson's theory of life stages (1963, 1968), particularly those emphasizing ego identity and a sense of autonomy; successful management of the crises associated with these life stages is seen to be essential to the process of CDM and to encompass it.

In all these concepts of life stages, the principal focus for CDM is the period of adolescence and young adulthood, when the genetic "schemata" for choosing have developed. Super and his associates (1957) have attempted to identify in greater detail successive career behaviors appropriate for this age span. They have defined the construct "vocational maturity" in two components to indicate the extent to which each of their (male) subjects (a) is engaged in the vocational tasks "typical" for a given age and (b) is handling such tasks effectively compared to his age group. (This construct is presented as analogous in some respects to that of mental age and may be equally counterproductive; it has also been advanced as representing "readiness" to engage in CDM, analogous to "reading readiness.") Their Career Pattern Study, following 142 ninth graders in 1951 to about age 36 in 1973 via periodic interviews and questionnaires has traced an intricate network of relationships among many variables. Still, these patterns seem mainly to corroborate previously established relationships and to provide scant insight into processes (Jordaan & Heyde, 1979; Super, Kowalski, & Gotkin, 1967). Indeed, judgments of outcomes seem to speak largely of subjects' failure to engage in the kind of process that is regarded as representing progress in (so-called) vocational maturity. Jordaan and Heyde (1979) asserted: "evidence is mounting that vocational goals, even in the last year of high school, are often poorly conceived and at variance with later work histories."

"The evidence indicates that the period following high school is more likely to be characterized by floundering—by haphazard and poorly conceived changes of jobs and even occupations—than by purposeful progress toward a clearly conceived goal."

Gribbons and Lohnes (1968, 1969) also assiduously followed up a sample of 111 eighth-grade males and females, selected in 1958, to about age 25. Data from early structured interviews in this Career Development Study were quite rich in describing individual differences in students' awareness of relevant factors in curriculum choice and occupational choice, their perceptions of linkages between curricula and occupations, their use of self-appraisals (abilities, interests, and values) in making such choices, and their independence in choosing. Unexpectedly, Grade 8 scores on these variables were more valid than Grade 10 scores in predicting various criteria of vocational adjustment 2 years after high school. Other evidence for maturational stages was also weak, particularly because of the large numbers of people who made little progress. Gribbons and Lohnes (1969) noted: "the majority of adolescents are poorly oriented with respect to career development tasks and . . . fully one-third to almost one-half of young adults at age 25 appear to be in career development trouble."

Perhaps by the time adolescence and young adulthood have been attained, it is proper to think of stages determined not so much genetically as culturally. The arrangements and expectations of the society, particularly the educational system, prompt people at certain points (possible discontinuities) to decide on one course or another. At these points, people tend—consciously or unwittingly—to reduce the number of options available to them in the future. There is usually at least one road not taken. Help is often needed if the choice is to be informed and rational. Katz (1963) stated:

> Decision-making at each stage may be regarded as a strategy for acquiring and processing information. If a decision is truly *to be made*, if it is not a foregone conclusion, it must involve some novel elements. [People] confronted with the problem of decision making either do not know what information they need, do not have what information they want, or cannot

good definition

use what information they have. Thus, the pressure for making a decision creates a discrepancy between individuals' present state of knowledge (or wisdom) and the state that is being demanded of them.

Regardless of the size of the discrepancy, some decision will be made at each choice-point—if only by drift or by default. . . . The role of guidance is to reduce the discrepancy between a [person's] untutored readiness for rational behavior and some hypothetical ideal state of knowledge and wisdom.

Nature of the Discrepancy

To spell out the nature of the discrepancy, we engaged in a series of interview studies as part of our early development of SIGI. We were interested in ascertaining students' own perceptions of the process of CDM. How much responsibility were they assuming for their own decisions? How free did they feel they were to make their own choices? What constructs did they use? What elements of self-appraisal did they regard as relevant? What evidence did they seek? What options did they see as open to them? What information did they have or seek about those options? What linkages did they make between their own perceived characteristics and the perceived properties of occupations? Had they planned steps to implement any decisions? Did their plans allow for contingencies? What actions had they already taken in respect to any of these questions?

In general, we found that college students tended to take responsibility for their own decisions. They recognized some constraints but for the most part emphasized their freedom to choose from a wide range of options. Individuals differed considerably in the number and nature of constructs they used in choosing an occupation, or describing occupations, or differentiating between occupations, or evaluating occupations (we used a variety of stimulus questions in these interviews). Some students readily produced five or six meaningful constructs. Others had great difficulty in dredging up more than two or three. Still others bogged down at the outset and then, after a bit of thinking, might shrug and say vaguely they wanted a "good job." Pursuing what they meant by a "good job," the interviewer might elicit a few such enlightening phrases as: "I want to make a good living . . . a desk job . . . no advanced math." These statements are meaningful, but one wonders (given the difficulty in eliciting them) whether they are comprehensive, whether the students have thought about and mentioned everything of importance to them. To test this concern without a canvass of all possible dimensions, the interviewer would suggest a few constructs not mentioned, for example: "How about security? Would you want a desk job that paid a high salary if the job was likely to be wiped out early in a recession, or if it depended on the success of a very risky venture?" To this, a student would often say, "No, I want a steady job."

Later, when they were exposed to a much larger array of constructs, including those they had mentioned and many others they had not thought of, students tended to weight heavily in importance some of those constructs that they had produced initially; but most students assigned at least as heavy weights to constructs that had been supplied by the interviewer. Thus, we could infer that the constructs or dimensions the students had generated were not sufficiently comprehensive. Matters that turned out to be quite important had not been made explicit.

Besides considering the range of constructs, interviewers probed for clarification of those constructs that had been expressed. What was the significance of "desk job" to this student? Was she concerned about the prestige of the occupation? Physical demands? Something pertaining to the work activities? Was "desk job" a surrogate for some other latent concern? Often, "desk job" did not mean the same thing to different students who had used the phrase. Similarly, a student might say he wanted an occupation that is "not boring." This phrase uses an individual language that is not helpful in CDM until it is translated into a language that is relevant to occupations. Pressed on what he means, the student might say, "I don't want to do the same thing all the time." This is one facet of an operational definition of a dimension that we labeled variety. Occupations can be described along that dimension. Or he might refer to another dimension labeled working in a main field of interest. If, for example, math is boring to him, it is to be *avoided*. But is there some field of activity or knowledge to be *sought?* Perhaps working with people appeals to him. Expressing a desire for a job that is "not boring" is, by itself, of no help in identifying occupations. Specifying some level of variety or work involving personal contact can help the student to identify occupations that are worth further examination.

In the realm of perception of options, most students could name one or more occupations of prospective interest to them. But later in the interview, when they had been helped by prompts and probes to state more extensively and clearly what they wanted in an occupation, the interviewer would ask, "Why not (such-and-such occupation)? Wouldn't that appeal to you at least as much as (one they had named)?" The answer was often that they had not known of such an occupation or had not recognized that it met their (now much clarified) specifications.

Indeed, surveys have generally confirmed the paucity of occupations considered by people in their own CDM. When the National Assessment of Educational Progress (NAEP) of 1973–1974 asked a national sample of 17-year-olds to name five occupations they had considered, 86% were able to name one and 78% named a second, but only 56% a third, 29% a fourth, and 15% a fifth (Katz, 1978a). Nor do college students appear to consider any greater number of occupations. Samples of students at six colleges, ranging widely in size, location, characteristics of student body, and other variables, were asked, "How many occupations have you explored as possibilities for yourself?" (Chapman et al., 1977). Distributions of responses tended to be quite consistent across schools, with a median of 5% indicating they had considered no occupations, 51% one or two occupations, 33% three or four, and only 12.5% more than four. (One of the effects of use of SIGI at those colleges was a very significant increase in the number of occupations considered.)

Similar fuzziness or downright ignorance was found in the amount and quality of students' information about occupations they were considering. They were uncertain about how to link the information they did have to their self-appraisals. They could not explain the process by which they had arrived at their stated decisions or choices. Planning was often nonexistent or vague or inappropriate. Little specific action was under way to remedy these deficiencies.

Summary of Students' Needs

In summary, then, we found that students were short on constructs, unable to bring latent matters of importance into explicit awareness and expression. They often used vague or idiosyncratic terms for a construct they did adumbrate, limiting themselves to a personal vocabulary that could not be linked to occupational properties. Thus, there appeared a need to help students define the domain of self-appraisal so that a comprehensive array of constructs about self (about what one wants, what one is interested in, and what one can do) may be linked to corresponding dimensions in the domain of constructs about occupations (the opportunities for various rewards and satisfactions, the fields of knowledge and activities, and the required preparation and skills in different occupations). Then, when a manageable array of options could be identified, there was a need to come to grips with decision making—to understand and use rational decision rules and processes in maximizing desirability and minimizing risks according to each person's own lights. There was also a manifest need to plan and take steps that would be productive in implementing decisions, including identification of checkpoints at which progress could be evaluated and decisions reviewed; thus it was important for students themselves to understand the CDM process so that it could be used during the future.

Special Needs of Adults

All the needs just stated were taken into consideration in the design and development of SIGI, as the description of the model for SIGI shows. Because SIGI was targeted mainly toward college students, however, the design of SIGI PLUS had to take into account the special needs of the rest of the adult population for career guidance.

One of the first questions to consider was whether the general population of adults construes occupations and values differently from the college population. For example, do they tend to place more or less importance on extrinsic or intrinsic values, on values relating mainly to occupations or to jobs? Does their satisfaction depend more on avoidance of things disliked than on opportunities to get what they like? Do likes and dislikes involve different dimensions? Or are they poles of the same dimensions? To begin to answer these questions, we first looked at relevant research. (Some of this work was cited in the previous chapter that discussed the relative prevalence of intrinsic and extrinsic values; so here only the findings for adults are summarized.)

In the 1973-1974 National Assessment of Educational Progress, a national sample of young adults (ages 26-35) were asked to "list ten different things that a person should think about in choosing a job or career." ("Job" and "career" were loosely used in the NAEP exercises as synonymous with "occupation.") They gave responses similar to those of 17-year-olds in frequency of mention of extrinsic and intrinsic values. As with the 17-year-olds, some global or holistic concept of intrinsic satisfaction, often vaguely expressed, seemed to come to mind right off the bat in response to the question; it was promptly mentioned, and that subject was exhausted. On the other hand, respondents were able to think of many items that had to do with extrinsic values, such as working conditions. Other categories of response – even some extrinsic values – do not seem to occur to people so readily. For example, security might be considered particularly important to many adults, especially during periods of high unemployment. Yet only 1% of the respondents mentioned tenure, resistance to seasonal, technological, or economic change, favorable outlook for demand and supply, and so on (Tiedeman et al., 1978). But other studies have shown that, when security is included in an array of specified categories, and young adults are asked to assign weights to the categories to indicate the relative importance of each one, security tends to outweigh working conditions (Chapman et al., 1977; Harris & Associates, 1979; Norris & Katz, 1970; Norris et al., 1978; Quinn et al., 1974).

This theme of significant discrepancies between examined and unexamined values has been substantiated in structured interviews and simulated occupational choice (Katz et al., 1969; Katz et al., 1976, 1978). The things that pop into people's heads when they have not subjected their values to close scrutiny but are only responding to a survey are often less important to them than the things they emphasize when they have thoroughly explored or examined their values, as in a more systematic process of CDM. At the same time, adults' emphasis on working conditions cautioned us to include job-related as well as occupational values in SIGI PLUS.

Adults' pattern of responses again resembled 17-year-olds' when questions were asked in National Assessment about things liked and things disliked in a current (or recent) job. Of the categories used to describe things liked, the most popular were job-related values such as Interpersonal Relations and Good Working Conditions, Hours, Location, Fringe Benefits (mentioned by about the same proportion of adults and 17-year-olds). Less frequent mention was made by both groups (again in equal proportions) of the occupation-related categories Good Pay and Specific Duties and Requirements. Given the different nature of the jobs characteristically held by adults and teenagers, these findings represent a remarkable convergence in what people tend to say they like about their jobs. Probably the 17-year-olds had lower expectations and liked their jobs in relation to the other jobs they saw as available to them at that stage in their lives. The two groups diverged only when the proportions were small: 13% of the adults but only 5% of the 17-year-olds referred to the opportunity for independent work; 13% and 3%, respectively, indicated the work was interesting or fun to do, and the same proportions liked the fact that the work provided a challenge and a sense of responsibility (whereas 4% of the adults and 11% of the 17-year-olds liked the *lack* of responsibility).

When it came to things disliked, the combined Don't Know and No Response categories accounted for about half the respondents in each age group – in keeping with the repeated findings that most people tend to say they are generally satisfied with their jobs. As pointed out before, likes and dislikes seem to be construed along the same dimensions. That is, although there are some differences between the "likes" and "dislikes" in rank order of categories, the most frequently disliked things fit in the same four categories as the most frequently liked things. Thus, similar constructs were elicited regardless of whether the question was phrased in positive or negative terms. This finding tends to contradict theories (Herzberg, et al., 1959) that the dimensions of job satisfaction are different from the dimensions of job dissatisfaction. Instead, the dimensions along which most people evaluate their job likes and dislikes appear to be bipolar (e.g., "good pay" vs. "low pay").

An earlier survey of a national probability sample of American workers in 1969–1970 (Quinn et al., 1974) obtained importance ratings of 23 "job facets." As detailed previously, most of the very important facets to a majority of workers were occupation related, and only a minority found job-related facets very important.

It is a truism to note that responses change according to the way a question is asked. A national sample of men ages 18 to 49 (Harris & Associates, 1979) were asked about 27 aspects of their work: 79% rated a "chance to use your mind and abilities" and 70% rated "job security" as very important. But the rank order changed when the task was to "name the four or five most important to you." Only 34% named the former and 50% the latter; "good salary" rose from sixth to first rank, chosen by 56%. Thus, comparative judgments result in changes in priorities. (This is one reason that SIGI asks users to distribute a fixed sum of value weights across the 10 values; it is an efficient method of making and recording comparative judgments for a substantial number of variables.)

Our own study of adult needs indicated four general types of situations in which career guidance might be sought:

1. people who want to stay in their current occupation but find it necessary or desirable to change jobs;
2. people looking for advancement in their present line of work or in a related line;
3. people currently employed who want to change their occupations; and
4. people wanting to enter or re-enter employment, who want to decide on an occupation and a job.

These types may often overlap or people may shift from one to another (e.g., a person who initially seeks a job change may later decide to change occupations, or vice versa). People in the various types also share some common needs. It is clear, nevertheless, that each type involves some distinctive needs.

Last (1978) suggested that Type 1 requires the following: a list of available vacancies; a means of identifying alternative job possibilities for which vacancies exist; information about training programs, grants, and assistance; advice on relocating; help in writing resumes and preparing for interviews. For Type 2 (according to Last), additional needs include details of educational opportunities and professional training programs. I would add information about "career ladders" and promotional opportunities in organizations where the person works or might seek work. Types 3 and 4, concerned with comprehensive aspects of CDM, present virtually all the needs identified for college students plus the means of taking into account previous education and experience.

Most adults lack the flexibility of youthful college students. The latter have not as yet accumulated an overwhelming investment in education, training, and work experience of a given kind, nor have they usually settled into a home and family life, a community, a stable network of friends and associates. Adults, by contrast, bring to career decisions both impediments and assets that are seldom part of the baggage of less encumbered young persons. To adults relocation may be seen as dislocation: What if one's spouse has a good job here? How will a move affect the children? Will a suitable house at a relatively low mortgage rate have to be sacrificed for one less suitable and more expensive? Previous education and experience may be a help or a hindrance in an occupational change: Is it relevant to the new occupation? Is it obsolescent? Is it likely to be credited or discounted? In general, adults are likely to want to make choices that will capitalize, as much as possible, on their assets and previous investments. If such possibilities cannot be found, they will at least want to minimize their losses. Thus, loss functions usually play an important part in their CDM.

To determine more precisely the ways in which SIGI should be amplified to meet the special needs of adults, in 1981 we conducted a questionnaire survey of 167 adults who had just used SIGI. We had already ascertained that adults found the general model and content helpful, but in this instance we wanted to focus on the gaps and shortcomings of SIGI for this population: What should be added? What should be changed? The findings were almost all in keeping with our expectations.

The largest number (more than 33%) of the respondents were concerned with a change of occupation and therefore with the full array of sections in SIGI. The next most popular response was for job advancement "in my present occupation." Each of the SIGI values was deemed important by significant numbers of people; thus the occupational values dimensions held up as well for this population as for college students. All the items on a list of 11 job values were also regarded as important (e.g., on-the-job training, fringe benefits, congenial co-workers, chances for advancement); free-response suggestions for "other" job values indicated that the 11 listed covered the concerns quite well. In response to a question about the kind of help they needed in CDM, the three items chosen most frequently were "assessing occupational characteristics as they relate to your values," "getting information about occupations," and "assessing job characteristics as they relate to your values." Each of the nine items listed, however, was checked by more than 31% of the respondents and warranted consideration in developing SIGI PLUS. They included assessing financial resources, information about financial aid for education or training, college credit for experiential learning, learning how to apply for a job, information about college training, and assessing family's priorities as they relate to "your occupation or job." Only 6% of the respondents indicated "other" concerns, and these were widely scattered.

All the occupational information in SIGI was of interest to most of the respondents (only two items were not regarded as important for adults by a significant minority). As for information that might be added to a system for adults, *local* information about "Where the jobs are" and "Employment outlook" were rated as very important by about 75% of the respondents. More than 65% rated as very important "Where to get additional training or education for a specific occupation" and "How to go about getting a job." There was a very broad scattering of "other" types of information suggested for inclusion in an adult system. These highlight the diversity of concerns in even a small sample of adults, although the salience of each item to the respondents is unknown.

Asked directly whether they would want to use a computerized career guidance system that we would design specifically for adults, more than 98% said yes. More than 65% would be willing to "come back" three or more times to go through the system at least once and would be willing to spend more than 4 hours on it. Preferred sites for such a system would be at a college, public library, "my place of work," or public school (the first two getting about 75% of the vote). Asked how they would like to proceed through the system, a plurality (47%) wanted the computer to lead them through from beginning to end and explain how to use each section to best advantage; almost as many (44%) wanted the computer to describe each section and suggest a path; only 10% wanted the computer to describe each section with no prescribed or suggested path, leaving users to skip around on their own. About 94% wanted to see identification of occupational skills included in the system. Clearly, adults want help in assessing their accumulated skills and experience in relation to occupational requirements.

While the respondents did not represent a scientific sample of any population, these questionnaire responses are consistent with findings from other surveys and extended observations. Having our expectations corroborated by these results confirmed our belief that the design of SIGI PLUS, therefore, must take into account job values as well as the occupational values encompassed in SIGI. It must treat preparation for an occupation not just from the standpoint of the young college student; it must be flexible enough to allow people with vastly varying kinds and amounts of education to judge what requirements they may have already met and what pathways may take them most efficiently from where they are to where they want to be. It must help them in coping with practical considerations of all kinds: child care, flexible hours, credit for nontraditional learning, and so on. It should include help in obtaining local information: the work environment, fringe benefits, and "career ladders" at particular companies. It should help them extract from their total experience and synthesize all that is relevant for exploring and examining options, making decisions, planning preparation, coping with problems, and taking next steps.

INTERACTION BETWEEN SOCIETAL AND INDIVIDUAL NEEDS

It is generally recognized that society and the individual both have a stake in career decisions. Society wants its work done well. It craves excellence, as Gardner (1961) said, in plumbers and philosophers lest neither pipes nor theories hold water. There are high economic and social costs for incompetence. Society also hopes for a nice balance between supply and demand in labor markets, one that will avoid both high costs and high unemployment. Society is also concerned with equity—equal opportunity for access and for socioeconomic mobility. These objectives are frequently also in the interest of individuals. By the same token, matters of paramount importance to the individual—such as success and satisfaction in work—generally are benefits also to society. There is, nevertheless, often a certain tension between the societal stake and the individual stake in the rules that govern selection and choice at various transition points.

Manpower Versus Guidance Models

As in any transaction, there are overlapping interests but also some elements of competition or conflict between social and individual needs. Government, for example, tends to focus on *manpower* models. To the extent that government policy dictates a planned economy, individual freedom of choice tends to be restricted. The United Soviet Socialist Republic represented an extreme example of such restriction according to manpower needs: Rutkevich (1969) said, for instance, access to educational institutions was severely limited, and "educational priorities [were] largely determined by the production goals of the state." In China during the Cultural Revolution, government-appointed neighborhood councils made all career decisions for each person in the community (France, Jin, Huang, Si, & Zhang, 1991).

In the United States, manpower policy has relied more on incentives than on restraints. In the 1950s, the National Defense Education Act, which provided for an unprecedented expansion of guidance services in education, was prompted largely by the federal government's perception of an urgent need to recruit able students for engineering and the sciences. At that time, it seemed of crucial importance to national interest to keep up with the Soviet Union in space.

More recent federal funding for guidance has emphasized reduction of unemployment (e.g., The Youth Employment and Demonstration Projects Act of 1977) and has called in the Comprehensive Employment and Training Act (CETA) Amendments of 1978 for special attention to improve the match of youth career desires with available and anticipated labor demand. CETA has been superseded in the 1980s by the Job Training Partnership Act, which aims to foster guidance, selection, training, and placement for the private sector. Because a shortage of good teachers has been perceived, a 1984 government program was designed to attract talented people to prepare for careers in teaching. In the 1990s there is again urgent concern for recruitment to occupations in engineering, technology, mathematics, and science – this time to keep up with Japan. Thus, the federal government has supported extensive interventions in career decisions as a means of inducing youth to adapt to societal needs and conditions and presumably *thereby* to ameliorate their own status. Government intervention was deemed necessary because the labor market was regarded as too slow or ineffectual to accomplish these aims.

Access. Manpower models of selection and guidance have the effect of erecting barriers and limiting access at relatively early stages in careers. They are dedicated to preventing failure, waste, and inefficiency in training or preparation and low productivity on jobs. Concepts of equity through compensatory education and selection are alien to this model but not to current social policy. So recent compensatory models (including special educational provisions and "affirmative action") aim to wipe out barriers, especially those that in the past have been associated with discrimination against minorities, women, and the handicapped. The thrust of these programs has been not only against discriminatory practice in selection but also against another constraint on equal access – the lack of appropriate information. Thus, the first component of equal access has been legislative and administrative programs to make more opportunities available. The second has been guidance to make people aware of opportunities and aware of their own capabilities, interests, and values as these characteristics relate to options. The first is directed against external barriers. Guidance is directed against internalized barriers.

This is an important distinction. Despite the emphasis in federal support of guidance to reduce unemployment, it is important to note that guidance does not create jobs. Guidance, along with compensatory and affirmative action programs, may affect the distribution of certain segments of the population in various occupations. Such programs could also reduce structural unemployment, particularly in a tight labor market, but are unlikely to have much effect on the magnitude of unemployment in loose labor markets. Thus, the argument that *any* approach to guidance can reduce general unemployment is a weak one, contingent on relatively rare circumstances. Similarly, manpower and guidance models converge only under special assumptions about the nature and purpose of guidance.

A Unidimensional Model. The manpower approach to meeting perceived national priorities for certain occupations depends partly on incentives but generally includes a substantial guidance component to steer people in the direction that is regarded as best for all concerned. The rationale for such a view of guidance often appears to assume that a single optimization rule applies to both the societal and the individual stake. The major premise seems to be that requirements, qualifications, and rewards are distributed along parallel scales. The rule is to select the best qualified people for the highest priority until the quota is met, then work down the list to fill the next highest priority, and so on. Rewards would presumably be set (by government support when market forces appear insufficient) in line with priorities. This parallelism between individual and societal benefits is readily achieved if the only rewards of concern are earnings and attained status, generally defined so as to be highly correlated, as by Jencks et al. (1979). In this case, occupational choice and membership is a zero-sum game (as indicated by the title of the Jencks book, *Who Gets Ahead?*). "Winners" and "losers" are all assumed to be striving to place as "high" as possible; "altitude" is the sole criterion.

Multiple Dimensions. Another view is that requirements, qualifications, and rewards are multidimensional. A selection rule to maximize societal benefits, then, might be analogous to minimizing the sum of squared differences between qualifications and requirements. But if rewards and satisfactions are also multidimensional, parallelism between societal and individual benefits may be absent. Variation in the importance attached to each dimension by different individuals means that they can "win" in different ways. For example, some may especially want high income, or an opportunity for altruistic service, or job security, or autonomy, or work in a main field of interest, and so on, and also various combinations of such rewards and satisfactions. Such differences in values may represent stronger and more variable incentives than those associated with meeting manpower requirements. Thus, manpower models are not optimal for individual benefits when (a) individuals are multipotential, (b) individuals vary considerably in their values, (c) occupational requirements are flexible, and (d) opportunities for rewards and satisfactions tend to vary considerably from one occupation to another. So the fact that at various times more people have persevered in wanting to farm or teach history than present or projected labor markets appeared able to accommodate may be attributed in part to lack of information or to skepticism about the validity of outlook information but may also in part reflect the gap between societal and individual values.

Democracy and Autonomy

Henri Marrou (1982) said: "Education is not an element that can be detached from one civilization and borrowed by another. It is the concentrated epitome of a culture and as such is inseparable from the form of that culture, and perishes with it." What Marrou said of education may be said also of guidance. The need of a society for a particular kind of influence on careers differs as the society is industrially advanced or undeveloped, warlike or peaceful, autocratic or democratic.

For example, what is most distinctive about a democracy may be its processes of decision making. A crucial characteristic for the processes by which national policy decisions are made in the United States is the recognition of pluralism. On every issue competing interests and pressure groups are heard. Sometimes they differ on predictions of outcomes – for instance, the effects of a particular change in tax laws on the economy. More often, and more significantly, they have different definitions of desirability, different objectives, even when they agree on predictions of outcomes. How do these differences get resolved, ideally? The necessary condition is freedom, the open marketplace of ideas, in which every voice can be heard and judged. Out of this confrontation of competing values, informed and reasonable people can hope to reach an informed and rational decision, to be translated into a mandate for action. But it does not stop there. The process is ongoing, permitting revision of content in accordance not just with outcomes but also with changes in values and objectives. This emphasis on process provides for change in content of decisions, for adaptation to new situations and circumstances, for solving new problems. It has perhaps insured the survival of democracy, up till now, through many vicissitudes.

We would expect, then, that this democratic process of decision making found in the larger society should be reflected in the principles of individual CDM. Individuals make order out of the rabble of impulses that beset them by recognizing that, essentially, they must choose between competing values. Neither suppressing nor blindly obeying impulses, they can control them by bringing them under the rule of reason, giving each "equal time" and attention. They can hold themselves open and receptive to different values, allowing each to speak to them as loudly as the others. This process involves active and systematic exploration of competing values to answer the central question, "What do I want?" Hence, the primary emphasis on exploration and examination of values in SIGI for career decision making reflects the similar emphasis for policy decisions in the larger democratic society. We would expect, then, that at least some forces in a democratic society and its government would recognize a stake in fostering democratic principles in CDM and guidance.

Societal influences on guidance differ also in accordance with perceptions of human beings and of their place in the environment: Are they unique and independent or interchangeable and determinable? Are they free to make choices about their own lives or bound by being part of a larger system of reality that ordains the shape and direction of their careers? In our democratic society, at this time, there are still obvious constraints on freedom of choice.

Yet, notwithstanding the biological, economic, social, political, and psychological limitations on freedom, individuals still cherish their remnants of autonomy in CDM. They seek opportunities and options that provide satisfaction relevant primarily to their own values. Willingness to incur some level of risk is often part of this interaction between values, satisfactions, and probabilities of entry. The approach to guidance embodied in SIGI, according to Katz (1974), aims to foster individual freedom by recognizing that:

> within whatever constraints are allowed by being a member of the human species, having inherited a given set of genes, being brought up in a certain culture and being subjected to selected arrays of reinforcements, most young men and women seem to want to become as independent as possible. They seem to want to use as much space as is left them for making their own decisions, for determining their own behavior—even those who decide to become behaviorists.

Freedom, Competence, and Process. A proponent of this approach goes on to recognize that freedom without competence is frustrating. Freedom and ignorance are an ill-fated pair. Information about risks is an important component of the trade-offs that must be made between probable risks and valued rewards. Collecting and interpreting information and providing structures and strategies for its use are functions appropriate for professional intervention. But the outcomes of this process depend on individual values. To use professional competence to dictate the content of a person's decisions is presumptuous. SIGI was designed, therefore, to provide the structure and information suitable for a free and rational process of CDM. Katz (1974) stated:

> Without directing the content of [individuals'] choices, we do think we can help them in the process of choosing. This emphasis on process does not pretend to insure the "right" choice—except insofar as the right choice is defined as an informed and rational choice. Our bias—our conviction—is that in education enlightened processes are intrinsically important. Therefore, we bend our efforts to increase [students'] understanding of the factors involved in choice (imperfect though our own understanding may be) so that [they] can take responsibility for [their] own decision-making, examine [themselves] and explore [their] options in a systematic and comprehensive way, take purposeful action in testing hypotheses about [themselves] in various situations and exercise flexibility in devising alternative plans.
>
> In short, we don't want to play the decision-making game for them. We want to help them master the strategies for rational behavior in the face of uncertainty so that they can play the game effectively themselves.

SPECIFICATION OF COLLEGES' NEEDS

Most colleges and universities have recognized a need to assist students in CDM and have accepted and even welcomed a role in meeting that need. Career planning and placement offices have been established almost universally in postsecondary institutions. Yet, until recently they have rarely enjoyed much "clout" on the campus. Staffs were generally not accorded faculty status, they tended to be few in number, and their budgets were usually low. Consequently, they have rarely been equipped to provide comprehensive career guidance services for large numbers of students. Instead, they have had to focus on certain functions that are consistent with institutional priorities or their own predilections. In many instances placement is the paramount function, with possible further specialization between placement in jobs and placement in graduate and professional schools. For many colleges placement represents the "bottom line," testimony to the quality of their "product." Placement helps establish the college's reputation and contributes to "marketing," to attracting and retaining students. So one of the first needs to be recognized was to extend and amplify the productivity of the career planning and placement officers.

Pragmatics

Contributions to recruitment and retention are often the strongest arguments that career planning and placement officers can make to administrators for their support. Obviously, recruitment and retention are boosted not only by placement but directly by a display of the quality of career guidance services offered. Such services may be made available to prospective students even before enrollment, to help them establish career objectives and see how a particular college's programs can help them move toward those objectives. Knowing that students (and their parents) are often greatly concerned about career decisions and plans, colleges make a point of describing and even demonstrating their resources to prospective enrollees. Counseling facilities and resources are pictured in catalogs and proudly shown on campus tours. The presence of a computer-based career guidance system is seen to enhance the "image" of the college: It speaks of concern for students' CDM, of being up to the minute technologically, and of high capacity for serving large numbers of students tirelessly.

To the administrator a computerized career guidance system speaks also of cost effectiveness. To hire additional counselors to deal with as many students for as much time as such a system does would exceed the cost of the system by more than an order of magnitude. The administrator would not supplant present counseling staffs with computerized guidance but would use it instead of trying to support a much more expensive increase in staff.

In short, there are various pragmatic bread-and-butter needs of colleges that a computerized system should be designed to meet. It should provide as comprehensive career guidance and planning as possible, showing the relevance of college programs for careers; it should be as self-sufficient as possible, capable of handling large numbers of students at low unit cost. Another important consideration is low capital cost; while all costs are important, career planning and placement offices have not traditionally been able to manage substantial capital budgets. Thus, an important need was to design SIGI for the least expensive hardware compatible with its mission. All these concerns were of great practical importance, but they omit some matters of intellectual substance that were of crucial importance in gaining acceptance of the system by faculties.

Academic Hostility to Career Guidance

Many faculty members, particularly those in the liberal arts and sciences, are at best lukewarm and very often downright opposed to career guidance on the campus. They tend to see struggle and conflict in the "threat" that "careerism" (as they call it) poses to the traditions of liberal arts education. For example, Loyal Rue (1982) wrote that professors "cry for a return to basics, to more rigor, to greater breadth," whereas administrators remind them it is "a buyer's market. And what the buyer wants is a good investment that will bring ample monetary returns" (p. 25). Students want "a narrowly instrumental education, well targeted for a specific lucrative job" (p. 25). Liberal arts professors then are quick to identify career guidance with such "careerism" and mark it as the enemy. To see how the needs and perceptions of liberal arts faculties can be met by a career guidance system like SIGI, it is necessary first to trace briefly the present plight of the liberal arts.

The Rise and Fall of a Community of Discourse

Historically, the ideal of a liberal arts education was centripetal. The quadrivium (a place where four ways meet) and the trivium (where three ways meet) converged on the baccalaureate. The new Bachelor of Arts was admitted to membership in the society of liberally educated persons, recognized as an initiate in the community of learned discourse. All who reached that status had traveled the same ways and had a shared background of knowledge and intellectual experience. Even as the content of the liberal arts changed over the centuries, it changed for all, so that a common core of learning prevailed for all. Thus, in their respective centuries, even a Newton or a Darwin, with radically innovative ideas, could address the community of educated persons and be comprehended.

But in modern times, particularly in our country, the liberal arts have fallen on hard times. There is less than universal agreement on what higher education should consist of. The founding and flourishing of land grant colleges, technical institutes, and community colleges exemplify a pragmatic view of education that has sometimes been at odds with the ideals, the goals, and the structure of the liberal arts. Furthermore, even at most traditional liberal arts colleges, the liberal arts themselves seem to have come unglued. The rapid expansion of knowledge and increasing specialization have exerted a centrifugal force, spinning apart the separate disciplines. Indeed, the disciplines themselves have fragmented into specialties, and the specialties, like stars in an expanding universe, have sped off at accelerating rates to distance themselves from one another. For example, today's physicists and biologists work beyond the comprehension not only of most "educated persons" but of many scholars in their own disciplines. So the cohesive force and binding energy of the liberal arts have been lost. As consensus disintegrated, the disciplines and subdisciplines of the traditional liberal arts – to say nothing of other fields – became less collaborative and more competitive, less coherent and more partitioned. This trend affected the objectives, content, and nature of instruction. Professors in each discipline sought and fostered disciples and often designed even their introductory courses for prospective majors. There has still been some obeisance to the concept of the liberal arts: Distributive requirements have given reluctant students exposure to those introductory courses and enabled them to acquire a "smattering of ignorance" in several areas. The outcomes of higher education have tended to be divisive, however, leading to not just "two cultures" but multiple cultures.

In the 1940s the late James Bryant Conant, as president of Harvard, led an attack on the pervasive neglect of general education. The Harvard committee that prepared the famous "red book," *General Education in a Free Society* (1945), invoked the social–political responsibilities of higher education: In a society that depends on "cooperation without uniformity, agreement on the good of man at the level of performance without the necessity of agreement on ultimates" the committee sought to redefine a "common core" of learning that might restore the community of discourse (referred to before) among educated *citizens in a democracy*. Consequently, there came into being at Harvard courses in science for nonscientists (Conant himself helped to design and teach one such course) and courses in humanities that would be attractive to nonspecialists.

Notwithstanding these heroic efforts, the red book, although widely read and discussed, had little impact on practices generally, and the centrifugal forces continued to drive elements of education farther apart.

General education courses that survived tended to have little rigor, or respect from faculty or students. Even at Harvard the curriculum that emerged from the red book fell into "innocuous desuetude." During the 1980s, new faculty committees attempted to redefine a liberal education and regenerate a new core curriculum; for example, a new Harvard report by a faculty committee chaired by Dean Henry Rosovsky received wide public attention for such an effort. A Secretary of Education in the 1980s (William Bennett) released a report on higher education that (among other things) decried the emphasis it found on "a highly specialized education that will lead to a specific job" and called for more emphasis on the liberal arts. (There are cynics who believe that a new required core curriculum appeals to liberal arts faculties, in a time of declining enrollments and faculty cutbacks, as a way of securing bread-and-butter levels of enrollment in otherwise endangered departments. Whether it will appeal to students in a buyer's market is another question.)

While the future of the liberal arts as the central theme of college education is not clear (although it seems safe to assume that they will continue to be important as individual areas of study), there appears no likelihood of achieving consensus on a stable universal curriculum such as marked the middle ages. Perhaps one can anticipate a continuing trend toward dispersed and pluralistic arrangements, with different institutions doing different things. It may also be anticipated that whatever distinctive arrangements for a core curriculum are reached at any institution (even Harvard) will tend to degrade as the energy that binds them is dissipated. Continual attention, redefinition, reconstruction, and revitalization will be required to forestall the effects of academic entropy.

Guidance to the Aid of the Liberal Arts

Certainly, the centrifugal forces of expanding knowledge and specialization that tore the liberal arts apart also established the need for guidance. When education no longer prescribed a common experience for all, when students were confronted with a perplexing and not readily visible variety of options, both educational and occupational, problems of choice became difficult and complicated. Of course, guidance too can be fragmented. There are guidance programs and so-called systems of computerized guidance that are not systems at all. They fail to integrate elements of self-appraisal and of occupational and educational information into a well-articulated structure for explicit CDM strategies. But let us speak of a coherent system.

How can such a computerized career guidance system come to the aid of the liberal arts in reconstituting a centripetal force? How can it be seen not as an enemy but as an ally? The liberal arts and a well-integrated guidance system have somewhat distinctive roles that may be regarded as complementary. I have suggested elsewhere that education, particularly the liberal arts, purports to deal primarily with the "universals" in a culture, whereas guidance deals primarily with the "alternatives." But this dichotomy is not just a distinction; it also suggests an interaction. Katz (1963) wrote: "If the role of education is to transmit the culture, the role of guidance is to help the individual come to terms with the culture–that is, to see himself in the culture. But first he must see the culture in himself. Thus, his first question should be, Where have my values come from? His second, Where are they taking me?"

Note that values mediate the interaction between education and guidance. The liberal arts contribute to an understanding of the genesis and development of the values of a culture. Guidance contributes to an understanding of the values of an individual in that culture, confronting the problem of selection between competing values in the individual's CDM. SIGI was designed to engage students in a dialogue that leads them sequentially through six subsystems, culminating in the section called Strategy. (The analogous section in SIGI PLUS is called Deciding.) This section takes into account the student's own values and interests, the characteristics of specific options, and the student's perceptions and informed assessment of external circumstances. It provides decision rules for balancing rewards and risks and leads to adjudication between options. Students then become "initiates" and are free to move directly to any subsystem in any order.

Thus, students use the system in *distinctive* ways: They follow different branches within each section, make unique self-appraisals, see and use different data–all consistent with their own needs, values, preferences, circumstances, plans, and particular stage of decision making–yet all work their way through a *common structure*. Each may deal with distinctive content, but all go through and learn a common process. The structure and the process of SIGI and SIGI PLUS, which all students share, provide a common core in guidance. This common core also provides a powerful centripetal force in education, gathering students from different disciplines to develop competencies in CDM. The very area in which individual differences are most pronounced–the area of distinctive career decisions, often including decisions to specialize–becomes a strong central focus of activity for all students.

This process of construing and choosing "alternatives" may be the most compelling "universal" in higher education. It fortifies the liberal arts because it suggests what should be liberating about the liberal arts: not just having freedom, but learning to use it to best advantage. The development of touchstones and competencies is a major objective of liberal education, which has been defined as "what you remember after you've forgotten everything you learned." A coherent career guidance system that contributes to that objective can be an important adjunct to or even component of the liberal arts. Thus, there is a need in liberal education for a guidance system that avoids purveying discrete gobs of occupational information using computer technology as an electronic page-turner. Such information is only a fragment of a guidance system and is irrelevant to a liberal education. It can be made relevant only by being integrated into a well-founded structure and a carefully conceived process of CDM.

Computerized guidance can aspire to be a "liberal" art form. It needs to delight students as well as instruct and guide them. "Art," said Whitehead, "is the imposing of a pattern on experience, and our aesthetic enjoyment is recognition of the pattern." Thus, guidance and the liberal arts can conspire to help students find order in the complexities of decision making, help them enrich their experience by examining it, and help them become the conscious artists of their own careers and of their own liberal education.

SIGI PLUS retains the integrated sequence and structure of SIGI for those who elect to use it. But in view of the wider variations in presenting needs and circumstances of adults (compared to college students), the "core curriculum" is not required of all. Users have access to any section in any order right at the outset. They may decide to use just one section and no other, although they will usually encounter suggestions to go to another section for certain types of information or assistance. Some college counselors who have seen SIGI PLUS during its development have expressed regret at the loss of the prescribed sequence of sections for "novices." But just as users must often make compromises, trading off satisfaction of one value for aggrandizement of a more important value, the developers of SIGI PLUS have also had to make trade-offs. We have given up the "core curriculum" universally required of college students in exchange for more flexibility in meeting the needs of a wider population of users.

SPECIFICATION OF CORPORATE NEEDS

Once SIGI came into prominent use in colleges, personnel and human resource directors of corporations expressed interest in offering a career planning system to employees. It seemed likely to us that they would represent a strong and ready market for SIGI PLUS. As we began planning for SIGI PLUS, therefore, we reviewed the literature on career development in business, industry, and labor unions, and we also convoked a meeting of representatives of such organizations to advise us on the characteristics that should be added to SIGI to make it most useful. We also engaged in individual conversations with various personnel directors.

The high level of enthusiasm we encountered led us to include use in such contexts in our plans for the development of SIGI PLUS.

From the corporate point of view, what are the major needs that a career planning system should meet? The review of the literature included a number of surveys asking this question of large companies (e.g., Cohen, 1977; Lancaster & Berne, 1981; Morgan, Hall, & Martier, 1979; Vetter, Winkfield, Lowry, & Ranson, 1977; Walker & Gutteridge, 1979). These surveys showed that most large corporations were involved in *some* kind of career development activities. In general, they identified six major types of needs that were mentioned frequently by the companies. These categories overlap somewhat but are listed separately to retain the flavor of the survey responses.

1. To meet affirmative action and Equal Employment Opportunity goals, it was deemed necessary to stimulate women and minority groups to consider a wide range of opportunities in which they were underrepresented. The purpose here would be to eliminate self-imposed or "internalized" barriers (mentioned earlier in a discussion of the role of guidance in improving access).

2. With the aging of the population of executives during the 1980s and 1990s and expectation of a high retirement rate, it seemed important to insure lines of succession and replacement. Career guidance and development programs would be expected to result in retention and training of competent and talented young people to fill the anticipated vacancies, particularly in middle management. By making clear the opportunity structure in the company (including "career ladders") and by demonstrating the company's interest in formation of career goals, such programs were also believed to help in recruitment of able people.

3. Companies expressed an interest in helping employees take responsibility and initiative for their own career planning. This includes not just preparation for specific opportunities for promotion but also increased commitment, involvement, satisfaction, and competence in CDM, largely through clarification of values (Yaeger & Leider, 1975). The frequent augmentation of income through a spouse's pay check was seen as encouraging a quest for "meaning" in work, often through lateral job enrichment rather than advancement. In fact, the phenomenon of people who decide to get off the "fast track," with its attendant mobility and tensions, was repeatedly mentioned.

4. Some companies believed that a prominent career development program would demonstrate concern for employees. It would improve the image of the company as supportive and flexible in helping employees formulate and assess individual goals in the context of organizational goals. Such a program was expected to improve morale, enhance the

quality of work performance, increase productivity, and reduce turnover and absenteeism. By the same token, it would help in recruitment.

5. Career planning was seen by some companies as an effective complement to performance appraisal. Supervisors were expected to make more productive evaluations of an employee's performance when such evaluations could be associated with advice, counsel, and assistance in improving performance to meet career goals and plans developed by the individual employee.

6. Some companies were concerned with providing assistance to employees in "outplacement." They recognized that the pain and disgruntlement generally associated with termination of an employee (for whatever reason) might be eased by a program that would help in the reassessment of career goals and plans.

A possible negative consequence of career development programs was occasionally mentioned. This was the fear of raising aspiration levels that were not to be fulfilled. Such an outcome might lead to disappointment, anxiety, dissatisfaction, and reduced commitment and performance. On the other hand, it was recognized that recent increases in the educational level of employees might produce this effect anyway (Bachman, O'Malley, & Johnston, 1978). A career guidance system might be able to suggest more options to people who felt stuck, or—through reexamination of values and "reduction of cognitive dissonance"—help them accept what they cannot change. The need for this "cooling out" function would depend in part on the capability of the system to warn of and perhaps prevent unrealistic expectations.

It was difficult to get a sense of the relative importance attached to these statements of needs. One survey (Walker & Gutteridge, 1979) reported the following frequencies in responses from 225 companies to a questionnaire sent by the American Management Associations: 88% cited the desire to develop and promote employees from within; 63% a shortage of promotable talent; 56% a desire to aid career planning; 39% a desire to improve worker productivity; 38% affirmative action commitments. Over 90% of the responding companies believed that career planning enhances performance, equips employees to use personnel systems more effectively, improves utilization of employee talents, and would not disrupt the organization.

To meet the needs expressed in survey responses and in direct conversations, it seemed appropriate to design a system that would retain the emphasis on values in SIGI but extend the scope of the values domain and other elements of self-appraisal; that would similarly augment the variables used in structured searches for occupations; that would provide for the addition of local company information (such as specific job titles and career ladders) to the occupational information data base; that would pay special attention to the skills required for entry to each occupation and successful performance in it; that would permit adding local opportunities for education and training to more general information on preparing for an occupation; that would suggest ways and means of coping with the practical considerations that might obstruct adults (particularly women and minority group members) from considering and embarking on new career goals and plans; that would pull together even larger and more complex elements of information than those in SIGI in a readily comprehensible framework for decision making; and that would assist in designating immediate actions to be taken.

SPECIFICATION OF DEVELOPERS' NEEDS

Recognizing, as we have just done, the needs of students, adults, society, colleges, and corporations requires systematic observation and inference, a form of research. But many who have given effort to such research do not commit themselves to taking action to meet the perceived needs, that is, to development. Intervention requires talents other than or additional to research and is presumably motivated by the developer's own needs. These needs often include meeting the needs of others, as befits members of a "helping" profession. Developers may also feel a need to be creative, that is, to solve problems not by choosing a "right" answer from existing alternatives but by constructing or creating a "new" answer. They may also feel a need to extend their reach to a larger population of clients than one person can ordinarily counsel. As in writing for publication, they may also feel a need for recognition, for reputation associated with the product of their endeavors, and for concomitant extrinsic benefits.

This sample of developers' needs is not exhaustive, and insofar as it represents needs common to most developers does not illuminate distinctions between computerized guidance systems. Other common needs pertain to the marketplace: keeping costs to developers and prices to users low enough to encourage wide use. Distinctive needs may be illustrated by examining differences between developers of other systems and the developer of SIGI in the context of their professional backgrounds, their organizational affiliations, and their sources of funding.

Efforts to develop computerized career guidance systems were undertaken during the 1960s by some variety of individuals and organizations concurrently with my work at ETS—for example, John Cogswell at System Development Corporation, Frank Minor at IBM (in consultation with Donald Super and associates at Columbia University), David Tiedeman at Harvard, Joseph Impelliteri at Pennsylvania State University,

John Flanagan at American Institutes for Research, JoAnn Harris at Willowbrook High School, and Bruce McKinlay at the University of Oregon. (Other names could be added, but this list seems to represent well the range of developers.) All these people except McKinlay participated in a kind of floating symposium held at their respective sites from 1966 to 1970, discussing problems and approaches; so it is possible, without being too presumptuous, to infer some of their distinctive needs. For a few developers, there was a patent need to relate a computerized career guidance system to a theoretical orientation consistent with a long-standing program of research.

Cogswell was interested in an application of systems analysis, as befitted his affiliation with System Development Corporation. With substantial funding from the Office of Education, he tried to study the objectives of guidance in a secondary school, determine why they were not being met, and provide a system to close the gap between objectives and current activities. One effort was to simulate, via computer, the counselor's interview with a student. Another effort allocated information processing to the computer, leaving to counselors the use of the information in counseling. Counselors were so bemused by their new capability in data processing that they spent more time than ever in doing statistical analyses and less time working with students. Dismayed by this unforeseen consequence, and responding to other personal needs, Cogswell left SDC and systems analysis and became a psychotherapist. Funding was cut, and the project became defunct.

ECES (most systems have become known by their acronyms; since the full names are cumbersome and forgettable, only the acronyms are used here) emerged from the work of Super and his associates on the Career Pattern Study and on their propositions about the continuity of vocational development involving age-linked stages in which career decisions are made and modified. ECES focused on the exploratory stage (adolescence); it included such functions as self-knowledge, browsing through occupational and educational information, considering plans, and reality testing. ECES also emerged from IBM's expectation that a secondary school market for its mainframe computers would be stimulated by the availability of such a system. It was IBM's policy to start more developmental projects than it would complete. Frank Minor therefore had to devote a considerable amount of time, effort, and money to compete for continuing support (e.g., an expensive motion picture was made during development to convince IBM executives of the merit of the project).

Strangely, despite extensive "human engineering" research by IBM, the student station for ECES was diffuse and inefficient, requiring the user to move back and forth between a teletypewriter for readouts and a set of film strips that had to be loaded and unloaded with considerable frequency and that would have added greatly to the expense of updating. IBM supported developmental efforts through the completion of ECES I and its field test in Montclair but then dropped out as market prospects looked dim and hardware had to be "unbundled" from software. (Results of the field test were inconclusive, and a second field test was held in Flint; rights in the system were eventually released to the Genesee County School District, where a revised version of ECES was running at last look.) Because CVIS had been developed (under the direction of JoAnn Harris, later Harris-Bowlsbey, for IBM mainframes), IBM then contributed some support to its further development and marketing and its metamorphosis into DISCOVER. Super also transferred his consulting activities to DIS-COVER.

In his early years of work at Harvard, David Tiedeman had focused on statistical methodology, offering the technique known as multiple discriminant function as "the answer to the guidance problem." This focus gave way (perhaps by some arcane rotation of the axes of personal needs) to an overriding concern with a "sense of agency" on the part of the "inquirer." In this shift of Tiedeman's philosophy, the student went from being the recipient of guidance to becoming the seeker and controller of activities, deciding which questions to ask, what decisions to make, and how to engage the system. Thus ISVD was developed (under a large grant from the Office of Education) with a view to stimulating inquiry and mastery by the user. For example, a heavy investment was made in an effort to implement processing of natural language so that the user's options would not be prescribed. But of course the user's options for input were circumscribed by the limited strings that the computer was programmed to respond to constructively. The inquirer then was confronted by a covert multiple choice array that had to be discovered by guesswork, trial and error, or – eventually, if patience held – experience. Overt multiple choice would have been more honest, effective, easy, and inexpensive. The magnitude of the investment made in language processing (to meet the developer's need) swamped attention to content and proved self-defeating: The system did not run in demonstrations, progress was slow, and support was not continued.

A member of Tiedeman's staff (Eugene Wilson), as an entrepreneur under the company name of Interactive Learning Systems, used some fraction of the materials developed for ISVD in a much less ambitious product, which became known as GIS. The natural language was abandoned, but multiple choice was not used either. Instead, the user was required to type in codes that had to be looked up in a booklet. This was a cumbersome system, so discouraging to users that they often had to depend on the counselor to help them through the system. ILS did not survive, but, after a series of corporate takeovers (including Timeshare, which was able to capitalize on judicious placement of computers), GIS became a financially successful product marketed by Houghton Mifflin.

Like GIS, Impelliteri's CACE, Harris's CVIS, and McKinlay's CIS were atheoretical in origin. CACE (funded by the Pennsylvania Department of Public Instruction) was a rudimentary system, designed for use by ninth-grade boys in choosing vocational programs; it contained information on only 40 occupations. The point was to get something out and working as quickly as possible and then revise it on the basis of field tests and advice from counselors. Development stopped with Impelliteri's untimely death.

CVIS (supported by the Illinois Board of Vocational Education and Rehabilitation) also started mainly as an electronic page turner to convey occupational information, with certain eclectic additions: Students' suitability for an occupation was determined by comparing rank in class and composite test battery scores to the "level" of an occupation, and Kuder Preference Record scores to its "field of interest." In the absence of a "match," a discrepancy message appeared. This simplistic matching system was useful in meeting the developer's need to produce an up-and-running system as quickly as possible to piggyback on an existing computerized student record system used by counselors. Counselors would receive, through their CRT's, not only students' cumulative records but a list of students who had received discrepancy messages during the day. Thus, the system met a need felt by the school counselor who developed it to keep counselors informed about students' use of the system and give them an opportunity to intervene. The developer was at that time innocent of any knowledge about the invalidity of the Kuder Preference Record (Bauernfeind, 1963; Katz, 1962, 1965) or about other elements of the matching procedure used.

Knowing what it takes to bring a computerized guidance system into successful use, I have high regard for all those who have developed systems that compete with SIGI and SIGI PLUS. This regard must not, however, diminish the candor of my comments on the development of DISCOVER (by JoAnn Harris-Bowlsbey), which offers a compendium of off-the-shelf instruments eclectically. For example, the student can use interests measured by UNIACT (DISCOVER is now a "service" of ACT), Holland's SDS, the SCII, the OVIS, or the Kuder E (again, pardon the use of acronyms by which the inventories are generally known) with no apparent concern over the differences between these instruments and between the various sets of occupations that they would retrieve. Perhaps this indiscriminate gathering-in of instruments was a sophisticated response to a perceived marketing need to include every counselor's favorite, rather than exercise selective judgment.

Easy eclecticism disconnected from any theory or principle appeared again in the early borrowing by DISCOVER of values dimensions and definitions that had been developed at ETS for SIGI. After several years, on the absorption of DISCOVER by American College Testing, these values dimensions were replaced by those in Super's Work Values Inventory. The ACT "World-of-Work Map" was also incorporated in the system, again presumably to meet the need to use "company" materials. There seems to be no concern that the axes of the map, Data *versus* Ideas and People *versus* Things, prevent the proper representation of occupations that combine activities involving data *and* ideas (such as computer programmers, research psychologists, engineers, and so forth). In the area of technical decisions, it must be granted that the principle of comprehensiveness has been more productive: Recognizing the need to run on some variety of computers in order to extend the market was a decision that cannot be faulted.

McKinlay's OIAS (later CIS) was funded by the U.S. Department of Labor as a demonstration project to indicate that statewide occupational information could be collected and presented through a computer-based or other system. As CIS, the procedures have become the basis for a number of state systems, with development in each state supported mainly by funding from the Department of Labor (originally) and (later) the National Occupational Information Coordinating Committee. McKinlay, an economist, was concerned with the need to focus on labor market information and to avoid getting involved in other aspects of guidance. So self-appraisal for OIAS and CIS was handled off line (through a questionnaire). There is no pretense at offering on-line "guidance."

As the developer and custodian of the vast Project TALENT data base (a probability sample of over 400,000 former high school students followed up at specified intervals), American Institutes for Research sought to set up a "computer-measurement" guidance system for high school students. The computer would store test scores on the TALENT battery and correlations between test scores and certain follow-up data for the original sample. It would advise students of probabilities of success and satisfaction and refer them to off-line "units" of study. Supported by the Office of Education, this plan – or PLAN, as the project was called – never materialized as a working system.

Thus, of the major early systems only a few survived. The others were not alone in their demise. For the record, it may be appropriate to call the roll of other well-subsidized projects that, like the SDC system, ECES, ISVD, CACE, and PLAN, also aimed at secondary schools but fell short of reaching full operational status. These included the Rochester Career Guidance Project (a multimedia system supported jointly by Eastman Kodak, New York State Employment Service, and New York State Department of Education); the University of Oregon GUIDPAK System; the Palo Alto Course Selection and Counseling System (supported by the

Office of Education); and (also funded by the Office of Education) the Total Guidance Information Support System planned by Oklahoma State University for the Bartlesville Public Schools. In retrospect, it seems that these systems tended to be as doggedly atheoretical as CVIS, GIS, and CIS, but perhaps their developers (all of whom had substantial funding) were less dogged in following through to completion, or less clear in defining manageable goals, or less adept in managing the intricate teamwork between guidance and computer specialists. Perhaps their needs were not sufficiently productive.

SIGI Developer's Needs

The development of SIGI drew on an extensive background of work on theory and research in CDM and guidance. The underlying principles and concepts were expressed in papers dating back to the early 1950s. Katz (1954, 1963) emphasized the role of values as the major "synthesizing element that orders, arranges, and unifies . . . interactions [between social and psychological forces]" and a model of informed and rational decision making that produced and combined indices of utility and probability (Katz, 1966a). Thus (like Tiedeman and Super), I felt a need to develop a system that was derived from a particular theoretical orientation, was based on a particular model, was supported by a body of research, led to additional research, and contributed to elaboration of a theoretical structure.

This posture was consistent with organizational goals and character. In the middle 1950s, ETS (under the presidency of Henry Chauncey) was concerned that its role as a testing organization was identified too much with "gatekeeping." It wanted to emphasize the use of measurement for self-understanding and individual decision making and development – that is, for guidance. To define the state of guidance and an organizational role in it, ETS launched a project known as the Guidance Inquiry. A National Advisory Board, composed mainly of past presidents of professional guidance associations, was appointed, met, and quickly disagreed about what guidance was, what should be done to improve it, and what part ETS should play. This dissension was disastrous in view of the ETS need for endorsement of its enterprises by appropriate external boards of review. In 1956 I was recruited to become principal investigator for the project, charged with reconciling the warring factions, proposing a course of action, and conducting whatever research and development might be agreed to.

The top ETS officers had harbored an expectation, consistent with the major activity of their organization, that a product should consist of a battery of tests and inventories to be taken and scored by students who would then make decisions in the light of prepared sets of interpretations for various score combinations. The officers proved open to my arguments to the contrary, however, and (along with an internal committee and the external Advisory Board) enthusiastically endorsed the alternative product that was proposed and developed. This commitment to autonomy for research and development staff, coupled with openness to professional judgment, was an ETS characteristic that also represented an organizational need.

A marketable product of the Guidance Inquiry was a text-workbook entitled *You: Today and Tomorrow,* designed for classroom use in eighth and ninth grades. The book took students through appraisals of abilities, values, and interests. It helped them get information about educational and occupational options and provided a structure for relating such information to their self-appraisals. It taught a process of CDM with copious examples and exercises. It was, in short, a kind of paper and print precursor to SIGI.

Manifesting another organizational need, we then gave this product a widespread field test and both intensive and extensive evaluations (Gribbons, 1960; Shimberg & Katz, 1962). Then, although there was great interest by various publishers in handling this book, ETS decided to do the marketing itself to satisfy its need to establish a visible role in guidance. The book sold well over a hundred thousand copies and set a precedent for an ETS involvement in developing and marketing a product for direct use in guidance.

In the early 1960s I was commissioned to write a further analysis of guidance by the College Board, which published it in 1963. Entitled *Decisions and Values,* this analysis led naturally into my development of a model of CDM that, I pointed out, lent itself readily to computerization in an interactive mode. I lectured and wrote on this model (for a summary of these speeches and papers, see Katz, 1966a), aroused considerable interest in it, and (still in 1963) tried to persuade the College Board to support development of an interactive computer-assisted guidance system. The Board was unwilling or unable to take this venture, and ETS— although eager to get into new applications of computer technology and willing to list computerized guidance system development as one of its "moon shot" prospects—also refrained from making a significant financial commitment. Furthermore, I had not yet found an appropriate computer expert to team up with. It was not until 1967 that I identified William Godwin, then an ETS research psychologist and a brilliant computer buff, as the person to provide the technical expertise necessary to configure the hardware and get the programming done. We still needed a source of funding.

At this point I noted that the Carnegie Corporation had recently sponsored an evaluation of community college guidance services that pronounced them to be "woefully inadequate." So I sent a preliminary proposal to Carnegie saying, in effect, you've just spent money identifying a serious problem: now how about investing in the solution? Carnegie invited a full proposal and awarded the full grant requested. Thus, it was an opportunistic effort to meet my perception of the foundation's "need" that led me to decide that the system would be initially designed for use at community colleges, although I took haste to add that there was nothing in its principles, concepts, or design to keep it from being extended to use by other populations. Indeed, the extension was made to 4-year colleges, in response to their expressions of need and interest, before development for the field test was completed.

A Carnegie "need" led directly to another decision. My original proposal was to complete research and development and then release the product into the public domain. Carnegie demurred from this (and only this) element of the proposal, on the grounds that "public domain" would result in the demise of the product. To insure that SIGI would be used and have an impact, Carnegie required that ETS make a commitment to maintain and market it or arrange with some other organization to do so. As with *You: Today and Tomorrow*, ETS chose to market the product itself. (Later, this commitment resulted in serious conflict when I had obtained funding from the National Science Foundation to support field tests, evaluations, and continuing development: NSF held that work supported by the government should be put in the public domain. Thus, the needs of two supporting foundations were in direct conflict, and we were caught in the middle. The successful resolution of that conflict is too long a story to tell here.)

The ETS decision to market SIGI was consistent with a long expressed need to assert some leadership and foster expertise in the development and distribution of interactive computer applications. Also consistent with ETS practice was the appointment of an external Advisory Committee composed (as for the Guidance Inquiry) of recognized leaders in career guidance.

Another element of "organizational culture" should be noted. SIGI was developed by research scientists specified as the Guidance Research Group under the aegis of a research division at ETS. Our research interests and identification led to a need not only to use research in the development of SIGI (as described in various chapters of this volume) but also to use SIGI to further a program of research in career guidance and decision making. It was an effort to meet this need that led to certain decisions in the design and development of SIGI, particularly the capability of automatically collecting data on students' use of the system (data that later served to answer questions on such topics as gender differences in CDM).

SIGI has two major advantages as a resource that meets certain needs for research. First, as a working model of guidance, based on an explicit theory and rationale, it opens up the "black box" of treatment. Research in guidance has been greatly hampered by difficulties in specifying "treatment." No matter how firmly counselors may subscribe to a given theory, philosophy, or method, there is no assurance that even the most experienced ones will behave consistently vis-à-vis students in a succession of counseling sessions. SIGI is flexible in letting students find their own distinctive paths through the system, but the totality of the system is specified, thereby defining the treatment in strictly operational terms. Furthermore, because the track of each student through the system can be recorded, and very large numbers of cases are available for study, a comprehensive taxonomy of individual variations in treatment can be objectively defined. So if the effects of a treatment are to be measured, everyone knows what the treatment has been.

The second advantage has to do with observations of career decision-making processes. Most research on career development has used responses to survey questionnaires and similar instruments. These responses are made by people who may or may not be actively engaged in CDM at the time they are questioned. The SIGI user record, on the other hand, provides a direct window on the process of CDM while it is known to be going on. Observations are made unobtrusively in the course of the user's interaction with the system; it does not interrupt the process, nor does it depend on often illusive retrospection or elusive recall of processes. The variables recorded are elements in the process itself, not made-up answers to made-up questions that may or may not have been salient to the respondent.

In short, the development of SIGI as a product of staff devoted to research led to a design that would enable development to feed back into research. One way to proceed in theory building is to construct a model, tease out hypotheses that are essential to the model, and then test each specific hypothesis in a series of rigorous studies. As these hypotheses are tested against plausible alternative hypotheses, and each one is confirmed, revised, or discarded, the entire model itself – bit by bit, piece by piece – begins to look more or less acceptable. This is a tedious and time-consuming labor, in which the parts begin to loom bigger than the whole.

An alternative procedure is to translate the model into a working system, give it a spin, and watch it run. Observations on the way it runs then provide feedback on the efficacy of the model as a whole and on the functioning of the parts in the context of the whole. As modifications are made the entire model can be retested. Thus, research on CDM and guidance was embedded in the development of SIGI, as was appropriate to an ETS division then labeled Developmental Research. Indeed, SIGI fit into a concept of developmental research as encompassing both research for development and research from development – that is, research pertaining to system construction and research deriving from system use.

Research and development for SIGI, however, were not conducted in an ivory tower segregated from concern for marketing needs. All development decisions took into account impact on costs. For example, we developed SIGI on a minicomputer rather than a mainframe, to reduce both our costs and those of customers. When costs of mass storage came down sufficiently, we abandoned our ingenious custom-made terminal station (combining a computer controlled carrousel slide projector with a cathode-ray tube) for a standard off-the-shelf CRT. To avoid compromising quality of occupational information, we kept the number of occupations in SIGI down to a manageable size. We kept our eye on microcomputers and converted to them as soon as sufficient storage became available. Notwithstanding all development efforts to make SIGI as marketable as possible, a near-fatal error was made by the person appointed to direct the marketing of SIGI. Meeting *his* perceived need to show an early breakeven date, he set the price of the annual license much higher than the traffic would bear (despite a market survey in which respondents called that proposed price structure "outrageous"). So an energetic and costly marketing campaign resulted in a sale to just one college (which obtained a Kellogg Foundation grant to support its use). When the original marketing director gave up, we dropped the price by about 85%, and sales began to accumulate to reach the breakeven point. Conversion to microcomputer then slashed the high cost of hardware and resulted in a multiplication of sales, with attendant financial success.

Funding for the microcomputer conversion (along with other activities) was obtained from the Kellogg Foundation. Here again, I had to consider the distinctive needs of a foundation. Kellogg had a strong commitment to adult and continuing education. It seemed appropriate to couple this with my own longstanding interest in extending career guidance to this broader population. Indeed, in my first proposal to NSF I had anticipated that extension in view of the fact that "more and more people . . . change their occupations in the course of their lives. This trend toward serial careers . . . will require extension of career guidance services to cope with individuals' recurrent needs." Hence my proposal for support from the Kellogg Foundation led to research and development for what was then called SIGI-A and is now known as SIGI PLUS.

RECAPITULATION OF NEEDS AND PURPOSES

Without attempting to summarize this lengthy examination of needs, some recapitulation of topics may be appropriate at this point. To stake out the theoretical foundations for the career guidance systems, SIGI and

SIGI PLUS, this chapter started with a focus on the needs of individual clients – particularly college students and the general adult population. It then emphasized that increments in chronological age often do not result in corresponding increases in CDM competencies. There is great variation in all components of CDM at all ages considered: in self-appraisal, in knowledge about options, in linking information about options to information about self, in evaluating alternatives, in planning for preparation and action, in managing practical problems, and in understanding the process of CDM. At the same time, note has been taken of certain distinctive needs of the general adult population compared to college students.

There are other players in CDM besides clients. An analysis of the societal stake in career guidance has indicated that to a great extent individual and societal benefits overlap. Nevertheless, there are conflicts and tensions between national and individual needs. Sometimes these tensions reflect misunderstandings of the capabilities of career guidance – such as the unrealistic expectation that increased availability of occupational information will by itself effect a substantial reduction in unemployment. But sometimes the conflicts arise from implicit discrepancies between two models, designated here as the "manpower" approach and the "guidance" approach. A proposed resolution of this conflict emphasizes certain common themes in the processes by which national policy decisions in a democracy and individual career decisions in a "guidance" model are ideally made. In each case, the necessary condition is freedom, the open marketplace of ideas, in which every voice can be heard, and competing values can be systematically defined, explored, and examined. To resolve this confrontation between competing values, whether on the national or individual scale, not only freedom but competence is required, to make order out of a rabble of impulses and bring them under the rule of reason. Then relevant information can be identified, interpreted, and brought to bear. Out of the interaction between values and information, it is possible to assess the utility of each option and then modulate utility with probabilities of success.

In an analysis of college needs, I have also shown this guidance model to be consistent with the purposes of the liberal arts. It supports and complements the liberal arts in providing a centripetal force and unifying principles at a time of increased specialization and fragmentation in higher education. While the liberal arts contribute to an understanding of the genesis and development of the values of a culture, guidance contributes to an understanding of the values of an individual in that culture. Like the liberal arts, a coherent guidance system helps develop touchstones and competencies. It is also seen to serve certain bread-and-butter needs of colleges in terms of services, recruitment, retention, and cost containment.

In a similar way an expanded system can serve a number of practical needs of corporations in such matters as meeting affirmative action and Equal Employment Opportunity goals, retaining and recruiting able people, filling lines of succession and replacement, increasing satisfactions in existing positions, improving morale and productivity, and assisting in outplacement.

Finally, an analysis of the needs of computerized guidance system developers summarizes certain common concerns and goes on to describe distinctions between various systems in the context of their developers' professional backgrounds, organizational affiliations, and sources of funding. This framework of analysis includes some brief historical notes on computerized guidance system development generally and a much more specific narrative account of factors affecting the development of SIGI and SIGI PLUS. Emphasis is placed on the research environment from which SIGI emerged.

In all these analyses of needs, I must caution that the space given to any need is not related to its importance. I have passed quickly over the obvious and universally recognized needs in order to dwell at greater length on those that are not self-evident.

The next chapter describes the rationale and model for SIGI and SIGI PLUS that emerged from these studies of needs.

3

Rationales and Models of Career Guidance

A ghoulish old fellow from Kent
Encased his wife in cement.
He said, with a leer,
"I was careful, my dear,
To follow your natural bent."
　　　　　　　　　　　　—Ogden Nash

The first chapter of this book dealt with the content of career decision making (CDM). The complexities of CDM led, in chapter 2, to a consideration of the needs for professional intervention in the process of CDM. Such needs imply the purposes of guidance and the *rationales* for treatments that might be designed to improve the process of CDM. The rationale for a treatment includes premises, problems, and principles. The content, structure, and functions of a treatment can be called a *model*. A particular model may serve as the framework for the design and development of a career guidance *system*.

As stated earlier, in the specification of needs for guidance, the process of CDM is difficult to observe directly. It was noted that most formal extensive studies of the sort traditional to the social sciences paid little attention to what was going on in the individual who had to make a career decision and live with it. Efforts at intensive studies, through interviews, have often foundered on the fuzziness of subjects' expressions and explanations in response to questions. People have generally seemed to lack both concepts and vocabulary to describe their own CDM processes. Perhaps the process was so often inaccessible simply because it had not got under way. Just as many people appear to need guidance to "jump start" their own career decision making, so does research into the CDM process often appear to require the existence of a structured guidance treatment before there is much going on to observe and record. Actions and reactions in the treatment provide substance for observations.

There are, of course, many treatments available. Some are based on various explicit theoretical foundations, rationales, and models. Others, however, are atheoretical, eclectic, or ad hoc. Their rationales have had to be inferred from their procedures. But often one encounters conflicts and contradictions within these ad hoc systems. *An implicit rationale is an oxymoron.* If developers know and state *why* they are doing something, they stand a better chance of avoiding anomalies. So in keeping with the previously announced strategy of viewing CDM and guidance through the lens of SIGI and SIGI PLUS – a particular treatment designed to meet the needs described and analyzed in the preceding section – at this point I briefly describe the model for that system and then compare some of its principles and components with those of other major rationales and models. Then in chapter 4, "Focus on Functions of Computerized Guidance," I examine closely the decisions made in the development of a system to meet the specifications of the model. The elucidation of *why* we did what we did instead of something else elucidates and reifies the rationale. Thus, theory leads to practice, and practice illuminates theory.

THE MODEL FOR A GUIDANCE SYSTEM

A model for a system represents a way of organizing, integrating, and applying major components of a theory and a rationale. It makes explicit their implications for practice. In traveling from theory to model, five premises that underlie the model serve as a useful point of departure.

Premise 1. My first premise is that in our culture making career decisions is each person's right and responsibility. At one time or another, choosing a high school curriculum, or a college, or an occupation, or a job *is* a person's job. So the model for SIGI, which aims to increase freedom and competence in CDM, is based on what may be regarded as a *job analysis* of CDM. Such a job analysis starts by recognizing the goals of a career decision, then goes on to identify the job tasks or functions that can best achieve those goals.

Premise 2. The next premise is that the goal of decision makers, in general, is to maximize utility. In CDM, this objective translates into

making choices that provide the greatest rewards and satisfactions. Pragmatically, these choices are usually modulated by a concern for avoiding
excessive risks or investment. Individual perceptions vary, however, on
the importance of each reward or satisfaction and on how much risk or
investment is tolerable. Such individual differences in the importance
attached to any given array of rewards and satisfactions make values and
interests central constructs in CDM. Similarly, differences in abilities,
skills, and resources constrain or ease people's access to various options—
for example, they account for different probabilities of success in entering
some occupations.

Premise 3. Furthermore, people differ in the extent to which they can
appraise and express all these characteristics—their values, interests,
skills, and resources. So another premise is that self-understanding,
through exploration and examination of all the relevant characteristics, is
an essential component of guidance if people are to gain competence in
making their own career decisions. To help people understand themselves,
to sort out and appraise their characteristics, a clear-cut structure is
useful. Such a structure includes all the relevant domains (such as values,
interests, skills) and, within each domain, well-defined dimensions along
which individual differences are to be construed.

Premise 4. It is also axiomatic that occupations (and other career options) vary in their attributes: the particular configuration of opportunities
for rewards and satisfactions that they offer (which I have called their
instrumentalities); the activities that they involve; their requirements for
entry; their outlook (that is, the competition for openings that may be
expected in the future); their visibility and accessibility; their criteria for
successful performance; the number and kinds of paths by which they can
be approached; and the quality of information available on all these attributes. So a structure of occupational information and procedures for
collecting, analyzing, interpreting, evaluating, and communicating data for
such information are essential components of guidance for CDM.

Premise 5. Also essential is a strategy for linking the domains of
individual characteristics to the domains of information about options.
Ideally, people might be expected to prefer an occupation that provides
ample opportunity to obtain *all* the rewards and satisfactions that they
value highly; can be readily entered within the scope of their qualifications
and resources; and presents a rosy prospect for their continuing success.
Needless to say, such an option can be identified but rarely. So help in
finding an appropriate compromise is often required.

As indicated previously, the domains of individual characteristics do not tend to be isomorphic with the domains of occupational attributes. Therefore, ways of linking the personal and occupational domains—for example, values to instrumentalities, interests to fields of knowledge, interests and skills to activities, skills and resources to requirements—may be ill fitting and awkward. Furthermore, even if complete self-understanding, complete information, and perfect articulation between the two sets of domains were possible, trade-offs and compromises would have to be made. For example, people would have to decide whether to sacrifice some degree of satisfaction in respect to one value in order to retain some other satisfaction; or they would have to compromise between rewards and risks associated with various choices. But of course all variables cannot be clearly recognized and perceived. Self-understanding of one's own characteristics is often dim. Information about occupations may be insufficient, misleading, or irrelevant. In all cases, outcomes are uncertain. So CDM is bound to be muddled and cumbersome. No unequivocal strategy may be apparent. These problems are not functions of technology. Private dyadic counseling may skim over them or brush them aside. But the attempt to apply technology, namely, the interactive computer, in a system that is open to scrutiny, stimulates us to take careful cognizance of them. The effort to develop a strong model for a computerized guidance system compels us to cope with them.

Principles

In the face of all these deficiencies and uncertainties, what is the path to wisdom? How can a guidance system best intervene and assist? Not by cranking out decisions, as it were; the system cannot "know" the "right" choice for a person. But it can help clients in the process of choosing. My major premise is that enlightened processes are intrinsically valuable in education and in guidance. So the model for SIGI aims to foster a process of learning—helping clients develop competencies by following and comprehending a model of informed and rational decision making. That is, they master the process by using it.

Features of the Model

For an overview of the practical purposes of the model derived from the foregoing premises, problems, and principles, four major functions can be defined. They are to help people:

1. know themselves in terms that are relevant for career decisions;
2. use these self-appraisals to narrow the staggering number and bewildering variety of occupations into a comprehensive but manageable list of options worthy of further consideration (I say "narrow" from the developer's point of view. For the user, the search does not merely eliminate occupations; it often suggests occupations not previously known or considered and may be seen as expanding options);
3. make distinctions between occupations on the list and so close on a choice that offers an optimal combination of desirability and probability of successful entry;
4. make plans and engage in actions designed to implement the choice.

These functions may be clarified by a brief statement of the operations involved in each, with more detailed description and analysis to follow in chapter 4.

1. *Self-appraisal* requires that appropriate domains and dimensions be clearly defined. Then people can consider in specific terms their values (what they want, what is more and what is less important to them), their interests (both in fields of knowledge and in activities), and their skills (what they can do well). Particular attention is paid to the domain of values because of its central importance in maximizing utility.

How the dimensions of values were identified and defined for SIGI and SIGI PLUS is described under *The Domains of Self-Understanding* in chapter 4. For now, let it be granted that we have established a comprehensive, albeit not exhaustive, set of values dimensions, each of which can be meaningfully defined, is important to substantial numbers of people but varies considerably in popularity, and can be linked to some corresponding dimension of occupational reward or satisfaction. Clients are guided through an interactive exploration and examination of these values dimensions, in the course of which they assign weights to each one indicating its importance to them. These relative weights are brought under close scrutiny through a series of dilemmas; clients are confronted by a need to make choices between competing values, with a number of opportunities for changes and consistency checks. Clients also appraise their interests and skills.

2. Clients are then ready to engage in a *structured search*. They begin by specifying (from appropriate menus) the level or category of the occupational attributes they want. These attributes should correspond to the values, interests, and skills they have deemed most important. Their specifications may also include how much education they are willing to invest in and what features of occupations they particularly want to avoid.

Each specification is used by the computer program to sort through a data base that includes ratings of occupations on all attributes relevant to the possible specifications. This structured search generates a list of occupations that meet or exceed the set of specifications. Clients can play "What if?" games by changing their specifications and arranging them in various combinations. Thus, they can slice different planes through the universe of occupational attributes to identify sets of occupations that offer opportunities for valued rewards and satisfactions, while avoiding their major aversions. Typically, these lists include occupations not previously considered by the client. Sometimes they omit occupations previously favored, and the user can ask, "Why not?" to find out in what respect such occupations failed to meet a given set of specifications.

After structured search, the user can query the data base extensively about each occupation, asking pointed questions and getting specific answers. This *direct access* to information serves to enrich the client's knowledge and usually results in refining the list under consideration.

These two modes of acquiring information, structured search and direct access, represent two related aspects of occupational information. For the search mode, summary information is required, such as median pay for an occupation, ratings on opportunities for independence, security, variety, and the like, and the presence or absence of specified activities. Summary ratings of this kind lose some information but gain in simplicity and power. The direct access mode reclaims the lost information: It captures more of the detail and diversity of each occupation, giving distributions for each attribute and showing variations within an occupation by region, industry, and subtitle.

Further scrutiny of occupations is accomplished through other sections providing detailed information about the skills and preparation required or recommended for entry and through predicting probabilities of success in such preparation. Often the view of steps that must be taken or of skills required to enter some otherwise attractive occupation leads to reconsideration of its inclusion on a list.

3. With a list of manageable size, the client is ready to make fine distinctions between the surviving occupations, gaining a greater degree of closure on *choice* of an occupation. The model recognizes two sides to the choice: One side represents the *desirability* of each occupation, that is, the extent to which it offers rewards and satisfactions that are most important to the client. The other side represents the client's *probabilities of success* in entering each occupation, taking into account the skills and education required and the outlook for openings. SIGI used a numerical algorithm to calculate desirability and its modulation by probability. SIGI PLUS provides "Deciding Squares" on which a summary of the client's conclusions about these two sides is represented graphically: With desirability repre-

sented along one axis of the square and chances of success along the other, the client can readily see the position of each occupation in the two-dimensional space. The system then provides decision rules to help students balance desirability and chances of success. The idea is for each client to maximize desirability while avoiding risks and investments that he or she regards as excessive.

4. Having made at least tentative choices, clients are then helped to make action plans and to cope with practical considerations and special problems. The transition between making a decision and acting on it may include such mundane matters as identifying local opportunities, finding out about sources of financial support for further training or education, establishing "networks," writing a resume, and starting on a series of "next steps" to set plans in motion.

As this model will be compared with counterpropositions, it is useful to note here that the basic principles for SIGI (now obsolescent) and its successor (SIGI PLUS) are the same. The latter differs from the former mainly in reflecting the needs of the broader population for which it was designed (as previously explained in the chapter on needs) and in taking advantage of the greater storage and other capabilities of more recent generations of microcomputers.

The four major functions summarized here apply to both SIGI and SIGI PLUS. For the most part, the latter enlarges on the former. There are some differences, however, between the two systems in nomenclature and content. For the sake of clarity in future reference, these differences are indicated in brief descriptions of the sections for each system, following.

The Sections of SIGI and SIGI PLUS

As mentioned in chapter 1 on the needs for guidance, SIGI was developed in the late 1960s and early 1970s (with financial support from the Carnegie Corporation and the National Science Foundation) to help college students make informed and rational career decisions (and learn a process of decision making). In the proposal to Carnegie, the intent to expand use of the system to other populations (when time and money permitted) was made explicit. In 1980, the Kellogg Foundation responded to this intent, supporting experimental use of SIGI by members of the general adult population. This enabled the SIGI staff to investigate changes and additions that would make the system more appropriate for the extended population. Findings from this study, as well as additional research, led to the design for SIGI PLUS (with development supported by Kellogg).

Both systems start with an Introduction: Users indicate where they are now in their CDM and what kind of help they want. Both Introductions give an overview of the remaining sections. Then they diverge. In SIGI, students proceed through the six other sections in order. Having at least sampled each section, the student is then declared an "initiate" and is free to use any section at any time. In SIGI PLUS, clients can go from the Introduction to any section at the outset, following or ignoring the path recommended for the status and needs they have expressed. The sections of SIGI and SIGI PLUS are named and briefly described in Exhibit A, SIGI at a Glance, and Exhibit B, A SIGI PLUS System Overview.

When it is appropriate to make the distinction, in the following chapters, each system is named. Otherwise, as a matter of convenience, SIGI is used as the generic term, with the understanding that all principles apply to the current version of SIGI PLUS.

SIGI® at a glance

☐ is an interactive computer-based aid to career decision making. . .
☐ serves primarily students in, or about to enter, two-year and four-year colleges. . .
☐ complements the work of guidance counselors. . .
☐ was developed on the PDP-11 computer. . .
☐ has been converted for other minicomputers, some mainframes, and certain microcomputers. . .
☐ includes six interrelated subsystems listed below. (Each subsystem raises a major question and helps the student answer it. These questions and answers form distinctive steps in decision making.)

Subsystem	What the Student Does	Questions Answered
Introduction	Learns concepts and uses of major sections listed below.	Where do you stand now in your career decision making? What help do you need?
I. VALUES	Examines 10 occupational values and weights importance of each one.	What satisfactions do you want in an occupation? What are you willing to give up?
II. LOCATE	Puts in specifications on 5 values at a time and gets lists of occupations that meet specifications.	Where can you find what you want? What occupations should you look into?
III. COMPARE	Asks pointed questions and gets specific information about occupations of interest.	What would you like to know about occupations that you are considering? Should you reduce your list?
IV. PREDICTION	Finds out probabilities of getting various marks in key courses of preparatory programs for occupations.	Can you make the grade? What are your chances of success in preparing for each occupation you are considering?
V. PLANNING	Gets displays of program for entering each occupation, licensing or certification requirements, and sources of financial aid.	How do you get from here to there? What steps do you take to enter an occupation you are considering?
VI. STRATEGY	Evaluates occupations in terms of the rewards they offer and the risks of trying to enter them.	Which occupations fit your values best? How do you decide between an occupation that is highly desirable but risky and one that is less desirable but easier to prepare for?

Exhibit A (Copyright © 1974, 1975, 1980 by Educational Testing Service. All rights reserved.)

A SIGI PLUS® SYSTEM OVERVIEW.
(SYSTEM OF INTERACTIVE GUIDANCE AND INFORMATION PLUS MORE)

SIGI PLUS is divided into nine sections with each one relating to a stage in making a career decision. Users can go through the entire program or just the steps needed.

Introduction

❏ Explains how simple the system is to use.

❏ Gives an overview of the program and recommends a pathway suited to the user's particular needs.

Self-Assessment

❏ Users evaluate their work-related values, interests, and skills. With the help of a new "values" game, individuals explore their work-related values in greater depth.

❏ Interests are examined by field of knowledge and types of activities.

Search

❏ Creates a personalized list of occupations based on values, interests, skills, and level of education.

❏ Allows a "negative" search; i.e., removes from the list occupations with features the user wants to avoid.

Information

❏ Users get answers to as many as 27 questions about occupations.

❏ Occupations can be compared two at a time.

❏ Local information can be added here.

Skills

❏ Users learn what skills are needed in an occupation and whether they have those skills.

❏ Users examine their skills and workstyle for managerial and supervisory positions.

Preparing

❏ Education and/or training requirements are described along with the skills needed for chosen occupations.

❏ Helps users estimate their chances of completing such preparation.

Coping

❏ Offers practical advice on securing financial aid, managing time, finding day-care facilities, and getting credit for learning through experience.

❏ Local information can be added here.

Deciding

❏ Directs users in weighing the potential rewards and chances for success in their chosen careers.

❏ Users can evaluate up to three career choices at a time, including the work they're currently doing.

Next Steps

❏ Short-range goals are established and steps outlined that must be taken to achieve those goals.

❏ Sample resumes are provided.

COMPUTERIZED CAREER PLANNING

MAJOR APPROACHES TO GUIDANCE

Computerized guidance (CG) must be seen against a background of development in the field of guidance generally. This is not to say that CG involves no more than application of new technology to old substance. Quite the contrary: The capabilities of computers have stimulated innovations in guidance. But the development of CG systems has taken place in a context of considerable variation in philosophies, rationales for guidance, and models of CDM. This variation in CG is probably more important than variation in individual counselors' beliefs. Each counselor works with a relatively small clientele, at most perhaps a few hundred a year. Furthermore, counselors' behaviors may vary from one occasion to another. The clientele interacting with a CG system in a year, however, may number in the hundreds of thousands. And the CG system is completely consistent: Although it may respond differently to different inputs, it always responds in the same way to the same input. Embodying a given approach to guidance in a CG system, therefore, usually leads to much more widespread implementation of that approach than does a counselor's espousal of one school of thought or another. The treatment represented by a CG system is delivered in toto at many sites and is standardized for all users. In a way that may be paradoxical but is consistent with the American genius, computerized systems enable a given approach to guidance–the most individualistic of educational enterprises–to be made widely available through mass production and distribution. So it is useful to ask: Out of what set of beliefs about human nature and the world of work have various systems emerged? On what basis do the interventions rest? What models of CDM are represented? Indeed, to what extent is any definable and consistent model discernible?

It was noted previously that three CG systems were explicitly based on theories formulated and research conducted over many years by their developers. Notwithstanding the manifest differences between these three systems (ECES, the system developed at IBM, with Donald Super of Columbia University serving as a consultant; ISVD, developed at Harvard under David Tiedeman; and SIGI), they emerged from theoretical positions that encompassed large areas of agreement on fundamental principles. Indeed, there have been notable continuities, as well as marked discontinuities, in theoretical formulations from the dawn of the "vocational guidance" movement at the turn of the century to current approaches to "career decision making" (Katz, 1963). A brief comparison of major theories will help to clarify the rationale for SIGI.

Parsons's True Reasoning

In his posthumously published book, *Choosing a Vocation*, Frank Parsons, a noted pioneer in both theory and practice, invoked a triad of activities that should constitute vocational guidance: appraisal of the individual, study of occupational information, and "true reasoning" to establish connections between the other two domains (Parsons, 1909). On the face of it, this does not seem far removed from many current conceptualizations of the guidance process. But it is revealing to look at this approach in operation in a case report by Parsons (Stephens, 1970) on a 19-year-old client who was "sickly looking, small, thin, hollow-cheeked, with listless eye and expressionless face" and wanted to be a doctor. Parsons told him, "You haven't the pleasant manners a doctor ought to have," and advised him to go "into some sort of work where you don't have to meet so many people as a doctor must." He suggested instead that, "Some mechanical or manufacturing industry or wholesale trade where you could handle stock, care of poultry, sheep, cows, or other outdoor work would offer you better opportunities and be better for your health than the comparatively sedentary and irregular life of a physician." Parsons said that the youth accepted his advice and changed his goal from physician to cow-herder, although "it was like taking medicine at the time."

Few counselors today would be so directive. Today, the appraisal procedure would almost certainly be different, the information about physicians would be somewhat different, and the rationale for selecting other occupations to be considered would probably also be different. The accompanying matrix (Table 1) highlights these and other distinctions between Parsons's approach and three other major approaches to guidance.

As noted in Column A, Parsons's work was limited in technical sophistication: Methods of individual appraisal and data bases for occupational information were primitive. There was virtually complete dependence on the counselor's knowledge and judgment. As is also evident, the delineation of goals failed to recognize issues that later had to be confronted. For example, Parsons believed that the right matching of aptitudes, abilities, and other traits with the characteristics of occupations would result in "economic efficiency and success" and *therefore* "a useful and happy life." He thus failed to see any possible conflict between social and individual benefits, such as were examined previously in the section on interaction between societal and individual needs. (These comments should not be construed as deprecatory of Parsons for not having been farther ahead of his time than he was! It seems worthy of note, in passing, that Parsons campaigned vigorously for inclusion in the public schools of both vocational guidance and what would today be called career education.)

As for individual assessment (Row 2), the report quoted earlier (of Parsons counseling a client) illustrates some of the quirks and perils of a counselor's perceptions and prejudices without any check or balance to his fallible judgment. The cell for occupational information (Row 3) perhaps does not do Parsons full justice. Data files about occupations were developed at Parsons's Boston Vocation Bureau, and bulletins describing a

TABLE 1

Four Approaches to Career Guidance (from Katz & Shatkin, 1983)

	A. Parsons	B. Selection for Success	C. Resemblance to Membership	D. Understanding & Competence in CDM
1. Purpose or objectives (implicit or explicit)	Choose occupation to maximize success and *therefore* satisfaction of individual and benefit to society.	Prevent waste & inefficiency in preparation by basing choice on differential prediction of success. Improve overall productivity.	Prevent waste & inefficiency, maximize satisfaction, by basing choice on resemblance to membership in occupation. Increase homogeneity of membership.	Learn career decision-making process to achieve individual satisfaction; make plans that take into account preparatory requirements and probabilities of entry.
2. Appraisal of individual	Counselor's observation and judgment during interview.	Standardized test battery, emphasizing differential aptitudes—off-line (e.g., Air Force selection, GATB).	Standardized tests and/or inventories, often emphasizing interests—off-line (e.g., Strong, Holland, TALENT).	Individual's informed self-appraisal of values, interests, abilities—interactive.
3. Occupational information	Counselor's knowledge, experience, impressions.	Job analysis to classify occupations by aptitudes and to specify requirements or criteria for success in each occupation (e.g., Air Force, Shartle, Minn. Employment Stabilization).	Differentiated characteristics (antecedent or concurrent) of members of each occupation—usually involving scores on same instrument as in (2), above (e.g., Strong, TALENT).	Systematic multidimensional analysis of opportunities for satisfaction (i.e., "instrumentality" of each occupation on each dimension).

4. Articulation between (2) and (3) above — strategies for "choice" or decision making	Counselor's judgment (i.e., "true reasoning" by counselor).	Counselor's judgment linking aptitude scores to occupations, or regression analysis — equation using predictor variables, from (2) above, selected and weighted optimally to predict success as specified by criterion, from (3) above.	Counselor's judgment linking interest scores to occupations, or discriminant analysis — showing degree of individual's resemblance to membership of various occupations differentiated by the characteristics measured.	Algorithm for combining individual's weighting of each value with rating of occupation's instrumentality — produces index of "desirability": decision rules for adjudicating between desirability and risks.
5. Effectiveness depends on data showing	counselor's omniscence and wisdom.	differential validities (which depend, in part, on relatively low correlations between criteria — i.e., differentiated requirements for success in various occupations — and relatively low correlations between predictor composites for various occupations).	differentiated distance of individual from various occupational memberships such that probability of resemblance vs. dissimilarity can be discerned at useful level of confidence.	differentiated opportunities for satisfaction and success in various occupations consistent with differentiated profiles of examined values, interests, and skills.
6. Evaluated by (a) short term (b) long term	(a) client's acceptance of counselor's judgment; (b) later success and satisfaction in occupations chosen.	(a) clients' choices of occupations offering highest probabilities of success; (b) later success in occupations on criteria specified in (3) above.	(a) "hit" ratio: clients' choices of occupations whose members they most closely "resemble"; (b) persistence in occupations so chosen.	(a) & (b) clients' competencies in CDM (e.g., understanding of own values, comprehensive specifications sought from occupations, knowledge of relevant occupational information, accurate interpretations of comparative probabilities of success in various preparatory programs). Choices of occupations consistent with desirabilities and risks.

number of occupations were published. The main source of occupational information for clients in Parsons's "system," however, was the counselor, who was expected to know the tasks, requirements, and rewards of many occupations and also to judge the traits necessary for success in each.

Then, as indicated by the "true reasoning" in Row 4, it was the counselor again who had to make the right connections between individual traits and occupational requirements in order to match the client to the "right" occupation. Note that this obsession with the "correct" choice, and the avoidance of waste, of floundering, of trial and error, did not stop with Parsons. It pervades the more recent approaches described in Columns B and C. Without ignoring the universal protestations by proponents of these approaches on behalf of the client's freedom to choose, one can observe the underlying conviction that the wise choice, the right choice, can be known to the expert counselor—but can be properly accepted and implemented only if "freely" reached by the client. This practical concession to individual freedom has been viewed more as a trick of the trade than as a basic goal of guidance (as indicated by the criteria listed in Row 6).

Using Tests to Predict Success

If indeed the client was "keyed" to one or a few correct occupations (see B1), the aim of individual appraisal was *discovery* of the key traits for predicting success in every occupation. During the decades after Parsons's death, there was growing dissatisfaction with the procedures available for appraisal and prediction. Counselors felt increasingly uneasy about the validity of their observations and forecasts. They believed that more "scientific" data would make them more persuasive. In short, guidance in the horse-and-buggy days was a set of practices in search of a technology.

Moving out of the horse-and-buggy days, a technology akin to putting the horses under the hood became available. Standardized tests gained rapid acceptance during the years after World War I in supplying the appraisal component of that search (B2), and the prediction component was supplied by use of statistical methods in which test scores appeared as independent variables (B4). After World War II the computer provided a great boon to the technology of prediction. By extending the size, ease, and speed of statistical manipulations, it made feasible and commonplace the computation of large correlation matrices, stepwise multiple regression equations, large-scale factor analyses, and so on. The prospect of such capabilities so bedazzled Clark Hull that as early as the 1920s he envisioned a "single universal battery" of 30 or 40 tests used to "sample all the important aptitude determiners," with scores fed into a machine. Hull (1928) wrote:

Upon the basis of this one battery there will be constructed separate forecasting formulae for each of the more important type occupations. . . . In its final form, this machine will have the different forecasting formulae placed in it permanently. . . . As the machine makes its forecasts it will stamp them down on . . . [a] card automatically . . .

The card of forecasts, when removed from the machine, will then present in orderly array and in units of single uniform scale, permitting of instant comparisons, forecasts of the individual's probable success in all of the chief occupations of the world.

Hull's logical extension and application of trait-and-factor theory, as he gazed prophetically into the brave new world of psychometrics and computing machines, did not anticipate the stubbornness with which the data would resist neatly differentiated forecasting formulas. Perhaps the closest approach to Hull's vision has been the Occupational Aptitude Patterns (OAP), based on the sets of General Aptitude Test Battery (GATB) scores that were found to be predictive of success in various occupations and training programs (U.S. Department of Labor, 1970). A detailed critique of the OAP and other techniques based on GATB appears in chapter 4 under a discussion of aptitudes. A salutary effect of the trait-and-factor approach has been the inauguration of large-scale programs of job analysis and the publication of occupational information; but an accompanying limitation has been the tendency to classify occupations mainly in terms of the aptitudes for which measures were available (B3).

Before working farther through this matrix, it should be mentioned that neither Column B nor C is specifically descriptive of any single existing guidance system. Rather B and C are idealizations of sets of practices and procedures. Neither of these approaches, as defined and described here, is necessarily recognized as a theory or school of thought by its practitioners. As indicated in the heading for Row 1, the purposes and objectives of many systems are seldom explicit and must be inferred from practice. The other rows also reflect abstractions from particular sets of practices that have usually been developed ad hoc. The question I have tried to answer is, in effect: If there is a point to some of these guidance practices, what is it? What is the rationale or model that could justify or explain them? This is not an apology, for the descriptions do them justice, and in some cases more than justice: Usually, in practice, data are not brought to bear in so rigorous a fashion as the mention of regression analysis or discriminant analysis implies. Many practitioners still substitute their own or someone else's impressions and judgments for the kinds of data and analyses listed here. Indeed, many use occupational information based on worker traits, which would be suitable for the approach under C, in a model that appears otherwise to be based on B.

Returning to the prediction of success, under Column B, we may note that the Air Force selection program (see Rows 2 and 3) developed in World War II seems to have served as the model. This program attracted many of the leading psychological measurement specialists of the time, such as Flanagan, Thorndike, Guilford, DuBois, and Horst. With success in training as a criterion and an aptitude test battery and some biographical data as independent variables, multiple regression techniques were used to weight the contribution of each score to a set of prediction indices. These were then used to assign candidates to pilot, navigator, or bombardier training. Factor analytic techniques were adapted by Guilford (1948) to refine both predictors and criteria. The development of the GATB by the U.S. Employment Service was strongly influenced by this model, which also led to the development of a number of multifactor aptitude tests (Differential Aptitude Tests, Flanagan Aptitude Classification Tests, Holzinger-Crowder Uni-Factor Tests, and the Guilford–Zimmerman Aptitude Survey). All these tests aimed at improving differential prediction through various combinations of some of the "most important" factors. Development of such tests might have been presumed to depend on extensive job analysis to identify the kinds of aptitudes that are likely to make for success in each occupation. The tests themselves, however, turn out to represent factors long familiar in measurement. It is clear that the factors have been derived from analyses of test space, not from analyses of occupation space. They were expected to deal, however, with many more than the three occupations of concern in the Air Force program.

Such dependence on a small number of factors for predicting success in a large number of occupations can contribute to very efficient *selection* even when validities are modest. The use of such tests for selection in a given setting can be justified in terms of increasing productivity–to an extent determined by the validity of the weighted composite and by the selection ratio (Brogden, 1949; Cronbach & Gleser, 1965). For use in *guidance*, however–if we were to accept the assumption for this model that maximizing productivity (i.e., success) benefits both society and the individual–evidence of differential prediction would be required. Because similar evidence would be required to validate the model for resemblance to membership, it is discussed in connection with both models, under *Differential prediction or classification* following.

Resemblance to Memberships

The approach in Column C derives from the observation or premise that certain characteristics of people in a given occupation tend to differ from those of people in general or those in every other occupation. This leads to the inference that occupational choice *does* take place in a "birds of a feather" way. Next came the assumption that it *should* take place in this way, only more so. Therefore, guidance practices were developed to increase the homogeneity of people in each occupation (on the given characteristics). So if these characteristics can be spotted in time, this approach also can avoid waste, vacillation, or error along the way.

Empirically, it often turns out that in a rather gross way aptitude measures tend to be associated with differences in *level* of occupation (which in turn is associated with predictions of success), and interest measures are sometimes associated with differences between *field* of occupation, especially those at a given level. Hence the special attention to interests in appraisal (C2). Note that in occupational information (Row 3), we move from an emphasis under Column B on job analysis and requirements for success to an emphasis under Column C on worker traits. Just as the Minnesota Employment Stabilization Research Institute (Paterson & Darley, 1936; Paterson, 1941) attempted to classify occupations according to aptitudes in order to predict success, Strong, Kuder, Holland, Campbell, and the more recent U.S. Department of Labor *Guide to Occupational Exploration* have tried to classify occupations according to interests. The reference to discriminant analysis as the method of choice for articulation (Row 4) is not limited to the method of analysis known as the multiple discriminant function; Strong, for example, used correlations.

A philosophical critique of what is common to the approaches described in Columns A, B, and C is implied in the limerick at the head of this chapter. But there are also evidential shortcomings that undermine the validity of differential prediction or classification, which is basic to the models represented in Columns B and C.

Differential Prediction or Classification

In considering evidence of effectiveness (Row 5), note that both Models B and C depend ultimately – for use in guidance – on differential validities. In *selection* of candidates for a given job, the selector may care only about absolute validity in order to get the best qualified person available. But for *guidance* in approach B or C differential validities are required. That is, the individual would have to be told that predicted success is higher or lower in various occupations or that resemblance to membership of various occupations is greater or less. Some reasonable degree of confidence is required in a rank ordering of occupations according to an individual's chances of success, or resemblance, or (using a technique like that proposed by Tatsuoka, 1956) both simultaneously.

Obtained differential predictions or classifications, however, have been very disappointing to proponents of the guidance approaches represented by Columns B and C – as reviews and studies by Cronbach (1956), French (1961, 1963), Hunter, Crosson, and Friedman (1985), Katz and Norris

(1972), Schmidt et al. (1983), Super (n.d.), Tiedeman (1958), Thorndike (1985), Thorndike and Hagen (1959), and others have demonstrated.

These consistent findings run contrary to an egalitarian spirit in the United States. For example, in respect to aptitudes, people would like to believe in a compensatory distribution: Everyone is not good at everything, but almost everyone is good at *something*. The trick in guidance is seen as identifying that something (call it aptitude or a combination of aptitudes) for each person early on (before choices have to be made), matching it to an occupation where it is in demand, and advising people to enter the occupation in which they will be most successful – and will be more successful than other people with other combinations of aptitudes.

No matter how often research data fail to confirm this model, there is a general reluctance to accept the findings: It would be such a well-made world if the assumptions were true. Surely, there must be something wrong with the measures, people feel, or the way the studies are conducted.

Perhaps there is. If so, the problems are stubborn; they refuse to yield to repeated and sophisticated efforts. Some years ago, at the conclusion of one of the studies cited previously, I tried to shed some light on the persistent difficulties in differential prediction (Katz & Norris, 1972). The diagram that follows is intended to represent all the elements, common and unique, of a test battery and criteria for success in two options:

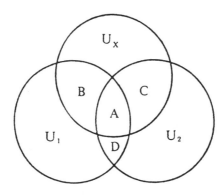

In this sketch,

U_x stands for what is unique to the test battery x;
U_1 for what is unique to criterion 1;
U_2 for what is unique to criterion 2;
B for what is common to criterion 1 and to the test battery;
C for what is common to criterion 2 and to the test battery;
A for what is common to both criteria and to the test battery;
D for what is common only to both criteria.

The multiple correlations for criterion 1 can be represented as

$$\frac{A + B}{A + B + C + D + U_1 + U_x}$$

and for criterion 2 as

$$\frac{A + C}{A + B + C + D + U_2 + U_x}$$

The correlation between predicted criteria, $r_a{}^*{}_b{}^*$, can be represented as

$$\frac{A}{A + B + C}$$

The correlation between the observed criteria, r_{ab}, can be represented as

$$\frac{A + D}{A + B + C + D + U_1 + U_2}$$

Usually r_{ab} cannot be calculated, because people rarely enter two options simultaneously. French (1954, 1961, 1963) tried to get around this problem by trying two assumptions in his computations for each pair of criteria: $r_{ab} = 0$ and $r_{ab} = .42$. This assumption of a fixed value for the correlation between criteria implies an independence between r_{ab} and $r_a{}^*{}_b{}^*$ that is mathematically possible but is not found in the real world. A moderate to high relationship between r_{ab} and $r_a{}^*{}_b{}^*$ must be expected, because test batteries are designed to provide good absolute as well as differential prediction. Under the assumption of a fixed r_{ab}, it is clear from the last two equations on the preceding diagram that any variation in $r_a{}^*{}_b{}^*$ must be offset by a function of D, U_1, and U_2 (the elements in the equation for r_{ab} that are not in the one for $r_a{}^*{}_b{}^*$). In other words, with r_{ab} held constant, the trick in enhancing differential validity would be to develop a test battery that could increase B and C "at the expense of" U_1 and U_2, while *minimizing* A. In other words, it would make maximum use of what is unique to each criterion and minimum use of what is common to both criteria.

In the real world, however, what is most predictable in most pairs of criteria seems to be mainly what they have in common. Thus, because test batteries must usually maximize the multiple correlation between the predictor and each criterion, it is almost impossible to construct them in such a way as to increase B and C without also *increasing* A. That is, the regression equations tend to include a set of predictor variables that have similar weights for each of the criteria. But to the extent that the regression weights are similar for the criteria in each pair of options, differential validity must be diminished.

To avoid high correlations between predictions, French used pure-factor aptitude tests as predictors. His reasoning was to cut into uncorrelated error rather than correlated error. Clearly, however, the larger the actual correlation between criteria, the more likely will be a large value of A (the area common to the test battery and *both* criteria). A large value of A in turn precludes a small value of r_a*_b*. Empirically, r_{ab} and r_a*_b* tend to vary together – a situation that limits attempts to develop batteries that will be useful simultaneously for both differential and absolute prediction.

The most fertile opportunities for differential prediction would be offered by pairs of criteria with low r_{ab} (although even with the assumption that $r_{ab} = 0$, French did not obtain useful differential validity). Low correlations between observed criteria are most likely to occur, however, when the criteria for success in a pair of options are distinguishable in so gross a way that a formal effort at differential prediction is hardly needed. Meanwhile, criteria for most options considered by a person are determined (as Thorndike, 1985, reported) mainly by some general composite of aptitudes; pairings with low r_{ab} (and low r_a*_b*) continue to be rare; and differential prediction continues to be a will-o'-the-wisp.

As for differentiating in terms of resemblance to membership, even if differential classification "worked," it would never (if followed to its logical extreme) "improve" the sorting of people into occupations: It would only tend to increase homogeneity of membership within each occupation. This effect might well be detrimental, as Katz (1963) observed:

> There is a big step from the observation that certain differentiations do exist to the conviction that they should exist – that, in fact, they should be sharpened, refined, and actively encouraged. . . . The logical conclusion of such attempts would be a monotype for each occupation. In the absence of convincing evidence for the existence of occupational monotypes, or arguments for establishing them, the theory for this trait-and-factor approach breaks down and much of the guidance based on it breaks down.

It is often the variety of talents and interests brought by people to each occupation that enables individuals to make *unique* contributions and enjoy special success and satisfaction.

This is not to say that predictions of success and descriptions of worker traits do not provide useful information. It is to say that they are inadequate for cranking out decisions. A given prediction or classification has different meanings for different individuals. For example, a prediction of a 50% probability of success is viewed by some as favorable to a course of action, by others as deterring. The difference is often a function of their values, which may make the option appear more or less desirable, more or less worth incurring a given level of risk.

Freedom, Understanding, Competence, and Satisfaction

In Column D the major focus is not on success or resemblance, but on learning a process of CDM that emphasizes a combination of satisfaction and success. In developing SIGI along this approach, we never pretend to tell the client the "correct" choice but attempt to enhance clients' freedom, understanding, and competence in CDM so that they can learn how to maximize satisfaction. V. S. Naipaul (1990) wrote of "the beauty of the idea of the pursuit of happiness," the existence of which can cause "other more rigid systems to blow away."

Democratic values inspire in us too much humility and too much pride to want to control decisions—humility concerning our own lack of omniscience, pride in human capacities for self-determination. We do not know what choice will be best for society *and* the individual. So we try to help clients find as much freedom as possible to work things out. But freedom without competence may be frustrating. While we do not pretend to know what the content of an individual's choice should be, we can intervene to help in the process of choosing. Enlightened processes are intrinsically important for education in a democracy. So we have set out both to expand freedom and to enhance understanding. The goal is informed and rational CDM.

Consequently, assessment in Row 2 appears as self-assessment. We recognize that college students and other adults already possess a great deal of knowledge about themselves. By the time they reach late adolescence and adulthood, they have lived a little (many of them a lot). They have had experiences, noted outcomes, developed a sense of identity. They have taken tests and courses, have obtained scores and marks, have had their work evaluated, and have swallowed or rejected the results. In short, they have at least the raw material for self-appraisal, even though much of it is latent. It is this knowledge that SIGI tries to help the client uncover, bring into full awareness, and make explicit through structured examination and exploration of values, recognition of interests, and informed self-estimates of abilities and skills. We are concerned with more than observations of relationships between such variables and success or membership in an occupation: We are concerned with what each individual's self-perceptions and concepts signify to him or her.

As suggested in Row 3, occupational information in SIGI is analyzed in terms that are relevant to the domains and dimensions that clients have used in self-appraisal. Thus, having specified the values that are important to them, clients can see what opportunities to obtain various satisfactions and rewards a given occupation offers. They can also see the kinds of knowledge and activities that are encompassed in the occupation, the skills and other qualities that are regarded as most important for it, the levels of education generally required or recommended, the conditions of work, and the outlook. Slices can be taken through many planes of the universe of occupational information to retrieve lists of occupations that have features (specified by the client) in common. Thus, an almost endless variety of occupational lists can be successfully retrieved, perhaps opening new horizons to the client, and then filtered in response to additional specifications entered by the client, including (in SIGI PLUS) features to be avoided. Note that this approach emphasizes occupational characteristics, not worker traits. It tries to describe the nature of the work and other features of the occupation, not the traits of the people who are engaged in it. The client is then enabled to judge relevance, not resemblance.

This distinction pertains particularly to the articulation between individual assessment (Row 2) and occupational information (Row 3). As indicated in Row 4, an algorithm in the decision-making sections (Strategy in SIGI, Deciding in SIGI PLUS) links occupational satisfactions, rewards, and activities to individual values, interests, and skills. The extent to which any occupation is instrumental in providing the total configuration of satisfactions, rewards, and activities that the client seeks is represented by a numerical index in SIGI, enabling the client to compare occupations in terms of their overall desirability. Estimates of the probability of entering the occupation are also made and can be combined with desirability according to explicit decision rules. In SIGI PLUS, the estimates of desirability and probability are combined graphically in "Deciding Squares." The point is not for the system to adjudicate between desirability and risks, but to provide the client with a structure for examining desirability, risks, and decision rules and with a process for informed and rational CDM.

Just as the approaches described in Columns B and C require differential prediction or classification to demonstrate validity (Row 5), the model for SIGI requires evidence of differentiated opportunities for satisfactions and rewards consistent with differentiated profiles of examined values and interests. In our research on SIGI (Chapman et al., 1977), we have demonstrated that clients' values vary greatly: That is, the standard deviation of weights assigned by college students to every dimension is high; every dimension is very important to some students and of relatively low importance to others; thus, no value is universally weighted high or low. We have also demonstrated that occupations vary greatly in the opportunities they offer for satisfactions and rewards, their instrumentality. Thus, no occupation is universally desirable or undesirable, and occupations have different levels of desirability for different configurations of values weights.

Finally, in Row 6, the four approaches are distinguished in terms of the criteria on which they are, or would be, evaluated. For Columns A, B, and C, short-term and long-term criteria are differentiated. These criteria are consistent with the other rows for each column. Because Parsons's approach depends heavily on the insight, knowledge, and reasoning of the counselor, a short-term criterion is clients' acceptance of the counselor's judgment and their acting on it; a long-term criterion would be their later success and satisfaction in the occupation to which the counselor has directed them. Presumably, their presence in another occupation would represent a failure. For Column B the short-term criterion would be clients' selections of occupations that offer the highest probabilities of success, and the long-term criterion would be later success in those occupations. Success in this case would have to be defined in terms of the criteria for which predictors were validated (Row 3). This approach is silent on satisfaction; if it figures at all in the reckoning, it must be assumed to accompany success. The short-term criterion for Column C is the "hit" ratio, clients' tendencies to choose occupations whose members they most closely resemble on the selected dimensions; the long-term criterion would be persistence in those occupations.

The criteria for evaluating effects of SIGI are treated at greater length in chapter 5. Suffice it to say here that no distinction is made between short-term and long-term criteria. Because CDM, in this view, is not a one-shot episode but usually a continual process, clients are expected to go on using, perhaps even modifying (a) the understandings of self they have gained through interaction with the system; (b) the competencies in identifying, obtaining, and interpreting relevant information about options; (c) the ways of linking information from the domain of options to the domain of self; (d) the ways of describing and applying decision rules; and (e) the planfulness involved in implementing a decision and getting from where they are to where they want to be. In short, they are expected to be sensitive to changes in their needs, values, interests, skills, and life situations, to remain open to new information, and to continue to make informed and rational decisions. While the avowed purpose of the other approaches is to help individuals make appropriate choices (however defined), their methods effectively tend to exclude the individual from the CDM process: Although they may purport to follow a person's "natural bent," they rest major control in external agencies or expertise, leaving the individual only the choice of acting or not acting on the output.

The developers of SIGI, on the other hand, assume that guidance should shun even benevolent control. We assume that we do not know what will be best for the individual (or society) except freedom to work things out. But even if we did, in some ineffable sense, "know" what was best for people, we would shrink from telling them what to do. We are suspicious of certainty. As Muller (1953) said, "Uncertainty is not only the plainest condition of human life but the necessary condition of freedom, of aspiration, of conscience—of all human idealism," and "pretensions to ... certainty ... are the ultimate source of corruption, the reason why the best becomes the worst and crusaders for heaven make a hell on earth." We believe that we must not deprive the clients of their right to understand the CDM process themselves and to act on their own understandings. Only then can they be free to take responsibility for their own decisions and to learn *from* their experiences (distinguished by Kaplan, 1964, from learning *by* experience). So the best choice is the one that is most nearly free. But we do not define freedom as laisser faire. Rather, it is the freedom (quoted earlier from Shaw's preface to *Man and Superman*) "to be able to choose the line of greatest advantage rather than yielding in the path of least resistance." Advantage in this sense involves some assessment of utility as well as probability. Then clients, recognizing that they and the world around them change, can formulate their plans as theories to be tested, can examine themselves and explore their options in a systematic and comprehensive way, take purposeful action in testing hypotheses about themselves in various situations, exercise flexibility in devising alternative plans—in sum, master the strategies for rational behavior in the face of uncertainty. This may be the closest one can get to wisdom.

4

Focus on Functions of a
Guidance System

*Theory is of practice, and must stand or fall with its practical-
ity, provided only that the mode and contexts of its application are suitably specified.*

— Abraham Kaplan (1964)

The main features of the model for a guidance system were summarized in
the preceding chapter on Rationales and Models of Career Guidance. The
major functions defined and briefly described were (a) self-appraisal, (b)
structured search for options and direct access to occupational information, (c) closure on choice of occupation, and (d) planning for action. As
should be clear from the discussion in that chapter of different approaches
to career guidance, there are differences of opinion on each of these
functions — for example, whether the function should be incorporated in a
career guidance system; if so, what it should include and how it should be
structured and handled.

This chapter focuses more closely on each function in turn. It identifies
the purposes, principles, and propositions that serve as the basis for each
function. It defines the main issues, summarizes and interprets relevant
research, and explains in some particularity the decisions bearing on the
design of SIGI and SIGI PLUS. It also poses and counters arguments for
alternatives. This application of theory to practice brings the theory into
the "real world," makes its consequences explicit, and illuminates its
implications.

THE DOMAINS OF SELF-UNDERSTANDING

Here it may be useful to consider more thoroughly the various components of individual appraisal and to explain the primacy of values in SIGI, particularly in comparison with interests, temperaments, and aptitudes or skills. The questions of whether to appraise individual characteristics, which ones to appraise, and how to appraise them are answered variously in different approaches to guidance. Logically, these answers should be linked to purposes, and usually are. Even when appraisal is not incorporated as part of a guidance system, there is generally an assumption that it has already taken place or will take place somehow at some time. Among the individual attributes that are often considered important for guidance are aptitudes, abilities, skills, values, interests, physical handicaps, financial resources, attitudes, and temperaments. Each of these domains is represented in some guidance system, although it is difficult to say whether any system includes them all: Nomenclature is sometimes fuzzy — for example, temperaments, values, and interests may be operationally defined to overlap and mingle. Before defending the primacy of values in comparison with interests, temperaments, and aptitudes, it is necessary to define these domains and refute the notion that the terms values and interests do not represent distinctive domains. Then it is appropriate to examine each domain worth consideration in more analytic detail.

Needs, Values, Interests, Temperaments, Aptitudes

Are these domains distinctive or redundant? Which should be retained in a guidance system? Perhaps the strongest argument for merging the domains of values and interests was made by Thorndike, Weiss, and Dawis (1968). They proposed that the previous findings of low correlations between measures of interests and values were attributable to inadequate statistical analyses. To test this explanation, they computed canonical correlations between Strong Vocational Interest Blank (SVIB) and Minnesota Importance Questionnaire (MIQ) scales, which they accepted as operational representations of interests and needs, respectively. (They regarded values and needs as synonymous.) From their results, Thorndike et al. (1968) concluded that vocational interests and needs, "which have heretofore been generally treated . . . as separate and distinct domains," probably belong "to the same class of variables."

They qualified their inferences by defining interests and needs "as measured by the SVIB and the MIQ, respectively." This qualification deserves particular emphasis because Strong himself classified interests with needs, wants, desires, attitudes, and the like as part of the total motivational system with which his instrument was concerned. The SVIB is a potpourri of items that were found empirically to differentiate men in certain occupational groups from a group called men-in-general. (The scales for women were similarly derived.)

A more primitive technique than canonical correlation proves illuminating here: It is called inspection of the items, and shows a substantial number of virtually identical items in the SVIB and the MIQ (Katz, 1969b). So obtaining significant canonical correlations should not have come as a surprise! Useful distinctions between such conceptual domains as values and interests are still warranted, even though particular inventories that purport to measure these domains are found to overlap.

It is not necessary to try to resolve these perseverant "jingle" and "jangle" phenomena here. Note, however, that distinctions between domains sometimes confused by research scholars with doctorates have been clearly comprehended and readily used in career decision making by eighth- and ninth-grade students (Shimberg & Katz, 1962), have been spelled out operationally at the item and inventory level (Katz, 1969b), and have been substantiated through factor analyses of test and inventory scores obtained from a survey of a national sample of high school juniors followed up 1 year after graduation (Norris & Katz, 1970): In an unrestricted maximum likelihood factor analysis, we found virtually no overlap between measures of values, aptitudes, and interests. The tenor of such useful distinctions may be suggested by attempts at clarification paraphrased from two previous papers (Katz, 1963, 1969b).

Needs may be regarded as basic motivating forces (often unconscious), the inner psychological and physiological drives for which satisfaction is sought. Maslow (1954) and Roe (1956) have been particularly active in directing attention to the importance of needs and need satisfaction in a theory of occupational choice, with particular emphasis on the hierarchy of needs that (it is postulated) determines the order and nature of attempted gratifications. Hoppock (1957) has also stressed needs (more broadly defined) in his formulation of a theory of occupational choice. The dominance of unconscious needs in occupational choice is stressed by writers with psychoanalytical orientations—for example, Brill (1949) and Forer (1953). Kline and Schneck (1950), Schaffer (1953), Segal (1953), and Small (1953) have each reported studies contributing to recognition of occupational choice as a means of basic need satisfaction.

To the extent that needs reside below the level of consciousness, they are best handled in guidance through their outer manifestations and expressions, as values. If CDM can be made a rational process, it depends on helping clients understand what they are doing. The process must therefore become explicit and overt, susceptible to the client's own grasp and management.

So if *needs* are regarded as basic motivating forces, *values* are the synthesizing element that orders, arranges, and unifies interactions among various psychological and social forces in CDM, that ties together an individual's perceptions of cultural promptings, motivating needs, mediating symbols, and differentiating characteristics, that relates perceptions to self-concepts, and that accounts most directly for a particular decision or for a mode of choosing. Values may refer to characteristic outer expressions and culturally influenced manifestations of needs. They are teleologically described, in terms of the satisfying goal or desired state or reward that is sought rather than in terms of the motivating drive, on the one hand, or instrumental actions, on the other hand. More specifically, values represent feelings and judgments about the satisfactions and rewards that may be expected as outcomes or results of a decision. They make it possible to anticipate the importance, purpose, or worth of an option.

Interests apply to the differentiated means by which the valued goal may be reached. They are concerned with satisfactions inherent primarily in the *process* rather than in the *outcome* of an activity. Thus, altruism and high income may be (often conflicting) occupational values. *How* one likes to help people or make money – by talking to groups, or repairing machinery, or solving mathematical problems – expresses occupational interest.

Confusion occasionally appears because the concept of interest – in the sense of engaging in an activity that is intrinsically enjoyable – may be more or less highly valued by various people. In other words, the *importance* to a person of doing work that is intrinsically interesting – as compared, say, with work that pays a high salary or work that helps others – is an indication of that person's values. The particular clusters of activities that a person finds intrinsically appealing are an indication of that person's interests.

The dimensions of interests, then, should not be mingled – in conception or in measurement – with the dimensions of values. Interest measures and ratings may be expected to identify and classify the activities that an individual finds intrinsically interesting. Such measures will not generally predict global satisfaction in various options; they can predict only the satisfaction of interests. When individuals have decided which clusters of activities are intrinsically interesting, they must still decide how much importance they want to attach to satisfying intrinsic activity interest – compared, say, with such other occupational value dimensions as altruism, wealth, autonomy, security, and so on. For this comparison, a measure of values is appropriate. Measures of values permit, ultimately, explicit estimation of the total satisfaction that a person may derive from various options, provided that the instrumentality of each option in respect to each value can be rated.

Guidance models differ in the extent to which they make or recognize such distinctions between domains and also in the attention or emphasis they give to any domain. Relative emphases are derived from the purpose of each approach. Thus, many models (like B in Table 1, chapter 3) start by trying to identify occupations in which the client is most likely to be successful. The pragmatic failure of this approach is described in the discussion of aptitudes, following, and in *Aptitudes Revisited*. But, more fundamentally, there is a problem in the meaning of success. It does not have the same meaning in all models. In a manpower model, it refers to successful performance as defined by others—such as society, an employer, a supervisor—who seek to select according to their own purposes, usually in terms of maximizing productivity.

In a guidance model, however, success comes into play in accomplishing the individual's purpose—that is, achieving occupational satisfaction. Therefore, it is necessary to begin with the dimensions along which occupational satisfaction is construed. Then, in structured search, it turns out that starting with rewards and satisfactions (the instrumentality of occupations) is more effective in differentiating useful lists of occupations than starting with aptitudes or other predictors that might relate to chances of success. The prediction of success in the occupation plays its role more effectively in the later stages of decision making. That is why, in SIGI, values play a primary role. They provide the major dimensions along which clients analyze their own desires and construe the instrumentality of various occupations. Further support for the primacy of values appears later, after an analysis of aptitudes.

In the original SIGI, interests, as indicated previously, were explicitly embedded in values, in a two-step appraisal: They were taken into account in searching for or evaluating occupations only if they had indeed been weighted as relatively important. In SIGI PLUS, interests are detached from values and treated independently on the implicit assumption that they will be used in structured search if, and only if, they are indeed highly valued. This is still a far cry from the exclusive use of interests alone, as in the type of approach summarized in Column 3 of Table 1 in chapter 3.

The use of *interests alone* (e.g., in Holland's Student Directed Search) assumes that interests are the sole or overwhelming consideration—an assumption that is not supported by evidence. For example, Beynon and Blackburn (1972), finding in a study of British blue-collar workers that job satisfaction was related to congruence between the workers' values and the attributes of their jobs, also noted that many workers perceived their jobs as "uninteresting." This perception, however, did not influence job satisfaction because of the lack of importance they attached to interest compared with such other dimensions as income and job security. While satisfaction of intrinsic interests is often a major consideration, other values are frequently regarded as being equally or more important. Many people do not expect to satisfy their major interests in their occupations. A better match can generally be found between interests and avocational pursuits than between interests and occupations. To place the main emphasis on occupational interests limits guidance to (at best) a fragmentary approach to appraisal, to occupational differentiation, and to CDM.

Furthermore, the approach that depends largely on interest measures to maximize resemblance to membership in an occupation assumes that birds of a feather do flock together, and that such a tendency toward homogeneity is desirable. But there is considerable evidence that contradicts the "birds of a feather" assumption. Strong (1943) himself, notwithstanding his sustained efforts to distinguish occupational groups by their responses to his inventory, once commented, in a passage often overlooked, on the striking *similarities* of responses to the SVIB among various groups of people:

> likenesses among the interests of individuals are far more striking than differences. All groups so far studied agree very well in their interests. Men regardless of age and economic or occupational status agree on all types of items to a high degree. There is also good agreement between the interests of men and those of women of corresponding ages. Only when differences in age and sex are both involved do we find correlations approximating zero for certain groups of items. The least similarity of interests occurs between 15-year-old boys and adult women; even here the correlation is .48 when all items on the interest inventory are considered.

A study of interests of employed women (Zytowski & Hay, 1984) tested similarities within each of a variety of occupations and differences between them. They concluded that birds of a feather in their sample did not flock together.

Interests are among the most widely studied of the "psychological" variables that are presumed to relate individual to occupational differentiation. Over many years, interest inventories developed by Strong and by Kuder have probably racked up heavier sales than any other test or inventory used for guidance. A major investment by the U. S. Department of Labor (1979) was made in the publication of the *Guide for Occupational Exploration (GOE)*. It also places interests in a position of paramount importance for appraisal, occupational differentiation, and CDM. It partitions the universe of occupations in the *Dictionary of Occupational Titles* into 12 "interest areas." It then goes on to divide these areas into groups and subgroups according to other criteria. The simplifying notion is that the user can start with interests (measured by an inventory with scales presumed to represent those same 12 areas of interest), then narrow consideration down successively to smaller groupings or "families" of occupations.

The mechanics of this are discussed in greater detail later, under *The Structure of Interests*, and are compared with our own procedures in SIGI and SIGI PLUS for linking individual interests to occupational attributes. For our purposes here, suffice it to point out that individual characteristics (such as interests) are not isomorphic with occupational attributes. "Interests" are often used loosely, as in the *GOE*, as if they characterized occupations. Strictly speaking, interests are not a property of occupations but of persons. *Activities* characterize occupations. Thus, the activities involved in an occupation tend to provide *opportunities* (more or less) for satisfaction of any of an individual's interests. But simple trait-matching – "square pegs in square holes" – does not work. Most of the occupations with which guidance can be concerned require some variety of activities. While people in these occupations may be able to emphasize some activities more than others, in keeping with their own preferences, they are rarely able to limit themselves to only the activities that appeal to them. At the same time, and conversely, people usually have a "surplus" of interests beyond those that correspond to occupational activities. Furthermore, some occupations require activities that hold low intrinsic interest for most people; activities in others may tend to be quite popular. It is clear that – even when corresponding dimensions are identified – the distribution of interests in the population is far from identical with the distribution of corresponding activities in the world of work. So the reductio ad absurdum of using guidance to make populations within occupations homogeneous in respect to interests is neither possible nor desirable.

That is why interests were considered along with values in SIGI: Clients first decided how important it was to satisfy some major interest; second, only if it was important, they identified occupations in which a large share of the activities tend to meet that interest. In evaluating occupations (in the section called Strategy in SIGI), the effect of interests was represented by the product of the weight assigned to work in one's main field of interest and a rating of the instrumentality of each occupation in providing activities that would satisfy such interests. (Since this product is one of 10 similar products, the numerical effect of interests can be compared directly with the effects of the other nine dimensions of values.) This weighing of importance and identifying of a linkage between main interests of individuals and main activities of occupations is a far cry from trying to judge the resemblance of a person's own interests to the presumed distinctive interests of people in different occupations and to make a choice based on such a matching of traits.

In SIGI PLUS, interests are appraised in two ways: according to fields of knowledge and according to activities. Occupations can be identified in structured search as they offer opportunities that correspond to the fields or activities designated by users. This correspondence is, again, just one of the features taken into account when the desirability of occupations is evaluated in the section called Deciding.

Note especially that in both SIGI and SIGI PLUS the client's interests are not linked to the interests of *people* in the various occupations, as in Approach C, labeled resemblance to membership (Table 1 in chapter 3). Rather they are linked to the fields of knowledge or the activities that characterize the *occupation*.

Guidance systems that emphasize resemblance to membership often use a domain labeled *temperaments* as a major variable. Several career guidance systems depend on the *Dictionary of Occupational Titles (DOT)* for definitions of temperament dimensions and for classification of occupations on those dimensions. The third edition of the *DOT* defined pairs of temperament dimensions as if to represent opposite poles of a single dimension—for example, (1) variety and (2) repetitive operations, (5) working with other people and (6) working alone. Many guidance resources, including CG systems, used these worker traits, perhaps rather mindlessly because occupations were categorized on the *DOT* Data Display Tape as to whether certain worker "temperaments" are or are not "important." Despite its popularity, this domain can be discounted because of conceptual problems. No rationale has been given for the domain or its dimensions. Relationships between dimensions are not clear: Just as some pairs of constructs, such as "variety" and "repetition," must be negatively correlated, other pairs—such as "direction, control, and planning" and "influencing"—must have high positive correlations. Illustrations in the *Handbook for Analyzing Jobs* (U.S. Department of Labor, 1972) point up the inevitability of this outcome: One illustration under "influencing" starts "*Plans and directs* educational campaigns . . ." (italics added).

The fact that developers of CG systems using the *DOT* "temperaments" have experienced a problem in identifying the domain points up the conceptual problem. For example, the QUEST questionnaire for CIS introduces paraphrases of some of the DOT temperaments by stating, "NATURE OF WORK: People have different *personalities* and so do jobs. Your personal *likes, values, and interests* will affect the kind of work you choose" (italics added.) GIS encompasses a number of the DOT temperaments under the rubric of interests, folding them into the major categories of "people," "ideas or numbers," and "things or machines." The Ohio Career Information System (OCIS) refers to them variously, under the heading, "Work activities which describe the occupation," as "personal adjustments," "job demands," and "work situations (activities)." These dimensions clearly overlap with a separate set of dimensions called *interests* by OCIS. While the developers of CG systems may be faulted for their mindlessness in mingling, mangling, and copying such ill-defined dimensions from such ill-differentiated domains, the *DOT* developers cannot be held blameless: "Temperaments" have been named without palpable foundations in research, theory, or rationale and have proven highly susceptible to the "jingle" and "jangle" fallacies. So we dismiss "temperaments" without further ado.

Aptitudes are emphasized in Approach B, labeled selection for success (Table 1, chapter 3). Modeled on the Air Corps selection battery, this approach has tended to use measures of aptitudes, skills, and knowledge as predictors of success in training or on the job. Typical criteria of success have been completion of training or perseverance on the job for a given period, productivity, and supervisors' ratings.

The question has sometimes been raised as to why aptitudes were not given primacy instead of values in SIGI and SIGI PLUS. Some systems, for example, use such dimensions of aptitudes as those named in the *General Aptitude Test Battery (GATB)* scales as search variables to identify suitable occupations. As we have seen, Hull gave aptitudes the main role in his vision of computerized occupational choice.

There is, to begin with, some risk in even mentioning aptitudes as a component of guidance. The term is freighted with many connotations of inherent characteristics that have stirred great controversy and emotion in recent years. Let us try to defuse the explosive elements of this discussion and give aptitudes the benefit of every possible doubt by defining them, pragmatically, as any variable measured prior to engagement in some set of activities that is used to predict performance in that set. They may include developed abilities typically measured by tests, knowledge, skills, experience – whatever; the measures range from GATB to biographical inventories.

Another source of concern over aptitudes is that, although they tend to have moderate validity for predicting success in education or training, they tend to show consistently lower validities for predicting success in occupations. As indicated before, however, even low validities can be effective in selection of candidates for improved productivity. So again let us give aptitudes the benefit of doubt and assume that they make a significant contribution to prediction of success.

The evidence for differential prediction from any battery of aptitudes, however, as has been pointed out previously, is even weaker, and we cannot give much ground there.

Of all aptitude batteries, probably the most noteworthy and widely used entry in the lists is the GATB. Developed by the U. S. Employment Service and used by the state employment services since 1947, it has been the subject of more research than any other battery for predicting occupational success. It has evolved into 12 tests contributing to scores on nine aptitudes, with extensive norming and validity studies for occupations and training programs. A description and critique of specific procedures ap-

..er in this volume. Here suffice it to say that the aptitudes are ..tively correlated, with a median correlation of .44 in an intercorrela-..on matrix based on 23,428 employed workers, applicants, apprentices, students, and trainees (U.S. Department of Labor, 1970). People at or above the mean on any one aptitude are quite likely to "qualify" on Occupational Aptitude Patterns (OAP) for a very large number of occupations. The only kind of consistently valid prediction to be derived from GATB involves some very broadly defined index of "level" comparable to that derived from the Army General Classification Test in World War II (Stewart, 1947). For example, Thorndike (1985) reanalyzed data from all cross-validated studies of GATB and found that virtually all the predictive validity was accounted for by the general factor.

One could perhaps get around this problem of negligible differential prediction from any one battery by designing, empirically, a unique set of aptitudes, skills, or knowledge for each occupation. While this unique set of predictors might be useful to employers for selection from applicants, it would be prohibitively cumbersome to administer in a guidance system designed to help identify a suggested list of occupations (out of a large population of occupations) for further consideration by a client. On the other hand, it is apparent that such a unique set might be useful later in evaluating a small, manageable number of options that had already been identified as desirable by other means.

It is just this latter function that is found in the SIGI Prediction system and the SIGI PLUS Skills section. They bring to bear information about chances of success in options that have already been screened in terms of desirability—which, of course, is a function of values and interests. Chances of success moderate desirability but cannot substitute for it. Any given probability statement for entry or success in an occupation has different meanings to different individuals, depending on each person's values. While successful performance is a goal from the employer's point of view, it is a means to an end for the candidate; that is, the goal is the satisfactions and rewards that would accrue from successful employment, which is instrumental in providing such returns in respect to important values. Chances of success (for which aptitudes are a surrogate) suggest constraints or opportunities to achieve what one wants but come into play most effectively after the population of options has been narrowed in terms of satisfactions and rewards. (See the sections on *PREDICTION IN SIGI* and *Aptitudes Revisited,* later in this chapter.)

Support for Values

So neither interests nor aptitudes is a viable alternative to values, although they may be useful complements in CDM. On the positive side, there is ample and longstanding evidence of the major part played by values in individual perceptions and self-concepts. For example, Postman, Bruner, and McGinnies (1948), Bruner and Postman (1948), and Bruner and Krech (1949) demonstrated in a number of laboratory experiments the effects of values as organizing and selective factors in perception. Values not only are an integral part of the self-concept but also give it its frame of reference, defined by Allport (1943) as any spatial-temporal or cultural orientation that relates many of an individual's attitudes, habits, and judgments to one another and influences the formation of new judgments, attitudes, and habits. Thus values mediate the organization of attributes within an individual's self-concept and muster them for decision making.

Emphasis on the role of values in CDM has received support from a number of research studies. Ginzberg et al. (1951), formulating from their cross-sectional studies a developmental theory in which interests, abilities, and values play successively major roles, concluded:

> The foundation for an effective occupational choice must lie in the values and goals of an individual, for it is these which enable him to order his current achievement with reference to the future. The essential element in occupational decision making is the effective linking of present action to future objectives. Certainly, capacities and interests must be considered, but the individual will not make an effective occupational choice unless he has support from his value scheme.

A number of specific studies of the relationship of job satisfaction to congruence between individuals' values and the relevant job attributes, involving different types of workers and occupations, reinforce this conclusion—for example, female employees of discount department stores (Betz, 1969); workers in a British food production plant (Beynon & Blackburn, 1972); telephone company employees (Hackman & Lawler, 1971); technicians and "professionals" in the U.S. Forest Service (Koch, 1974). Locke (1976) marshalled extensive additional evidence to support these examples.

Cronbach and Gleser (1965), in their treatise on personnel decisions, also emphasized the dominant role of individual values: "The decision for each must be evaluated on a different scale of values. Since the student will make a particular choice only once, it is manifestly impossible to seek a strategy which is superior on the average, for the average has no meaningful definition. A particular decision must be evaluated on the basis of the expected outcome and its value for this individual."

They concluded that it is impossible for anyone save the decision maker to determine the "correctness" of a decision: The utility of the decision depends on whether the individual "brings to bear a consistent and fully acceptable value system" (i.e., "fully acceptable to himself" and "consistent within itself"). On the importance of increasing the client's awareness of values and consistency of values, Cronbach and Gleser (1965) said:

> Those who have proposed follow-up studies to evaluate the counseling process have been most concerned with the client's growth in 'objective self-knowledge' (i.e., knowledge of the probable outcomes of his decisions) and with the 'success' of those decisions as judged by some objective standard. But one of the main contributions of the counseling process may be to alter the person's verbalized value systems, particularly by eliminating contradictions between various wishes and hopes. It seems worthwhile therefore to study how the client's evaluation system itself changes during counseling. No one can say whether a given change is 'good' or 'bad,' since the person is the judge of his own values. In view of the central place they play in the decision process, however, any knowledge of the nature and development of such personal evaluation systems could be helpful.

Other distinguished psychologists, such as Anastasi and Tyler, have endorsed the emphasis on values in CDM. Tyler (1978) has herself carried out an extensive program of research in this field; Anastasi (1964), in her chapter on the psychology of vocational choice, specifically praises the treatment embodied in *You: Today and Tomorrow* (Katz, 1959), a text that, like SIGI, emphasizes values.

That text, incidentally, was one of the few in the field of guidance ever to be thoroughly evaluated, as Anastasi (1964) and Kroll, Dinklage, Lee, Morley, and Wilson (1970) emphasized. The results of the evaluation (Gribbons, 1960; Shimberg & Katz, 1962) led to further studies by Gribbons and Lohnes (1968), who followed up the sample of junior high school students well into adulthood; they concluded that guidance programs should foster awareness of values and "the integrating of [clients'] values and their aspirations and plans."

Cooley and Lohnes (1968), in their Project TALENT report on ways in which psychometric information can serve in the guidance process, endorse a trait-and-factor approach. But they quote *Decisions and Values* (Katz, 1963) extensively and acknowledge that "maintaining and deploying of a viable and satisfying set of values is absolutely central to the [decision] process." Hansen (1970) also cites and supports my rationale for the central role of values in CDM as a major theme for community and school guidance programs. Super and Tiedeman in numerous publications have also endorsed this emphasis on values. Rokeach (1971, 1973) regards values as "more fundamental components within a person's makeup than attitudes" or interests; he sees values "as determinants of attitudes as well as of behavior," as demonstrated by a procedure – analogous in many ways to the values game in SIGI – of confronting students with situations designed to make them aware of inconsistencies in their values systems.

All these authors accept the premise, emphasized in this book, that self-understanding is essential to CDM – and that examination of values is essential to self-understanding. There is, however, a school of thought that rejects self-understanding as a goal of guidance and counseling. Its alternative doctrine, behaviorism, focuses exclusively on interventions designed to change behavior without necessarily involving understanding by the client. This view has been accepted by a number of practitioners and warrants brief review and analysis. The foremost exponent of behavioral counseling has been John Krumboltz.

Self-Understanding Versus Behaviorism

In a series of papers, Krumboltz (1965, 1966a, 1966b) proposed as goals of counseling those specific and observable behavior changes that are desired by each client and are compatible with the counselor's values. (This implies that counselors must understand their own values even if clients need not!)

In a paper for the *Review of Educational Research* (Katz, 1969a), I observed that there is less than complete clarity in Krumboltz's deemphasis of a client's self-understanding in the formulation, definition, and acceptance of goals: It is difficult to see how clients can adequately designate desirable changes in behavior unless they first perceive their present state and "proceive" the new state to which they aspire. The setting of goals itself is to a great extent an expression of values and therefore a component of values.

Granted, answering these questions of self-understanding – Who am I? What do I want to become? What is the nature of the discrepancy between these two states? – is not the only goal of guidance. There remain the planning and the accomplishment of the change. It may also be granted that, as Krumboltz has said, behavioral changes can take place (e.g., through reinforcement) without self-understanding. But it is difficult then to demonstrate that these changes were in accordance with the counselee's goals. And does *specific* behavior change alone suffice? One of the generally accepted aims of guidance is to work itself out of a job – to help clients grow increasingly able to solve their own problems, independently and self-sufficiently. Some insight, then, into how the change took place would appear to be desirable for future self-direction.

Furthermore, in deprecating self-understanding, does not Krumboltz tend to limit perception of the counselee's goals? The Rogerian would ask: "What keeps counselees from engaging in appropriate goal-directed behavior? If they want to get better marks, say, don't *they* know, as well as

the counselor, that they must–let us say–spend more time studying?"
What may be overlooked is an implicit value conflict: "I want to get better
marks" may leave unsaid "but I don't want to spend more time studying."
Krumboltz does not explain how the unspoken clause gets into the counselee's statement of goals, or problem, without some attention to self-
understanding.

Guidance is not concerned just with the goal that counselees say they
want at the moment–say, at report card time. It is concerned with
examined goals. It tries to stretch the counselee's perceptions, without
losing sight of present wants, to include a systematic exploration and
examination of relevant values, resulting in some adjudication between
competing or conflicting values. Self-understanding, then, may be not just
an instrumental element in changing behavior; it may survive as a higher
order goal of guidance. Here we may note Shoben's (1965) suggestion that
problem solving is less the aim of counseling than its raw material. The
chief aim of counseling, in his view, is "developmental experience."

Krumboltz also seems to have slighted the bases on which the individual
counselor determines that a counselee's specific goal is "acceptable." Has
he ducked the question by simply delegating the responsibility to each
counselor without specifying the social, cultural, ethical, and individual
components of the standards to be used by counselors? To what extent
does their stand depend, say, on their affiliations? To what extent on their
own values? If counselors decide for themselves and advertise which kinds
of goals they consider compatible with their own values, counselees may
simply shop around to find a counselor who agrees with them. This is not
likely to challenge counselees to explore and examine their *goals* systematically.

Krumboltz's emphasis on problem solving and behavior changing as
aims of counseling may be better suited for a model of instruction, in which
the goals are given (the "universals" again), than for a model of guidance, in
which the goals are to be chosen (the "alternatives"). In the former model,
it has been suggested that society (rather than the individual being
counseled) is the counselor's "real" client. If so, the theory should indicate
how the counselor helps society to define its goals.

Indeed, we may ask how the behaviorist would contribute to society's
definition of goals without involvement in "self-understanding" by society,
that is, without examination of competing goals (or values) and adjudication between them.

I have not been able to refrain from asking Krumboltz whether he
believes he "decided" to become a behavioral psychologist; that is, did he
engage in value judgments? Did he consider information and reason about
it? Or was he just led blindly along by contingencies of reinforcement? I am
pleased to note that in more recent work (Krumboltz, 1979) he accepts the

premise that "a good decision is one yielding consequences consistent with the decider's values." His criterion instrument, Career Decision Simulation, is borrowed directly from our Simulated Occupational Choice (Katz et al., 1976, 1978), described in chapter 5.

THE DIMENSIONS OF VALUES

In the course of defining the domain of values, some indication has already been given of the dimensions it comprises. How were those dimensions determined for SIGI and SIGI PLUS? We wanted users to take cognizance of the full range of occupational values, without undue redundancy. The dimensions had to be comprehensive, including all values of importance to significant proportions of the population using the system; yet they had to be restricted to a manageable number. They had to show individual variation; there would be no purpose in appraising values that were universally held to be of no account. They had to be meaningful and relevant, capable of definition in operational terms, and capable of linkage to occupational rewards and satisfactions. They had to be relatively independent; the degree of importance attached to one must not automatically subsume the same degree of importance for any other.

From reviews of the literature and our own research, we compiled lists of occupational values. Most of these had been studied to ascertain their relevance to occupational satisfaction—as, for example, in Mortimer's (undated) review for the Work in America Institute, which lists such values as "autonomy and freedom from close supervision, good pay and other economic benefits, job security, . . . variety, . . . interesting work, . . . prestige" (p. 3) (all included in SIGI), along with "promotional opportunities," which is job specific rather than occupational and is included in SIGI PLUS.

Our own studies made considerable use of intensive interviews. In a variety of interview schedules, we asked questions devised to get at the common dimensions along which people construed their values and perceived and evaluated occupations. We built some redundancy of questions and techniques into the interviews so that we could check on consistency of responses: Confronting individuals with inconsistencies often seemed to evoke particularly illuminating insights. One schedule for college students asked them to name the "occupation(s) you plan to enter (are considering)." The interviewer then said, "I don't know much about [occupation named]. Can you tell me about it?"

This open-ended question got at the students' own perceptions of an occupation that appealed to them, in terms of the constructs they used to define it and differentiate it from other occupations. An interviewer's checklist provided for coding the descriptive and instrumental attributes mentioned, according to priority of mention and emphasis, extensiveness, or specificity. We then asked: "What information would you like to have that you don't have now?" After some intervening questions, we resumed this line of inquiry in a slightly more structured way: "Tell me more about why you chose [occupation named]. What appeals to you most? What do you expect to like about it most? What do you expect to like least? What changes would you make in it, if you could, to make it more appealing or satisfying?" (It is interesting to note, in Louviere's 1988 book on *Metric Conjoint Analysis*, that a similar line of questioning has more recently been used to identify "determinant attributes" – values, in our vocabulary – as a first step in many market researchers' efforts to analyze utilities of "brands.")

We then asked respondents to turn their imagination loose and describe, as fully as they could, an ideal, or "dream," occupation. The interviewer followed up by asking, "In view of what you've said about an ideal occupation, why didn't you decide to become [name of another occupation chosen by the interviewer to resemble the "ideal" in some salient features] instead of [the occupation first named]?" (This item depended for its effectiveness on the interviewer's insight and ingenuity in proposing alternatives that would challenge the respondent to reconcile value conflicts expressed or implied in the earlier responses.) The next question asked for a description of the converse, a "nightmare" occupation. These three items proved to be extraordinarily productive. They seemed to stimulate respondents to specify reasons and distinctions that had not occurred to them before.

Moving to a still more structured sequence, we showed respondents a list of 10 values with one-line definitions and asked them to tell of an incident in their lives in which they had received some (specified) "payoff" on each of these values. (If they could not recall an actual incident, they were asked to describe something that might happen.) This was used to clarify their perception of each value.

These values then formed one axis of a matrix, the other axis consisting of titles of 16 occupations plus a space to write in the occupation previously mentioned by the respondent if it was not included in the 16. In each cell, the respondent wrote an estimate of the level of satisfaction each occupation was perceived to offer in respect to each value. We analyzed the responses in this matrix to answer several questions: Are individual differences in values related to systematic differences in perceptions of occupational instrumentality? For example, do people who value altruism themselves tend to see more opportunity for altruistic satisfactions in various occupations? More generally, are values and perceptions of occupations independent? (They are.) Does a person's "sense of agency" moderate the relationships? (If so, the data were not unequivocal on the hypothesis that people with a strong "sense of agency" tend to perceive occupations as subject to shaping according to their own values.) Was there a "halo effect"—that is, did some occupations tend to be rated very high or very low on all dimensions? (There was not.)

The next two items were modeled on the Role Construct Repertory test (Kelly, 1955), which we adapted to evoke the constructs each person used to compare or differentiate between occupations. Each person named five occupations: your ideal occupation; the occupation you are most likely to enter; a parent's (or other family member's) occupation; your best friend's occupational preference; an occupation that you think is desirable in some ways but that you would not want to enter. These occupations were grouped systematically in triads, and the respondent was asked (a) to indicate which two of each triad offer satisfactions and rewards that are more alike than the satisfactions and rewards offered by the third member, (b) to describe the basis for the perceived similarity and difference. A similar comparison was made using the five occupations that had the highest appeal in the previous list of 16 occupations. (Variations of these questions were asked in later questionnaires designed for small-group administration.) Responses to these items revealed sharp individual differences in the richness, variety, and breadth of constructs used: Some people sounded the same note repeatedly in comparison after comparison—for example, "make more money versus make less money." It was clear that they construed the universe of occupational rewards and satisfactions along only one—or at most two—dimensions. Others used several constructs but almost always used each one more than once. Kelly called such constructs *permeable*.

A later item asked students to distribute a fixed sum in weighting the importance of a list of 13 values. Their scaling of the values ran the gamut of possibilities, with a wide distribution of weights assigned to each dimension.

The point of all these items, ranging from open ended to highly structured, including a variety of occupations selected to represent different attributes and to involve specified affects and connotations, was to acquire evidence, by a variety of methods, of the consistency, permeability, breadth, and rigidity of people's constructs. (The interview schedules used are appended to Katz et al., 1969.)

As another component of this sustained research and development effort, we devised a game-like exercise called Simulated Occupational Choice (SOC), for standardized administration to one respondent at a time. The task for the respondent was to choose one occupation out of three unknown "occupations of the future," designated as X, Y, and Z. In one version of SOC (four versions in all were constructed and field tested), the respondent was told that the interviewer had full information about these occupations, and the respondent could get whatever information was deemed important by asking appropriate questions and could then choose the occupation that was most attractive. There was a great deal more to SOC than this (see chapter 5), but this portion proved productive in eliciting people's values in terms of what they wanted to know in order to make a choice. Their responses served as an additional check on the comprehensiveness and relevance of the values dimensions that we had by then chosen to use in SIGI. They also served as a corroboration of the need for systematic examination of values: Respondents often failed, on their own initiative, to ask for information relevant to a value that later (when they were given an array of unmentioned values to choose from) turned out to be one of their most important or even crucial values (Katz et al., 1976, 1978).

Previous reference (Norris & Katz, 1970) has been made to unrestricted maximum likelihood factor analyses that helped us document the independence of the domains of aptitudes, interests, and values (using a large national sample of secondary school students followed up 1 year after completion of high school). These analyses shed some light on the structure of values and particularly on the relative independence of the dimensions. They contradict some sociologists' views that prestige is dependent on income and education. Such perceptions of redundancy, however, are largely an artifact of the procedure commonly used to derive an index of prestige (or social status of an occupation, as the sociologists are likely to call it): Most such writings appear to rely on Duncan's Index (Duncan, 1961), which predicts the index of prestige from the weighted sums of indices of income and education. But Duncan's scales were coarse, and his index has not held up well in reanalyses of his own data (Curry & Walling, 1984). In our own studies of SIGI users, who have been exposed to operational definitions of each value, the relationship of prestige to income and education (although positive) has not been so high as to be redundant.

An example of a value that we initially considered for inclusion in SIGI, but eventually deleted, is one often called creativity. The term has achieved great popularity. Indeed, Jacques Barzun (1990) complained that the word creativity has been rendered meaningless by overuse: "It fits all situations, pointing to nothing in particular. . . . Creativity has become what divine grace and salvation were to former times."

In our own research, we could not come up with a viable operational definition for it, nor were respondents at all consistent in their perceptions of it. "Creativity" was construed sometimes as general and sometimes as specific: It was not clear whether those who said that "creativity" was important to them valued a chance to be "creative" in a pervasive sense or in some particular type of activity or field, such as verbal, scientific, or artistic. (Sternberg, 1988, concluded that researchers in creativity had also failed to reach a consensus on such issues.) Some people who gave a high weight to creativity said they would be content to be creative in avocational fine arts (say, painting or ceramics) or in cooking, but did not as a rule seek opportunities (and demands) for "creativity" in an occupation. We were unable to define the value with sufficient clarity and relevance to link it to corresponding rewards and satisfactions on which each occupation would have to be rated. As we discussed the opportunities for "creativity" with people in various occupations, their responses indicated that there is a chance to be innovative in effective ways (our best definition of creative) in any occupation that permits some degree of freedom to its members. But we account for that in the value called autonomy or independence.

Another example of a value we did not use (although, again, it is used widely) is variously called sense of accomplishment or pride in work. Our judgment was that, although rewards and satisfactions corresponding to this value might differentiate between some unskilled and higher-level occupations, it did not seem useful in differentiation between the occupations to which guidance programs are usually addressed and which were likely to be considered by the population of SIGI users. (Most unskilled positions are chosen as a function of job characteristics, indicated later, rather than occupational characteristics.) There is a doctrine that all socially useful work can be a source of pride or sense of accomplishment, and we had no desire to provoke protests from believers in that doctrine or members of any occupation rated low on this dimension. (Indeed, who would dare rate an occupation low on it?)

In several research studies and guidance resources, values labeled "work that seems important or interesting to me" (used in the National Longitudinal Study), "self-actualization" (used in DISCOVER), "work satisfaction," and the like are often encountered. Such labels represent an attempt to wrap up virtually the entire domain of values and interests in one all-encompassing dimension, leaving the work of self-assessment still undone. As far as I can tell from these labels, something akin to a composite of all of an individual's important values seems to be the referend. These global labels cannot be linked to the attributes of occupations. An attempt to rate an occupation on such a composite of all attributes of importance should be the *outcome*, not the *starting point*, of an analysis of what a person wants and what opportunities an occupation offers to obtain it. It appears to represent a fuzzy attempt to express at the outset what SIGI derives from an analysis of the desirability of each occupation in terms of the total configuration of the person's values and the occupation's ratings on corresponding rewards and satisfactions – what we call the "Desirability" of an occupation for each person.

Other values frequently found in the literature tend to be linked to attributes not so much of occupations as of jobs. While a desire for pleasant co-workers, flexible hours, easy commute, chances for advancement, and the like may be important to many people, the opportunity to obtain these desiderata varies more between jobs within an occupation than between occupations. Their flavor is local rather than generic, and they do not tend to differentiate between occupations. So as explained before, they were not suitable for SIGI, which provided information only on occupations, but have been included in SIGI PLUS for consideration of specific jobs and places of employment.

In field tests of SIGI (Chapman et al., 1977), we found that the values dimensions stood up well. College students perceived the dimensions as independent (intercorrelations of the weights were not high); the weights given each value varied greatly across students (as indicated by the standard deviations); each value was regarded as important by substantial numbers of students; and students did not feel that values of importance to them had been omitted (as determined by interviews and questionnaires after their use of SIGI). Similar findings on values dimensions held for adults in general in the field trial of SIGI PLUS (Norris, Shatkin, Schott, & Bennett, 1985). The aforementioned findings on these values dimensions were confirmed in paper-and-pencil and interview use with high school students (Tittle, 1981). Nevertheless, we have added for SIGI PLUS not only job values but, to avoid frustrating individuals who may have other important values, an opportunity to choose a value from a supplementary list or to name one themselves.

For future research, it may be appropriate to hypothesize about the facets of this system; the hypothesis can later be tested by use of Guttman's smallest space analysis. (SSA relates distance between points inversely to observed relationships between items and thus can be used to partition space according to a hypothesis.) I propose, therefore, a first cut involving two facets: (a) locus or source of reward–satisfaction; the rubrics for this would be occupation and job; (b) nature of reward–satisfaction, that is, higher order clustering of values according to type of need or desire met. These clusters are based mainly on armchair logic, with a slight intrusion from knowledge of outcomes of previous correlation matrices and factor analyses, and involve three categories:

1. achievement–striving, which includes high income, prestige, leadership, and independence among the occupational values, and advancement, challenge, on-job learning, and recognition among the job values;
2. pleasure–comfort–convenience–ease, which includes work in main field of interest, variety, leisure, and security among the occupa-

tional values, and fringe benefits, easy commute, stay put, pleasant co-workers, flexible hours, and pleasant environment among the job values; and

3. nurturant conscientiousness, which includes helping others and contribution to society among the occupational values and moral-ethical employer among the job values.

The value placement of which I would be least certain is security. From time to time it might shift between Categories 1 and 2.

Stability of Values

If values play a major role in CDM, it is appropriate to consider their stability over time. In the absence of longitudinal studies, we have not been able to check specifically on the stability of the values weights assigned by SIGI users. There is some research, however, on long-term stability of the importance attached to similar values dimensions. For example, Mortimer and Lorence (1979) examined the impact of work experiences on 512 males whose values were assessed in their senior year at college and then 10 years after graduation. Values were found to be "significantly stable over the 10-year period," with changes appearing mainly in the strengthening of those values that constituted the basis of initial work selection. A re-analysis was carried out (Mortimer & Lorence, 1981) to assess the effects of "situs" of work: for example, legal, economic or financial, education and research, health and welfare, aesthetic and entertainment. They found some significant situs differences in extrinsic but not in intrinsic values; the significant situs effects disappear, however, when other variables are controlled—for example, previous values as college seniors and opportunities offered by the occupation. They (Mortimer & Lorence, 1981) concluded that "earlier [that is, college senior] values have the most consistent effects on values a decade later" (p. 711).

In another longitudinal study Lindsay and Knox (1984) compared values of high school seniors measured as part of the National Longitudinal Study in 1972 and again in a 1979 follow up. They found strong evidence for value stability. They too, like Mortimer and Lorence (1979), found indications of "occupational socialization"—the effects of an appropriate (instrumental) occupation in strengthening values that had appeared earlier.

These longitudinal studies of stability probably represent the lower bounds of stability of values that would be obtained for a sample of SIGI users. The values dimensions used in the research reported previously were not so clearly and operationally defined as those in SIGI. Nor was there a systematic effort to help subjects examine their values, resolve conflicts between competing values, scrutinize inconsistencies of responses, and so on, as in SIGI. Nor were all the subjects actively engaged at the time in CDM, as were the SIGI users; therefore, for many of the subjects the weighting of values may have had little salience and may have been done quite casually. So it is not unseemly to infer a strong tendency toward stability of the weights given various occupational values by SIGI users.

This focus on stability, however, need not lead to the assumption that change is necessarily undesirable or that SIGI cannot accommodate changes in clients' values. There are probably dominant elements of constancy in all components of personality: Identities retain a sense of continuity. But many things do change, in individuals, in the culture, in occupations. Values weights reflect a person's state of mind, of beliefs, at a particular time under particular circumstances. A guidance system should help to make values explicit and internally consistent, with close attention to their implications for CDM. But it should not aim to freeze any person's system of values. SIGI recognizes the possibility of change. Even within the system, it gives users the opportunity to reconsider and reweight their values. This opportunity demonstrates an acceptance of the possibility for change. Users are encouraged to use the model of CDM iteratively at appropriate intervals, and certainly whenever there is some likelihood that change has occurred. The very act of providing a vocabulary for values, of making values explicit, of seeing them interact with attributes of occupations in determining the desirabilities of occupations helps develop a keen awareness of values among users and a sensitivity to changes, particularly as a result of experience. It may foster a greater readiness to re-explore, re-formulate, and re-examine values. It also provides a model of CDM in which the changes can be registered and their effects seen. Thus, users are encouraged to retain flexibility: If they attain an occupation that offers rewards and satisfactions for certain values yet find little pleasure in the outcome, the appropriate response is to re-examine values.

It is intriguing to speculate that some people who once used SIGI as college students may at a later time, considering an occupational change, use SIGI PLUS—perhaps some have already done so. As they recycle through the process of self-assessment, it may well be that age, experiences, and different circumstances will have brought about some changes in values. Perhaps just such changes have thrown their careers out of balance. Re-examination of values will then be the first CDM step toward restoring equilibrium. Early recognition of the possibility of such successive value systems may, indeed, constitute a necessary condition for maintaining a kind of "mobile equilibrium" (to borrow a phrase from Piaget).

THE STRUCTURE OF INTERESTS

Different structures of interests are used for SIGI and SIGI PLUS, the latter being considerably more elaborate and detailed. Without attempting a comprehensive review of the vast literature on interests, it is useful to consider a few of the persistent issues that have dominated research and practice, both in the measurement of interests and the role of interests in CDM.

The domain of interests has been construed, defined, and measured in different ways for a variety of purposes and criteria. Some measures have been keyed for specific occupations; others for occupational clusters (e.g., "engineering, physical sciences, mathematics, and architecture"); some to types of activities (e.g., "persuasive"); others to objects of activities (e.g., "plants and animals"); some to the purpose of activities (e.g., "protective"); others to the setting of activities (e.g., "industrial"). Item responses have been chosen for *occupational* scales because of their empirical resemblance to the responses of a criterion group, and items have been chosen for *homogeneous* scales on the basis of their correlations with other items in the scales presumed to measure major themes, factors, fields, or areas. In some instances (e.g., the Strong-Campbell Interest Inventory), item responses have been keyed both for an occupational scale *and* for a major theme scale. Various interest inventories may have over 100 empirically derived occupational scales, or 6 or 10 or 12 or 24 analytically or logically derived scales, representing a considerable variety of names and constructs.

In addition to standardized tests or inventories, clients' own estimates or ratings are often used—sometimes quite formally, as in questionnaires, notebooks, and computerized guidance systems, sometimes informally, as in interviews with a counselor. To make such ratings, clients—instead of responding to many items that comprise a scale, with responses aggregated into a score on each scale—make a single response to a definition or representation of the sense or theme of a scale or field of interest. Information tests have also been used as measures of interests (e.g., Project TALENT). Finally, "expert" appraisals sometimes come into play, as counselors make judgments from clients' "manifest" interests, as demonstrated by activities actually engaged in. A few specific examples of the various approaches to defining, measuring, and using interests in CDM may help in explaining what we have done, and not done, in SIGI and SIGI PLUS.

Edward K. Strong, one of the best known pioneers in interest measurement, took an empirical approach to occupational scales. He asked, in effect, what sets of items will produce responses that differentiate men in various occupations from "men-in-general"–the total population to which he administered the items. (He later followed a similar routine in developing a blank for women.) Having found item-response configurations that tended to be distinctive for certain occupations, his purpose then was to determine the resemblance between a new user's responses and the pattern of responses representative of each occupational group. The assumption made in using these scores for guidance was that people whose response patterns resemble those of members of some occupation would gravitate toward that occupation–the "birds of a feather" theory. Measurement of this tendency in advance would be expected to prevent error, vacillation, and waste along the way.

It is interesting that the largest section of Strong Vocational Interest Blank (SVIB) items consists of occupational titles, to which the client responds Like, Indifferent, or Dislike. (This item type is dominant in many other inventories also, such as Holland's Vocational Preference Inventory and his Student-Directed Search.) If identical responses to an item by different people are to have the same meanings (weights for occupational scales), it must be assumed that the stimulus (the occupational title) is perceived in a similar way. But this consistency of perception implies a *common basis* of knowledge or stereotype or even misinformation. If the responses reflect common knowledge, then they provide no new information; that is, clients must already know their likes or dislikes for the occupations to respond in a stable and meaningful way. In that case, they are being asked to invest the very coin they hope to earn. If, on the other hand, the responses reflect idiosyncratic perceptions, they cannot be expected to contribute to the validity of a score–they will provide more noise than information.

Another problem is the effect of response styles. As Bonynge (1991) demonstrated, many scales of the Strong–Campbell Interest Inventory (SCII), the successor to the SVIB, have a predominance of items keyed the same (say, L or D). Scores are thus susceptible to yea-saying or nay-saying response styles. For example, marking all items to show a pervasive dislike for work produced scores high enough to render such diverse occupations as Farmer, Broadcaster, Marketing Executive, Restaurant Manager, Optician, and more as worthy of "consideration" by the respondent.

In contrast with Strong's empirically built scales for specific occupations, most other developers of interest inventories tried to construct homogeneous scales. Out of conglomerations of items representing activities of many kinds, as well as occupational titles and various other stimuli for expressing likes or preferences, they tried to group items that seemed to be associated with logically selected *types* of interests. These items were then usually refined into scales by item analysis: Items were chosen that correlated relatively high with other items in their own scale and low with items in other scales.

The Kuder Preference Record-Vocational is the best known example of this approach. Its 9 (Form B) or 10 (Form C) scales include such rubrics as mechanical, computational, scientific, persuasive, literary, and artistic. The items range from atomistic activities ("Read a story to a sick person") to virtual occupational titles ("Be a bookkeeper"); the latter are subject to the same comments made earlier for the SVIB occupational titles. The items are grouped in triads, with instructions that, in effect, rank order preferences for the three items in each set. This is an ipsative procedure, comparing the client's preference for an item representing one scale with that for an item representing another. The sum of preferences for items representing a given scale yields a raw score for that scale, which is then converted into a percentile rank in an appropriate norms group (e.g., adult males). The manual says that scores above the 75th percentile rank are to be considered "high." There is very little evidence to substantiate the validity of any inference about the relevance of "high" scores for particular occupations.

Furthermore, *any* interpretation, either ipsative or normative, is nullified by a totally illogical alternation of ipsative and normative procedures (Katz, 1962, 1965). That is, a higher percentile rank on one scale than on another does not mean that a person's interest in the first area is greater than his or her interest in the other; nor does one person's higher percentile rank than another person's on a given scale mean that the first person has more interest in that area than does the other.

This inventory was probably the most successful, financially, of any standardized measure sold for use in guidance: According to the publisher, it was purchased for use by over 2 million students in 10,000 schools annually (over a period of several years). Notwithstanding such financial success, after severe criticisms by Katz (1962, 1965) and Bauernfeind (1963), Kuder and his publisher focused their efforts on a new instrument with empirically keyed scales. This inventory, the Kuder Occupational Interest Survey (KOIS), essentially attempted to emulate the SVIB by correlating each subject's responses with keys for occupations or college majors based on responses of reference groups presumed to represent those occupations or majors. Studies comparing college students' occupational scores on KOIS and SVIB have shown considerable divergence, and interpretations for a given client would often be quite different from one inventory to the other. It is not clear whether the differences between the inventories are attributable mainly to differences in reference groups for the same occupations or to differences in items and procedures.

Incidentally, in the course of reviewing various interest inventories for Buros' *Mental Measurements Yearbooks*, I have found that my sometimes severe criticisms seem to prompt a consistent defense: that the scores are to be interpreted only tentatively and that the primary purpose of an inventory is exploratory and heuristic – to get people thinking about their interests and the relation of their interests to CDM. I grant immediately that youthful experience is often limited and that tryout, or enlarged experience, is the logical remedy. But interest inventories are ineffectual tryouts. The items seldom describe activities in such a way as to provide insights or vicarious experience in an occupation (as noted before, many of the items in existing inventories are merely occupational titles). If exploration is the primary objective, it seems possible to provide more active or enlightening tryouts through description or simulation.

Indeed, a section called Sample in the earliest version of SIGI, using a computer-controlled slide carrousel, presented samples of work problems typically encountered in occupations students were exploring. They could then discover whether trying to solve these simulated work problems was congenial enough with their interests and skills to warrant further investigation of each occupation. As costs of multimedia technology come down, such simulated work samples should play a prominent role in computerized guidance systems of the future. Combining sound, graphics, motion picture, and text, they can provide realistic interactions to help students explore their interests and skills – in Emerson's words, "to eat of every apple." Such explorations are more useful than mere measurement.

The main point is that interest inventories do not, as a rule, offer items that substitute for experience. Rather, their express contribution is to organize or classify items and responses according to some formal procedure (resulting in scales). The underlying rationale is that young people are not able, on their own, to classify their discrete likes and dislikes, to organize them, make sense out of them, and relate them to occupational or educational options. Thus, it is important to consider the structure of the scales and the procedures used for interpretation of scores.

While the Kuder inventories went from homogeneous scales to occupational scales, Campbell (1971) added homogeneous scales ("basic interests") to the revised edition of the SVIB occupational scales. Then, in the Strong-–Campbell Interest Inventory (SCII), still using essentially the same items, he adopted the six "theme" scales from Holland's SDS. Emphasis on these scales appears to reflect a desire to give a more "psychological" interpretation of interests than could be derived from the curious mixtures of items in the occupational scales. It also appears to offer an escape from the endless labor of adding and updating occupational scales without much hope of achieving a comprehensive array in the immediate future.

These SDS dimensions bear some resemblance to the six dimensions of interests that we had used in SIGI. It may be enlightening to list the rubrics in parallel:

SDS & SCII	SIGI
Realistic	Manual-Technical
Investigative	Scientific
Artistic	Aesthetic
Social	Personal Contact
Enterprising	Verbal
Conventional	Administrative

It is evident that the nature of the language used differs. The first column uses words that purport to apply to "personality" traits; the second is meant to apply to clusters of activities. Both sets of rubrics are designed to apply to both the individual and occupational domains. In the first instance, combinations of up to three rubrics are used to characterize persons or occupations. In the second, each occupation is weighted on a scale of 1 to 4 on the extent to which it involves activities linked to each interest field.

While these and other differences could be amplified and emphasized, it may be useful also to consider some similarities. Definitions and examples of the rubrics suggest that the pairs across the first three rows and in the sixth row represent at least roughly similar constructs. Aside from these four pairs, the structures seem to diverge.

"Social" in the SDS appears to share some of the "Personal Contact" activities of SIGI but also partakes of the purposes and needs embodied in the SIGI and SIGI PLUS values that refer to altruism ("Helping Others" and "Contribution to Society"). "Enterprising" in Column 1 seems to cut across elements of the SIGI and SIGI PLUS values, "Leadership" and "Independence." The SDS appears to have no counterpart for the SIGI "Verbal" interest; perhaps the closest it comes to incorporating verbal interests and activities is under the "Artistic" personality rubric, in that some occupations that involve writing (e.g., author) are listed there.

The main difference between the two structures, however, is that the six rubrics of the SDS are meant to encompass the *entire structure* of personality and occupations and serve as the *sole* dimensions for choosing occupations. The six rubrics of SIGI, by contrast, are meant only to serve as dimensions for linking individual *interests* to occupational *activities*, and they are attached to a structure incorporating nine other dimensions linking individual values to occupational rewards and satisfactions. For example, a person's value of high income and an occupation's capability of providing monetary rewards do not appear in the SDS system at all. Yet such values as "High Income," "Security," and so on, which are ignored in the SDS structure, are of great importance to many people (as indicated previously in the discussion of the derivation of the values dimensions used in SIGI).

Thus, in Holland's SDS, all occupations are classified rigidly within the system of six "personality" rubrics and their combinations up to three at a time. In SIGI, occupations can be clustered much more flexibly, permitting different sets of occupations to be summoned by many more combinations of specifications. Such glaring omissions of values that are important to many people diminish its usefulness for structured search and fatally weaken the claims (made by Holland) for the SDS as a comprehensive guidance procedure.

A final point should be made about the so-called hexagonal structure attributed to the SDS. Holland (1973) and many of his disciples have claimed that the relationships among the six personality types are modeled as a hexagon with each point representing one of the types. The geometric distance along a straight line representing every pair of points is said to correspond to the psychologically meaningful relationship between the types. (For example, Realistic is supposed to be most closely related to Conventional and Investigative and most dissimilar to Social.) Gati (1982) reanalyzed 13 data sets of published studies that supported the hypothesized ordering of types. Using more rigorous methods, he found that the model was supported by only 2 data sets and rejected by the other 11. (Gati proposed a "hierarchic" or tree structure that better fit the data sets for the interests represented by the SDS and by Roe's, 1956, "circular" structure of fields of interests.)

The *Dictionary of Occupational Titles* (U.S. Department of Labor) incorporated in its earlier editions five bipolar interest factors that purported to describe occupations. These five factors emerged from a factor analysis of the Minnesota Multiphasic Inventory, and the Strong, Kuder, and Bell interest inventories (Cottle, 1950). Each factor was then rated merely as "important" or "not important" for each occupation. For many reasons, these factors and ratings were found to be virtually worthless. We need not go into the reasons here, because the dimensionality of the domain has since been revised and the classification of occupations by interests has been transferred to a more recent publication, the *Guide for Occupational Exploration* (U.S. Department of Labor, 1979).

The *GOE* partitions the universe of some 20,000 occupations into 12 "interest areas" (then subdivides them according to "capabilities and adaptabilities" and, further, according to a mix of criteria involving materials, products, methods, etc.). Each occupation is assigned to one, and only one, interest area. So an occupation involving activities that appeal to two or more kinds of interests is not retrieved from each area. For example, engineering occupations, including research engineers, appear in the Mechanical but not in the Scientific area. On the other hand, the 9 defined psychologist titles are split between the area designated Humanitarian (for clinical, counseling, and school psychologists) and one labeled Leading–Influencing (for comparative–experimental–physiological, developmental, educational, industrial–organizational–personnel, social, and engineering psychologists).

Mention of the rubrics for *GOE* interest areas highlights some of the questions raised by the peculiar way in which the interest domain has been defined in the *GOE*. Many of the labels seem to pertain to the *object* of activities (e.g., Plants and Animals), to the *purpose* of activities (e.g., Protective, Humanitarian), and to the *setting* of activities (e.g., Industrial) rather than to distinctions that might reside in the nature of the activities themselves. This problem is illustrated by the definition of the interest factor called Leading-Influencing: "Interest in leading and influencing others through activities involving high-level verbal or numerical abilities." Logically and semantically, this definition seems to identify two kinds of activity interests: verbal and numerical. These might be applied to a variety of purposes – protective, humanitarian, and leading–influencing presumably being among them. Thus the problem of confounding values and interests is revisited.

It is not necessary to dwell on the conceptual limitations and misdirections of all these approaches to the measurement of interests. The only reason they warrant as much detail as they have been given is that most of them have been used in other guidance systems and have received extensive use in CDM generally. Perhaps it is more important to note that the items in interest inventories are not interesting. Whether they are lists of occupational titles or fragmented activities, they tend to be dull, dreary, and time-consuming. There is nothing in the items themselves that reveals to people their interests. The items are transparent. Indeed, the paradox is that in filling out an inventory people have to know their interests in order to respond to the items! They are thus asked to invest the very coin they hope to earn. If people do know their interests, the items are redundant. If they do not know their interests, their responses are likely to be misleading.

Interest inventories, in short, do not differ so much in the nature of their items as in their conceptual structures – the definition of the domain and of the dimensions that it comprises. That being the case, are the items really necessary? Is more valid and useful information obtained by having a person respond to hundreds of items, then totting those responses up into scores on scales, with all the attendant cost and complexities of scoring, reporting, and so on? Or is it sufficient, particularly for adults, to see a definition of each dimension and rate their interest, once, on that dimension?

The way to find out is to pit the inventory against the direct rating of interests in longitudinal validity studies. In a review of relevant studies of just this kind, Dolliver (1969) concluded: "The predictive validity of expressed interests is at least as great as the predictive validity of the SVIB. In no study where direct comparison was made . . . was the SVIB as accurate as the expressed interests in predicting occupation engaged in." Furthermore, although one might assume that the SVIB predicts best for students whose expressed interests are least valid, this assumption was not borne out: In the studies reviewed, the validity of the SVIB tended to vary directly with the validity of expressed interests. In a review that encompassed other inventories besides the SVIB, Whitney (1969) also concluded that expressed choice was as valid as inventories in predicting future occupation.

The criterion in the Dolliver and Whitney reviews – occupational membership – may be faulted. One wonders why it has been so widely accepted by developers and publishers of interest inventories when nine studies, cited by Laing, Swaney, and Prediger (1984), have shown that "Regardless of interest inventory taken, length of time between initial and final measures, and index of predictive success, expressed choice has been found to be a more accurate predictor of eventual choice than measured [inventoried] interest." This and other criteria, such as success and persistence in an occupation, are known to be affected by factors other than interests – abilities, for example. General satisfaction may also be too inclusive a criterion, encompassing values besides interests. It may also be, according to Strong (1958), too *elusive* a criterion:

> Years ago I contended that there was . . . no better criterion of a vocational interest test than that of satisfaction enduring over a period of years. . . . I have actually never used satisfaction as a criterion on the ground that there seemed to be no good way to measure it. Such correlations as have been reported between interest scores and satisfaction have been for the most part too low to be of practical significance.

The criterion that an occupational interest measure should most reasonably be expected to predict is *interest* in an occupation – that is, intrinsic interest in the occupational activities.

One study that did compare the relative validities of inventoried and expressed interests for predicting occupational interests (as well as other criteria) used measures of academic interests (Katz, Norris, & Halpern, 1970; Norris & Katz, 1970). A national sample of secondary school juniors responded to an inventory with items describing activities assembled into 12 highly reliable scales of interest in fields of study. A random subsample also gave simple one-response ratings of their interest in each field represented by a scale. In follow-up studies through senior year in high school and 1 year after high school, these ratings were generally just as valid as the scale scores for predicting high school or college grades, differences between grades in various fields, academic interests in high school and college courses, *occupational* interests (1 year out of high school), and differences between interests in various subjects in Grade 12 and again in college. Furthermore, the factor structure of the ratings was virtually identical with that of the scales. In short, by late adolescence or early adulthood, interests seem to occupy a rather well integrated and coherent territory in the individual's awareness, such that expressed interests "behave" in very much the same way as inventoried interests.

With this background of analysis and research, it is possible to see why expressed rather than inventoried interests were used in SIGI and SIGI PLUS. College students and adults should not have to waste their time responding to a multitude of tedious and transparent items when a single rating on a scale name (with a brief definition) is just as valid. Nor is it necessary for purposes of CDM to devote any attention to norms (although normative comparisons, such as between males and females, may be useful for research into group differences and similarities in studies of the "natural history" of CDM). What clients really want to know, if interests are indeed important to them in CDM, is not how their responses to a set of items compare with some norms group's. They want to know whether they will derive "enough" interest from the activities that characterize a given occupation or group of occupations: enough to stay in that occupation, be attentive to their work, and enjoy it as long as other rewards and satisfactions are also met. Or, conversely, will lack of interest tend to make them unhappy, bored, and unstable in it? In brief, they need a structure that is well designed to help them express their interests in a way that permits linkage to the activities of occupations. Or, to state this need more specifically but less concisely as a client's question: "If satisfying such-and-such a kind of interest in my occupation is important to me, which occupations offer greater or lesser opportunities to engage in activities that will tend to satisfy that kind of interest?"

The designation of the six main fields of interest for SIGI took cognizance of the massive body of research on interest measurement and dimensions of occupational activities. The name of each field was presented with a concise definition, followed by a short list of occupations with high ratings on the field. The rating of each occupation on each field of interest was determined not by the interests of the *people* in that occupation but by an analysis of occupational *activities*. Hence, no assumption of isomorphism between individual interests and occupational activities was required. The fields were introduced with directions indicating that some people may want to choose only one main field of interest, others two or more; some may want to insist on choosing an occupation that is in a main field of interest, while others may not—perhaps feeling they can satisfy their main interests best in avocational pursuits. Thus, interests were not treated as if they were the only factor of importance in CDM; desire to work in a main field of interest was weighted along with other values. Occupations were not evenly distributed among the six fields: As might be expected, fewer occupations in SIGI were rated high on Manual–Technical and on Aesthetic activities than on the other fields.

In general, this structure of interests can be said to have "worked." College students, with very few exceptions, had no difficulty understanding and choosing the fields. Every field was chosen by substantial numbers of students, although Manual–Technical and Aesthetic were generally chosen with distinctly less frequency than the other fields. Research assistants were able to rate the occupations in SIGI on each of the six fields with a high degree of inter-rater reliability, and reviewers consistently corroborated these ratings.

Notwithstanding the success of the structure of interests used in SIGI, a new structure was developed for SIGI PLUS. It was felt that interests should not be confined to activities but should be extended also to fields of knowledge. The argument was made that interest in content of a field as well as in activities had been implicit in at least two of the fields, scientific and aesthetic. For example, scientific interest was held to include not just scientific activities (including the process of acquiring knowledge) but also a preference for acquiring knowledge about some kinds of topics more than about others. Thus, social and behavioral sciences were believed to represent a field of knowledge that should be distinguished from physical sciences. This argument was fortified by the notion that types of knowledge used to assess interests should be consonant with classifications of types of knowledge represented in higher education curricula.

This line of argument led to a decision to assess interests in terms of two separate (although not necessarily independent) structures: fields of knowledge and activities. It was further decided that, because activities were being used to describe skills required by occupations, the same set of activities could well serve as one of the structures for interests. The rationale for this structure is explicated later, under *Skills*. Here is a list of the "seven interest fields" that are used to represent "types of knowledge" in SIGI PLUS. They are called Arts and Humanities; Business; Health; Science and Mathematics; Social and Behavioral Sciences; Sports and Physical Education; Trades and Technologies. Each is defined by a list of "subjects that might be included in this field." For example, Arts and Humanities subjects are given as "architecture, art, dance, drama, education, English, foreign language, music, philosophy, religion." One proposed advantage of this structure, then, is to relate interest fields to curricula, in the manner of Academic Interest Measures (Katz, Norris, & Halpern, 1970; Norris & Katz, 1970).

These two structures of interests—activities and fields of knowledge—are defined and illustrated in such a way as to make inventory items unnecessary. They help clients, first, to express their main interests quickly and simply; second, to judge how important it is to pursue those interests in an occupation; and third, to identify occupations with activities that meet their interests well enough to be desirable or acceptable—given the other rewards and satisfactions they offer and the qualifications they require.

PREDICTION IN SIGI

Once clients have explored and examined their values and interests, have linked what they want and like to the rewards and satisfactions of occupations, and have thus obtained a manageable list of occupations desirable enough to warrant further investigation, they are ready to consider their chances of success in meeting the requirements for entry and successful performance in such occupations. They must usually grapple with two main questions: What are my chances of doing well enough in a preparatory program to reach the next step in a (frequently) long path toward entry into a given occupation? What are my chances of getting into an occupation and then of performing well in it?

The previous discussion of the primacy of values in SIGI noted that counterpropositions giving primacy to aptitudes (and, more generally, to prediction) in CDM were less justifiable. Some of the fallacies identified dealt with philosophical issues, but others were pragmatic. For example, comparative or differential predictions based on a single battery of aptitude tests have been notoriously weak. Yet the sequential use of a set of distinctive predictors for each occupation would be a hopelessly tedious approach, at best, to identifying occupations that offered good chances of entry and were therefore worth checking out in terms of desirability. As we saw, then, prediction, or evaluation of chances of success, plays its most effective role in CDM *after* the total population of occupations has been reduced to a manageable number of desirable ones. This accounts for the fact that Prediction did not appear in SIGI until the student had gone through the sections called Values, Locate, and Compare. It was originally designed so that students could move back and forth freely between Prediction and Planning. Although the Prediction system in SIGI was discontinued and does not appear in SIGI PLUS, there may be more than historical interest in describing it at this point before revisiting the issue of aptitudes and considering the Skills section of SIGI PLUS.

It was our expectation that the main users of SIGI at colleges would be students in their first 2 years. For them, choice of college program–particularly choice of major field–was the most immediate concern. Because college programs were linked to occupations in the Planning section, we could help these students focus on probabilities of success in the programs associated with various occupations that appeared desirable to them. Like Planning, Prediction was tailored distinctively for each college and for various programs at a college.

Many colleges have used some form of prediction as part of their admission and placement procedures. For admission, the criterion has usually been grade-point average, and predictors have tended to be scores on mandated tests (such as the SAT and ACT) and high school rank or average. Neither the criterion nor the predictors, however useful for selection, are entirely suitable for purposes of CDM.

The criterion of GPA might be useful in helping a student decide whether to attend a college; but SIGI was being used by students already enrolled in a college and concerned with choices between programs of study linked to various occupations. So the criteria of more urgent concern were grades that represented the different programs available at a college: What are one's chances of success in an "accounting" program, in a "visual arts" program, in a "computer science" program? Chosen to stand in for each program was a "key course"–a course identified by faculty as required for a program, coming early in the sequence for a program, representing the entire program well, distinguishing between students who perform satisfactorily in the program as a whole and those who do not, and (ideally) unique to one program. These criteria focus on what is distinctive in each program and thereby avoid high correlations between criteria insofar as possible.

As for the predictor variables, the limited number of tests typically available and the similarity in factors (such as Verbal and Quantitative) usually tapped by them and by high school rank or average decrease the likelihood of useful comparative or differential prediction across the full variety of programs offered at most 2-year and 4-year colleges. Furthermore, many open admissions colleges do not mandate tests, and test scores could not be expected to be available for large numbers of students at such institutions. The SIGI research and development staff therefore compiled, with the help of college faculties, descriptions of factors that might be expected to make for successful achievement in each key course (and its associated program). In a series of studies at various colleges, students in key courses were asked, at the beginning of the term, to rate themselves on these factors. They were also given a great deal of information on the criterion side, describing the activities of the course and including a distribution of grades obtained by previous students in that course. Then they were asked to make their own best estimate, in the light of all the knowledge made available to them, of the grade they would obtain.

At the end of the term, actual grades obtained and all predictor variables (including test scores if they were available, selected biographic data, ratings on achievement factors, ratings on commitment to the program, and "informed estimates" of grades) for each key course at each college were put into a regression analysis. Then the next cycle of students, seeking predicted grades in a key course, responded to prompts and put in their self-ratings on each achievement factor and also their informed estimates of grades. The computer program selected the best composite of optimally weighted predictors and displayed probabilities of getting A, B, C, or below C in that course.

In general, validities based on these informed ratings and estimates turned out to yield higher validities than test scores (especially for such programs as "visual arts," which tend to be poorly predicted by conventional tests). Multiple correlations, using only the two or three best "informed rating and estimate" variables, tended to fall in the range of .45 to .65, and the addition of test scores to these variables failed to improve validity appreciably (e.g., Norris & Cochran, 1977). Furthermore, because only predictors that had a logical relationship to each criterion were used, there was no shrinkage on cross validation. These high validities are consistent with an extensive body of literature on self-predicted performance. Summarizing this literature, Baird (1976) wrote that:

> self-estimates of ability seem to be relatively efficient predictors of academic performance. . . . Most students should be able to do this quite well after twelve years of comparisons with their peers, feedback on test scores, and the daily evidence of their performance in classwork. . . . Such experiences should provide students with a conception of their own capacities that incorporates ability, past achievement, and motivation. In any case, estimates of this type seem valid.

There is more to commend this prediction approach than validity. Because students became involved in the prediction process, they learned a great deal about what to expect in a course. They also tended to believe the predictions (expressed as probabilities of getting various grades) more than those based on test scores, which they often felt did not represent them at their best. They understood that if they fed false information in they would get false information out ("GIGO"). The method worked because students had no incentive to falsify – everything was done in private, and no decisions about them were to be made on the basis of their ratings.

(The same system would probably not work well for admissions purposes.) The procedures carried many side benefits as well: College faculties became active participants. They nominated achievement factors, an act that stimulated them to think about the basis of their grading. Sometimes factors that they expected to predict well had low correlations with their grades. Thus, they could re-evaluate their grading practices as well as their expectations of what makes for success in their courses.

Like local Planning systems, Prediction had to be tailored specifically for each college. Although ETS provided manuals and work sheets and performed the data analyses, the colleges had to bear costs in money, time, and effort. We expected that one staff person at each college's career planning office, working part time, could handle the data collection necessary for tailored Prediction and Planning. This expectation was confirmed for the first group of colleges during the first few years. The staff people initially assigned to this work were well trained and did a good conscientious job. As they grew more familiar with the procedures, they became more efficient: The time required for maintenance and updating was reduced significantly each year. But as staffs turned over and new people had to be trained, enthusiasm for tailored Prediction and Planning dwindled. As some colleges faltered in maintaining their Prediction and Planning systems, we found that their data were getting obsolescent. (As a dramatist once said after an opening night, "The play was a success; the audience was a failure.") Priding ourselves on the relevance, accuracy, and currency of our occupational information, we did not want to see college-specific information that was of lower quality put into SIGI. So we developed a new "universal" Planning section to replace the original Planning section. The replacement was not tailored to any one college but represented common elements in curricular programs across colleges.

We also dropped the Prediction section. In the absence of a locally tailored Prediction system, the only approach left in SIGI for estimating probabilities was the assessment of chances of success in entering an occupation based on the overview of possible pathways. This overview, taken from the Planning section, was used in Strategy. We thought of attempting to develop a generalized Prediction section, analogous to the "universal" Planning section. But a major virtue of the SIGI Prediction system was its use of empirical data: The probability statements for each key course could be documented. A generalized Prediction system that avoided real data would be of dubious validity. We have been critical of other systems that use "armchair" predictions, and we did not want SIGI exposed to a similar loss of credibility. For example, several guidance systems and other resources use the *Dictionary of Occupational Titles* *(DOT)* ratings of aptitudes as "requirements" for entry into an occupation. These ratings are conveniently available on the *DOT* Data Display Tape.

Having rejected the use of aptitude tests represented by the General Aptitude Test Battery (GATB) and Occupational Aptitude Patterns (OAP) based on extensive empirical studies, we were obviously unenthusiastic about ratings made at some remove from the body of research associated with GATB and OAP. To explain our rejection of this popular counterproposition takes some space, which may be justified just because of the widespread use of the DOT aptitude ratings. What follows is a brief description and a critique of the derivation of those widely used ratings.

Aptitudes Revisited

The *DOT* aptitude categories were taken essentially from GATB, developed by the U.S. Employment Service and used by the state employment service offices since 1947. As described in the 1970 edition of the *Manual* (U.S. Department of Labor, 1970), the GATB had evolved into 12 tests contributing to scores on 9 aptitudes: Intelligence or General Learning Ability (G), Verbal (V), Numerical (N), Spatial (S), Form Perception (P), Clerical Perception (Q), Motor Coordination (K), Finger Dexterity (F), and Manual Dexterity (M). Norms had been derived from a sample of the "general working population" (in the age range of 18–54), and scores had been converted to a standard score scale with a mean of 100 and a standard deviation of 20 for each aptitude. Studies had been accumulated of the relationship between GATB scores and successful performance in occupations and training programs. Job analysts had also continued to rate the relevance and importance of the various aptitudes for each occupation and groups of occupations.

To derive norms for specific occupations, the kinds of data indicated above were considered together. That is, for each occupation a preliminary set of aptitudes was selected from some combination of those with relatively high mean scores, relatively low standard deviations, significant correlations with the criteria of successful performance, and ratings of "critical" or "important" in job analyses. From the preliminary set, an Occupational Aptitude Pattern (OAP) was determined using dichotomized criterion groups: The OAP set minimum scores on three aptitudes for a given occupation such that most of the individuals in the high criterion group would be "qualified," most of those in the low criterion group would be screened out, and the proportion screened out would approximate the proportion in the low criterion group. The standard used for judging the validity of the OAP was its relationship with the criterion – a positive phi coefficient significant at the .05 level.

There has been, as might be expected, some difference of opinion about these procedures. Much of the criticism has focused on the use of multiple cutting scores rather than a multiple regression analysis for selection and guidance of prospective workers, the absence of tables of "hit rates" for predictions of success and nonsuccess, the particularly low validities for white-collar occupations (Weiss, 1972), and the high correlations between aptitudes such that people at or above the mean on General Learning Ability (G) are quite likely to qualify on OAP for a large number of occupations (Chapman & Katz, 1981).

To supplement Weiss's (1972) criticism of the use of multiple cutting procedures, it should be pointed out that such use is incontrovertible when strength in one relevant aptitude cannot compensate for deficiency in another: For example, airplane pilots require good vision, and people who are tone deaf—regardless of their other aptitudes—have not been able to succeed in sonar training. But aside from such obvious situations, the more general finding in predicting success in most occupations is that strength in one predictor tends to compensate for weakness in another. Then multiple regression techniques that weight and sum aptitudes into a composite are usually more valid. Lord (1962) provided a strong demonstration that this conclusion holds particularly when the predictors are fallible, as in the case of aptitude test scores,

> because the desiderata in the selection procedure are surely unrelated to the errors of measurement. . . , yet the selection is determined in part by these errors of measurement. . . . Other things being equal, either low reliability of predictors or high correlations between them tends to increase the difference between the multiple-cutting-scores selection region and the optimum selection region. . . . Anyone now using multiple cutting scores with . . . [such] predictors would do well . . . to allow a high value on one predictor to compensate at least partially for a low value on another.

Perhaps the definitive empirical demolition of the principles underlying the use of GATB for differential prediction was Thorndike's (1985) notable meta-analysis of all cross-validated studies of the predictive validity of GATB. He found that the predictive validity of this battery of aptitude tests is mainly a function of the common factor (G). This factor is almost invariably as valid as or more valid than the best predictive composite of tests for an occupation. Obviously, then, there was virtually no evidence of differential validity.

These and other criticisms of the use of GATB and the OAP for CDM are cogent. Nevertheless, there is much to be said for the long-term large-scale development and research undergirding this use. In this research, the U. S. Department of Labor has confronted problems of enormous complexity and difficulty and has had to make compromises: Getting representative samples and good criterion measures for large numbers of occupations, following up samples for longitudinal data, and interpreting data obtained under diverse circumstances present great obstacles; nothing comparable in scope and accumulated research over 4 decades has been accomplished. So whatever the shortcomings of GATB and OAP for selection (in which even modest validities may be useful) and guidance, and whatever compromises have been made between scientific rigor and pragmatic expedience, one marvels at the body of information that is *there*. One wishes it could be used judiciously.

Unfortunately, this massive research basis for GATB is virtually abandoned—or compromised too much—in the use of GATB categories in the *DOT*. Only the factor categories have been retained, and even these have not been kept up to date; for example, by 1970, Eye–hand Coordination (E) had been merged into K, with which it was highly correlated; yet the *DOT* tape—used by guidance systems—retained E.

Of greater concern is the abandonment of "hard" data, accumulated through so much travail, providing norms and validities for the aptitude scores based on samples of people in many occupations. Presumably, it was decided that continuing the data collection necessary to establish OAP for a sufficiently large number of occupations was too laborious a process. To accumulate OAP for the first 60 occupations had required many years. To establish them for hundreds and even thousands of occupations would have required a prodigious and evidently prohibitive level of effort. So the decision was made to substitute for these empirical data the judgments of job analysts, who decide which aptitudes are relevant for an occupation and what level of each is "required" for "satisfactory (average)" performance.

The levels are defined on the following scale: 1 = the top 10% of the "general working population," 2 = the next 23%, 3 = the middle 33%, 4 = the next 23%, and 5 = the lowest 10%. The *DOT* Data Display Tape contains the job analysts' ratings on aptitudes judged significant for over 12,000 occupations. This tape is used directly by such widespread CG systems as GIS and CIS, although there have been some minor differences from one resource to another in the transformation and use of the scales, as illustrated in the following examples.

In the GIS Guide for student use, Edition 11, an aptitude was listed for an occupation "only if the job requires a high degree of that aptitude (i.e., the top 40% of the population)." In other words, aptitudes deemed relevant and scaled at Level 1 or 2 on the *DOT* tape were regarded as requirements for a given occupation. (The use of 40% in this context rather than 33% appears to be a misinterpretation by GIS of the *DOT* scale.)

Level 1 or 2, according to the scale just defined, is at or above the 67th percentile rank in the general working population. This rank is tantamount to a standard score of 109 on a GATB aptitude. Of the 62 occupations with OAP listed in the 1970 Department of Labor Manual, only one has all three components above this level, and 57 have all three components below this level. When an aptitude is above this level, it is invariably G, N, or S. There are *no* OAP at Level 1 or 2 for P, K, F, M, Q, and V. In other words, research data on OAP would support the use of only G, N, or S as "required" for an occupation under the GIS rule!

I examined the consequences of the procedure that was actually used by GIS for a few occupations chosen at random. GIS listed 7 "aptitudes required" for Architectural Drafter: N, S, P, Q, K, F, and M. Reference to the Manual (U.S. Department of Labor, 1970) shows an OAP of NSP (90, 95, 90), with a phi coefficient of .22. The correlation coefficients for K, F, and M with the criterion are not significantly different from 0. Thus students who take the GIS (DOT tape) list of "aptitudes required" seriously might disqualify themselves from the occupation on grounds of low K, F, and M abilities even though the research data showed no relationship between scores on these aptitudes and performance on the job. Furthermore, they could be *below* Levels 1 and 2 on N, S, and P and still "qualify."

GIS listed 6 "aptitudes required" for Dental Hygienist: V, N, S, K, F, and M. The Manual shows an OAP of GSP (105, 95, 100). The phi coefficient for this OAP is given as .54. Again, K, F, and M are not significantly correlated with the criterion. And again, people *below* Levels 1 and 2 on G, S, and P would "qualify" according to the research data.

GIS listed only one aptitude required for Plumber, M. The OAP is NSM (80, 95, 85) with a phi of .19. Correlations with the criterion are significant at the .01 level for N and S, as well as for M: The Manual lists them as .30, .29, and .20, respectively, in the validation sample; of the 3 aptitudes, only N was significant (at the .05 level) in the cross validation, with a coefficient of .25. Incidentally, Q was significantly correlated with the criterion in both samples, the coefficients being .30 and .22, respectively. If aptitudes below Levels 1 and 2 were included for Architectural Drafter and Dental Hygienist, why were N and S not included for Plumber, especially since the cutting score for S (95) is higher than for M (85) on the OAP? Thus, the *DOT* tape as represented by GIS is not even consistent in the direction of its departure from a research base.

CIS, as indicated previously, used the *DOT* tape in a slightly different way from GIS. It designated Level 1 as High, Levels 2 and 3 as Medium, and Levels 4 and 5 as Low. The instructions to the student also took on a somewhat different connotation: Whereas GIS spoke of aptitudes that an occupation *requires*, listing only occupations that are at Levels 1 and 2 on the DOT tape for a given aptitude, CIS invited students to "Mark the highest level of [the aptitude] you *want to use* on a job" (italics added). Then, any occupation rated at or below that level would be retrieved.

Another important distinction between GIS and CIS is that GIS makes students' use of aptitudes optional–a student can bypass the entire array–whereas in CIS the "abilities" section is part of a universal sequence. A student can, in effect, duck a given aptitude by responding "not sure" instead of Low, Medium, or High–but *some* response is called for on each of *eight* abilities. GIS includes 10 aptitudes from the DOT tape; it omits G, reasonably enough since G is a function of tests that overlap those contributing to V, N, and S. CIS, however, includes G but omits Color Discrimination and the GATB S and M; it also adds "Physical Activity" to the aptitudes–hence, the total of eight.

Notwithstanding these differences between GIS and CIS, the use of the DOT tape results in essentially similar departures from a research base for one system as for the other. Thus the criticisms addressed at GIS apply equally to CIS. There is at least one serious additional anomaly in CIS. *The aptitude domain is defined under direct access differently from the way it is defined under structured search!* That is to say, the written descriptions of aptitudes for an occupation include dimensions quite distinct from the aptitudes used to retrieve occupational titles. For example, in direct access CIS describes "aptitudes" for Salespersons as follows: Average ability to do arithmetic; ability to stand for long periods of time, communicate clearly, and to deal with the public. The punctuation here is troublesome: It is not clear whether everything after the semicolon represents one aptitude or three. In either case, there is no such one aptitude listed in QUEST (the questionnaire in which students specify the aptitude levels) for structured search, nor does QUEST contain any aptitudes remotely resembling either "stand for long periods of time" or "deal with the public."

All this confusion in the use of the so-called GATB aptitudes in various CG systems may seem messy and inconsistent, but it seems almost orderly when compared to the chaos that prevails in many other resources. A sampling of the various state microfiche systems (VIEW) indicates that they have conceptualized the aptitude domain in rather indiscriminate ad hoc terms. For example, in Florida VIEW the following "Scholastic Aptitudes" were listed for Plumber: mathematics, chemistry, welding, blueprint reading, mechanical drawing, metal and wood shop. Oklahoma VIEW listed the following "Aptitudes" for Plumber: work from awkward positions; work without direct supervision (but "prefer working alone" appears in an adjacent column under "Personal Traits"); bear responsibility for correct decisions; work indoors or out; tolerate dirty, unpleasant conditions; tolerate unpleasant odors. For Sales Clerk the following "aptitudes" were listed: meet the public; speak and write clearly; aptitude for basic arithmetic; adapt to fluctuating situations. Florida VIEW listed these "Scholastic Aptitudes" for Salesperson: catch on quickly; remember things well; think up new ideas; understand instructions; talk easily with people; do math problems quickly; use math to figure costs; pay attention to details. "Abilities" for Accountant were described by Missouri VIEW as follows: Understand and apply instructions and principles of a complex nature; reason and make judgments; organize complex data, make reports both orally and in writing; think mathematically; do accurate work. "Abilities" for Accountant were listed by Tennessee INFOE as follows: be able to write clearly in a small space; be able to concentrate for long periods of time; be able to do detailed work; be able to figure mathematical problems. Under "Personality" is listed "work accurately."

It is apparent from all this that the "aptitude" domain is construed in many occupational information resources just as chaotically as the "interest," "temperament," and "personality" domains. In each case, there appears little agreement on the dimensions that constitute the domain. Even those that use the *DOT* tape select different components from it and apply them in different ways. Research, such as it is, is virtually ignored. "Aptitude" appears to mean whatever a given developer decides it is to mean in describing a given occupation, with no consistency across occupations. There is also little consistency across resources for any occupation. An aptitude may sometimes be synonymous with a physical demand, a temperament, a working condition, an interest, a preference, a requirement, or some other characteristic of personality or occupation. Its use appears, in general, to lack rigor, clarity, definition, consistency, or logic. It often runs contradictory to the empirical data that have been reported. There is little to commend the use of aptitudes in other resources, and we had to reject the use of any comparable system as a substitute for the Prediction section in SIGI.

Chances of Success

How then should we deal with the problem of evaluating chances of success in entering each occupation that the user is considering? (As I have pointed out, in the Strategy section of SIGI and the Deciding section of SIGI PLUS the client's estimate of chances is combined with the estimate of desirability of each occupation.) Recall that SIGI Prediction had provided copious information on the criterion side, describing the achievement factors in each course. Similarly, we decided to rely heavily in SIGI PLUS on descriptions of major activities involved in each occupation and the skills required by these activities. Then, as in SIGI Prediction, users could assess their own status on these skills. Because many skills might be developed through further education, experience, and study, we also relied on estimates users might make from the Preparing section on their likelihood of completing a preparatory pathway to the occupation. Another major effect on chances of entering an occupation is the outlook for the balance between supply and demand; clients can obtain outlook projections in the Information section and review them in Deciding. Finally, because many adults have to find their way through a host of obstacles and problems, it also seemed appropriate to consider the conclusions they reached after use of the Coping section.

A client's assessment of chances of success, then, derives from an amalgamation of inferences: Do I have or can I acquire the requisite skills? Can I complete the necessary preparation? Is the outlook acceptable? Can I cope with all the obstacles and problems (such as worries about money, time, day care for children, lack of confidence) that beset my efforts to prepare for, obtain, and succeed in the kind of work I want to do?

Clearly, skills play the leading role in this amalgamation, with preparing, outlook, and coping playing off them. But this treatment of skills raises questions about structure. It is possible to describe specific activities for each occupation and ask people to assess their skills in respect to these activities. But is it possible to find some overarching structure that subsumes these specific activities, groups them in appropriate and useful ways, and enables skills to be linked to requirements? We searched for such a structure first at the simplest level, as used in SIGI.

SKILLS IN SIGI PLUS

SIGI dealt with occupational skills primarily in response to the questions (in Compare) about the "Level of skill in interacting with data, people, and things" and about "Personal qualifications." Responses to "Other requirements" in Compare also occasionally mentioned some skills. The latter two questions evoked a broad array of skills (and other characteristics) determined ad hoc for each occupation. Data, people, things (DPT), however, represent a longstanding structure of skills or, as labeled in the *DOT*, "worker functions." According to the fourth edition of the *Dictionary of Occupational Titles* (U.S. Department of Labor, 1977), this structure is based on the premise that "Every job requires a worker to function to some degree in relation to data, people, and things," and that these degrees can be represented by hierarchic scales. The level of each function is expressed by the middle three digits in the *DOT* code for each occupation, with 0 representing the highest level and increasing numbers representing successively lower levels. It is assumed that a worker who can handle a function at any level can also handle higher numbered (less demanding) levels of that function. Here are the scales as they appear in the fourth edition of the *DOT* (compressed slightly from 9-point scales in the third edition):

DATA (4th Digit)	PEOPLE (5th Digit)	THINGS (6th Digit)
0 Synthesizing	0 Mentoring	0 Setting Up
1 Coordinating	1 Negotiating	1 Precision Working
2 Analyzing	2 Instructing	2 Operating–Controlling
3 Compiling	3 Supervising	3 Driving–Operating
4 Computing	4 Diverting	4 Manipulating
5 Copying	5 Persuading	5 Tending
6 Comparing	6 Speaking–Signalling	6 Feeding–Offbearing
	7 Serving	7 Handling
	8 Taking Instructions–Helping	

Thus, a Chick Sexer, *DOT* code 687, is rated at the lowest level on each function: 6 Comparing, 8 Taking Instructions–Helping, and 7 Handling. A Crown Pouncer, Hand is also rated 687, but Crown Pouncer (hat and cap) is rated 685, the last digit representing Tending. A Developmental Psychologist is rated 061 (?) and a Personnel Psychologist 107. Presumably, each rating applies to the highest level *typically* required in an occupation. *DOT* rules are not clear for adjudicating between one level and another when there is an apparent conflict between frequency of use of a given level of function and its importance in the occupation (an infrequently used level may nevertheless be important for performance).

The *DOT* system has several shortcomings. The hierarchic scales for rating DPT are presented in such a way as to imply parallelism. Thus one would assume that the developmental psychologist works on a higher level in respect to Things (1 = Precision Working) than to People (6 = Speaking–Signalling). But note the nature of the activities involved for the first six scale numbers under People: Mentoring, Negotiating, Instructing, Supervising, Diverting, Persuading. On the face of it, these all appear to represent a high level of complexity. Under Data, on the other hand, just the first three levels (Synthesizing, Coordinating, and Analyzing) and under Things only the first two (Setting Up and Precision Working) appear comparably high in complexity. These apparent anomalies bothered me, and so I tried to resolve them for DPT in SIGI.

First of all, the ceiling set by the Things scale seemed too low. It neglected a higher level of complexity in working with Things. I decided that a reasonable addition would be to establish a top level designated "Inventing or Designing" that could include (for example) mechanical invention and work in the fine arts. The *DOT* rates occupations like Sculptor and Painter as 061. Synthesizing (the 0 on Data) is defined by the *DOT* as "Integrating analyses of data to discover facts and/or develop knowledge of concepts or interpretations." This definition does not fit the design and workmanship required of the sculptor or painter who works with visual and material elements rather than data. Furthermore, the rating of Precision Working (the 1 on Things) falls short of describing the high level of skill involved in sculpting or painting, while Setting Up would be obviously inappropriate. (Because the arrangement of levels purports to be hierarchic, Precision Working and Setting up would be subsumed under Inventing or Designing.) Adding Inventing or Designing at the 0 level would bump the other descriptors down a notch on the scale; so the scale would be brought closer to equivalence with the other two scales. At the same time, we changed Data to Data–Ideas so that high-level conceptualization could be included, such as drawing conclusions from data, or translating ideas into artistic performance. This would help in rating Painter, Sculptor, Writer, and others whose functions are better described in terms of ideas than data.

Then we telescoped the six to eight levels used by the *DOT* into three – High, Medium, and Low. For Data–Ideas, the top three levels were classified High, the next two Medium, and the last two Low. For People, the cuts came after the top six levels and after the next level. For Things, the cuts were after the top three (after Inventing–Designing had been inserted) and the next three. This provides a closer and more useful approximation to equivalency of the scale across the three functions while avoiding finer discriminations than the concepts and data permit.

Thus, by telescoping the scales into High, Medium, and Low, we preserved distinctions useful for guidance and eliminated the need to discriminate between Inventing–Designing, Setting Up, and Precision Working. The problems in ranking the first six levels under People and the first three under Data–Ideas also disappeared.

It was also evident that the labels and brief descriptions of each level in the *DOT* would be awkward to apply to many occupations. Work descriptions for many occupations are not (could not reasonably be) limited to these terms; yet they would have to be rated. What we did was to develop a comprehensive thesaurus of verbs for work activities at each level to help raters determine which activities other than the ones designated in the *DOT* scales warrant rating an occupation at a comparable level. The resultant system for rating DPT in SIGI is best summarized by the following Exhibit C, extracted from the handbook, *Occupational Information in SIGI* (Pears & Weber, 1976, 1978, 1980, 1982). It was this system for rating DPT in SIGI that served as our point of departure for developing the structure of skills for SIGI PLUS.

We started by trying to classify *all* the major work tasks for a representative sample of SIGI occupations according to the DPT structure as we had amended it. It did not take long for us to acknowledge that, while the structure was useful as far as it went, many work tasks of considerable importance in SIGI occupations did not fit well. Often, an activity might

Exhibit C
Rating Categories and Thesaurus for Data–People–Things

*Data–Ideas**

		HIGH	
0 Synthesizing (to develop knowledge)		"drawing conclusions"	
1 Coordinating			
2 Analyzing			
Adapt	Evaluate	Study	Edit (revise)
Apply principles	Explain	Survey	Translate
Arbitrate	Forecast trends	Translate ideas into artistic performance	
Calculate	Integrate	Translate ideas into practical application	
Classify	Interpret	Write reports, directions or specifications	
Decide	Investigate		
Design	Make policy		
Develop ideas	Organize		
Diagnose	Originate		
Discuss ideas	Plan		
Do research	Predict		
Estimate	Solve problems		

	MEDIUM
3 Compiling	"performing prescribed actions"
4 Computing	
Apply information	Follow diagrams
Assist – carry out instructions	Handle applications
Check	Enforce standards
Collect facts, information, data (survey)	Memorize
Fill out reports	Supply information
	Transcribe
	Use maintenance manual

	LOW
5 Copying	"observing or copying"
6 Comparing (checking)	
File reports	Record observations/transactions
Keep files	Review
Keep log	Verify
Not related to work activities	

*People**

	HIGH
0 Mentoring (counseling)	"changing behavior, giving advice
1 Negotiating	or instructions"
2 Instructing	
3 Supervising (maintaining harmony)	
4 Diverting	
5 Persuading	
Advise	Instruct (teach)
Consult	Lead
Counsel	Arrive at joint decisions (confer)
Guide	Modify behavior

Exhibit C *(continued)*

Cure	Order
Direct	Prescribe for
Employ	Rate
Entertain	Rehabilitate
Evaluate	Remedy
Influence	Resolve disputes
Be responsible for	

6 Speaking–Signaling	MEDIUM
(giving instructions to helpers)	"cooperating, exchanging information"
Answer inquiries	Participate in team effort
Assist	Protect
Confer (discuss)	Refer
Correspond with	Represent employer
Examine people or animals	Rescue
Inform	Treat (minor cases)
Interview (using prepared questions)	
Notify	
Observe	

7 Serving (attending to immediate needs)	LOW
8 Taking instructions-Helping	"following other people's orders"
Serve the buying public	
Visit	
Greet	
Guard	
Little direct interaction with people as part of work activity.	

Things*

0 Setting-up	HIGH
1 Precision working	"using considerable judgment & knowledge combined with a high level of manipulative dexterity"
Build	Fabricate
Calibrate	Identify complex objects
Construct	Invent (SIGI addition)
Create	Make
Design (SIGI addition)	Trouble shoot
Draft (detailed sketches)	Use precision tools & equipment
Experiment	

2 Operating-controlling	MEDIUM
3 Driving-operating	"some latitude for judgment and
4 Manipulating	moderate dexterity"

(continued on next page)

Exhibit C *(continued)*

Adjust	Modify
Arrange	Overhaul
Combine	Purchase equipment
Cultivate	Regulate
Drive	Repair
Examine equipment	Test equipment
Inspect	Type
Install (routine)	Use simple tools or equipment

5 Tending	LOW
6 Feeding-offbearing	"little judgment or manipulative
7 Handling (moving or carrying objects)	dexterity needed (push buttons or keys; monitor lights or dials; do minor repairs. Use pencil, paper, telephone, common devices.)"
Carry	Pass to someone else
Monitor	
Make minor repairs	
Not related to work activity.	

*Numbered words are taken from the *Dictionary of Occupational Titles* (1977). Appendix p. 1369–1371.
Source: From Exhibit II-5, Pears and Weber (1982).

straddle two or three types of function and yet be more convincingly represented as a distinct entity in itself rather than be decomposed into separate functions.

For example, in communicating plans to clients, architects may be using data they have synthesized and things (models) they have designed and built, as a basis for mentoring, negotiating with, and persuading people. Thus, the act of communicating involves skills in working with all three functions: Data–Ideas, Things, and People. So Architect is rated high on all three functions. But the direct act of communicating (speaking, writing, drawing) specific kinds of information or ideas to particular kinds of people under certain defined circumstances can easily get lost in the generalized DPT functions. We wanted to preserve the specifics of the nature of the communications engaged in by Architect with a structure that would link it to acts of communication in other occupations.

The converse problem arose in trying to classify various mathematical work tasks under Data–Ideas. One could make them fit, but mathematics appeared to have a particularity that could be handled more comfortably if broken out of Data–Ideas into a separate category, leaving the residual components of that function in a category called Organizing Information.

It should be emphasized that the new structure came about through an alternation of conceptual and empirical efforts. First, research assistants encountered difficulty fitting work tasks for occupations into the highly generalized DPT structure. New structures were developed independently by research staff members, then pooled, to accommodate the problems without losing sight of several major objectives: (a) The structure had to remain simple and manageable; while the major categories might have to be extended to more than the original three, it seemed unwise to exceed six or so; (b) the terms used in all headings had to be familiar to users; (c) the category headings would obviously have to stay at a high level of generalization, with the subcategories (again no more than six for each category) also applying across a substantial number of occupations; yet each subcategory would have to be applied in specific terms to the work tasks of each of the occupations in SIGI PLUS. Thus, the user could see examples of how each subcategory skill might be used in a given occupation. (It was also decided to include, for users who requested it, an illustration of use of each subcategory skill in "everyday life.")

The resultant structure of activities used for both skills and interests in SIGI PLUS is as follows:

I. Working with People
training, instructing
advising, counseling, interviewing
persuading, negotiating, selling
assisting, protecting, physical care
coordinating work with others
supervising, directing, assessing

II. Working with Hands or Equipment
operating machines or equipment
using tools, measuring
maintaining, inspecting, repairing
installing, setting up, constructing
drafting, drawing
designing equipment, developing systems

III. Communicating
following written/oral instructions
explaining, answering questions
making presentations
writing, preparing reports
public speaking, broadcasting, entertaining

IV. Organizing Information
keeping records, cataloguing
gathering information, conducting research
making diagrams
analyzing, interpreting, evaluating
developing ideas

V. Working with Mathematics
mathematical reasoning
calculating, computing, applying formulas
developing budgets
analyzing numerical data

VI. Special Activities
attention to detail
quick thinking
memorizing
fine & performing arts
spatial visualization

Note that Categories IV, I, and II are respectively very close to Data, People, and Things; as just noted, Communicating represents a conceptual recombination of communicative activities that had been parceled among the DPT categories, and Working with Mathematics breaks out a specific subset of Data–Ideas. These two categories are congruent with everyday parlance and are instantly recognizable by users. The last category,

Special Activities, is a catchall; it includes the miscellany of activities that are important in some occupations but cannot be comfortably classified elsewhere.

The subcategories listed under these six rubrics do not purport to be hierarchic. Each stands on its own feet and must be mentioned separately if it applies to an occupation; it is not subsumed under any other activity. For use in Search, the activities are not rated on any numerical scale. They are included only if they are important in an occupation, with no attempt to differentiate levels of importance: If they are included, they are considered above the threshold level that represents a requirement. For example, most occupations require some level of skill in such activities as following instructions and paying attention to detail. But these skills are ascribed only to occupations in which they are part of the essence of the work tasks, such as Forestry Technician and Accounting Clerk.

The iterative nature of the development of this structure, with testing of each new formulation on a sample of occupations, seems to have produced a system that "works" from the point of view of occupational analysts: They have been able to classify work tasks for all occupations in SIGI PLUS without serious problems, and reviewers for each occupation have agreed with the classifications. The important activities seem to be described accurately, comprehensively, and distinctively for each occupation. Indeed, the strength of the Skills section is apparent in the examples of how a given kind of skill is used in a given occupation. The meaning of the category and subcategory is immediately clarified and enriched by its particular application to the occupation.

Besides covering skills for every occupation in SIGI PLUS, the Skills section provides a separate treatment of the skills needed for management. This was included because management is a frequent advancement step for mid-career adults in many occupations. Management skills are displayed like the skills for any occupation, with illustrative work tasks. Also included are key aspects of work style for management—like handling stress, providing leadership, and taking responsibility—leading clients to evaluate the desirability of management work for themselves. Messages advise how they might explore management opportunities in their current line of work.

Clients are introduced to the structure of the Skills domain in the Self-Assessment section. They can then use its elements, along with those of the other domains of self-understanding (such as values and interest in fields of knowledge), in structured Search, as they seek a manageable list of occupations for further consideration. Their use of the Skills structure then reaches its culmination as they work through the Skills section. There, the objective is to enhance their understanding of the requirements of an occupation that is being considered. With this understanding, they are capable of making an informed judgment of their chances of meeting these requirements. This judgment can be combined, in the Deciding section, with judgments about preparation, outlook, and coping to produce an informed estimate of chances of success in each occupation still under consideration. These estimates and estimates of desirability are simultaneously displayed in "Deciding Squares." With this graphic display, clients can readily be helped to apply decision rules and can come to at least tentative closure on a choice that is informed and rational.

Thus, clients can progress from self-appraisal to closure on decision. Mediating their progress is command of relevant occupational information.

OCCUPATIONAL INFORMATION

What can we reason but from what we know? (Alexander Pope)

Occupational information nourishes a career guidance system. It is the food and liquid that renew the system and keep it functioning in good health. But scholars and practitioners of guidance are not much interested in bread and water and give occupational information scant attention. The professional journals include few articles about it, and doctoral candidates do not include it among the topics they consider for their dissertations. As a developer of a career guidance system who has given considerable attention to the subject, I would like to share in comprehensive detail the challenges and delights of solving problems in the collection, analysis, evaluation, interpretation, deconstruction, reconstruction, and presentation of occupational information. For in the architecture of occupational information, as of buildings, "God is in the details," as Mies van der Rohe said. But I suspect that most readers' interests will not resonate to the intrinsic attractions of those divine details; so I limit this discussion of occupational information to an overview of its place in the system and its structure, with illustrations of some of the issues, problems, and procedures involved in attaining and maintaining the highest possible standards of accuracy and currency.

Occupational information appears to abound. Sources include people (counselors, teachers, family, friends), publications (books, monographs, briefs, periodicals, directories), audiovisual materials (film strips, motion pictures, videotapes, videodisks, microforms), experiences (oral discourses, observations, courses, simulations, work), sorting materials, and computerized systems. This apparent abundance can be deceptive. It is often difficult for clients to get a grasp on the material, to relate it to what they have learned about themselves, and to translate it into relevant differentiation between options (Chapman & Katz, 1981).

Earlier, I suggested that one component of career guidance is a strategy for helping people acquire and process information. Most people don't know what information they need, can't get what information they want, and can't use what information they have. Guidance can intervene to provide structures, information, and procedures to reduce the discrepancy between people's present state of knowledge and the state that is required for informed and rational CDM.

Self-appraisal helps people know themselves (their values, interests, and skills) and thereby know what information they need. Then they can seek the information that is most useful and salient to them – provided that the information has been organized and structured to articulate with the dimensions of self-appraisal. The structure in which the information is framed can cue clients to select appropriate specifications in structured search and to ask the "right questions" in direct access so they can get the information they want.

Finally, clients need guidance in integrating discrete pieces of information in some rational way to use what information they have – to arrive at a decision.

Self-appraisal has been discussed in the preceding chapters. Decision making is addressed in the chapter immediately following this examination of occupational information.

Here, the focus is on the structure, content, and quality of occupational information. Perhaps the macrostructure can be pictured as a matrix, with occupational *titles* along the horizontal axis, occupational *attributes* along the vertical, and *information* in the cells. Each of these three components has its own microstructure.

Occupational Titles

How many titles are needed in a career guidance system? Which ones should be used? The subject of occupational titles has not attracted much thought or attention. To many people, they have simply always been *there*. Just as Adam named all the cattle and the birds in the sky and the wild beasts, some early descendant of his presumably named the occupations.

Many titles appear merely to transform verbs that represent a major set of activities into nouns. Thus, one who bakes is a baker. But how many kinds of bakers should be titled? Should "baker" include both those who bake pizzas and those who bake pastries? Should it include those who bake products in bakeries and those who bake in restaurants? Or should each of the "bakers" have its own separate title (e.g., "baker, pizza")? Sometimes separate titles are used to emphasize the differences; sometimes a single title encompasses all the variations to emphasize what they have in common.

Obviously, there is much more to an occupation than its main set of activities. The number and nature of titles to be used depend on one's purpose. An occupation is defined by all of its attributes that relate to the purpose for which a title is used; well-known purposes include the census, economic forecasting, licensing, salary equity, guidance, and employment. For example, the census probably requires less differentiation between titles than analyses of "equivalent worth"; guidance permits more aggregation than listings for employment.

For guidance, as I indicated earlier, an occupational title represents a generalization or abstraction from such selected observations of phenomena as sets of activities, requirements for entry, configurations of opportunities for rewards and satisfactions (like earnings, independence, contributions to society, prestige), conditions of work, outlook, and the like. A guidance system would violate the law of parsimony if it designated by separate titles two or more occupations that were identical in almost all relevant attributes. On the other hand, there is the question of how many differences, of what kind and magnitude, would call for using two or more titles instead of one. Differentiation of occupations by titles requires careful study and precise judgment by a developer of a career guidance system to "carve at the joints."

The first step is to compile a list of occupations appropriate for the people being guided and for the nature of the choice-point at which they have arrived. Existing compilations, like the *Dictionary of Occupational Titles (DOT)*, may be inappropriate for some populations. The *DOT* has always been imbalanced in favor of industrial occupations: Even the most recent (fourth) edition and its supplement (U.S. Department of Labor, 1979, 1986) define in detail more than 20 different "welders" (according to process, materials, and so on) but only one "secondary school teacher" (without differentiation by subject); "oceanographer" appears only as a related title, with no separate definition. Apparently, job analysts for the *DOT* have tended to make site visits mainly at large industrial establishments, and job analysis procedures permit distinctions to be made more readily in terms of activities that are visible and physical rather than intellectual. The *DOT* sample of titles is less appropriate for students enrolled in or bound for college (who, if they were considering secondary school teaching, might be concerned with such differences between subjects as interest fields, preparation, and outlook) than for students in vocational education or unemployed adults at State Employment Services.

What is appropriate for a given population, however, is sometimes not so simple a question as it may appear. A bit of empirical evidence may overrule armchair judgments. When SIGI was originally developed for use by students in or about to enter postsecondary education, initial lists of occupations were compiled from many sources, including surveys that asked former students to name their current occupations. Responses to these surveys produced, as expected, a broad range of professional, technical, and managerial occupations, but also a considerable number of occupations for which a college education was not required–for example, bank teller, carpenter, chef–cook, electrician, flight attendant, florist--floral designer, keypunch operator, machinist, plumber, police officer, receptionist, secretary, and welder. The early SIGI included each of these titles (just one "welder"), because, clearly, college students entered many occupations that did not require postsecondary education. On the other hand, very few people without such education enter professional, technical, and managerial occupations. So amount of education and type of occupation entered are related, but not symmetrically.

For SIGI PLUS, designed for the general adult population, more occupations not requiring postsecondary education were added. Unskilled occupations (which would certainly appear in lists of titles for other purposes) were never included, however, because they do not seem to be chosen. People tend to enter them when they have no choice, or when the choice is between *job* environments, not *occupations*.

The number of start-up occupations for the initial version of SIGI was severely limited by storage space and the amount of work necessary to collect, evaluate, analyze, interpret, decompose, recompose, and put in the first arrays of information. Occupations with very small numbers were, therefore, excluded; still, the first 155 occupational titles included in the system accounted for the occupations entered by about 95% of the former students who had responded to surveys. These 155 titles actually included information on about 225 occupations: Sometimes we saved space by telescoping information about two occupations into one title, like the doublet interpreter–translator; court reporter was subsumed as a specialty under stenographer; information about different kinds of welders appeared under one title; members of a survey crew, like rod worker and chain worker (formerly rodman and chainman–nomenclature became unisex in the early 1970s), were described under surveyor. A cross-reference list helped clients use alternative titles to gain access to information. An occupation similar to one already in SIGI was added only if it was rated differently on one or more of the dimensions used in structured search or required a different route for preparation. For example, a relatively large number of engineering occupations were included because students usually have to decide while still in college to major in one specialty or another.

Even now, with ample storage available for SIGI PLUS, the original thrust toward economy in the number of titles has been maintained. A doctrine of making each new title "earn its way" prevails, with no desire to play a "numbers game" by padding the number of main titles to indicate that the coverage of occupations is exhaustive.

The question may be raised: Why bother to aggregate and select titles? As long as there is enough storage space, why not just put all possible titles into the system separately, without regard for redundancy? One reason is that, if occupational titles were not well differentiated, clients would often be swamped with titles in structured search. The search function, as described previously, is to provide a manageable list of occupations that meet or exceed the client's specifications. From this list, the client can choose occupations for further investigation through direct access to information. But if the list gets too long, it is no longer manageable. There are costs in time and frustration to clients who have to deal with such unwieldy numbers of titles. There are also nontrivial costs to developers in entering and maintaining a superfluity of occupational titles.

The list of occupational titles included in the system is not static. Occupations are added every year, and occasionally a few are deleted. It has always been the practice of the development staff to poll career planning and placement officers at colleges for suggested additions and deletions. Clients have also been asked to name occupations they would like to have added to the system. Obviously, other compilations, such as the *DOT* and the *Occupational Outlook Handbook*, published biennially by the U.S. Department of Labor, have been consulted to avoid inadvertent omissions. Extensive searches have been conducted to pick up early indications of "emerging occupations." A substantial file of "candidate occupations" for inclusion is maintained and examined every year. (In general, some priority is given to occupations with favorable outlook and to occupations for which the colleges offer preparatory programs.)

Often, the best sources for picking up emerging differentiation in an occupation are the panels of people in the occupation who serve as consultants and reviewers. For example, the panel for "metallurgist" suggested that differences of such a number and kind had developed as to warrant distinguishing "materials scientist–engineer" from "metallurgist." Further research corroborated their suggestion; so the new occupation was added.

Differentiation within an occupation, however, does not always result in bifurcation of titles. For example, staff occupational analysts had for some time recognized that "chiropractor" included two kinds of practitioners: "Straight" chiropractors, in the tradition of the original development of the occupation, limit themselves to the manipulation of the spine; "mixed" chiropractors additionally use ultrasound or galvanic currents and prescribe corrective exercises, shoes, and diets. Each kind of practitioner is represented by a professional organization, but the "mixed" are clearly dominant both in numbers and in influence over the direction the occupation is taking. Most members of the "straight" association hold dual membership and favor merger of the associations. Because of the numbers in each group, their ages, and the unmistakable trend, occupational information in SIGI PLUS represents the "mixed" group, although the occupational analysts admit that a small number of diehard "straight" chiropractors would "probably disown it."

Occupational titles are deleted when the occupations they represent become obsolete, are merged into other occupations, or fail to develop as anticipated when they were installed. For example, "robotics technician" was deleted from SIGI PLUS in 1989 when use of robots in industry, which had initially accelerated with deceptive urgency, was clearly seen to have faltered (cf. Kilborn, 1990); companies that used robotics said they preferred to hire applicants with associate or baccalaureate degrees in mechanical or electronic engineering, who could be trained in-house as robotics specialists as needed, but whose greater versatility would allow them to be employed more flexibly. So it would be a disservice to lead clients to prepare in a narrowly specialized program for robotics. Another example: In 1990, occupational analysts noted a trend toward merging inventory control specialist, industrial traffic manager, and materials manager into one occupation with a new title, logistics manager. Further research was undertaken to confirm or modify this observation.

These anecdotal explanations, which could be multiplied, illustrate the dynamic nature of occupations and titles. New occupations are born, obsolescent ones fade away, and many undergo metamorphoses. As mentioned in chapter 1 on Career Decision Making, the fourth edition of the *Dictionary of Occupational Titles*, compared with the third, added about 2,100 new occupational definitions and deleted about 3,500. Editions of the *DOT* come out at long intervals. A computerized career guidance system is (or should be) kept up to date annually. The anecdotal accounts also illustrate the crucial need for "inside" information—what is known by members of an occupation, of professional associations, and of labor unions long before it appears in published materials. Use of such sources is important not just for getting occupational titles right but for the quality of information that goes into the system.

Occupational Topics

Sections with overlapping, but not identical, topics are used to address the occupational information in a computerized career guidance system. For the *structured search* section, clients specify the occupational attributes that are most important to them. These may be chosen from designations of (a) levels of rewards and satisfactions corresponding to their values, (b) fields of knowledge corresponding to their interests, (c) activities corresponding to their interests and skills, (d) amount of education corresponding to the investment in education they are willing to make, and (e) features that they may particularly want to avoid. The computer program uses each specification chosen from these sets to sort through a data base that contains ratings or categorizations of occupations on the attributes specified. This structured search generates a list of occupations that meet or exceed the specifications. Clients can play "What if?" games by changing their specifications and arranging them in various combinations to see what titles will be generated by each array. They can also ask "Why not?" to find out in what respect a previously favored occupation may have failed to meet a given set of specifications. A 1990 addendum also permits a search for occupations related to each major field of study. Thus, the client starts with specifications and gets lists of occupational titles.

Another set of topics is used in *direct access* to information. Here, the client starts with occupational titles and chooses questions from a menu (see Exhibit D, Menu of Topics in Information). In response to each question, the system displays appropriate concise information. This direct access to information serves to enrich the client's knowledge of each

Exhibit D
Menu of Topics in Information

DEFINITION AND DESCRIPTION	PERSONAL SATISFACTIONS
(1) Definition of occupation?	(16) Contribution to society?
(2) Description of work activities?	(17) Leadership?
(3) Typical job titles/specialties?	(18) Prestige level?
(4) Work setting(s)? Indoor/outdoor?	(19) Leisure/flexible time?
(5) Special problems/satisfactions?	(20) Independence on job?
	(21) Variety?
EDUCATION, TRAINING,	(22) Interest Fields?
OTHER REQUIREMENTS	
(6) Educational requirements?	
(7) Examples of college courses?	OPPORTUNITIES AND OUTLOOK
(8) Specific occupational training?	(23) Employment outlook?
(9) Personal qualifications?	(24) Where employed?
(10) Skills required?	(25) Security?
(11) Other requirements? Experience?	(26) Advancement?
INCOME (national figures)	MORE INFORMATION
(12) Beginning income?	(27) Where to find out more?
(13) Average income?	
(14) Top earning possibilities?	
(15) How earnings vary?	(0) none of these

Press the number (plus ENTER) for each question you want to ask.
When you have chosen all the numbers you want, press ENTER a second time.

occupation and usually results in further refining the list of occupations already under consideration.

As indicated before, in the description of the model for SIGI, these two modes of acquiring information, structured search and direct access, represent complementary aspects of occupational information. For the search mode, the specifications address summary information, such as scale levels and ratings, or presence or absence of some feature. Summary ratings of this sort lose some information but gain in speed, simplicity, and power – suitable for a first cut. Questions used in the direct access mode are devised to reclaim the lost information: The responses capture more of the detail and diversity of each occupation, showing distributions and variations within an occupation, by region, industry, type of organization, and subtitle. (Just as structured search compresses the more detailed information that appears in direct access, so does direct access abbreviate the more extensive treatment of skills and of preparation in special sections devoted to those topics – as seen in the earlier description of the Skills section.)

Sometimes it is expedient to set specifications for structured search and questions for direct access at different levels of specificity or generality. For example, a client's general concern about income can be summarized along a scale of average income in structured search; in direct access, however, it can also be translated into specific questions about beginning income, average income, top earnings possibilities, and variation in earnings (Items 12 to 15 in Exhibit D). To include all the latter items in structured search would dilute its brevity and diffuse its summary power. At other times, however, the same rubrics can be used both for specifications in structured search and for questions in direct access (as in Items 16 to 21 and 25 in Exhibit D). The output will be a summary rating in one case and detailed information in the other.

Of course, the nature of the medium prevents detailed information from being too lengthy. It is not just a question of the number of lines and characters per line that can be accommodated in a display; for various reasons, people do not tolerate reading lengthy and unrelieved text on a computer terminal. So direct access provides additional sources of information (Item 27 in Exhibit D).

Obviously, the menu of topics for direct access is more comprehensive than the specifications for structured search. The information addressed in direct access is developed first and serves as the information base from which the ratings and categories used in structured search are derived. So every specification in structured search must have a counterpart in direct access, but not *vice versa*. Needless to say, the ratings in structured search are always consistent with the information in direct access. (This use of *praeteritio* – mentioning what is "needless to say" – is attributable to *in-*

consistencies observed between structured search and direct access in some computerized guidance systems.)

Although the menu of topics in direct access may appear comprehensive, it is not exhaustive. Additional topics have been considered; one was included for a while but later deleted. The controversy surrounding it illustrates the amount of thought and debate underlying some of the decisions. I originally planned to include questions on the number of women and of minority groups in each occupation. Representatives of organizations that often speak for women and minority groups advised that such data be omitted: If the number were small, women or minority-group members might construe it as a "Keep Out" sign. My reasoning was that the information was better than its absence; a small number might be construed in various ways by various people–deterring some and challenging others–but the information was useful in any case. (A similar argument holds for telling the total number of people in an occupation, as in Item 23, on outlook.) The number of women and members of minority groups might also suggest occupations in which affirmative action was most likely to have an impact. So I proposed an empirical test: We would try the question for women (deferring the problem of determining how many minority groups to include) and see how the information affected female clients. In follow-up interviews, I found no sign of detrimental effects, but an objective determination was admittedly difficult. (We had no opportunity to do a controlled experiment with two versions varying in respect to this item of information.) Meanwhile, occupational analysts found the data were volatile–as affirmative action programs did take effect, it was hard to keep up with the pace of change in many occupations. Besides, I did not want to ignore the advice I had sought from competent advisers. So we decided to omit reference to numbers of women and minority-group members and trust that clients would assume that all occupations were open to them.

The topics for structured search were determined by the research, previously described, establishing (a) the independence of such domains as values, interests, and skills (and the fuzziness of "temperaments") and (b) the dimensions comprised by each of those domains. Beyond that, the dimensions often required division into scales or categories that the client could use as specifications to generate a list of qualifying occupations. The output is clearly sensitive to a number of decisions, rules, and procedures that govern scales, intervals, and screening. For example, how many scale values or categories are suitable for each feature? How should interval sizes be determined? Is there an "ideal" distribution of occupations on each feature? Most of the solutions to these problems have worked well, and it would be tedious to detail their effective development and use. Instead, it may be more interesting and enlightening to focus on a trouble spot.

An issue in structured search is which of the following search rules to use for each feature or set of features: "equal to," "not equal to," "equal to or more than," or "equal to or less than." In screening occupations on a desirable reward or satisfaction, we assumed that the appropriate rule was "equal to or more than." Thus, if a client specified a certain level of income as acceptable, it seemed reasonable that an occupation that returned a higher amount of income would not be unacceptable. For fields of knowledge and for activities, the rule was "equal to"—that is, only occupations that lie in the specified field or that involve significant amounts of the activity specified would qualify. For amount of education, the rule would be "equal to or less than," because willingness to invest in a specified level of education would include all lower levels. For features clients particularly want to avoid, the rule would be "not equal to"—so that only occupations that did not include a significant amount of that feature would qualify.

The neatness of this array of rules may obscure some of the difficult definitions that had to be developed—like how much is a "significant amount." As it happens, such definitions could be made with some precision and the resultant judgments proved to be reliable. But we have been troubled by an even more fundamental problem in using the "equal to or more than rule" for two of the dimensions in the domain of rewards and satisfactions. These dimensions are Leadership–Responsibility and Leisure. Short-form definitions and a summary of the rating rules for each of these values appear in Exhibit E for Leadership and Exhibit F for Leisure. These exhibits are extracts from the *Handbook* that was developed and used by occupational analysts for SIGI. They illustrate the ways in which rewards and satisfactions are defined and rated generally in the system. The rating rules have proven robust for all the dimensions, and inter-rater reliabilities have been maintained at a very high level. But for these two dimensions client attitudes have not always corresponded to the assumptions governing the "equal to or more than rule." We have learned from structured interviews that some clients prefer an "equal to" rule. For example, if they specify an "average" amount of leadership or leisure, they do not invariably regard a greater amount as equally acceptable. Thus, "too much" leadership may be regarded as involving "more stress" than a client wants, and "too much" leisure may leave some clients feeling that their lives would lack a necessary modicum of structure. Perhaps the solution to this problem will be to return to a procedure that allows clients to designate the rule they want to use: "equal to" or "equal to or more than."

As a sidelight, note that the verbal "tags" for the 4-point scale ratings for leisure differ from the tags for leadership (and the other dimensions of rewards and satisfactions). Deviations for leisure *above* the "average" 36-

Exhibit E
Definition and Rating Levels for Leadership

Definition:
You want to guide others, tell them what to do, get them to work together, be responsible for their performance. You're willing to accept the blame when things go wrong.
Rating Levels:
The amount of leadership is judged on two factors: (1) the number of co-workers one directs and is responsible for, and (2) the number of clients influenced and the importance and duration of the activity.

4–**A great amount:**
(1) Directs many co-workers and is responsible for their performance or (2) exerts influence over many clients in areas of activity that are important and of long duration (e.g., teacher, hospital administrator, psychologist).

3–**More than average:**
(1) Directs a moderate number of co-workers and is responsible for their performance or (2) exerts influence over clients in areas of activity that are of moderate importance and/or moderate duration (e.g., correction officer, recreation worker, registered nurse, retail store manager).

2–**Average:**
(1) Directs a few co-workers and is responsible for their performance or (2) exerts influence over clients in areas of activity that are of minor importance or duration (e.g., oceanographer, dancer/dancing teacher, legal assistant).

1–**Less than average:**
No opportunity to direct others. Not responsible for the performance of others (e.g., bank teller, computer operator).

to 40-hour work week (that is, fewer hours per week) are too infrequent to warrant two higher steps in degree of leisure; deviations *below* the average, however, are more common and permit two lower scale steps in degree of leisure to be differentiated. We used to hear a great deal from futurists about the "new leisure" to come. Concern was expressed about the use to which the time off from work would be put: Would it be possible to foster more constructive use of the extra leisure than idling in front of a television set with a glass of beer? The alarm about excess leisure has so far proven false. The standard work week has not diminished in the United States in over half a century, and the number of occupations requiring longer hours still far exceeds the number requiring shorter hours. Indeed, a Louis Harris survey showed a steady decrease in leisure from 1973 to 1983, and a 1989 Bureau of Labor Statistics study showed that 24% of the 88 million people employed full time worked 49 or more hours per week (U.S. Department of Labor, 1990). Further documentation appears in *The Overworked American* by Juliet Schor (1992).

Quality of Occupational Information

With the axes of occupational information defined (occupational titles and topics), the next concern is the stuff that goes into the cells of the matrix.

Where does it all come from? How accurate and current is it? Can clients trust it in making their career decisions?

Each item of information in the system is the product of dogged applied research by dedicated occupational analysts. While sources vary from one occupation to another, they typically include professional and trade associations, labor unions, employers, publications of many kinds (including those put out by the Department of Labor and other government agencies, occupational briefs and monographs, psychological and sociological studies

Exhibit F
Definition and Rating Levels for Leisure

Definition

You want short hours or long vacations. You feel that the satisfactions you get off the job are so important that work must not interfere with them.

Rating Levels:

Three factors contribute to the amount of discretionary time available for Leisure: (1) extended periods of time off (vacations or seasonal unemployment); (2) length of work week; and (3) degree of flexibility of work schedule. Complete flexibility of scheduling (the opportunity for setting one's own schedule) exists for very few occupations. Some free-lancers (e.g., fine artists), self-employed, or persons with a minimum of "scheduled" hours (e.g., college teachers) have a high degree of flexibility. Other self-employed or sales persons (such as physicians, retail store managers, or farmers) may set their own schedules but their flexibility is limited because they must adjust to the time demands of patients, customers, or the weather.

As for irregularities, scheduled "on call" time or overtime affects the length of the work week; unpredictable "on call" or overtime affects the degree of flexibility, as well as the length of the work week. Shift work, while it may be required at unusual times, does not usually affect the total length of the work week and is predictable. For some people it may be considered a disadvantage; for others an advantage.

4–**More than average:**

A great amount of discretionary time may be due to one or more of the following: long vacations (teacher); seasonal work (professional athlete); short work week (pilot, flight attendant); or highly flexible free-lance or self-set schedules (fine artist, college teacher). Long vacations or seasonal work with frequent or more than occasional overtime, however, would be lowered to an average rating (3).

3–**Average:**

Average amount of discretionary time. Regular vacation; regular work week (receptionist, legal assistant, industrial engineer), *or* long vacation/seasonal work but long work week with frequent overtime (merchant marine, farmer, construction worker). NOTE: Shift work or "on call" hours which average out 36 to 40 hours per week (e.g., nurse, claim agent) are also rated average.

2–**Less than average:**

Somewhat limited discretionary time. Regular vacation; longer than average work week due to occasional overtime or "on call" hours, whether scheduled (X-ray technologist), voluntary, or unpredictable (newspaper/broadcast journalist).

1–**A small amount:**

Little discretionary time. Regular vacation; long work week due to frequent overtime or "on call" hours, whether scheduled, voluntary, or unpredictable (physician, business administrator).

(continued on next page)

Exhibit F *(continued)*

Clarification of terms:
- regular vacation = 2–4 weeks*
- long vacation = over 4 weeks – may include work at home, e.g., college teacher – so defined when over 60% in college teaching
- seasonal unemployment = over 4 weeks at regular times during the year
- short work week = less than 36 hours per week.
- regular work week = 36–40 hours per week.
- longer than average work week = the equivalent of about 41–44 hours per week (regular work week plus occasional overtime [1–4 hours per week] or one weekend "on call" per month).
- long work week = the equivalent of 45 or more hours per week (regular work week plus frequent overtime [5 or more hours per week] or "on call" evenings and more than one weekend per month).

---

*Frequent layoffs are not considered as vacation or seasonal unemployment; much of the workers' "free" time may be spent looking for employment and is not discretionary. Occupations with frequent layoffs are considered to have the vacation or work week scheduled for regularly employed workers in that occupation.

Notes: Verbal Tags:

The verbal "tags" for the scale ratings for Leisure differ from the other values dimensions, because deviations above the "average" and modal work week are too infrequent to warrant two higher scale steps. It was possible, however, to identify two lower scale steps that differentiated a significant number of occupations. In other words, relatively few occupations offer "more" leisure than the modal amount; a substantial number offer "less."

Factors in Ratings:
- Flexibility:

In assigning ratings we found that with highly flexible schedules it is difficult to ascertain the hours worked per week or vacation time, and there tends to be much discretionary time. Therefore, flexibility is used as a substitute for the other two factors in certain occupations which are highly flexible (Rating 4). When the amount of discretionary time is definitely not "great" due to one of the other two factors, the amount of flexibility is thereby reduced and is not considered a factor in the ratings.

- Vacation

Regular vacation (2–4 weeks) is the lowest possible category for vacation because 2 weeks is the minimum for the majority of workers in any one occupation (excluding free-lance).

- Part-time Work

Part-time work, while offering more discretionary time, cannot be a factor in the ratings because no occupation is exclusively for part-time workers.

A uniform short work week, as in the case of pilots, is not part-time work because full-time pay is received for the shorter hours. Nevertheless, the possibility of part-time or shift work should be mentioned in the INFORMATION write-up for those who would consider it an advantage.

---

of occupations, economic forecasts, and commercial surveys), and consultant panels of members of the occupation. Information gathered from these diverse sources is winnowed for each occupation, and a draft written in form suitable for the system is sent to as many as 12 selected reviewers – the number varies according to the number of specialties and environments for the occupation. The reviewers usually represent associations and unions, educators in fields preparatory for the occupation, and practitioners. Sources of information, including reviewers, are entered into a data-base management program to be consulted for updates. The many sources used for a current update have been distilled from a larger number over a period of years, having been demonstrably valuable. When a new occupation is added, however, the various possible sources must be evaluated. Salary surveys, for example, need to be examined closely: Thus, scrutiny of sampling procedures and response rates helps in judging the trustworthiness of each survey.

Acquiring and assembling material from the numerous sources, evaluating and interpreting them, decomposing and then recomposing information from them to extract the elements needed for the system, "scripting" these elements to fit the structure, format, and style required, and finally entering the information into the system takes, on the average, three person-weeks per occupation (2 to 4 weeks is the range). This investment of time reflects a reduction over the years due to accumulated experience and sources. It is still difficult and expensive work, but necessary to retain a high level of quality. If information were taken "off the shelf," from the readiest sources at hand, that difficulty, time, and cost could be significantly reduced. But quality would suffer.

Early in the development of SIGI, torn between conflicting motives – to get information on a lot of occupations quickly for an early start-up and to establish a high standard of quality of information – I tested the difference between two modes of developing occupational information. One occupational analyst was assigned three occupations, with instructions to work as fast as possible, using the first respectable source (such as the *Occupational Outlook Handbook* or an occupational brief) that provided a basis for answering each of the questions posed by SIGI. Another analyst was instructed to do the most thorough job possible on the same three occupations – not settling for the first answer available but digging as much as necessary to get the most accurate and current information. For another set of three occupations, the same two analysts were given the reverse instructions. This procedure controlled for possible individual differences between the analysts. We then compared the results of the two methods. Perhaps not surprisingly, the information for all six occupations that were thoroughly researched was at so much higher a level of accuracy and currency that we knew we could never be satisfied with the faster, less expensive approach. We vowed not to compromise on quality of information, despite the higher cost or smaller number of occupations.

A good example of the difference in quality (on a larger scale than our six-occupations experiment) came some years later. The operating program had been moved out of the control of research staff and under a program director who knew nothing of the content of SIGI and whose main concern was the bottom line. To cut costs, he decided to "contract out" to a university the update of occupational information. When the work was completed, it was possible to demonstrate that the information in the *previous* year's version was more accurate and recent than what had been furnished for the *current* year. In other words, no update at all would have been better than the contractor's "update." After this demonstration, responsibility for updating was returned to the research staff, and a high standard of quality was reinstituted.

The distinction in quality can be illustrated in reference to income, an area of information especially sensitive to change. The *Occupational Outlook Handbook*, published biennially by the Department of Labor, provides data over 2 years old as each edition is issued; by the time an edition is superseded, the information on earnings is over 4 years old. Indeed, the data for various occupations are not of uniform vintage; users who want to compare earnings for two occupations have no way of knowing when they may be looking at data from different years. The *Handbook* serves as a common source for other publications and information systems; so their information is likely to be considerably older. The annual SIGI update, on the other hand, shows salaries and wages for the calendar year just completed. No secondary sources are used. By dint of energetic scouting, occupational analysts identify good, useable, current or very recent surveys of earnings for some 60% of the occupations (up from about 35% a few years ago – the fruits of experience). Such surveys are cast in various forms. Some may report ranges in salary for different segments of the occupation, according to situs of work, region, experience of workers, and so on. Analysts retain these distinctions for direct access, but for structured search must weight them by the proportion of workers in each segment to calculate an average.

Data for the remaining 40% of the occupations must be obtained through our own surveys. Questionnaires are sent to panels of participants strategically positioned to observe segments of the occupation. That is, they are selected as representative of the various specialties, regions of the country, and situs of work (e.g., industry, government, education). Returns are compared; apparent anomalies are cleared up by telephone consultations with some of the respondents, as appropriate. The resultant figures are then checked against projections from the last good survey.

To make the projections, we depend mainly on percentages of changes for various groups of occupations published quarterly by the Bureau of Labor Statistics in the Employment Cost Index. These percentages are based on data collected from a sample of employers weighted to cover all occupations and industries in the nonfarm economy and are disaggregated for large occupational groups according to their proportion in each industry. Percentage changes are given for 3- and 12-month intervals. We first identify the group of which each SIGI occupation is a member. Then, working from the date of the last good survey, we project by 12- and 3-month increments, as appropriate, to the year on which we are working. We have tested the validity of this procedure by making "retrospective" projections; that is, we have applied the procedure to old data on occupations for which we had collected good current data. Even in periods of high inflation, we found no significant differences between such projected and actual current data for any occupation. Periodic checks are made for slippage in this procedure, but there is undoubtedly a limit to the duration of periods over which this level of accuracy will hold.

Fortunately, success in finding primary sources keeps at a minimum the number of occupations for which projections of earnings must be made in any given year. In any case, the earnings reported for all occupations are for the same year. This is preferable to the frequent practice of reporting earnings data from various years, according to the availability of data. In such practices, if the years are not designated, clients may make inappropriate comparisons; if the years are designated, clients will be puzzled about how to compare two occupations with data from different years. The high level of accuracy and currency in information about earnings contained in SIGI has always been applauded by reviewers, and the staff takes pride in it. Although reviewers generally find no fault with information on any topics, I feel considerably less satisfied with the information that can be provided about *outlook*—job market projections for each occupation over the next 5 to 10 years. This topic is important enough to warrant attention.

Information and misinformation about outlook play a crucial role in many career decisions. Even people who are considering an occupation they can enter immediately may want to know whether they can expect to remain employed over the long haul—especially if they value stability of employment. Outlook can be excruciatingly important, however, to students who are considering an occupation that requires a commitment to lengthy education or training; they need projections of opportunities 5 to 10 years ahead. The current demand–supply ratio is usually easy to observe. But that may change by the time the preparation has been completed.

Indeed, because the effects of responses to the market at a given time are delayed, decisions made in the light of publicity about the current market rather than sound projections for the future may tend to amplify oscillations in imbalance between supply and demand. Often people flock to programs that prepare for occupations visibly in high demand and shun those for occupations in which people are currently being laid off or finding stiff competition for jobs. Once they are in the pipeline, it is often difficult for them to change even when they do get news of changing market information. Those who emerge into the job market after supply has overtaken demand help tip the new imbalance even more steeply. Meanwhile, the occupations that had been shunned may have developed shortages. Since occupations that require long preparation tend to be "impermeable," market forces cannot be counted on to correct the imbalance. (The dynamics of such oscillations, or "cobwebbing," were illustrated earlier, under the heading, *Labor market information and educational decisions*, in chapter 1.)

Sound, comprehensible, well-disseminated projections can dampen such oscillations and reduce the severity of the imbalances, if they are timely. A computer-based guidance system can increase greatly the speed of communicating such projections to people who are in the throes of making educational decisions, plans, and commitments. Thus, the supply side of the equation may be affected by reducing the lag in information about outlook. On an individual scale, timely projections of outlook can help people assess future employment opportunities more rationally before making a long-term commitment. Of course, even carefully made projections do not necessarily turn out to be veridical. Here, it may be helpful to examine the methods by which projections are made, and their virtues and weaknesses.

The most comprehensive periodic projections of outlook on a variety of occupations are provided by the Bureau of Labor Statistics in such publications as the *Occupational Outlook Handbook*, the *Occupational Outlook Quarterly*, and the *Monthly Labor Review*. Periodic projections are also published by various associations and commissions for appropriate groups of occupations—as in the *Allied Health Education Fact Sheet* (by the Division of Allied Health Education and Accreditation of the American Medical Association) and *Scientific, Engineering, Technological Manpower Comments* (by the American Association for the Advancement of Science Commission on Professionals in Science and Technology). Occasional in-depth studies project outlook in a single occupation or occupational sector—for example, *Prospects for Faculty in the Arts and Sciences* (Bowen & Sosa, 1989), which projects for 5-year intervals from 1987 through 2012. This last book not only offers projections but attempts to provide a *machine* for generating projections, permitting the comparison of outputs from different assumptions and models. It provides an exemplar of what can be done in the best of circumstances, with conclusions that are robust enough for practical use across a range of reasonable assumptions. Of course, the authors are careful to emphasize—as does the Bureau of Labor Statistics—that they are in the business of making projections, not predictions. The distinction is that a "prediction" purports to forecast what is most likely to occur, including effects of probable interventions. A "projection" describes what would be expected in the absence of an intervention or response to its own output and implies later modification as such effects are observed.

By definition, the conclusion of projected outlook for any occupation should include some statement about the number of openings expected and the balance between supply of people available to fill those openings and demand for their services. Since the *Occupational Outlook Handbook* is the eponymous source of most outlook projections, it may be useful to glance at an overview of the procedures followed for that work. To arrive at its projections for industrial occupations, the Bureau of Labor Statistics traces a long and complicated process. It begins with the simplifying assumption of no major war or depression – otherwise, all bets would be off. Demand consists of two major components: *growth* and *replacement*. Projections of growth (which may be positive or negative) in an occupation are most prone to error. In one study (Carey, 1980), errors in projections for occupations aggregated into major groups tended to be quite tolerable, but differences between actual and projected employment in specific occupations ranged from −43% for personnel and labor relations workers to +136% for plasterers, with the error for all 76 occupations evaluated averaging 20.8 percentage points. Briefly, the projections for industrial occupations are based on projections of growth for each industry, derived from a model of the economy in the target year. These industry projections are then allocated according to the distribution of about 500 occupations among approximately 260 industries in a National Industry-Occupation Matrix.

The results of these projections are featured in the *Occupational Outlook Handbook*, which usually starts the outlook section for each occupation with a statement about its expected growth. This tends to be an extensive statement, covering the expectations for the various industries in which the occupation manifests itself. In our observation (Chapman & Katz, 1981), many readers tend to misunderstand such featured growth projections as representing outlook projections. They fail to place such phrases as "growth much faster than average" or "little or no growth" in proper context. Thus, they often construe the first phrase as good outlook and the second phrase as poor outlook. But the first example might refer to only a few hundred openings in an occupation in the target year, and the second to many thousands of openings. So a statement about expected growth in an occupation is meaningful only in conjunction with the number employed in the occupation, replacement needs for people leaving the occupation, and the prospective relationship between supply and demand. Yet these topics are often not mentioned at all or sometimes buried after a lengthy discussion of growth. Perhaps the emphasis on growth reflects a wish to justify the magnitude of the effort devoted to estimating growth in an occupation.

Consider the quantity and nature of the data that go into the projections of growth by industry. Among the most reliable are demographic studies of the size and composition of the labor force for the target year (for a 10-year projection, the people have already been born). Indeed, for a nonindustrial occupation like elementary school teacher, growth in demand can be estimated quite effectively from demographic data (projected enrollments) and assumptions about class size. But for industrial occupations, the economic model cannot be content with demographic data. It attempts to anticipate such factors as gross national product and its distribution, productivity, inflation, and unemployment, along with trends in consumer expenditures, investment, government spending, and foreign trade, leading to estimates of demand for goods and services in each industry combined with input–output tables to estimate worker hours and, finally, detailed industry employment growth projections.

Such projections of growth tend to be unreliable. For example, Bishop and Carter (1990) pointed out that the Bureau of Labor Statistics projected in 1981 that professional, technical, and managerial jobs would account for only 28% of employment growth between 1978 and 1990 and that operatives, laborers, and service workers would account for 34% of growth. In fact, they indicated, professional, technical, and managerial jobs accounted for 52% of employment growth during this period, and operatives, laborers, and service workers accounted for only 9%.

Currently, different analysts using similar models emerge with strikingly different projections of growth in specific occupations and occupational groups. For example, Pool (1990) pointed out that the Bureau of Labor Statistics projects only a 13% increase in demand for aeronautical and astronautical engineers between 1988 and 2000 (slightly less than the projected 15% growth in the work force as a whole). But the National Science Foundation projects a 48% increase in demand for aeronautical and astronautical engineers in that period—near the highest rate projected for any occupation. While analysts at the BLS and NSF could not pinpoint the reason for this inconsistency between projections, Pool speculates that perhaps different assumptions were made on cuts in defense spending. Given such unreliability of growth projections, to emphasize the growth component of demand, as the *Occupational Outlook Handbook* and many other sources of outlook projections do, requires an act of faith in the capabilities of economic forecasts at a range of 10 years.

The macro-miasma emanating from the "dismal science" should not obscure from view, however, some firm and valuable data contained in the National Industry-Occupation Matrix: (a) the number of people in each occupation for the base year, derived from surveys of employment in the occupations (it is from this relatively firm base number that a sometimes infirm projection to the target year is made by adding a percentage derived from the weighted expected growth of the industries among which the occupation is distributed); (b) the separation or exit rate of people from each occupation, derived from the Current Population Survey; (c) the distribution by age for each occupation (16–24, 25–54, 55 and over), also derived from the Current Population Survey. (It would be useful to have the exit rate by age, but this is not provided; one could assume for most occupations, however, that for a 10-year projection virtually everyone in the 55 and over group would have retired.) These three elements of data can be combined to project the *replacement* component of demand. Fortunately, for most occupations, replacement (compared to growth) is by far the more important component of demand.

In my view, then, outlook projections should begin by giving the number of people currently in the occupation. This emphasis is appropriate because current number is the firmest relevant datum, and the demand – the number of openings projected for the target year – will almost always be proportional to this number. Combined with the separation rate and the proportion of members who will reach retirement age by the target year, the size of the occupation can also serve in estimating the replacement component of demand. (For most occupations, the refinement of this estimate achieved by Bowen & Sosa, 1989, who start with the age distribution and the exit rate by age and then feed in changes in the distribution and consequent new exit rates due to a continual stream of new entrants, is not readily attainable; such a refined analysis is not crucial, however, because it affects mainly short-term replacement needs and has very small effects on replacement needs 10 years out.) The *absolute size* of the growth component will also be a function mainly of the number of people in the occupation (a low growth rate added to a big base results in more openings than a relatively high rate added to a small base). The first impression the client gets, then, should be the size of the occupation.

The second statement should be the projected number of replacements, estimated as indicated previously. The third statement should give the projected balance between demand and supply. The demand side will be composed, in most cases, mainly of replacement needs but can be modified by the growth projections. Growth projections are most likely to be valid and can be given appropriate weight when they are a consequence of robust demographic data (such as a "baby boom" or a rapid increase in the proportion of the elderly segment of the population) or of technological change that has already taken hold. (Futurologists' speculations about the effects of technology not yet in place may be interesting to read but are rarely valid enough for clients to bet on at a range of 10 years.) The language expressing the balance between "demand" and "supply" should probably not use those terms, because they are not readily understood by many clients. Instead, the following verbal tags for outlook in an occupation have proven clear and useful:

EXCELLENT: Many more job openings expected than trained job-seekers.

VERY GOOD: More job openings expected than trained job-seekers.

GOOD: Number of job openings expected to equal number of trained job-seekers.

FAIR: May face competition for jobs.

POOR: Keen competition—more job-seekers than jobs.

NOT CLEAR: [whatever information is available can be offered, including expectations for growth.]

Of course, these statements about outlook require information about the supply side of the balance scale as well as the demand side. Data and procedures for projecting supply are not so well developed as those for demand. The inadequacies of growth projections on the demand side are redeemed by such firm data as the number in an occupation and the projected replacement needs due to expected transfers, retirements, and deaths. But the supply side presents more intractable problems. The Bureau of Labor Statistics and other sources have little to say about methods for projecting supply.

Fortunately, all is not bleak. Supply can be projected quite well for occupations with long periods of preparation, such as graduate or professional study. For example, the median time from bachelor's degree to a doctorate in the arts and sciences in 1986 and 1987 was 9.5 years (Bowen & Sosa, 1989). Even if this time were accelerated *after* the expected tightening of the academic market during the 1997–2002 interval, there would still be time to monitor supply in the pipeline for each field: Bowen and Sosa point out that there tends to be a lag of 7 to 11 years between perception of a new strong demand and an increase in the output of new doctorates; the lowest median time to doctorate was attained in 1972, 7 years after the peak demand. (Bowen & Sosa provide excellent models for projecting supply, including in their projections the increasing proportion of doctorates gained by nonresidents of the United States and the rate at which they enter the U.S. labor market.)

Hard data contributing to supply projections are also readily available on the number of people in the age cohorts from which total labor supply will be mainly drawn, and some reasonable assumptions can be made about the effects of immigration. The proportions of people in each cohort likely to attain various educational levels can be estimated and combined with data on the amount of education obtained by people in various occupations, thus indicating the potential supply "pool" for occupations requiring each level. Periodic surveys show the numbers of college students majoring in each field. There are also occasional questionnaire studies of occupational plans of students by major field. But all these potentially useful data that affect supply fall short of a systematic, continual, coherent collection and integration of information.

Such a systematic collection of information for supply projections would require a well-coordinated research effort, which could build on work already under way. For occupations requiring postsecondary education, it would be possible to track the flow of students into and through various programs of study. Extensive information is now routinely gathered by the College Entrance Examination Board and the American College Testing Program on the abilities, records, and plans of applicants to college. A great deal of information about supply can be obtained simply by asking students about their aspirations, expectations, and plans. These change, of course, and it is necessary to repeat the questions at regular intervals. In addition, follow-up surveys could answer such questions as: What proportion of applicants who say they plan to enter a certain program actually do so? What proportion remain to completion of the program? What are the characteristics of those who persist and those who drop out or transfer? What is the net gain or loss of students in each program, and what are patterns of transfer? What is the distribution of occupations entered by those who complete each program? How many from each program go on to which graduate or professional studies? What proportion of those entering each graduate or professional program complete it and/or enter an occupation for which it is preparatory? Information from such surveys could help to categorize connections between academic programs and occupations entered.

Continuing the surveys over time would help define the nature of the supply pool for each occupation requiring postsecondary education and recognize (and take into account) the conditions that influence it. Annual collection of such data permits comparisons from year to year, and trends can be traced as the data base matures. Some elements of such a continual data collection are already in place. For example, the National Center for Educational Statistics and the National Science Foundation have recorded numbers of students entering various fields. Their work demonstrates the feasibility of the kind of data collection envisioned here. But at present, each set of numbers is compiled, reported, and interpreted separately by the agency initiating a survey. For the purposes envisioned here, such elements need to be combined and coordinated in a continual tracking of cohorts through the postsecondary educational system and into occupations. The late William Turnbull, former president of Educational Testing Service, wrote a prospectus in 1981 for "the development of information and services related to the flow of students into and through higher education and their subsequent entry into different occupations." He proposed annual surveys and interpretations in terms of supply for all the occupations for which postsecondary education was found to be appropriate. Circumstances prevented development of the concept then, but perhaps the time is ripe now. At any rate, the idea should be kept alive for periodic consideration until the time is ripe.

As for occupations not generally entered via postsecondary education, perhaps a less elaborate approach is appropriate. These occupations tend to be more "permeable." They require relatively short-term training, and thus the supply is more quickly responsive to immediate market conditions and training opportunities. The main question is likely to be, how many people have (or will have) the basic skills to handle the work or the training for it. Periodic large-scale inventories of skills and abilities are already being undertaken through a variety of sponsors and measures. The National Assessment of Educational Progress, the Armed Services Vocational Aptitude Battery (administered widely in high schools to students who are not planning military careers, as well as to those who are), the General Aptitude Test Battery (also administered in many high schools, as well as at State Employment Services), and statewide testing programs are all sources of relevant data for such an inventory. Again, there would be an advantage in coordinating the data collection and analyses. A systematic research effort could determine the connections between skill and ability levels and success in training and occupations. A continuing inventory of relevant skills, abilities, and talents in the nation's youth would appear to provide a major contribution to policy planning as well as guidance.

Who would carry out these coordinated, systematic surveys, inventories, and analyses? Presumably interested agencies that come first to mind include the national Departments of Education, Labor, Commerce, and Defense; the National Science Foundation; large testing, survey, and research organizations; professional associations concerned with career guidance; and many others too humorous to mention. But this is not the place to get into detail on the roles of various agencies in a coordinated continual survey of the flow of students through education and into occupations. An article in the *New York Times* that appeared on the day I was concluding this chapter (May 21, 1990) quoted veteran negotiators on arms control as saying: "The devil is in the details" (p. A14). Perhaps now that "details" have descended from divine (at the beginning of this chapter) to diabolic (at its conclusion), it may be best to leave the question of who will collect the data for supply projections and return to focus on the use of the data in career decisions.

At any rate, to avoid overselling the idea, the new systematic program of research that I have been advocating here would not guarantee a high level of accuracy in projecting specific supply for every occupation. But it would contribute to a greater level of confidence in verbal tags, such as those listed on a previous page, for the balance between supply and demand in most occupations. After all, clients do not need to know the exact number of people likely to be available for an occupation they are considering. Each tag could tolerate the amount of error likely to be incurred in the derivation of such numbers from continual surveys and analyses. It would then be up to clients to judge whether the projected outlook for a given occupation was "favorable enough" for them – in terms of their own propensities for risk-taking or risk-avoidance. Outlook is one more piece of information that may play a greater or lesser part for each client in closure on an informed and rational decision – the subject of the next section.

A STRATEGY FOR DECIDING

Seek simplicity and distrust it. (A. N. Whitehead)

In previous sections of this chapter, we have seen the drama of career decision making unfold as clients explore and examine their values, interests, and skills, get a manageable list of occupations that meet their specifications, and then inform themselves further about those occupations. The drama does not reach its climax, however, until clients pit the remaining "candidate" occupations against one another and gain closure on a *choice* of an occupation. Other computerized guidance systems stop short of the climax. Their apparent rationale is that once clients have gone through some exercises in self-understanding and have been exposed to some occupational information, coming to grips with a decision is easy.

Easy, perhaps – but logical and consistent, no. Leaving the client to select appropriate elements from the seething, buzzing swarm of knowledge and information collected through extensive self-appraisal and gathering of occupational information, then to consider them and to combine them, somehow, without further guidance, into a decision represents a failure of nerve and commitment on the part of the system developer. Having labored so far up the slippery slope toward a choice, clients are abandoned on the very verge of climbing the cusp of competence in career decision making.

Pitz and Harren (1980) cited a number of studies showing that, left to their own devices at the point of decision, people tend to recall and use only a small portion of the relevant information they have obtained. They may neglect a feature they earlier deemed essential. They may give inappropriate weight to the most recently acquired information or emphasize

unduly some item of information that was presented more vividly th
rest. They often have no idea how to manage and reconcile different
of information in coming to closure on a choice. Pitz and Harren (1980)
wrote: "When . . . left to integrate such information by themselves, they
often fail to do so consistently and appropriately." Thus, Pitz and Harren
(1980) concluded from an extensive review of research on decision making:

> The literature . . . provides a clear documentation of the need for helping
> people to integrate complex information. For optimal decision making to
> occur, it is not sufficient to provide a person with a clear understanding of
> the problem and all relevant information. Without further assistance, people
> resort to simplifying heuristics for coping with the information, which
> results in potentially serious inconsistencies in their behavior.

Or, as Einstein is reputed to have said, somewhat more succinctly,
"Everything should be made as simple as possible, but not more so."

Formal Decision Analysis

Pitz and Harren (1980), having cited SIGI for its explicit model of career
decision making, concluded that decision analysis offers "something no
other procedure can offer. It provides a means of ensuring logically
consistent choices in the presence of complex information, uncertainty
about future outcomes, and conflicting values."

Similarly, endorsing the advantages of formal decision analysis through
the computation of "Expected Utilities," Shepard (1964) posed this "key
question": Do people collapse the various component dimensions to one
over-all evaluative dimension in any optimum way? His review of experimental literature provided a negative answer. He concluded that judgments are better when the dimensions are combined formally, even
mechanically, rather than intuitively and holistically: "Even when the
underlying factors combine according to a nonlinear rule, a machine using
a purely linear rule of combination can yield estimates of 'true' worth that
surpass in accuracy those of trained subjects who are not constrained in
this way."

In *Decision Analysis*, his book on the calculations of "Expected Utilities," Raiffa (1968) described the basic strategy in these terms: "The spirit
of decision analysis is divide and conquer: Decompose a complex problem
into simpler problems, get one's thinking straight in those simpler problems, paste these analyses together with a logical glue, and come out with
a program of action for the complex problem."

Raiffa, Shepard, and others who have worked on decision theory are
unanimous in accepting the superiority of formal mathematical combina-

tions of the basic components to rank the options on an "Expected Utilities" (EU) index. Agreement on a mathematical solution for combining components, however, leaves the basic questions of defining and quantifying the elements that go into the equation. To Raiffa (1968), "The trouble is that these basic questions *are the most difficult to answer.*" But he emphasized that mathematical decision analysis provides advantages even in defining and quantifying the basic elements because it encourages decision makers to scrutinize a problem as an organic whole, to communicate about the problem, to come to grips with interactions between various facets of a problem, to see the need for relevant information and seek it, and to distinguish between preferences for consequences and judgments about uncertainty.

The "basic questions" are, of course, what the structure and substance of self-assessment and occupational information in SIGI were designed to answer. But the guiding principle in organizing the quest for self-understanding and knowledge about occupations was to enable clients to marshal in one section all the relevant insights and information to be obtained from other sections and to combine them in a formal process of rational decision making. Indeed, SIGI had its origin in an explicit model of career decision making that I developed in 1963.

The Original Model of Decision Analysis for SIGI

At that time, EU theory had been applied primarily in economic and business decisions. These tended to deal with a single criterion, financial gain. Stated in its simplest terms, this theory posited that one could choose between options by combining the prospects for gain and loss to be obtained from each course of action with the probability of each outcome. Most applications were more complex than that simple statement might suggest, because each choice is likely to have ramifications; so the calculation of EU must often be accumulated through the branches of a decision tree (Raiffa, 1968).

For career guidance, clearly, multiple criteria, or objectives, or values (nomenclature varies) were needed to represent all the major dimensions that compose the worth of each option. It was also clear that quantifying these objectives, and the attributes of options that bear on these objectives, would not be transparent, as in the case of financial gain.

What was required, then, was first to identify and define the major objectives that people sought to satisfy in an occupation (or any other career decision). Then came some difficult steps in quantification: Clients had to weight the importance of each objective (or value); experts in the structure and substance of information had to rate the attributes of each option relevant to each objective (that is, the opportunity it offers people to get what they want on each dimension); probabilities of entry and success in each option had to be calculated or estimated. Exhibit G (Katz, 1966b) illustrates how I put these quantities together in this first pass at the model.

The mock-up is generalized for any career decision—occupational or educational. So letters stand in for the names of values dimensions (A–E, the number being limited to five and the scales for B, C, and D curtailed to save space) and of options (W–Z). In the column headed Magnitude, a high school student, Joe Doe, identifies for himself what may be called a "crucial magnitude" (or "threshold level") or a "specified segment" within each dimension and circles the corresponding interval(s). Each circle can specify either a single interval (such as E3) or all intervals above a threshold (A1–3). So the problem later encountered in the SIGI intervals for Leadership–Responsibility and Leisure (mentioned in the previous section, on occupational information) was prevented. For example, if the options are occupations, and if A1–A5 represent levels of annual incomes, Joe can weight the importance (in the next column) of earning an amount *equal to or greater than* A3. Or if E1–E4 represent levels of leadership and responsibility, Joe may prefer to weight the importance of an amount *equal to* E3. He may run through the exercise several times, trying out the effects of choosing different levels and weights. He puts the numbers representing weights in the column headed Importance, distributing a fixed sum of points among the various dimensions (Metfessel, 1947). He reaches a trial balance first and then revises the allotments as many times as necessary to establish the proper relationships between values dimensions. This exercise could serve as a useful *reprise* of an earlier examination of Joe's values or as an *introduction* to self-appraisal and getting relevant information (I return to the latter alternative at the end of this section). If it is a reprise, inconsistencies and intransitivities are called to Joe's attention—his resolution of such anomalies are likely to be particularly productive of insight. Thus, Joe may be asked to verify that he is saying A1–3 is worth as much as B1 and C2 together, B1 is worth twice as much as C2, and so on.

The rating of "Strength of Return" reflects the fact that some options tend to offer greater opportunities than others for satisfying each desire or value that Joe has expressed. It might also be called instrumentality, opportunity, likelihood of encounter, or availability in respect to each magnitude of each value dimension. In this model, I used a 5-point scale, "standard fives," based on the frequency of appearance of the chosen magnitude within each option; the dummy ratings on this scale appear in the columns headed Coefficient. The Product (in the adjacent columns) is of

Exhibit G
Model of Guidance for Career Decision Making (from Katz, 1966b)
Illustrative Chart for Joe Doe

OPTIONS
Strength of Return

VALUES			W		X		Y		Z	
Dimension	Magnitude	Importance (Sum = 100)	Coefficient	Product	Coefficient	Product	Coefficient	Product	Coefficient	Product
A	A_1 A_2 (A$_3$) A_4 A_5	30	5	150	2	60	4	120	2	60
B	(B$_1$) B_2 B_3 C_1	20	4	80	5	100	5	100	3	60
C	(C$_2$) D_1	10	5	50	1	10	3	30	1	10
D	(D$_2$) E_1 E_2	5	5	25	3	15	1	5	1	5
E	(E$_3$) E_4	35	3	105	2	70	3	105	4	140
Sum of value returns				410		255		360		275
Joe's probability of success				0.7		0.8		0.7		0.5
Expected value				287		204		252		137.5

the weight under Importance and the corresponding rating under Coefficient. These products are summed to represent the overall desirability of each option in terms of Joe's values.

The "Sums" are then modulated by a decimal representing the probability of entry and success in each option to provide an "Expected Value" (or utility). Where does the decimal come from? When the options are educational choices, as of a high school course or of a college, formal prediction systems using previous scholastic record and standardized tests as independent variables have generally demonstrated useful validities, and expectancy tables showing probabilities can be derived directly from regression analyses. Attempts to predict entry and success in occupations, however, have not achieved an equal claim on confidence, and it is necessary to fall back on well-structured but nonmathematical analyses (as described previously under the headings, Prediction in SIGI, Aptitudes Revisited, Chances of Success, and Skills in SIGI PLUS).

A major purpose in devoting this much space to an illustration of the generalized model is to emphasize that CDM is indeed a continual (not continuous) process; that is, the process is enacted through a sequence of choices: Decisions, whether long range or short range, tentative or binding, must still be made at various choice-points—made, expressed, acted upon, lived with, and perhaps reconsidered. Thus, as I (Katz, 1966b) explained in presenting the model, a student in high school can, at appropriate intervals:

> use the model to make firm decisions involving close-range options—curriculum for next year; to make tentative and contingent decisions involving intermediate-range options—college or other post high school educational plans; and to make even more fluid decisions involving long-range options—occupations. The more distant decisions require less commitment and may be recycled through the model as often as seems desirable—particularly as the outcomes of earlier decisions take effect. Thus, this iterative use of the model is not inconsistent with the concept of a continual *process*, while allowing realistically for distinct discontinuities in the *content* of choices.

Modifying the Model for SIGI

Inevitably, when a theoretical model is applied to practice, it is subject to contextual changes. The compromises made in adapting the original concept for a particular treatment may be instructive. Throughout the development of SIGI, we were torn between two motives: to make the application of the model as complete as possible and to keep it short. In an operational program of this kind, with a large number of users and a limited number of terminals, total time per client had to be kept as low as possible. Thus, more people would be able to use the system, and delays in scheduling clients for repeated sessions would be reduced. (Some time between sessions is desirable for examining print-outs, thinking over implications, and carrying out off-line investigations, but ideally it should not exceed 3 weeks.) We expected great variation between clients in time of use, but we aimed at an average of about 4 hours per client (and we did hit this target).

To see where we cut, compare the decision analysis of the Strategy section of SIGI (Exhibit H) with the original model (Exhibit G). In this example (extracted from an early client's record), a student was comparing three occupations: Pilot, Oceanographer, and Landscape Architect.

The client had previously (in the Values section) examined each of 10 values dimensions (carefully defined in operational terms) and weighted its importance to him, one at a time, on a scale of 0 to 8. The weights for all 10 values had then been assembled and displayed, graphically and numerically, and the student had been given a chance to compare them, have second thoughts, and make adjustments in the weights. Next, to stimulate clients to scrutinize their values more closely in a clearly playful and game-like (nonthreatening) context, they were confronted with a series of values dilemmas. The first step was to choose between two hypothetical occupations named and described to represent a pure manifestation of

	VALUE	WT.	OCCUPATION					
			Pilot		Oceang		LnsArc	
(1)	High Income	5	5	25	5	25	4	20
(2)	Prestige	3	4	12	4	12	3	9
(3)	Independence	6	3	18	3	18	3	18
(4)	Help Others	5	2	10	3	15	2	10
(5)	Security	3	1	3	4	12	2	6
(6)	Variety	3	3	9	3	9	4	12
(7)	Leadership	4	3	12	2	8	3	12
(8)	Interest Field	6	3	18	4	24	3	18
(9)	Leisure	1	4	4	2	2	2	2
(0)	Early Entry	4	2	8	2	8	2	8
				119		133		115

Your weight for income(5) × the rating of Pilot on Income(5) = 25, etc.

The sum of the products appears at the bottom of each column.
The occupation with the highest sum is probably the one that would fit your Values best. The highest possible sum is 168; the lowest is 40.
In general, a difference of 10 points or more between sums is significant.

For a copy press PRINT; otherwise press NEXT.

Exhibit H This student designated "Scientific" as his main field of interest. The sum of the products shows Oceanographer to be more desirable (in terms of his values) than Pilot or Landscape Architect (Katz, 1974–1981).

each value (e.g., the titles included Buckster, Benefician, Autonomist, Tenurist, Charismat, and the like). These were paired at random for the client's initial choice. Having made a choice, the client encountered a series of problems or opportunities, each featuring a different value. For example, the fictitious occupation chosen might be deficient in independence; or there might be an offer to move to an occupation providing higher income. The decision to stay or switch indicated the relative importance, to this student, of the two competing values in a given context.

At the end of each "round" of the game, the client saw a display in the form of a balance scale, showing which values had "outweighed" which others. Another display pointed out any inconsistencies between the client's previous weighting of values and the preferences indicated in the course of the game. The game was intended to stimulate further thinking about values, and the client was not held accountable for inconsistencies. Clients' own evaluations of their inconsistencies showed up when (after completing as many rounds of the game as they wished) they reweighted their values. A new constraint was introduced at this point: to distribute a fixed sum (40 points) among the 10 values. This constraint reflects the sad truth that one can rarely expect to get all of everything desired in the real world. Hard choices must be made – to give up a little on one value in order to retain more on a value of greater importance. The result of the adjustment was a profile of the client's "examined values."

Unlike the original model, however, the weights applied to the values in general; the step of applying them to scaled "magnitudes" had been cut. The scales of "magnitude" appeared as specifications made by clients in structured search but then disappeared again in the formal decision analysis. Deleting the "Magnitude" column and its associated activities in Exhibit G from Exhibit H was a simplification that did save a significant amount of time, but at a cost – particularly in dealing with values that do not "scale" for all clients, like Leadership and Leisure. Ah, there, Whitehead!

To allow for a band-width in the components of the Desirability Sums – that is, the client's values weights and the system's ratings of occupational attributes – a difference of 10 points between Desirability Sums was estimated to be significant. Thus, the sum for Oceanographer was interpreted as significantly higher than the sum for either of the other two occupations in the illustration; the sums for Pilot and Landscape Architect were treated as a tie.

Another deletion in applying the original model to SIGI is the decimal for "probability" by which the "Sum of Value Returns" or "Desirability Sum" was multiplied to give "Expected Value" or utility. As indicated before, these probabilities could be calculated with some confidence for educational options, but not for occupations. Instead, students were given an opportunity to review (from the Planning section) the steps required to enter each occupation and (from the Prediction section) their chances of success in preparatory programs. They could also consider (from direct access) the outlook for each occupation – that is, the competition for jobs. They were asked to combine these components to rank the three occupations in probability of successful entry.

Decision rules were then used to guide them in balancing the rank orders of rewards and risks for the three occupations. An occupation with both the highest desirability (by 10 points or more) and highest probability would clearly have a strong claim on choice; but if an occupation with the highest desirability did not have the highest probability, other decision rules would be invoked, asking in effect: Is the high reward offered by one occupation worth the extra risk? Or does the comfort of choosing the highest probability compensate for the lower desirability of another occupation? Or is an occupation with neither the lowest desirability nor the lowest probability a good compromise? Clients' choices were usually consistent with an expected utility model.

Thus, in SIGI, students were guided through a process in which they combined elements of data in a systematic but less stringently numerical way. Many students appeared more comfortable with this leeway than with the apparent numerical precision of the original model. As developers, we too were uncomfortable with the sense that the strictly numerical model, especially for probabilities, might be deceptively precise. While rank order on Desirability was still obtained directly from numerical computations, we could not calculate Probability in any way that would improve on the students' derivation of rank orders from interpretations and combinations of Prediction, Planning, and Outlook data. So the structure of the Strategy section of SIGI made sure that clients "touched all the bases" – took all relevant data into account, explored alternative strategies for choice, and evaluated each in terms of their own values and tolerance for risk. This approach appeared to give clients more sense of control and mastery of the decision-making process than did a more mechanical and strictly numerical algorithm.

Further Modification for SIGI PLUS

The model has since undergone additional changes in SIGI PLUS to help the client engage even more actively in the decision analysis. In developing a system for the general adult population, and for secondary schools as well as colleges, there was a fear that the remaining numerical tables and operations might seem forbidding. Furthermore, the use of newly available color and graphic capabilities seemed likely to make the formal decision analysis easier and more attractive. In short, there was the inevitable urge to simplify.

One significant change was in the values weighting scale. In place of the scale ranging from 0 (no importance) to 8 (highest importance), SIGI PLUS uses a categorical scale: At the highest level is Essential; the other levels are Very Important, Desirable, and Not Important. Clients are permitted to weight no more than 3 values as Essential, and no more than 5 as higher than Desirable. A weight of Essential has "veto power": An occupation lacking in that value cannot qualify for further consideration no matter how attractive its other attributes may be. So in the Deciding section, the occupations designated by the client are first examined to see whether they satisfy all the values weighted Essential. If not, they are eliminated.

In the Strategy section of SIGI, *all* the values entered into the decision analysis. The Desirability Sum (the sum of products of weights and ratings for each occupation) thus allowed high satisfaction of less important values to compensate, to some extent, for lower satisfaction of more important values. Deciding in SIGI PLUS, however, uses only the five values that the client judges to be most important. This (arguable) tactic responds to the finding, mentioned earlier in this chapter, that people generally prefer to simplify – to make decisions on a smaller set of variables. It can also speed up the analysis, countering the old problem of requiring too much time. Indeed, SIGI PLUS is "layered": Clients can take a quick route through the system or can uncover additional layers of information, interactions, definitions, and instructions.

So in Deciding clients can quickly make a summary judgment (especially useful if they include their current occupation in the analysis) of the Desirability or "Rewards" of each occupation on a 4-point scale (Poor, Fair, Good, Excellent), indicating how well it satisfies their values, involves their preferred fields of knowledge, and includes activities they enjoy. Or in a closer scrutiny, for each occupation they can first see a display in which their five most important values are listed along with an adjacent column showing the corresponding attributes of the occupation. If the occupation satisfies their Essential values (otherwise, it must be dropped from consideration), they rate it on the 4-point scale for satisfaction of values. Through consideration of analogous displays, clients then make similar evaluations of the extent to which their preferred fields of knowledge and activities, respectively (no more than two each), are matched by corresponding attributes of the occupation. Their ratings (Poor, Fair, Good, Excellent) on all three domains (values, fields of knowledge, activities) are then displayed, and the client rates the overall Rewards of the occupation on the same scale. This rating determines the position of the occupation on the vertical axis of the Deciding Square (colored red for Poor, green for Excellent, and yellow for intermediate levels).

An analogous routine governs the rating of each occupation on "Risks," or "Chances" of success in entering the occupation. Clients may quickly make a summary rating of Poor, Fair, Good, or Excellent based on their chances of success in (a) performing the work tasks (in reference to their Skills), (b) completing the necessary preparation, and (c) getting a job (considering employment outlook for the occupation). Or, again, they can take the longer course: Compare their skills with a display of skills required in the occupation and rate the correspondence on the same scale; and similarly rate their chances of completing the preparation, displayed in overview form, and their chances of finding employment, from a display of outlook for the occupation. The ratings on all three components of Chances (skills, preparation, outlook) are then displayed, and the client makes an overall rating of Poor, Fair, Good, or Excellent. This rating determines the position of the occupation on the horizontal axis of the Deciding Square (also color-coded).

Eventually, all three occupations are placed in the Deciding Square (Exhibit I). The client is then asked: "Based on everything you know, which occupation looks like your best choice?" One of the options is, "I can't decide," and this response is followed by further inquiry and interaction to resolve the difficulty and (usually) to return to the question. When an occupation is chosen as "best," the system responds in a way consistent with the EU model, based on a latent computation attributing a numerical rating to each cell of the Deciding Square. This computation assumes that rewards and chances should receive equal emphasis, in keeping with the concept of the Square (since its two dimensions are symmetrical). Of course, that assumption is not appropriate for all clients: In their choices, some will attend more to the payoff represented by the Rewards axis, while others will prefer to "play it safe" in terms of the Chances axis. Special messages are used to acknowledge that either emphasis is legitimate, provided that the client has considered both kinds of information. If

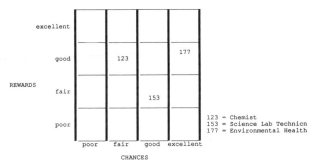

Exhibit I Deciding Square

a chosen occupation does not excel on either dimension but represents an acceptable compromise, a display merely notes that the choice is as good as any other on the Square. If a client chooses the "wrong" occupation according to EU theory, the message is that "it doesn't look like the best choice on this Square." The client may then select one of two reasons: "I simply made a mistake," which recycles the choice display, or "The Square doesn't tell the whole story." The latter leads to a message acknowledging limitations of Deciding, but also indicating the implications of emphasis on rewards or chances inherent in the choice. In all, messages are drawn from a repertory of 23 possible displays, according to a set of precisely defined rules governing all possible permutations of relative positions of the three occupations in the Square.

In summary, the following features of decision analysis in SIGI PLUS illustrate the direction of change:

1. It depends on graphic rather than numeric displays; graphics and color provide more visual appeal and enable clients to use perceptual faculties in comparing occupations.

2. It employs only the five "most important" values, reducing the number of variables to be considered.

3. Aside from the "veto power" exercised by Essential values, differences in the weights assigned to the five "most important" values are not explicitly emphasized (or even translated into numbers).

4. Attributes associated with "Rewards" of occupations are described rather than rated by the system; from the descriptions (aligned with values, fields of knowledge, and activities designated by clients), clients make evaluative ratings (Poor, Fair, Good, or Excellent).

5. Clients combine their ratings of these three distinct aspects of "Rewards" into a single overall rating, subjectively (for example, they decide themselves whether an occupation they have rated "Good" on two aspects and "Fair" on one should be called "Good" or "Fair").

6. A similar procedure having been followed in rating occupations on three aspects of "Chances" (skills, preparation, outlook) and then combining the ratings into an over-all evaluation, the occupations are positioned on a Deciding Square to show at a glance their relative positions on both dimensions, Rewards and Chances.

7. Although clients compare the occupations visually rather than numerically, a latent computation in the system assigns a numerical equivalent (not displayed) to each cell; decision rules based on these cell numbers and the configuration of positions in the square generate a repertory of possible messages responsive to the client's choice.

8. The interaction is "layered" so that clients can take a "short route" to an evaluation when they already have enough knowledge to rate an

ipation on an aspect of Rewards or Chances; or they can elect a longer route to acquire or solidify their knowledge before rating.

This SIGI PLUS decision analysis appears simpler, less formal, and less rigidly numerical than its predecessors. In the division of labor between client and computer, it seems to move further toward reliance on the client's judgments. At each stage, the client's judgments may seem subjective and even, to some extent, impressionistic. For example, it would have been easy to convert ratings on aspects of Rewards and Chances into numbers and use the median for each over-all rating. Thus, an occupation rated "Good" on two aspects of Rewards and "Fair" on the third would automatically be assigned an overall rating of "Good." But leaving this judgment to clients allows them to decide how important each aspect is in relation to the others. In some cases, one "Fair" may outweigh two "Goods," or ratings of "Excellent," "Good," and "Poor" might be combined to yield an over-all rating of "Excellent." As an alternative, having the client first assign a weight to show the importance of each aspect would have enabled the system to take over the task of combining the ratings. But the question is whether such a procedure would add useful knowledge. Or—in a context that carefully defines and describes all the relevant variables and sets the judgments in a structure and sequence invoking systematic analysis of information and synthesis of evaluations—would it be redundant? Would it be worth the cost of added time and complexity? Even though clients would really control the output by virtue of the weights they might have put in, should a loss of *visible* control and mastery be risked? Is it not better to leave the trade-offs in a decision to be defined by the system but resolved overtly by the client? Such questions are open to experimental research, of course, and we hope to investigate them and similar questions before another revision of the Deciding section of SIGI PLUS.

Common Principles

Despite all the changes noted in the form of the decision analysis model for SIGI PLUS, the basic concepts of the earlier models endure. In all the systems, clients first explore and examine what they want. They are helped to identify a manageable number of occupations that offer opportunities to get what they want. They compare the most promising occupations both on possible rewards and satisfactions and on probabilities of entry and success. They get closure on an informed and rational choice that may be more or less firm or tentative—perhaps a hypothesis awaiting confirmation or revision from outcomes at early milestones. In short,

Deciding in SIGI PLUS, like the earlier models of decision analys
people who face the problem of choice under uncertainty t(
occupations in terms of desirability and likelihood of attainment. Then it
helps them synthesize these two components and gain closure on a choice.
Most important, it helps them develop competence in the process of career
decision making. These accomplishments should make Deciding the "jewel
in the crown" of SIGI PLUS.

And yet. Although all sections of SIGI PLUS have been deemed by
clients to be comprehensible, helpful, and popular, in a tryout by a limited
sample Deciding was used a little less often than some of the other sections
and was rated a little less understandable and helpful. More research and
development are needed to pinpoint the difficulties. One obvious concern
is the length of the system and the number of sections. If people spend a lot
of time on Self-Assessment, Search, Information, Skills, and Preparing,
they may simply not reach Deciding or feel rushed when they do. Or they
may feel satisfied to get a manageable number of occupations for consideration.

It would be interesting, for comparison, to "begin at the end" (proposed
as an alternative in the original model); that is, we might start the system
with a blank Deciding Square and ask clients to place in it occupations they
are considering—*before* they use any other sections of the system. If the
concept of combining Rewards and Chances is implanted first, then the
other sections may be seen as a source for the substantial knowledge and
competence needed to position occupations appropriately in the Square.
This procedure would at least ensure that clients see how the other
operations feed into Deciding. Then, as in I. A. Richards's (1968) doctrine
of "feedforward," in its end will be the beginning. The circuit through the
other sections for self-appraisal and information will bring them "home"
again, where feedforward and feedback meet in an informed and reasoned
decision that may corroborate or replace the initial choice.

In both SIGI and SIGI PLUS, the opportunity to recycle through the
CDM process in the light of new information emphasizes that a choice is
not necessarily forever. A client need not be locked, with no chance of
release, into a decision that turns sour. Unhappiness with a decision
signals a disequilibrium, a time to re-engage in CDM. But perhaps worse
than such a decision is floating in a state of perseverant indecision when a
decision is called for. Even a decision that begins to look bad gives
information: Why isn't it working out? What has gone wrong? Was
assessment of values, interests, or skills mistaken? Was information about
options wrong or misleading? Were there unexpected changes in self or in
options? What should be done differently now? Answering these questions
can lead to a new and presumably better decision. But perpetual indecision

is less likely to lead to a revised assessment or new information, to stimulate useful questions, or to provide guidelines for improving CDM. In short, the CDM process should lead to a decision.

In any case, whatever the specific form of the decision analysis, the basic principles provide a structure or pattern for decision making without prescribing the decision itself. There is still art as well as science in this guidance. "Art," said Whitehead, "is the imposing of a pattern on experience, and our aesthetic enjoyment is recognition of the pattern." Such re-cognition leads not just to art appreciation but to mastery in use of the structure. Mastery has a liberating effect. It enables people to transcend the apparent limitations of the pattern, just as mastering the structure of a language or any other art or science frees people to become more expressive and creative in its use, to capitalize on their competence – in this case, to make career decisions wisely and perhaps even to develop wisdom in decision making.

DECISIONS INTO ACTIONS

If it were done when 'tis done, then 'twere well it were done quickly.
(*Macbeth*, I, 7, 1)

Deciding may be the climax of the CDM drama, but after the climax comes the denouement. Decisions have consequences. A choice of an occupation is rarely self-fulfilling. To enter it successfully requires actions and more choices. Three sections of SIGI PLUS are designed to help clients take appropriate action, to get from where they are to where they want to be.

Preparing

The Preparing section is useful both before and after Deciding. The previous section has already shown how clients can use information from Preparing in Deciding: They judge their chances of success in completing the preparation for a given occupation and feed this judgment (along with similar judgments based on skill requirements and outlook) into their over-all rating of chances of success in entering the occupation. More detail, however, is available for planning how to prepare for an occupation that has been chosen.

Preparation for some occupations is straightforward and universal (e.g., actuary, physician, and each of the engineering occupations). For many others, there are multiple pathways, with various permutations of education, training, and work experience. The "best" route may depend partly on clients' current credentials, partly on what they know and can do, partly on their own preferences, and partly on employers' tendencies to accept one path or another. Preparing tries to help clients choose the route that is best for them.

Preparing in SIGI PLUS evolved from the Planning section in SIGI. Originally, it may be recalled, because SIGI was designed primarily for use by college students, the Planning section was "tailored" for each institution. Students saw the pathways for entering an occupation, followed by a specific semester-by-semester course of studies recommended at their own college (along with other particular information, such as financial aid). Later, a "universal" Planning section was developed for use at colleges that did not provide local information. This section displayed generic education and training *programs* for each occupation; for each program, sequences of common *subjects;* for each subject, a *description* written in nontechnical language. These generic displays replaced the course titles and numbers that were specific to each college.

The Preparing section in SIGI PLUS built on this work. For SIGI PLUS, however, the assumption could not be made that clients were enrolled in college. Clients in the general adult population might represent a wide range in previous education, training, and work experience. So it was necessary to design Preparing to help any client, regardless of background and current status, to prepare as efficiently as possible for entry into a chosen occupation. (For most of the following description, acknowledgment is due to Laurence Shatkin, who was mainly responsible for developing this section of SIGI PLUS; Norris et al., 1985).

The purpose of Preparing may be viewed as finding the unknown quantity in an equation: the client's current education, training, and experience plus x equals total preparation needed. The unknown quantity, "x," represents the gap the client will have to bridge. The more education, training, and experience the client has that are relevant for entry into the occupation, the smaller "x" becomes.

An early version of Preparing tried to identify "x" by working from the "supply" side of the equation; that is, it started by assessing the client's status from past education, training, and experience. Unfortunately, the script of menus and submenus became long, tedious, and complicated even before reaching an adequate level of detail (e.g., to determine what portion of a client's previous education is relevant for a different field of study; to equate "units" of academic and work experience; to evaluate the extent to which experience in one occupation might qualify as preparatory for another). In addition, the "supply" side approach required consideration of a critical set of resources: time, money, talents, and commitment. Even a small amount of additional preparation may make demands on these resources. Of course, the system could take stock of these resources (again a lengthy process), but it would also have to manage their interactions with "x." It seems unlikely that a computerized system can manage this "supply" side approach adequately without natural language input – the cost of which the market cannot presently support.

Therefore, to simplify (that word again), the emphasis in Preparing was shifted to the "demand" side of the equation. Clients first see an overview outlining what preparation is typically required (or recommended) for entry into an occupation. They then see detailed and specific descriptions of (a) typical education and training programs (what they need to *know*) and (b) typical work tasks (what they need to be able to *do*). The former, as in the SIGI Planning section, was layered into programs, subjects, and descriptions. The latter was also layered: For each occupation, clients see a list of work tasks; then, for each task they can call in a paragraph of description. After seeing both aspects of the "demand" side of the equation, clients are guided through a workout of the "supply" side for themselves.

First, they see a graphic representation of the pathway to the chosen occupation; from what they have just seen of the preparation required, they are asked to estimate, in general terms, how far they have already traveled: "I've barely started," "I've come part of the way," or "I'm almost there." According to the response, the display colors in a portion of the pathway; the remaining uncolored portion represents the preparation that lies ahead. They are then asked to make a tentative rating of their chances of completing the preparation.

Next, clients are questioned on their resources for completing the preparation: time, money, ability to handle the difficulties, and motivation. They rate themselves on each of these resources and have the option of changing their earlier tentative estimate of their chances of completing the preparation. The system responds to this reconsidered estimate, either confirming it as consistent or challenging it as inconsistent with their ratings on the four resources. Clients who are challenged can decide for themselves whether they want to keep the rating or change it. The final ratings are stored in memory and retrieved in Deciding for use as one component in the evaluation of "Chances." The system also displays messages specifically designed to recognize the resources in which clients may consider themselves deficient and to offer guidance (when possible) in overcoming perceived barriers. For example, clients who indicate a problem with time are referred to the Coping section, which provides many suggestions for improving time management.

Coping

Indeed, the Coping section crept into SIGI PLUS as a small supplement to Preparing. It was prompted by the special needs of adults in transition, whether entering an occupation, re-entering the labor force after having left it for a while, or changing from one occupation to another. Somehow, it did not seem enough to leave them with a road map showing the route to an occupation while ignoring the problems frequently encountered in traveling the road. Interviews with adults in transition left the developers with a keen sense of practical problems that loomed large to them. Besides such concerns as time and money (already mentioned), people worried about arranging care for children or elderly parents, getting credit for what they knew, trying to compete after an absence from the job market, and so on. Penelope Schott, who was mainly responsible for the development of the Coping section (Norris et al., 1985), found serious gaps in the materials available to help people deal with these practical concerns. Many of the publications take a "You can be anything" tone. They pay little heed to real-world obstacles and worries. "Indeed, the closest to practical help has been an almost obsessive concern with what clothes you should wear to work" (ibid.). Clearly, real information was needed – the kind of concise, pointed, useful information that SIGI PLUS offers in other areas. Eventually, the small supplement grew until it threatened to equal the rest of the Preparing section. At that point, Coping was removed from Preparing and developed as a separate section.

Like the Information section, the format of Coping provides a menu of questions, 21 in this case, under 6 general headings. Each of these generates a submenu of up to 8 more specific questions or topics. For example, under the heading of Money, the question "Can I get paid for Preparing?" allows the client to follow with any of these topics: (a) entry-level jobs, (b) educational benefits and tuition aid, (c) company training programs, (d) government training programs, (e) apprenticeships, (f) internships, (g) uniformed services (nonmilitary), (h) armed Forces. For many questions or topics several layers of information are available; clients can pursue a topic in more or less detail, according to their need or interest.

In addition to providing generic information, Coping – like Information – allows the site manager to add local information. This appears to the client as a follow-on screen after the display of generic SIGI PLUS information. Thus, clients can get names, addresses, and phone numbers of local people and organizations that are able to help with the matter in question. Times and places of relevant workshops can also be posted on the local information screen. For example, under the major heading, Credit For What I Know, Coping describes criteria, procedures, and common methods for converting experiential learning into practical credit, and national sources for information. A local screen might indicate when and where tests for credit are given, what nearby institutions grant credit (and whom to write or call for more information), where the nearest external degree-granting institution is, and so on. Such local information, when put in by a conscientious site manager, can help ease clients over many apparent barriers. It would be interesting to know how widely and creatively the capability is used.

Without such local assistance, Coping often cannot provide complete solutions to practical concerns. But at least it does structure the main problems and offer an orderly approach to investigating possible solutions. When solutions are still not apparent, it may resort to a rudimentary counseling interaction. For example, the question "How can I find the time?" gives rise to a submenu of eight more specific questions, dealing with such topics as organization of time, avoiding interruptions, and so on. But inevitably the eighth is: "What if I've tried everything and still can't find the time?" The client is then asked to choose one of the following responses:

1. You don't really want to do it.
2. You would like to do it, but you aren't willing to pay the price.
3. Right now it truly is impossible.

At this point the system branches to gentle confrontational techniques appropriate to a counseling session.

It is probably clear that the impetus for Coping derived largely from the feminist movement insofar as it was directed toward the entry or re-entry of women into occupations. Many women about to re-enter the work force, enter it for the first time, or seek advancement in it were using SIGI. They seemed particularly vulnerable to the obstacles and worries that Coping addresses. It is fair to say that our awareness of their plight sensitized us to the fact that it was often shared by men just entering the work force or seeking advancement (often through further education or training). They too were beset with such problems as time, money, credit for experiential learning, and family responsibilities. So Coping, like the rest of SIGI and SIGI PLUS, is an equal opportunity section. It would be interesting to see to what extent Coping as a whole and each topic in it are used by each gender. At any rate, it does pay attention to common problems.

As Schott said: (Norris et al., 1985),

a crucial function of Coping is simple acknowledgment. Virtually anyone in career transition, especially a responsible adult, will experience some problems of logistics or nerve. But here in Coping what feels like a purely personal dilemma or secret inadequacy is shown to be common: After all, the computer wouldn't include it if you were the only one. Thus, the user's private concerns are legitimized – an important first step. Embarrassment, fear, or ignorance [is] sure to compound any problem; the simple act of stating that problem can become the beginning of its solution. Although the practical problem is still out there, this external validation may alleviate enough anxiety to help the user absorb and learn from the material in Coping.

Next Steps

There is no guarantee that clients who have worked assiduously through self-assessment, structured search, direct access to occupational information, skills and preparation required for occupations, decision analysis, and means of coping with practical concerns will achieve entry to the occupation of their choice. Beyond understanding, knowledge, and thought comes action. People can rarely depend on a seamless transition between completing preparation and getting the job they want. Getting a job in our country tends to be in the "free enterprise" tradition. The Next Steps section of SIGI PLUS is designed to give people a running start on appropriate actions.

Much of the initial work on Next Steps was undertaken as a doctoral dissertation by Susan Rogers. Hers was an ambitious agenda. It included summarizing what the client had done, developing an action plan, and writing a resume. For example, a series of "worksheets" developed for the client was to be compared with the relevant data in SIGI PLUS for the occupational goal. Whatever was required but absent from the worksheets was supposed to appear on a set of "to do" lists, such as skills to be developed, education or training to be completed, financial aid to be sought, and so on. The problem with this approach was that it tended to be redundant – rehashing much of the material in other sections of the system – and very long. Next Steps seemed to be a misnomer if it stretched out in time without much immediate forward progress. As Macbeth said, "Words to the heat of deeds too cold breath gives." So the total autobiographical review and comparison with the data base was dropped.

But Developing an Action Plan and Writing a Job-Hunting Resume survived and were incorporated in the current version of Next Steps. For the Action Plan, entry into the chosen occupation is broken down into component short-term goals with a next step for each one. For each goal there is a series of questions. The ones the client cannot answer appear as a list for further investigation and action. For example, one short-term goal is building a network of "contacts"; the relevant next step is to identify people who can help. Questions include: What friends, neighbors, relatives, or co-workers do the kind of work I want to do? Is there a local professional association, union, or other organization for people who do this kind of work? Are any workshops or classes on the subject offered locally? Can I do volunteer work in the field? Clients may ask to see a display of suggestions on how to start getting answers to each question.

After this screen, the site manager can again put in messages giving local information. Clients can thus get names, addresses, and telephone numbers of specific resources for help in their investigations.

The format for each of the six goals is identical except for the goal, "writing a resume." There, clients have the option of going into successively deeper levels of detail, including the nature and purposes of chronological and functional resume forms, with a number of practical suggestions and a sample for each.

Because the whole purpose of Next Steps is to move from decision to action, every print-out in this section includes the following "push":

The first place I should call is: _____ .
The phone number is: _____ .
When I'm going to call: _____ .

Any attempt to reach a long-term objective requires careful step-by-step planning and action. The message in Next Steps is to begin immediately. Although clients can go through SIGI PLUS in almost any order, many people will come to this section last. Its "do it now" emphasis provides an appropriate finale. Its trumpet charge calls on clients not to be passive "consumers" of guidance but active agents in the development of their careers.

This description of Next Steps completes the summary of the content of SIGI PLUS. So far, this book has tried to demonstrate that the strength of SIGI and SIGI PLUS depends heavily on their underlying theory. It has tried to describe, explain, and justify the premises, purposes, and rationale for the systems, particularly as compared with counterpropositions. It has examined related research and has shown how the premises, purposes, and rationale led to a model. This chapter has focused on the implementation of the functions in the model. It has shown how the content implied by the functions has been translated into an operating system. But there is more than content in this translation. One other notable feature of any operational system, although not independent of content, is its style.

STYLE AND DESIGN

Guidance for CDM is at least as much art as science. Style and design are the elements of a system that conspicuously partake more of art than of science. They are the most visible aspects of the system and should not require much explication. It is important, however, that the integrity of the logical progression from premises and purposes to rationale to model to content and design of a system not be violated. The art must not betray the science.

Obvious differences in style tend to be inherent in the various media used for guidance. Some tend to be relatively passive, like an occupational monograph filed in a cabinet; others, like a display on a bulletin board, are more visible; still others, like a counselor seeking out a student, are active. Some sources of information are vivid and memorable, like first-hand work experience in a slaughterhouse; others, like perusing the *DOT*, may seem dull and forgettable. Dramatization and exposition have different impacts. Pictures are different from words. Whether the same words are written or spoken may make a difference. Each medium of communication has its distinctive characteristics, inherent virtues and disadvantages, and each style of communication may encounter a responsive or resistant style in the person to whom it is addressed. Computerized guidance (CG) systems employ a medium that offers special opportunities and notable constraints.

Of course, stylistic variations within each medium may be as great as variations between media. A book may stimulate intense activity in a reader, who will be spurred to frame questions, seek answers, carry on an unvoiced dialogue; or a reader may be moved only to scan it dutifully, fulfilling an assignment to cover certain pages. CG systems also each have their own styles and design features; one of the most important elements in CG styles is interactivity between the user and the system.

Interactivity: A Historical Progression

A batch-processing system like the one Hull (1928) envisioned would be active but would seem to engender passivity in clients. They would not interact directly with the system (indeed, its processes would be invisible to them); they would only be recipients of the output. A step toward greater involvement of clients appeared in batch-processing systems for choice of a college: Typically, clients selected specifications for college region, size, curriculum, and the like on an answer-sheet form, mailed the form in, and then received by mail a list of colleges that presumably fit the specifications. The interval between the client's input and the system's output tended to limit the number of exchanges (usually to one) and dampened the sense of interaction. So most such systems have failed and have been replaced by systems that interact with the client in real time.

In most of the interactive systems, clients can see immediately the effects of a given specification or set of specifications and can then add, subtract, or change specifications to get a revised list of suggested options. This immediacy and flexibility make the search process for identifying options (such as occupations or colleges) highly visible. The client becomes an active participant and indeed a partner of the CG system. Among such systems, variations in degree of interactivity are a function of hardware, system design, and script writing.

Hardware

Many of the early CG systems used teletypewriter terminals. They are inexpensive but write slowly, and their style must be linear. Special formats and graphics are cumbersome and are rarely used. Cathode-ray tube (CRT) terminals, on the other hand, can write at speeds many times faster than teletypes and allow for graphics at various levels of sophistication; revisions and substitutions in text and graphics can be seen taking place on the screen, and elements of a display can be made to move from one part of the screen to another–in general, dynamic displays can be created. Principles from the visual arts can be used to direct, change, and focus a user's attention. Obviously, some systems have employed these CRT capabilities more effectively than others.

Paradoxically, the first operating version of SIGI did not do as much with visual effects as the earliest experimental version did. Limitations of CRT technology and the cost of mass storage at the time the prototype was developed forced us into ingenious coupling of two screens under one hood (see Figure 1): One screen was the display for a computer-controlled Kodak RA950 random-access slide projector; its adjacent "twin" was a

FIG. 1 The first SIGI terminal.

Sanders 720 CRT. In the space between the screens were two columns of six response buttons, each column governing one screen: Material on the screen for which a response was appropriate (such as options to be chosen by the user) were aligned with the buttons. Only active buttons for a given display of options were backlighted; the others remained dark. A green "Next" button at the top of the median strip lit up when no other response was appropriate. Thus, users, in effect, "pointed" to the option that they wanted—that is, pushed the backlighted button next to it. No keyboard was necessary, and users did not have to look away from the screen to find a response key. The displays could be presented on one screen at a time or both simultaneously. Carefully timed visual cues made the sequences easy to follow. The slides, of course, provided many advantages, including use of a variety of type faces, color, photographs, and other pictorial material, while the CRT provided dynamic displays, virtually simulating animation at times. This terminal eventually had to be abandoned in favor of off-the-shelf equipment, but it was fun while it lasted and taught us much about what a skilled and artistic programmer could do in the way of "choreographing" displays so that the user's attention was directed smoothly and efficiently from one point of focus to another.

So when we moved to a single monochrome state-of-the-art terminal for the operating system, we felt a bit of a comedown. SIGI PLUS, however, in the version developed for the IBM XT with a color monitor, made full use of color and "windowing," although the lack of a true graphics package prevented fully dynamic displays. Nevertheless, it is interesting that the use of "windows" (division of the screen into two or more clearly demarcated areas), one of which may carry a variable message, while another remains constant, lends itself to many of the display techniques in the old "twin-screen" SIGI terminal. It is worth noting that the "look and feel" of SIGI PLUS was enhanced by the expertise of a graphics design specialist in formatting displays. As costs of advanced graphics packages come within reach of developers and customers, system developers will find work for such experts.

Other display media may still be used to supplement a CRT. Under computer control, slides, filmstrips, audio, and video tapes or disks can be presented at appropriate points in the sequence of a guidance system, or they can be incorporated by reference, with activation in the hands of the user. For example, DISCOVER has offered a videodisk option. At present, the "high-tech" image and cost of the option raised a level of expectation that was disappointed when the content turned out to be only slides that picture people in each occupation. A cheap slide projector would have sufficed for such material. The obvious point of this venture, however, was to get acquainted with the technology in anticipation of the time when videodisks can be used to show people at work in each occupation and hear them talk about their work. The costs of making such videodisks are now too high for developer and customer. No doubt DISCOVER management counts on being well positioned when costs come down.

True multimedia work stations have been developed that make all the capabilities of those media available in one hardware and software package. They are still (at this writing) too costly for the budgets of educational institutions, but the history of computer technology encourages the belief that costs will eventually come down within reach.

System Design

A given configuration of hardware can be used in various ways. We mentioned that ECES users had to shuttle between keyboard, teletype, and filmstrip viewer, and that in the earliest version of SIGI users pressed backlighted pushbuttons to control the system. In recent years, microcomputers with the standard keyboard and CRT combination have become most common. Even so, response modes vary. A major distinction lies in the extent to which the dialogue between computer and user is self-contained. That is, all the necessary instructions, prompts, and cues may appear on the CRT in a "menu-driven" mode made popular by SIGI and SIGI PLUS. Some other CG systems, however, have required users to refer frequently to off-line material, such as function codes. This tends to interrupt the flow of the dialogue and, in some cases, discourages clients from using the system.

On the face of it, use of codes may appear to provide clients with more flexibility than responding to options (menus) displayed on the screen. At any given point in any CG system, however, there is a limited number of real options either available or logically desirable to the client. It is often easier for the client, and makes for a more fluent dialogue, if these are forthrightly specified on line – cuing the client to choose – than if the client is expected to search through the total range of codes off line, establish the population of options appropriate at this time, and from these select the one that is preferred. Indeed, such codes represent a gross and covert multiple-choice scheme. A refined and overt procedure is actually more flexible as well as more fluent, because it can tailor the options more specifically to the occasion.

A similar line of reasoning holds for attempts to process natural language inputs by users, of which ISVD was the only CG example. The ISVD objective in making this investment was to capitalize on clients' curiosity, give them the illusion of free-wheeling conversation, and enhance their "sense of agency." Laudable as these objectives are, the achievement was probably not worth the disproportionate share of resources consumed by this attempt. The latent multiple-choice array was still what counted. If the system asked the user, "What do you want to do today?" and the user replied, "Play basketball," the system would have to admit that basketball was not in its repertory and request the user to choose something else. It was not until the user said, "Choose a college," or "Get information about an occupation," or something else in the repertory that the system could be truly responsive. It would take less time, and be less frustrating to users, to list the options available at the outset. Furthermore, since natural language inputs can often be incomprehensible, the system must often seem to the user to be uncomprehending. Thus, it seems particularly costly to trade a forthright and transparent style for one that appears devious and opaque.

Interactivity in a CG system has many manifestations besides the modes in which the client communicates with the system. There are variations in the ways in which different components (e.g., appraisal, information, prediction, planning, decision making) of the system involve direct participation. Do they (at one extreme) unroll very much in linear fashion, inexorably, like a filmstrip or motion picture without much regard for individual clients' wishes? Or, at the other extreme, do they go any which way the client wants them to go, without regard for previous inputs or interactions? Or do they monitor and guide the client, giving reminders and suggestions but still allowing plenty of opportunity for branching within a logical structure? These three possibilities offer both different levels and different kinds of interactivity.

In SIGI, as has been pointed out, the sequence of sections for the novice was fixed. There was a logic to this progression that represented the logic of CDM, according to the SIGI model. But within each section there was almost no end to branches that could be taken; and after users had completed the sequence of sections, they became "initiates"–they were in full control, and could return to any section in any sequence. The aim was to foster diversity within unity. The model and structure of CDM were the same for all students, but the particular content might vary for every student. This unity in the model provided coherence in the interactions between components or sections of the system. (Interactivity can characterize not only the relationship between student and system but also the relationship between the parts of the system itself.) For example, the importance that students attached to various values in one section reappeared for use in other sections. Occupations that were retrieved in structured search were saved for consideration in direct access, planning, and strategy. Predictions of success in key courses interacted with plans for curriculum programs, and the overview from Planning was considered in estimating probabilities of success in Strategy. In this way, the design of the system itself provided visible bridges that carried users from one section to another. By contrast, in many other systems the connections take place only, if at all, in the minds of the users – or else only in the system, without close participation by the users. In SIGI, we tried to instruct the student in the topography of the components and the linkages between them, not just by means of a map but a guided exploration.

The clientele for SIGI PLUS, however, could not necessarily be expected to want to go through the entire system. Needs for this population are, as we have indicated, much more diverse. Some people might want to focus on only one section – perhaps seek answers to a few of the questions in Coping, perhaps look directly to Next Steps for help in preparing a resume. So the Introduction to SIGI PLUS provides a map of the system. Instead of bridges, the appropriate analogy might be a helicopter, by which clients can hover above any section, perhaps traverse it at high altitude to discern its main features – the woods, the roads, the buildings, perhaps descend to low altitude to examine a particular house or tree, perhaps put down and walk inside a house or scrutinize the leaves of a tree. Information and explanations can proceed from the macro to the micro level, at the user's wish. Thus, users can go once over lightly or get copious detail, according to their circumstances and inclinations. If they choose to omit some information at one point, they may take a suggestion to return to it later. This design seems appropriate for the general adult population. Do people understand it and can they use it to best effect? So far, it seems to have worked. We aspire, in further research, to probe more deeply into the differential effects of different designs.

In short, the design of SIGI PLUS includes the following features (paraphrased from Norris et al., 1985):

1. The sections cover all the functions of career decision making.
2. Each section can be used independently and in any sequence.
3. Information is carried between sections, as appropriate.
4. At any point in the system, there is easy exit and return.
5. The monitor (display screen) echoes and reacts to users' responses.
6. SIGI PLUS is highly interactive and provides continual branching; "page-turning" (reading screen after screen without doing anything) is kept to a minimum.
7. Frequent "layering" allows users to request deeper levels of detail.
8. Visual techniques are used to enliven and reinforce text: Colors are consistent within each section; related sections use the same set of colors; questions and response cues are highlighted.
9. Language is clear, familiar, simply structured, and economical.
10. "Back-up" allows users to go back and review a previous screen.
11. Users can readily get printouts of information or summaries.
12. At critical points, SIGI PLUS checks users' responses for consistency and provides appropriate messages.

13. SIGI PLUS suggests use of outside resources for reality checks and for additional information.

14. SIGI PLUS makes its procedures explicit; it avoids looking like a "black box."

The *hardware* and *software* represent a medium for communication. The *design features* indicate approaches to cope with some of the constraints and capitalize on some of the opportunities of the medium. But the medium does not begin to communicate until someone writes a *script* for it.

Script Writing

Writing for any medium is a distinctive art form. If, as McLuhan proclaimed, the medium is the message, the *distinctive* message conveyed to the script writer by the medium of computerized guidance is interactivity. There are other messages too, but they are common to other media. Since CG involves language, all the elements of prose style can be invoked: fluency, diction, clarity, flavor, syntax, and so on. But CG also requires particular writing skills. How, for example, does the writer fit the message to best advantage within certain limits of space? How choreograph the substitutions and movements of elements of a display on a CRT? How direct attention from one part of the screen to another, and then back – smoothly, quickly? How build up graphics and link them to text? How use multiple choice to convey the illusion of a dialogue? How handle even linear sequences to avoid the impression of page turning? There are tricks of the trade to be learned in answering these questions, and there are also differences in talents of writers that go beyond tricks.

Some writers perform these tasks with distinctive elegance and verve. Others are less conscious of the opportunities afforded or handle them with less imagination. Clients may not be conscious of the relative sophistication of a script. But they know whether it holds their interest or drops it, flows freely or sluggishly, grinds along monotonously or springs occasional variations (surprises!), talks with them or down to them, is clear or muddy, stimulates them or puts them to sleep. They can recognize good writing – or good design – without being thereby able to account for it.

Bad writing is easier to identify and explain. The computer medium seems to demand clarity and conciseness. Murkiness and prolixity are cardinal sins. Perhaps only a venial sin is the pretense of a homunculus in the machine – greeting clients with a cheery (but phony) heartiness, repeatedly addressing them by name, "personalizing" each message: "Hello, John, glad to see you." "Okay, John, let's go on." These vocatives ring false. A machine pretending to be a person seems no more tolerable than a

nding to be a machine. Honest machines are no less desirable
)eople.

ɔƈɾιρι writers for computerized guidance cannot digress or elaborate in
the manner of the preceding paragraphs. They have to get right to the
point. They have to be "perfectly clear." In writing scripts for SIGI and
SIGI PLUS, we have often labored over repeated revisions of the simplest
directions. We kept asking: Is there any way this direction or bit of
information can be misunderstood? Can we make it shorter with no loss of
clarity? Sometimes there was no substitute for trial and error and retrial.

There are several reasons for brevity of text. We were writing for
generations bred on visual and aural, not verbal, media. Television and
computer games made them impatient with strings of words on a screen.
The CRT itself is not reader friendly. Flicker, blurring, and glare were
particularly annoying in the early models, but long sessions still leave
readers feeling bleary-eyed. Users wearing bifocals have found particular
difficulty in establishing a comfortable posture in relation to the screen.
But above all, our approach to career guidance is to involve users as active
participants in the process of CDM. We want to get them thinking and
responding. We want to get them out of any passive mind set that expects
the system to make a decision for them. We want to get them into a
dialogue with this system of *interactive* guidance and information.
(Nothing is so fatal to a sense of dialogue as verbosity on one side.)
Eventually, we want them to become masters of the system, to learn how
to use it and play it as an instrument. So versatile writers may be
discursive in their books and journal articles; but when they write for an
interactive system, they must be clear and concise.

Finally, notwithstanding the headings of this section, design features
and style are not readily divisible, except for purposes of critical analysis,
into hardware, system design, and script writing. The smooth interaction
of these components (and I should not ignore the programming) produces
an effect that is greater than the sum of its parts. Hence, systems are not
readily differentiated by descriptions. Rather than just read about them,
one must use them and experience the stylistic distinctions at first hand.

This chapter, "Focus on Functions of a Guidance System," has attempted to suggest and illustrate the content and the design of SIGI and
its offspring, SIGI PLUS. It shows how the theory and model have been
translated into a specific treatment. It should also indicate that, while
some of the specifics have changed from year to year, the main principles
have endured. The next chapter raises explicitly the question: Is the
treatment good? In a way, all the preceding pages have been an indirect
response to that question. Now I try to deal more directly with the issues
involved in evaluation of a guidance system.

5

The Evaluation of a
Guidance System

*The meeting place between theory and experiment is one of
those dangerous intersections at which neither vehicle is
allowed to proceed till the other has gone by; the remarkable
thing is that traffic moves most freely only when both roads
are well-traveled.*

— Abraham Kaplan (1964)

"Does it work?" is the big question usually asked about a treatment of any
kind. ("Treatment" here includes all manner of resources, products, and
interventions in education.) In evaluating career guidance, a big question
like this is seen by many to call for a big answer in terms of career
outcomes. Some propose that the only outcomes of career guidance worth
measuring are long-term success and satisfaction attained in occupations.

BIG QUESTIONS AND LITTLE QUESTIONS

Precious few have tried to conduct long-term studies aimed at answering
such big questions. Longitudinal research is difficult and expensive. It is
difficult to keep track of people and collect data from them after a
considerable passage of time; to define trenchant criteria and develop
appropriate measures; to distinguish effects of the treatment from those of
other events and circumstances (". . . time and chance happeneth to them
all"; *Ecclesiates*, 9:11); and (a crucial question) to determine at what point
in careers to appraise success and satisfaction.

205

..er, for example, people of middle age who have worked success-
..ully in an occupation for some years, only to have their jobs suddenly
wiped out through no fault of theirs. If we survey them now, during a
period when they are unemployed and feel unsuccessful and dissatisfied,
can we conclude there has been a failure in their CDM and guidance? If so,
would we not have reached a different conclusion if the survey had been
made a year earlier? Abrupt changes in the job market are not uncommon,
and they are generally not predictable at long range. So to evaluate CDM
and guidance on the basis of a snapshot of a long-term outcome of decisions
is not only difficult – it is presumptuous. Tennyson wrote, "No man can be
more wise than destiny."

Must one, therefore, wait until careers have been concluded for one
to draw conclusions? Is it only on Judgment Day that criteria will be
sharply enough defined and measures sufficiently reliable and valid? Even
then, there is no assurance that the same treatment at a new time,
probably under new conditions, would produce a similar outcome. Besides,
the treatment (if it has survived) is likely to have changed by the time the
results are in. So in any case the findings of long-term evaluations tend to
be obsolete.

Tumin (1970) has called big questions like "Does the treatment increase
long-term success and satisfaction?" the "fool's questions – because they
are absolutely right to ask and impossible to answer as put." The question
of what should be evaluated cannot be divorced from the question of what
can be evaluated. To assume that the information in long-range career
outcomes that is valid for assessing CDM and guidance can be teased out
of the noise in which it is embedded puts an insupportable burden on our
methodologies. The lines connecting initial status and treatments, on the
one hand, and eventual outcomes, on the other, are almost impossible to
trace and disentangle.

Instead, evaluators typically focus on short-term outcomes, attempt to
break a big question into a series of subquestions, define each subquestion
in operational terms, generate new sets of "little" questions, sample from
the new sets of questions, and identify or develop relevant observations or
measures that are administered and interpreted according to conventions
that have become familiar in educational evaluation. Then the direction
must be reversed, in the hope that answers to little questions can eventually be assembled into ever larger fragments, leading ultimately to some
kind of answer to the big question: "Does it work?" (Katz, 1979).

But the big question usually involves constructs of considerable scope.
Cronbach (1969) pointed out that measures of specific behaviors may be
indicators, but not definers, of these constructs. It is the constructs, the
network of relations and characteristics, that are crucial to evaluation –
not a single specific incident of behavior.

Consider this illustration. Evaluators start with a big question: Doe particular treatment provide good career guidance to students? Then they try to define appropriate subquestions. At this point if they ask, as many have done, "Are students making wise decisions?" they are lost. This question leads them inexorably to make judgments about the content of students' choices. Typically, in the tradition of trait-and-factor theory, they compare the occupation chosen by each student with occupational titles derived from an interpretation of his or her scores on an interest inventory and a battery of aptitude tests. I hope that my discussions in previous chapters of the fallacies inherent in such use of these measures have thoroughly discredited this practice.

Fortunately, the question that has been asked more frequently in recent years is: "Are the students making their decisions wisely?" This is a useful step; it shifts the focus from evaluating the content of the decision – Have they made wise decisions? – to evaluating wisdom in the process of decision making (Katz, 1968). It is in this sense of wisdom that Tennyson's line is contradicted by the Latin motto, "Fato prudentia major" (Wisdom is stronger than fate).

Of course, this subquestion must also be sliced into many smaller pieces before it can be answered. No single piece suffices. A notable expert on evaluation, in association with other scientists (Cronbach et al., 1980), wrote: "instead of promoting single definitive studies that promise unquestionable guidance on a narrow issue of policy, evaluators should be contributing to the slow, continuous, cumulative understanding of a problem or an intervention"

For example, one reasonable query might be: Are students seeking occupational information? One of many ways in which students might seek occupational information is reading printed materials in files or a library. Aha! Now the evaluators have some behavior they can observe or measure. They can count the uses made of these materials, ask students about such use, test students on the information contained in them. But this kind of observation or measure does not tell us *by itself* whether students are making career decisions wisely and whether they are getting good guidance. Cannot positive results be obtained without affecting the outcome of real concern? For any single observation or measure, effects may be attributed to plausible alternatives to the treatment being evaluated. After all, students can be assigned to go to the library and told they will be tested on the occupational information materials filed or shelved there. So this indication that students are seeking information might, by itself, be no more valuable than, in E. L. Thorndike's phrase, boiling the thermometer to heat the house. Many little questions like this must be answered in order to make an inference about the big question.

Another problem in reviewing attempts to answer "little questions" is the ripple effect of interpretations of studies that measure such specific behaviors. By the time the report of the study gets cited, the specificity of the behavior and the measure that underlie the findings is often lost. A summary of the conclusions may be quoted and requoted: "A significant increase in information-seeking behavior of students contributed to an improvement of wisdom in decision making and is evidence of the efficacy of the guidance program." An indicator has now become a definer. The network of lines from specific measures to constructs has been short-circuited.

A Dilemma

Cronbach's distinction between "definers" and "indicators" of a construct is enlightening, but it leaves some difficulties. Constructs like wisdom, a sense of agency, competence in the process of career decision making, career maturity, and the like seem somewhat orotund. Behind the facade of such rubrics often lurks an amorphous fuzziness. When the constructs are translated into behaviors to be observed or questionnaire responses to be scored, they tend to provoke objections. For example, a widely used set of instruments that purport to measure facets of "career maturity" is the Career Maturity Inventory (Crites, 1973), which I examine in detail later in this chapter. Other instruments used with some frequency purport to measure "locus of control," "decidedness," and so on. Suffice it to say here that even those who subscribe to such constructs as criteria for evaluating guidance often find the specific measures irrelevant or trivial.

So the problem of demonstrating what has come to be called the "validity" of a guidance treatment leaves a dilemma. "Big questions" are difficult to define in operational terms. But chopping them up into many "little questions" may lose sight of the essential construct. On the one hand, no one wants to swamp an evaluative enterprise with meaningless rhetoric about goals and theories that offer no clues to measurement of people's progress in CDM. On the other hand, there is a reluctance to limit observations to trivial and low-level behaviors that seem, at best, only dimly and tortuously related to constructs and that might be directly coachable. We need a way of conceptualizing validity that will avoid the pitfalls at the extremes of what Tumin (1970) called "trivial precision and *apparently* rich ambiguity."

Furthermore, an important practical point is that effects cannot be observed until the treatment has been developed and used. But decisions about development and use must generally precede even preliminary tryouts and formative evaluations. Before a treatment can be tried out, it has to exist. Should not its development be guided by some concepts of "validity"–that is, based on some logic that emerges from analysis and synthesis of a body of research and thought? So to validate a par treatment, it is generally useful to consider other kinds of evidenc ... before there are outcomes to be observed and measured. Thus, "validity" comprises more than effects and outcomes of a treatment. It involves the concepts—the theories, rationales, and models—that underlie the treatment and shape the content and design of the treatment.

In short, we need a way to bring together definers and indicators, principles and behaviors, deductions and measures. Perhaps a model can be derived from the field of educational and psychological measurement.

ASPECTS OF VALIDITY

In the social and behavioral sciences, the concept of validity has been applied most formally and specifically to the evaluation of psychological and educational tests. *Standards* for such tests (American Psychological Association, American Educational Research Association, & National Council on Measurement in Education, 1985) define validity as "the appropriateness, meaningfulness, and usefulness of the specific inferences made from test scores. Test validation is the process of accumulating evidence to support such inferences." Through various editions, committees writing the *Standards* for tests have categorized and carefully defined (and redefined) types of evidence as *content-related, criterion-related,* and *construct-related.* The emphasis in many measurement texts on differentiation between these categories sometimes obscures the reminder that the types are not mutually exclusive: For example, evidence related to content or to criteria also contributes to understanding of constructs; in turn, the specification of content and the selection of criteria depend on constructs.

The prominence of the concept of validity in test evaluation has led to attempts to apply the term in other contexts. Thus, in career guidance the question of validity is often raised about resources, products, treatments, and interventions of various kinds, including publications of occupational information, computerized guidance and information systems (which are included with tests in the chapter on Counseling in the *Standards*), and counseling interviews. In many instances, the meaning of the question is rather fuzzy. Because the term *validity* has been virtually pre-empted as a "technical term" in the context of testing, its application to these other contexts is often awkward. The analogues of content- , criterion- , and construct-related evidence are not self-evident for transfer to a career guidance (or any other) resource, treatment, or intervention. Nevertheless, validity is too useful a concept and too good a word to be reserved exclusively for the realm of tests. What follows, therefore, is an attempt to define appropriate analogues and later apply them in a consideration of the validity of a computerized System of Interactive Guidance and Information. (Of course, the application of these analogues and related principles is not limited to one particular system; it should be equally appropriate for any career guidance treatment.)

The major dictionary definitions of "validity" include *strength, accuracy,* and *efficacy.* Each of these connotations of validity in the context of a career guidance resource or treatment requires a distinctive kind of evidence. *Strength* in a treatment can be defined as analogous to construct-related validation in the context of testing; *accuracy,* to content-related validation; and *efficacy,* to criterion-related validation.

Strength in this context can be taken to mean well founded, established on sound principles and clearly stated premises, supported by logic and evidence to form a coherent and well-integrated rationale – what has been called the tightness of the nomological net. In this sense, *strength* is a function of the theoretical structure on which a treatment is based. So to evaluate the *strength* of a particular system of career guidance, one must start with questions about its underlying theory – its premises, purposes, and rationale – or its lack thereof. Out of what set of beliefs about human nature, the world of work, and the aims of career guidance has the rationale for the system been derived? How do these premises and this rationale compare with counterpropositions? What domains of individual differences and occupational information have been defined for this system? How have they been justified? Along what dimensions has each domain been construed? What are the advantages of these constructs over other constructs? To what extent are the theory and rationale supported by a body of research? Has the rationale been reflected in a clearly expressed model of the system? More specifically, have these components of theory – and the progression from premises and purposes to rationale to model to design features – been stated explicitly? Are they coherent and internally consistent? Or has the system been built *ad hoc?* How does it compare with other approaches? From answers to these questions inferences can be drawn about the integrity of the system's structure, the *strength* of its constructs.

Accuracy, on the face of it, can be taken to refer to content: For example, are the purported statements of facts about occupations in the system of career guidance correct? But accuracy of facts is often difficult to determine. Absent some accepted standard like the platinum bar kept at the Bureau of Standards as the measure of a meter, the accuracy of one source cannot be ascertained by comparing it with another source. Consider a best case involving "hard" data: Suppose, for example, two sources give different "average" salary levels for an occupation. Which source is "correct"?

The only way to judge is to look at the *procedures* for data collection, analysis, and interpretation on which each statement is based. Do the sources refer to different time periods? Do they use a mean in one case and a median in the other? Do they include experienced workers only in one instance and beginners in the other? Usually, even allowing for such frequent sources of variation, differences remain. Then it is necessary to probe more deeply into many other *decisions, definitions,* and *rules* involved in the procedures. How comprehensively and defensibly have they been formulated and applied? Are the specifics of the system consistent with the model? Is the content derived from a proper application of the procedures? Is the chain from theory to content unbroken?

Occupational information is not just "there," prepackaged and ready to be plucked from a shelf and inserted into the system. It usually needs to be constructed from interpretations of raw data, which may appear in odd packets that must first be decomposed and then reconstituted.

Like content-related evidence for test validity, *accuracy* also refers to the adequacy of sampling from a universe of content for a defined purpose. In the beginning, one can assume that there is a universe of occupations and that there is a universe of facts about these occupations. Some of these occupations and facts have come under observation (according to what decisions and by application of what rules?). Observations are collected and organized as data (by what rules and definitions?). Data, in turn, are interpreted and transformed into information (what decisions, rules, and definitions govern such organizing features as intervals, scales, and categories?). So the accuracy of the information is judged by the nature of the systematic winnowing process. This process and particularly the decisions, rules, and definitions governing it are subjects for close scrutiny, critical analysis, and evaluative comparison with other resources. Then a crucial test of the application of the procedures would be whether independent analysts following the same decisions, rules, and definitions produce essentially the same information. Thus, *accuracy* of a guidance system is a function of the fidelity of its entire content to underlying constructs, as mediated (and judged) by the consistent application of explicit procedures.

Efficacy is evaluated by outcomes in relation to purposes. What are the consequences of use of the system? Does it accomplish what it was intended to do? Are there unintended side effects from interaction with the system?

To continue the progression just outlined (from universe to observation to data to information), information when filtered and absorbed by a user becomes knowledge, which usually feeds into decisions, plans, and actions. What do users learn and how do they behave as a result of interaction with the system? Do they become more competent in many facets of CDM? Are the effects generalized, or differentiated from one population of users to another? For what kinds of persons does use of the system result in what kinds of knowledge and behavior? Can effects of different parts of the system be isolated? How do the benefits and costs of this system compare with those of other treatments?

These questions are elements of the big question at the beginning of this chapter: "Does it work?" As indicated before, answers must be assembled from many studies undertaken at various times and places, with various populations, under various conditions. When such empirical evaluations have been completed, the interpretations of results feed back into a greater understanding of the treatment itself. They may support its constructs and augment its strength – or challenge its constructs and weaken its theoretical foundations, requiring reconstruction or abandonment.

Thus, this third segment of validation can be depicted as completing a triangle (Figure 2), formed sequentially. The base comprises inferences about strength – the structure of premises, theory, rationale, and model – evaluated in terms of logical integrity. The next leg turns to a characterization of accuracy – the formulation of procedures for applying the model – evaluated by the consistency of explicit decisions, definitions, and rules with the model for the system and by reproducibility of content from

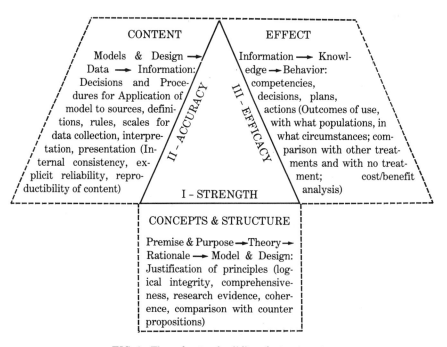

FIG. 2   Three facets of validity of a treatment.

the application of those explicit decisions, definitions, and rules. The triangle is closed by observations of efficacy—the outcomes of use—evaluated by the desirability of consequential behaviors, knowledge, and competencies. The progression then recycles: The interpretation of accumulated studies of outcomes may confirm, modify, or disconfirm components of theory. Ideally, the decision can then be made to maintain what has been developed, to make minor changes, to redo the entire development process (given time and money enough), or to dump it.

Note that accuracy and efficacy are founded on strength. Theory, rationale, and model should lead to procedures for development, which must precede use and outcomes. Furthermore, explicit purposes (an element of strength) help to define the scope and relevance of content (accuracy) and to develop criteria used in judging efficacy.

It follows that the three facets of validity, as just defined, are not to be construed as options for demonstrating validity: That is, it is not implied that one or another can be used at a developer's or an evaluator's discretion. Rather, they are presented as conveniently distinguishable aspects of a complex entity. With each facet in Figure 2 is associated a distinctive array of evidence and analyses that may be offered in support of a given treatment or intervention; criteria to be used in judging the evidence and analyses are also suggested (in parentheses). At various stages of development, tryout, use, and dissemination of a treatment, the focus may shift to one or another facet of validity. But at some point, when developers or advocates believe the treatment to have matured sufficiently, they should take responsibility for assembling and integrating the accumulated evidence in support of continued use of the treatment. This material, presented in such forums as professional publications and meetings, should then be subject to comparison with other treatments and to responsible criticism and rejoinder. Such an open marketplace of competing ideas can promote greater use of strong, accurate, and effective treatments, along with selective discard of others.

As indicated before, however, time is a critical factor. A treatment such as a career guidance system takes long to develop and must be in use for a considerable period before much evidence of efficacy becomes available. Meanwhile, decisions about development and decisions to use the system must be made on the basis of inferences of validity derived from critical analyses of strength and accuracy.

Previous Accounting for Strength and Accuracy

All the preceding chapters of this book are germane to the questions of *strength* and *accuracy* of SIGI and SIGI PLUS. A concise review of topics suggests their relevance.

   The first chapter, on career decision making, served to provide helpful handholds on the sometimes slippery substance of CDM. A number of issues in the concepts, content, and context of CDM were identified, defined, and examined. Included were such topics as the sorting of people into occupations; the components of CDM; dilemmas, domains, and options in CDM; definitions of work, position, job, occupation, and career; degrees of work centrality and commitment; the relative prominence of intrinsic and extrinsic values; distinctions between "vocation" and "employment"; problems in classifying or "clustering" occupations; similarities and differences in choice of occupation or job; linkages between individual characteristics and occupational attributes; the roles of education and training in CDM; the effects of labor market information on decisions; and factors in decisions about education and training.

   That chapter defined CDM in terms of information processing. It showed that career decision making is not a one-shot episode, not a single major determining choice of occupation followed by a few subsidiary decisions for adjustments along the way. Instead, decision making is a recurrent activity. At each stage, new options are confronted, and new information generally becomes available for processing. This information pertains to both means and ends. Feedback mechanisms suggest course corrections for a given destination; they may also suggest changes in destinations. So the content of career decisions varies from time to time. At each choice-point, decisions about goals can be reiterated or modified in response to the information and insights gained from experience and development, and these decisions can interact with decisions about immediate options. But as the *content* of decisions changes from one set of options to another (options embedded in such contexts as education, training, occupations, jobs, and positions), much remains constant in the *process* of career decision making.

   With this background in CDM, an early step in examining the strength, accuracy, and efficacy of a guidance system was to ask what needs it attempts to meet. An explicit identification of needs then serves to clarify the purposes of the system (an important element in its theory and rationale), the content that it should incorporate (relevant to judging accuracy), and the outcomes or results that are expected from its use (necessary for evaluating efficacy). A gross need was implied in the first chapter, which showed that CDM, unaided, is often characterized by ignorance. Many people at all ages make their choices unaware of most of the options that might be appropriate, with a paucity of information about the options and themselves, with little sense of linkages between the domains of self and options, unable to evaluate alternatives in a systematic and rational way, limited in their planning for preparation and action, frustrated in their attempts to manage practical problems, and with no grasp of a process of CDM. These conditions suggest a need for guidance. The second chapter is explicitly devoted to needs and considers in some detail the needs of individuals, groups, society, educational institutions, corporations, and system developers – and the possible tensions and synergies between these players in the CDM process. An important example is the apparent conflict between a "manpower" model, often used by government planners, and a "guidance" model. This conflict is resolved by identifying common themes in the processes by which national decisions in a democracy and individual career decisions are ideally made. In each case, the necessary condition is freedom, the open marketplace of ideas in which every voice can be heard, and competing values can be systematically defined, explored, and examined. To resolve this confrontation between competing values, whether on the national or individual scale, not only freedom but competence is required, to make order out of the rabble of impulses and bring them under the rule of reason. Then relevant information can be identified, interpreted, and brought to bear. Out of this interaction between values and information, it is possible to assess the utility of each option and then modulate utility with probabilities of success. Thus, the theory of guidance on which SIGI and SIGI PLUS are modeled is grounded in democratic principles.

Similarly, in the analysis of college needs, this model of guidance is shown to be consistent with the purposes of the liberal arts. It provides a centripetal force and unifying principles at a time of increased specialization and fragmentation in higher education. While the liberal arts contribute to an understanding of the genesis and development of the values of a culture, the guidance model complements them by contributing to individuals' understanding of their own values in that culture. Like the liberal arts, a coherent guidance system helps develop touchstones and competencies.

Some major needs of corporations are identified for the development of SIGI PLUS – for example, meeting affirmative action goals, retaining and recruiting able staff, filling lines of succession and replacement, improving morale and productivity, increasing satisfactions in existing positions, and assisting in outplacement.

Finally, an analysis of the needs of computerized system developers distinguishes between various systems in the context of their developers' professional backgrounds, organizational affiliations, and sources of funding. It emphasizes the research environment from which SIGI emerged.

Thus, the second chapter suggests the role of SIGI/SIGI PLUS in meeting the varied needs of many groups as well as individuals.

From this examination of needs, the argument progresses, in the third chapter, to rationales and models for career guidance, including an analysis of major approaches to guidance. Within this context comes a focus on the model and design for a particular guidance treatment, SIGI and its offspring, SIGI PLUS. It starts with a statement of premises and purposes, and concludes by comparing the model for SIGI with counterpropositions.

The fourth chapter focuses more closely and specifically on the design and functions of SIGI and SIGI PLUS. It explains and justifies such principles as commitment to self-understanding (e.g., versus behaviorism), selection of domains for self-assessment and dimensions for each domain, the importance of values, the stability of values, the structure of interests, the omission of interest inventories and of aptitude tests, the role of prediction and approaches to predicting chances of success, and the structure and role of skills. It deals also with the resolution of issues in occupational information: selecting occupational titles and topics and establishing and maintaining the quality of occupational information (matters that are most relevant to the facet of *accuracy*). Strategies for the guidance of decision making are examined, with some attention to formal decision analysis and its modifications in SIGI and SIGI PLUS. Procedures for translating decisions into plans and actions are described.

All in all, these preceding chapters provide the theoretical formulations underlying the development of SIGI and SIGI PLUS. These formulations derive some support from research and other evidence cited; this support leads to conclusiveness. Additional support has been derived from logical analysis; this makes for inclusiveness. One may provide depth; the other, breadth (Oppenheim, 1957).

Counterpropositions and competing approaches have been examined, and some comparisons have been made with other computerized guidance systems. It has been noted that other surviving systems seem generally to have been developed atheoretically. While decisions about procedures and content for SIGI and SIGI PLUS have emerged from a specific rationale noted in the preceding chapters, the rationales for other systems have had to be inferred from their procedures. Such inference assumes a logical connection between theory and practice. But, as has been illustrated, one encounters contradictions and conflicts within these *ad hoc* systems. An "implicit rationale" is an oxymoron. If developers know and state *why* they are doing something, they stand a better chance of avoiding anomalies in what they develop. Otherwise, incompatibilities may grow like weeds and choke out any beneficial activities.

On the other hand, a developer cannot afford to be smug about the depth and breadth of the theory in which a system is rooted. An explicit rationale is a necessary but not sufficient condition for worth. The system must be strong and accurate. But it must also make its way in the world by demonstrating effects on clients' behavior. So at long last we turn to the evaluation of *efficacy*.

EFFICACY: THE CRITERION PROBLEM

The most slippery issue in evaluating efficacy has long been recognized as the definition of criteria that are worth measuring and that can be measured. Katz (1966a) stated: "Like a fussy fisherman who cannot eat what he can catch and cannot catch what he can eat, the . . . evaluator has found angling for data on long-range outcomes overtaxes his patience and resources, while the short-term data that are easily netted often lack nourishment or flavor and may well be thrown back."

As was suggested earlier in this chapter, use of long-range, real-life outcomes as criteria asks "too much" of evaluation, while use of ongoing microactivities asks "too little." We need to identify criteria that (to complete the immortal categories of Goldilocks in the three bears' house) are "just right."

Perhaps it is appropriate to ask whether we should put a greater strain on the evaluation of guidance than on the evaluation of other educational programs and topics. In education generally, it has been possible to gain consensus on *competencies* that are regarded as desirable, and these have served as acceptable criteria of efficacy. For example, competencies in reading comprehension, mathematics, science, social studies, graphic arts, music, and so on are measured at appropriate stages in education and development without imposing the additional demand that they be traced to "real-life" outcomes much later. It may be we take too much for granted in all these areas. Or it may be that competency in CDM is less universally accepted as worthwhile in its own right and must go further to defend its legitimacy in the educational system. Still, recent emphasis on career development as a crucial component of education may allow us to feel more secure and less defensive about the prima facie value of competency in CDM. If so, the compulsion to troll for long-term real-life outcomes may be less urgent than it has seemed, while we can angle for bigger fish to fry than the microactivities that are so easily captured. In short, when a consensus has been reached that a given set of competencies is important for informed and rational career decision making, it should suffice to assess the state of that set of competencies at appropriate career stages.

For measures of such competencies, one tends to turn first to published tests and inventories. Probably the best known and most widely used is the Competence Test of the Career Maturity Inventory (Crites, 1973). Because of its popularity, it merits close examination.

Competence Test of the Career Maturity Inventory

This test is said to measure five competencies, with 20 items devoted to each scale: Self-Appraisal ("Knowing Yourself"); Occupational Information ("Knowing about Jobs"); Goal Selection ("Choosing a Job"); Planning ("Looking Ahead"); and Problem Solving ("What Should They Do?"). This array of competencies seems reasonable and should provoke no major disagreement in the profession. A thoughtful *Theory and Research Handbook* describes development of the measures and relates them to Crites's (and Super's) model of career maturity. Whatever criticisms are made here, this measure merits recognition for the care that has been taken to make the rationale explicit. Unfortunately, as an examination of the items demonstrates, these competencies are easier to identify than to measure. The following comments are derived mainly from a review (Katz, 1978b) in which I focused on the content and construction of each of the five scales in turn.

Knowing Yourself (Self-Appraisal) has nothing to do with the "self" who is taking the test. Like the other parts, it is all about hypothetical others. The task is to read a "description of a person" (four to seven lines) and select the appropriate appraisal, opinion, or action from a set of five options. The "description" is irrelevant, because the options form an invariant pattern, as illustrated by these options in a typical item:

A She has the makings of an astronomer; she should definitely go ahead with her plans.

B Before she decides about college, she should ask an astronomer's advice.

C Her interest in astronomy is strong enough, and she knows enough about it, to plan further study.

D She can't possibly decide if she has either aptitude or interest in astronomy from a backyard telescope.

E don't know

One option is always "don't know," as in E. Another involves dependence on other people, such as an appeal for help or advice, as in B. Of the remaining three items, one always represents a positive extreme, as in A; another, a negative extreme, as in D; and the third purports to be a balanced and moderate position, as in C, which is keyed correct.

It is apparent that recognition of this facet approach to the construction of options allows the test taker to choose the keyed response without even reading the stems (i.e., the introductory descriptions). Thus, these exercises called Knowing Yourself, or Self-Appraisal, not only fail to require knowledge of the self who is taking the test; they require no knowledge or appraisal of any person, real or hypothetical. Once the pattern has been perceived, they generally require only the ability to read the options well enough to distinguish the moderate statement from the two extreme statements, the dependent statement, and the "don't know." Perhaps it is just as well that the stems can be ignored, because they often provide flimsy data for the kinds of decisions involved. It is also just as well that finer discriminations between options are not required. Consider, for example, the "negative extreme" for one item: "On the one hand, he might make a good doctor, but on the other hand, maybe he should be a guitarist. It's hard to say which he would be better at." I find it difficult to distinguish the sense of this long-winded option from the more succinct "don't know."

The fact that the options deal with decisions rather than with self-appraisal suggests that this subtest is mislabeled not only in respect to "self" but also in respect to "appraisal." Indeed, it appears to attempt to tap the same kind of decision making or "problem solving" that the fifth subtest purports to measure (as described later).

Knowing about Jobs (Occupational Information) asks the test taker to match an occupational title to a description (five to eight lines) of work activities. The options are four occupational titles, plus "don't know." In this subtest, Roe's (1956) two-dimensional classification of occupations by level and field is used to determine the facets: One option is always the right level, wrong field; another is the right field, wrong level; and a third is in a different level and field from the keyed occupational title.

Selecting the appropriate occupational title to match a description may measure reading comprehension and knowledge of a particular selection of occupational titles. But this exercise is a very limited sample of the domain of occupational information and one of dubious utility for CDM. Competent decision makers need occupational information that is relevant to their own decisions; how would the ability to fit a title to a brief description help them in CDM? Perhaps whatever is measured here is thought to be correlated with more useful knowledge. However, cognitive abilities generally tend to be intercorrelated. One would like to see the items in each subtest represent as directly as possible the competency it purports to measure. In this case, the kinds of occupational information needed for informed and rational CDM include knowing which occupations may be worth considering in terms of the rewards and satisfactions they offer, the activities and conditions of work they involve, the education, training, and other investments they require, and their outlook, insofar as these attributes are related to the test taker's own values, interests, skills, and other resources.

Choosing a Job (Goal Selection) provides statements (five to seven lines) about hypothetical persons and asks the test taker to select the "best occupation" for each. Again, as in the previous subtest, the options reflect "field" and "level" facets; test takers presumably choose the option that best corresponds to inferences drawn from the stem about interests and abilities. This exercise exemplifies the trait-matching approach to guidance at its worst. It makes bland and unvalidated assumptions about relationships between the inferred traits (sometimes the inferences must be quite weak) and success and satisfaction in a set of occupations. I would say that for the information given in the stem the best response would almost invariably be the "don't know" option. For example, consider this item:

> Marty has many interests. He has been in the Debating Club for three years; he has written stories for the school newspaper; he has worked on the school yearbook; and, at the same time, he is one of the best students in the school. He is very good at words and can say exactly what he means. He is also quite persuasive and can often win people to his point of view. Which one of the following occupations would be the best for him?
>
> F   psychologist
> G   literary agent
> H   insurance agent
> J   lawyer
> K   don't know

The key is lawyer. Perhaps psychologist and literary agent were ruled out by the trait "can say exactly what he means"! (But doesn't that exclude lawyer too?)

Looking Ahead (Planning) presents three steps a hypothetical person must take to enter a given occupation and then asks the test taker to select the correct order of these three steps. The correct order is generally, first, take the appropriate training; second, get a job; third, pass an examination for certification or advancement. Again, one does not have to read the full stem or know the occupation involved, but can simply select the option that orders the three elements in this sequence. And again, one feels that the items may be good measures of test-taking savvy but miss the major components of the competency they purport to measure. The sequence of steps is not a decision that students have to make – it takes care of itself. Planning requires, more centrally, knowing what the steps are – for example, knowing *what kind* of education or training is appropriate for each occupation, how long it will take, how much it will cost, and where it can be obtained – not whether it comes before or after getting a job in the occupation!

What Should They Do? (Problem Solving) is very much like the first subtest (Knowing Yourself–Self-Appraisal). The stems are shorter, however–two sentences, presenting a thesis and an antithesis. Consider this example:

> John wants to be an engineer and has the ability to be one. *But*, his grades are poor, and he thinks he may not get into college. What should he do?
>
> A   Work harder and get better grades.
> B   Talk with his teachers or a counselor.
> C   Expect to get into college despite his grades, because he has the ability.
> D   Change his occupational choice to something else that doesn't require college.
> E   don't know

The facets represented by the options are described as A, compensation; B, consultation; C, denial; D, compliance; and E, the ubiquitous "don't know," said in this section of the *Inventory* to express confusion or indecisiveness. The key here is given as B (consultation).

We encounter an interesting phenomenon when we compare the keys for the items in this section of the *Inventory* with those for the so-called Knowing Yourself (Self-Appraisal) items in the first subtest. There, consultation was said to represent "dependence upon others" and was taken as a sign of "career immaturity" or incompetence. Here, it is taken as a sign of "career maturity" or competence! Even on the occasions when the consultation option is not the key, one must often quarrel with the option keyed correct on grounds of internal inconsistency. For example, in one instance the keyed option violates the very facets of level and field that were used as a criterion in the subtests Knowing about Jobs (Occupational Information) and Choosing a Job (Goal Selection):

> Betty wants to be a lawyer. *But*, her guidance tests indicate that she does not have enough ability. What should she do?
>
> F   Get married.
> G   Go into law anyway; tests can be wrong.
> H   Increase her ability to be a lawyer.
> J   Enter a related field at a lower level, like legal secretary.
> K   don't know

The key is J. Obviously, there is no reason, in terms of the principles expressed in this book, to accept this response as the correct one: Legal secretary is not likely to provide experiences, rewards, and satisfactions similar to those of lawyer. But even (and especially) by the standards invoked in the other two aforementioned subtests, this keyed response is out of bounds. According to the two-dimensional classification (after Roe) in the *Handbook* for the test, lawyer is Level 1, Field 7 in the matrix; secretary is Level 4, Field 3!

Moreover, even if one were inclined to accept dogmatic judgments, like the one illustrated, about the appropriateness of the choices keyed correct in the Goal Selection items, one would still stumble on the point I emphasized earlier: In a recent study (Westbrook, Sanford, & Donnelly, 1989), no relationship was found between the scores on the Goal Selection test and scores on a measure of "appropriateness of career choices." That is, this test involving a student's decisions about hypothetical others is unrelated to a measure of appropriateness of the student's own decisions.

A final point must be made about the "career maturity" construct that serves as an important element of the theoretical foundation of the test. Even though items were selected on the basis of a monotonic curve increasing with grade, the 8th-grade means for four of the five competence subtests were higher than the 9th-grade means in the standardization sample. Indeed, the 8th-grade mean was also higher than the 10th-grade mean on the last subtest (Problem Solving). So the data fail to provide persuasive support for the construct of career maturity (which I think has been as troublesome to the field of CDM as the Intelligence Quotient has been to education and measurement).

In summary, although a great deal of thought and care have gone into the development of the Competence Test, it cannot be recommended as a measure of competencies involved in CDM. This close attention to the CMI, however, should not be misunderstood. I have singled it out not because it is the worst case, but because it is well known and widely used, and its aims and rationale are better articulated than other published measures of competence in CDM, most of which warrant even more severe criticism.

It is understandable that the CMI and a hodgepodge of other standardized criterion measures – of so-called career maturity and career development, of locus of control, of decidedness, and the like – have been used in previous studies of status of students or efficacy of treatments. Many of these studies have been done by graduate students, who appreciate the "credentials" of such published tests, inventories, and questionnaires. It is a great temptation for a graduate student under pressure of writing a dissertation to want to take something off the shelf, an instrument that seems to have a ring of authority to it, with a manual, a publisher, and citations of supporting research. But I must state candidly that I have seen no standardized criterion measure in this field that stands up well to critical scrutiny.

This opinion is not sour grapes: Evaluators have generally reported "high marks" for SIGI/SIGI PLUS on such measures. For example, Salters (1984) and Grant (1985) found that SIGI significantly increased "decidedness" and decreased "undecidedness"; Pyle (1976) reported that use of SIGI resulted in significantly higher scores on the CMI Attitude Scale than either group counseling or no intervention; Hafer (1987) found that SIGI PLUS was more effective in reducing career indecision than either the Strong–Campbell Interest Inventory or Holland's Self-Directed Search.

Nor do I limit my criticism to the work of others. My colleagues and I have often labored in these vineyards. For example, we have developed tests, interviews, and questionnaires for evaluating the efficacy of a guidance text and workbook (Gribbons, 1960; Shimberg & Katz, 1962), of SIGI (Chapman et al., 1977; Katz, 1980), and SIGI PLUS (Norris et al., 1985); we have constructed a diagnostic measure of CDM, called Simulated Occupational Choice (Katz et al., 1976, 1978), and tests for a comparative evaluation of the effectiveness of career information systems (Chapman & Katz, 1982, 1983). The fruit of the vines has left our thirst for good measures of competencies still unslaked. Nevertheless, a quick look at some of our efforts may be useful in illustrating what has been done and what problems remain to be solved. The first example is Simulated Occupational Choice (mentioned previously in describing our research on the structure of values). Then, in keeping with the focus of this book, the second and third examples are from the field tests and initial evaluations (intended to be more formative than summative) of SIGI and SIGI PLUS.

Simulated Occupational Choice

In the course of criticizing instruments like the Competence Test of the Career Maturity Inventory, I have pointed out that they fail to serve as work samples of CDM because (among other reasons) they do not engage each person in his or her own identity. That is, none of them involves people in the CDM process as themselves, making their own choices. None evokes or observes behavior based on their own values, interests, skills, and resources. None involves a dynamic logic and sequence in which the components of CDM interact. Yet the unique content of CDM, as distinct from the content in other kinds of educational competencies, resides primarily in each person's sense of identity. People must first know themselves. Then, when they deal with data from other domains (occupations, education, and training), they can seek and find relevance to the personal domain in terms of what is salient to them. In short, the domain of personal constructs and specifications defines relevant slices through the universe of external domains.

Simulated Occupational Choice (SOC) was developed to measure competencies in CDM. It is a structured, game-like, individually administered exercise designed to elicit career decision-making behaviors and enable those behaviors to be observed, recorded, and scored in meaningful ways, particularly for diagnosis. Components of CDM, such as specifying what information one wants and being able to interpret the information one gets, can be observed both separately and in interaction. The array of occupational options available and the universe of information about each option can be standardized. The recorder can then focus on each person's behavior in identifying, seeking, and using information to choose between the options. Like simulations generally, SOC presents a standard set of exercises that are representative of real-life tasks, but (for the expedience of measurement) purified and time-compressed.

Initial development was followed by iterative cycles of tryout and revision to test and improve the procedures, materials, and scoring. In all, four successive forms were constructed and tried out with groups of secondary and college students (described fully in Katz et al., 1976). In all forms of SOC, students were given the task of choosing which one of three occupations would suit them best. The occupations were called X, Y, and Z, designated as "occupations of the future," so that students would not be tempted to try to guess the names of the occupations or to assume that certain characteristics tend to go together. Starting with no information, the students were instructed in the original version to ask the questions that would produce information most helpful to them in choosing the occupation. As the administrator provided answers to each question, the students moved markers along a scale to rate each occupation. Analysis of these moves, however, led to discovery of ambiguities inherent in this procedure. There were individual differences in the way students interpreted the answers for some of the occupational characteristics they said they wanted, like opportunities for leisure and for leadership: More was not always better. The effect of such individual differences was to muddy the interpretation of marker moves and scores.

Consequently, in later versions students were asked to solicit information by specifying what was desirable to them, rather than by asking questions. Administrators laid out response strips indicating the likelihood that each of the three occupations would meet each specification made by students. Again, students moved markers along a scale for each occupation to show the impact of each bit of information taken separately, and then the cumulative impact of an entire configuration of information at each of the following stages: Phase 1, the set of information provided in response to all specifications generated by students; Phase 2, the set of information provided in response to characteristics selected by students from a list of those previously unmentioned by them; Phase 3, both sets of information combined. In Phase 4, students assigned numerical weights, from 0 to 8, to show the relative importance of each of the characteristics in the pool (whether generated by them, selected by them, or residual).

The SOC Recording Form and scores for one student from the college sample can be used to illustrate the derivation of the scores and the nature of the diagnostic interpretations that can be made (Figure 3). Written headings aligned with "SPECS" represent the four occupational characteristics that were specified by this student in Phase 1 (Help Others, Income, Leisure, Security). If students know what is important to them in choosing an occupation and therefore what information they want, they should be able to generate specifications for virtually all their most important desiderata. A crude index of this competency is a simple tally of the number of specifications generated in Phase 1 (listed as N SPECS 4 under the heading, SCORES, in the lower left corner of the figure). This student's score of 4 is about a standard deviation below the mean of 5.4 in this small sample of college students who had participated in a career planning course.

The three characteristics that he chose in Phase 2 from a list of nine named and defined characteristics appear at the upper right of the figure

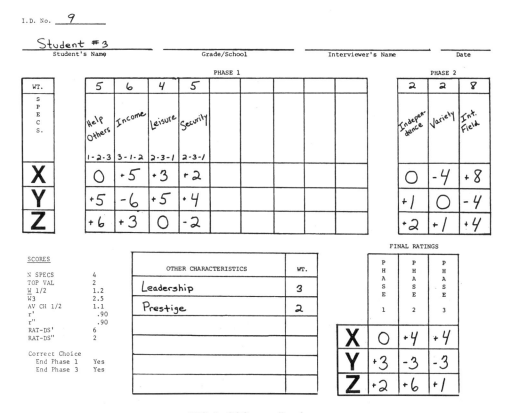

FIG. 3 SOC recording form.

(Independence, Variety, Work in Main Field of Interest). The residual characteristics are listed under the heading OTHER CHARACTERIS-TICS in the lower middle of the figure (Leadership, Prestige).

A second simple score, called TOP VAL, is a tally of how many of the student's three highest weights were assigned during Phase 4 to the specifications he initiated in Phase 1. The weights (on a scale of 0 to 8) appear in the top row labeled WT for Phases 1 and 2 and in the right-hand column of the box headed OTHER CHARACTERISTICS. TOP VAL for this student is 2 out of the possible 3. A characteristic selected in Phase 2 (an opportunity to work in his main field of interest) received a higher weight (8) than any of the four specifications he initiated. His score is almost a standard deviation below the group mean of 2.4 for TOP VAL.

A more refined measure of this principle (that people who know what they want can specify what is most important to them) is the ratio of mean weight in Phase 1 to mean weight in Phase 2. For this student, the ratio (W1/2) is 1.2, showing that over all he tended to assign higher weights to Phase 1 specs than to Phase 2 characteristics. This ratio was pulled down, however, by the high weight he assigned in Phase 2 to an opportunity to work in his main field of interest, and his score was slightly (about a quarter of a standard deviation) below the mean of 1.6.

The average weight he gave the residual characteristics (W3 = 2.5) was slightly above the group mean of 2.1; a desirable W3 score should be *lower* than the average weights in Phases 1 and 2, because people should attach greater importance to the characteristics they specified as desirable in Phase 1 and selected from the residual pool in Phase 2. W3 may be a function in part of N SPECS and any response set for using high or low weights. Indeed, none of the scores mentioned so far is independent of the others; they are included for descriptive and explanatory rather than summative purposes.

Just below the specs appear various combinations of the digits 1-2-3. These represent the predetermined information that was given in the "answer strips" for the various specifications. For example, the 3-1-2 under Income means that the level of income specified by this student was "very likely" to be found in Occupation X, "very unlikely" in Occupation Y, and "possible" in Occupation Z. The numbers in the column below this box show the student's reaction to this bit of information: He moved the marker for X up to $+5$, for Y down to -6, and for Z up to $+3$. The distance moved is defined in this instance as 11, the distance between the highest and the lowest marker position. Now, if the most important specifications have been specified in Phase 1, the impact of Phase 1 information should be greater than the impact of Phase 2 information. That is, the mean distance (or "Average Change") in Phase 1 should exceed the mean distance in Phase 2. Thus, AV CH ½, the ratio of mean Phase 1 distance to mean

Phase 2 distance, represents in a gross way the student's competence in interpreting and using the information he gets. If he has asked the right questions, his response to the information he has sought should be greater than his response to unsolicited information. In this case, AV CH $\frac{1}{2}$ = 1.1, a quarter of a standard deviation below the group mean of 1.2.

Correlations provide a convenient index of the consistency between the magnitude of weights a student has assigned to occupational characteristics (to indicate their importance) and the impact of information about the respective characteristics (represented by the distance moved). The correlation (represented by r') between this student's weights and moves for Phase 1 alone is .90. The correlation for Phases 1 and 2 combined, r'', is also .90. These coefficients show a very high level of consistency, comparing favorably with the group mean of about .7 for both r' and r''.

The two final scores require considerable explanation. RAT stands for ratings, represented by the numbers in the appropriate column of the box headed FINAL RATINGS in the lower right quadrant of the Recording Form. These numbers show the marker positions that the student assigned to the three occupations when a total array of information was considered at the end of each phase. They indicate the student's over-all evaluation of the attractiveness of the occupations when various amounts of information were displayed (in response to the student's self-initiated specifications at the end of Phase 1, in response to selected characteristics at the end of Phase 2, and for Phase 1 and Phase 2 information combined in Phase 3).

DS stands for Desirability Sum. It is computed by multiplying the weight the student assigned to a given characteristic (to show its importance) by the likelihood of finding that characteristic in each occupation (represented by the digits 1–3), and then summing the products for each occupation. The Desirability Sums were rescaled to put them on the same scale as RAT, the student's ratings of each occupation's attractiveness. Expected positions on the attractiveness scale were computed from the rescaled Desirability Sums. The discrepancy between actual and expected positions on the attractiveness scale was then calculated for each occupation and summed across the three occupations to give the scores RAT–DS$'$ and RAT–DS$''$. The former refers to ratings at the end of Phase 1, the latter to ratings at the end of Phase 3. Thus, a low RAT–DS score (i.e., a low discrepancy) is desirable. For this student, the discrepancy scores of 6 and 2 were relatively low, compared to group means of about 9 and standard deviations of about 4.1.

Note the changes that take place in this student's final ratings from Phase 1 to Phase 3. These are clearly a function of the fact that he neglected to specify in Phase 1 his single most important value – working in an occupation that involved his major field of interest (scientific). His marker moves in Phase 1 were consistent with his weights, and he chose the occupation with the highest Desirability Sum. So he was able to process information about his four specs consistently and logically. But when he reached Phase 2, he recognized his error of omission as soon as he saw the card with the label and definition of Work in Your Main Field of Interest. He gave this characteristic maximum weight, and the information he received about it exerted greater impact than any other item on his marker moves (the distance between Occupations X and Y in this column being 12).

Surveying the total array of information in Phase 3, he showed a very high degree of consistency. Although, over all, Occupation X was "very likely" to provide satisfaction for only two characteristics (Income and Interest Field), these were the two he had given the highest weights (6 and 8), a combination which accounted for the fact that X had the highest Desirability Sum. So in the end his choice was a "good" one, in the light of what was important to him and what information he had.

One might quibble over a small inconsistency. He assigned a weight of 3 to the residual characteristic, Leadership. If this weight was an accurate reflection of his values, he should have selected Leadership in Phase 2 rather than Independence or Variety, to each of which he gave a weight of 2. Ideally, no residual characteristic should have a higher weight than any characteristic specified in Phase 1 or selected in Phase 2.

In summary, notice that some of the scores are quite straightforward but others rather complex. Although this student's scores have been compared to group means, the group was a small one and was not a representative sample; because most members of the group had been exposed to an intensive guidance program, it is likely that their scores tended to be higher than would be obtained by a random sample of college students. For interindividual interpretation of such scores as N SPECS, national or local norms would have to be developed. However, although relative fluency in initiating specifications is of some interest, what is more to the point is the *quality* of the specifications: Do they include those characteristics that are most important to the student?

In this case, the criterion-referenced score, TOP VAL = 2, showing the student failed to generate a specification that tapped the occupational characteristic of greatest importance to him, reveals a meaningful and readily understood deficiency. This deficiency would presumably hamper his unguided search strategy in seeking out occupations and screening them. Yet he was able to identify and select that characteristic when it was presented to him in a way that a systematic guidance intervention might provide. Thus, he lacked a competency for making an unaided career decision; but he was competent to profit from a guidance treatment that would cue him on characteristics to consider. At the same time, as the "r" scores (which are mainly ipsative) suggest, he was competent in relating information to the characteristics. The RAT–DS scores also show that he knew how to use information rationally and consistently when he had it.

Thus, we may say that he grew in awareness of his values in the course of the exercise, and that he behaved in a way that was consistent with his (clarified) values in making a decision. The latter behavior reflects the criterion suggested by Cronbach and Gleser (1965): "The decision for each [student] must be evaluated on . . . its value for this individual."

A different pattern of scores–for example, TOP VAL = 3, W1/2 = 5, r' and $r'' = .5$, and RAT–DS = 20–would indicate counterbalanced strength and weakness. In this case, we would say that the student knows her values well but is not competent in interpreting and using information. Unguided, she would tend to make decisions inconsistent with what she wants and with the relevant information available to her.

So the scores are useful for gross diagnosis, for screening and classifying competencies and deficiencies. But the picture one gets from a close examination of the Recording Form is much richer. Here one sees in detail the entire sequence of interaction with the task. The dynamics of each person's decision making come alive–one has a window on the process. It is in this context that the scores become most meaningful.

For example, in the Recording Form displayed here, one picks up the fact that it is not just one of the three highest weighted characteristics that the student failed to specify in Phase 1 (TOP VAL = 2): It was the very highest, the one he gave maximum weight. Other aberrations and inconsistencies also become apparent, as already noted. In addition, one can see the range of weights used and the differentiation in marker moves. The interaction of these variables tends, of course, to affect such scores as r' and r''. But for purposes of diagnosis and guidance, if r is low, it is useful to know whether there was considerable differentiation in weights but not in moves, or vice versa, or relative lack of differentiation in both, or ample but inconsistent differentiation in both. Thus, once students have been screened and classified in diagnostic categories on the basis of scores, a close scrutiny of the entire Recording Form is invaluable as a guide to interventions. It also serves as an instructional resource itself; going over the record with the student in a focused interview may be one of the best remedial tactics.

I have emphasized the diagnostic capabilities of SOC, because diagnosis represents the proudest purpose of measurement in education and guidance–and also the least practiced. A good diagnostic measure should at least imply guidelines for remedial action and at best incorporate remedial instruction in the very process of measurement.

To accomplish such a goal, diagnosis depends–ultimately–on a distinct theory concerning the structure of the competencies to be mastered, the logical connections between them, and the sequence in which they are applied. Thus, it is based on a series of linked premises: Some outcome – in this case, competence in CDM – is the product of a number of components; each component makes a contribution that can be identified, defined, and measured; a deficiency in any one component, or in an interface between components, is an obstacle to an individual's progress toward competence in CDM. Recognition of an obstacle can then lead to remedial action, or may in itself be the beginning of remedial action.

Indeed, as an integral part of the administration of SOC, students who had just completed the exercise were briefed on the discrepancies between their behavior and an ideal of logically consistent and effective behavior in CDM. If, for example, they had given higher weights to characteristics selected in Phase 2, or to residual characteristics, than to the specifications they had initiated in Phase 1, they quickly recognized that they had been deficient in explicit awareness of their own values. This recognition started them one giant step toward values clarification and self-appraisal: "I hadn't even thought of security, and yet that turned out to be the most important thing to me in choosing an occupation in SOC." Or, if their final ratings were not consistent with desirability sums for the three occupations, they realized they had been deficient in sorting out, manipulating, and interpreting a mass of information. But what is more, they also realized that in the computation of desirability sums they had been handed a paradigm that they themselves could use in processing information of this kind in the future. Thus, the SOC measures do not merely indicate status. They point to actions that can be taken, and they can start students on a path to more rational CDM.

Many of these greatest advantages of SOC as a diagnostic and remedial instrument may be seen as drawbacks to its use in the kinds of evaluation studies most doctoral candidates and other researchers want to do. Clearly, the manifestation of the Heisenberg principle just described – the process of measurement may affect the competencies being measured – must give them pause. They are loath to evaluate the efficacy of a treatment with a measuring instrument that itself has a significant effect.

Another problem is the emphasis on diagnostic scores. SOC does not provide a single summary score indicating competence in CDM. This is a drawback to those who would seek the cozy refuge of a single index of "career maturity," or "decidedness," or the like.

Indeed, the problems of summary scores have plagued SOC (like most simulation exercises) from the beginning. The difference between the rich observations of behavior in the Recording Form and the sterile-appearing, sometimes complex numerical scores is hard to accept. Our best efforts at quantification fail to represent some interesting and relevant individual differences. We have not used SOC with large enough, well-drawn samples to determine the factorial structure of the scores and then to resolve problems that must exist in the interactions between scores, which may particularly cloud intergroup or interindividual comparisons.

Some of these problems derive from a more general and pervasive problem: the time and cost of large-scale administration of SOC. By its interactive nature, it must be administered to one person at a time. Each administration takes about 30 to 45 minutes. So giving SOC to a large sample would require a number of trained administrators, a lot of person-hours, and a bigger budget than we could muster. Cost was not the only difficulty, but the others proved manageable. Experience showed that a group of administrators could be trained in 2 hours. Although some of the scores require computations that appear forbidding, we had written directions to compute them on a hand calculator for small samples and had developed a computer program for large samples.

As might be expected, we played with the idea of reducing costs by computerizing the administration of SOC. All the steps of administration by interactive computer were feasible except for Phase 1. The student's own specifications had to be generated in his or her own words and had to be recognized by the computer. At the time, we could not get sufficient funds to develop a program for natural language recognition. We have done no work on SOC for well over a decade now. Perhaps the time is ripe for someone to pick up the tattered remains of this instrument and refurbish it with some additional research and development. But as it stands, for evaluation of a treatment, SOC must be rated as no better than a promising start for an interesting approach—with the promise still unfulfilled.

THE EVALUATION OF SIGI

When SIGI was deemed ready for use, it was sent out to six colleges for field testing and evaluation under regular operational conditions. The colleges represented great diversity in region, size, population, curriculum, and career guidance program. The design and procedures of the evaluation were for explicitly formative and summative purposes. We wanted to know not just whether SIGI "made a difference" on some criteria, but what we could do to improve it.

More specifically, formative evaluation required answers to such elementary questions as whether the system could be installed and run smoothly; whether the *Manager's Guide*, the *Counselor's Handbook*, and the manuals for the local Prediction and Planning sections were being used efficiently; what problems or gaps were noted by students or counselors; whether changes should be made in the reading level of text in the displays; whether all elements of the system were used by students; how SIGI was integrated with the total guidance program at each college.

Method

Straightforward methods were used to answer these questions. Each college kept a log to record any problems, and a telephone "hot line" was staffed at ETS to deal with anything urgent, such as a hardware or software malfunction. System response times were checked at the colleges with the largest numbers of terminals. The clarity of the *Manager's Guide* was tested by having technically unsophisticated staff members at most of the colleges handle all details of system operation. Counselors reported on their use of the *Handbook* as a guide to dyadic counseling with students who were using SIGI and as a resource for career development courses. The use of the manuals for the Prediction and Planning sections by paraprofessionals, graduate students, or counselors (varying with the colleges) was evaluated by the quality and timeliness of the data they collected for these sections and by asking them to report any problems or difficulties. Students and counselors filled out questionnaires, and some were interviewed. Summary and individual records of students' use of SIGI were scrutinized. In a small number of cases, "focused interviews" allowed student and researcher to discuss the student's path through SIGI.

Similar methods were used for "summative" purposes to evaluate the effects of SIGI on students' competencies in career decision making and its impact on counseling activities and career guidance programs. The research design called for each college to assign about 200 students randomly to an experimental or a control group. The experimental group used SIGI and then filled out a combined questionnaire and test, while the control group responded to the questionnaire and test before using SIGI. Between 10 and 17 students at each college (77 in all) were interviewed by the research staff. Another questionnaire was also completed by 57 counselors at the six colleges to assess the nature of their interactions with SIGI users, their acceptance of SIGI, and changes in their activities and programs attributable to SIGI.

Volume 1 of a final report submitted to the National Science Foundation (Chapman et al., 1977) provides a detailed account (over 700 pages) of this field test and evaluation. (Volume 2, an Appendix similar in length, includes all the evaluation instruments and the various manuals and guides and the handbook mentioned previously.) What follows is a summary of the results, with a few highlights.

Results

In the formative evaluation, no single aspect of SIGI stood out as a problem. Installation and operation of the system (after a brief "break-in" period) ran smoothly, response times were excellent, and documentation was judged clear and helpful. Students gave the system high grades on interest, clarity, and helpfulness. They wanted to use it again and recommended it to their friends. Both students and counselors rated the quality and amount of occupational information as high, better than other sources. Some would have liked data on local jobs. (Enabling institutions to add local information was always in our plans, and SIGI PLUS provides this capability.) There were several suggestions of occupations to be added to the data base. (Occupations have indeed been added every year.) The vocabulary and style of the display texts were judged "just right" by 92% of the students; only 1% found them "too difficult," and 7% said "too easy." Only two counselors thought that reading level was too hard for their students, one being concerned with the difficulty experienced by deaf students with some of the text, the other with its difficulty for foreign students. Over 98% of the students and over 90% of the counselors thought that SIGI was free from sexual, racial, and other bias. Some students complained that the scheduling (controlled by each college) made them feel rushed–they wanted more time for each session. Every section was judged "most helpful" by some students: More votes were cast for Values, Locate, and Compare, but the other sections (Predictions, Planning, and Strategy) were the ones they would most like to use when they returned to the system. (This response seems linked to the scheduling problem; because the latter three sections follow the first three, a number of students hadn't completed them–or had to rush through them–at the time they filled out the questionnaire.)

While the feedback was useful to us in improving the next version of SIGI, colleges also derived a dividend from formative evaluations. Their collection of local data for the Prediction sections highlighted for them differences in the distribution of grades in key courses and instances when faculty-selected grade predictors turned out to have low correlations with final grades. This information stimulated reviews of grading policies and practices. Similarly, specification of programs for the Planning section brought to light some anomalies in requirements and sequences of courses as stated in catalogues; some of the colleges revised their curricula.

Interviews with students were intended mainly for formative purposes, because the subjectivity of interpretation made them suspect for summative evaluation. Nevertheless, they seem to illustrate in some depth the effects quantified by data from questionnaire responses. Intensive and exhaustive interviews with a total of 77 students from the six colleges revealed many different ways in which SIGI helped students progress toward autonomy and rationality in making career decisions. The interviews (usually conducted with printouts at hand) reviewed each student's progress through the system. They served to flesh out the bare bones of questionnaire responses. The flexibility of SIGI in meeting a diversity of needs came through clearly. Consider five students who exemplified differences in initial status.

George started without a glimmer. He said, "I don't have any idea what occupation I want. All I know is I want something I'll like." After his first lengthy session at the terminal, he felt that he had a grip on what was important to him, and he was seriously considering four occupations, derived from his use of Locate, that seemed likely to satisfy his values and interests: Political Scientist, Optometrist, Civil Engineer, and Industrial Engineer. He was insatiable in his quest for more information about these four, not only using Compare, Prediction, and Planning in a later session, but also reading voraciously and talking to local people in these occupations. After his use of Strategy, he found that Optometrist and Civil Engineer emerged in a virtual tie. "I hadn't thought of Civil Engineer at all before I used SIGI. Now I'm leaning toward it, but I'll try to take courses that will hold open Optometrist as long as possible." When asked how SIGI had helped him, he said: "I guess it gave me a jump start. It made me realize I had to take responsibility for deciding what I wanted to do. . . . It gave me a foundation, a way to make decisions."

Jason had made at least a tentative choice of occupation and was looking for confirmation when he went on SIGI. He had wanted to become a mathematician but found that SIGI made him more explicitly aware of some of his values and of their relevance for occupational choice: "Once I started weighting values, it gave me a better idea of what I was looking for and what direction I was going in. . . . Something I realized going through SIGI was that I put a high value on Helping Others, and I would like to have that as part of my occupation. . . . SIGI didn't really tell me what occupation to enter (I didn't expect it to), but it helped point me in a direction. . . . After going through SIGI, I now lean more toward a social direction rather than a technical direction. Clinical psychology, therapy, social work, and teaching (in math, possibly) are occupations that I now see appeal to me."

Marilyn, a first-year community college student who wore hearing aids and had a slight speech defect, also sought confirmation of a previous choice. She was emotional about a conflict with her father, who thought that her ambition to become a secretary exceeded her abilities and that she should not be attending college. The combination of physical handicap and family conflict had sapped her self-confidence. SIGI helped her gain focus and confidence. She said of the Values section: "It is a fantastic thing for people who are confused, like me. . . . It really helped me know what I wanted in a job." The Prediction system was especially useful to her. It boosted her self-esteem: "I've always been knocked down. . . . It [Prediction] gave me confidence in how I feel about what I'm going to do, not how other people feel." Although she explored two other occupations, she returned to Secretary on a higher plane of understanding, with some assurance that it satisfied her values and lay within her reach. "I'm looking forward to my future more than I ever have before."

Sally, age 28, married and with a 3-year-old daughter, had dropped out of high school in senior year, but had since earned an equivalency diploma and enrolled in a community college. She had served a prison term for a felony, and went on SIGI knowing that she wanted to prepare for an occupation that would enable her to "help people in jails or prisons." The Values section was fascinating to her: "It really made me think, and I've thought about my values even more since then." Among the occupations she considered after using Locate were Rehabilitation Counselor, Social Worker, and Social Service Aid, and she explored them thoroughly in Compare. In Prediction she found her chances of success in sociology were satisfactory to her, and she said that Rehabilitation Counselor was what she "really wanted." But she was "sponsored" for only 2 years of education, and she noted in Planning that she would need a master's degree to become a Rehabilitation Counselor. After using the Strategy section, she decided that her best strategy would be to settle on Social Service Aid as her immediate goal, while planning to prepare to become a Rehabilitation Counselor later.

Mike had just entered college at the age of 22. He had been working happily as a plumber since graduating from high school and had never expected to reconsider his occupational choice. But he had seriously injured his legs in an accident, and he could no longer do the work he liked so much. "I needed to find another job. . . . It was something my mind had been closed to – other fields and occupations." During his first session, Mike went through Values, Locate, and Compare. He said that since the accident "I've had to change completely around. I've had to pick up new values, new ideas, new ways." In Locate he retrieved a number of occupations that he had never thought of before. "One that came up that I'm considering now is Accountant. It really appeals to me." He followed Accountant through Prediction and Planning, read as much as he could about it, and managed to talk with accountants and a teacher of accounting. In Strategy, Accountant had the highest Desirability Sum of the three occupations he was comparing and appeared to offer favorable chances for successful entry. "At first," he said, "I wasn't entirely happy with the idea of becoming an accountant. I still longed to be physically active. But the

more I looked at Accountant, the better I liked it. . . . Really, I didn't know
about my values and all those things until I used SIGI."

Lest these five obvious successes transport us beyond the bounds of a
decent humility, let us listen to a lone voice uttering some negatives. Carla
had reached her sophomore year with no idea of what she wanted to do.
She considered herself to be "the one student SIGI didn't help." She had
always had a hard time making decisions about anything: "If I was the kind
of person who could make up my mind, it would have helped me." She was
frustrated at not being able to decide which values were important and
which were not. She did like SIGI as a source of occupational information,
but she could not accept any occupations that appeared in Locate. For
example, she would not want to be a teacher "because there may be kids in
the class who don't want to be there." She rejected Ornamental Horticul-
ture "because there are so many prerequisites." During the interview
Carla said she recognized that she needed the help of a counselor for her
chronic and pervasive indecisiveness and in fact began a series of weekly
appointments soon afterward.

The first five examples illustrate how SIGI provided for people with
different needs. Some who had not even begun to consider any decision
(like George), or who were totally undecided, got started and moved along
toward definite, informed, and rational decisions. Some, like Jason, sought
corroboration for a decision they had made but, through SIGI, discovered
new directions to explore and a new set of options from which they
expected to choose. Others, like Marilyn, did find corroboration of a
previous preference and felt that the reassurance they received gave them
greater confidence, relieved tensions, and helped them move "full steam
ahead." Some, like Sally, were helped to translate a general goal into
specific decisions, concluding with a balance between two occupational
choices: one that was practical and expedient in the short term, the other
more desirable but necessary to postpone as part of a long-term plan.
Finally, some, like Mike, forced by circumstances to change from a favored
occupation, found that SIGI helped them become aware of new options
from which a satisfying choice could be pursued.

Even Carla accepted the method of decision making she found in SIGI.
From initial bewilderment about how to start choosing an occupation, she
recognized now that she had to explore and clarify her values to answer
the central question: "What rewards and satisfactions do I want from an
occupation?" She also came to recognize that her inability to decide on
anything was probably symptomatic of an emotional problem, and she was
motivated to seek the help of a counselor.

The first five cases were chosen to represent recurrent themes. Naturally, there were many variations on these themes; every user brought
some unique elements to the interaction with SIGI. Nevertheless, inter-

viewers were struck by the frequency with which certain messages were conveyed throughout the 77 interviews.

First, almost all the students said that SIGI had had an important effect on them. In describing the experience, they felt they had learned a lot—about themselves, about occupations, about making decisions.

Second, a common vocabulary emerged: They talked much about their values—how they had become aware of the importance of some values, how certain occupations related to their values, and how values could be used systematically in decision making. If there was any "Eureka" effect, it was this discovery of values as a basis for investigation and communication in CDM. Besides "values" and "aware," other words that they used often were "logical" and "reasons." They came to recognize that decision making can be structured, that there were steps involving self-appraisal, information about options (getting a list of occupations to be considered and exploring them in depth), balancing desirability and chances of success, and other components of the process they had used in SIGI. It was this structure that they referred to as "logical" and that helped them see "reasons" for what they chose and what they rejected.

Third, there was much evidence of purposive behavior. Students who used SIGI engaged in autonomous and rational activities as part of their decision making. These activities took different form with different students. Some sought occupational information off line, sending for materials, talking with members of an occupation. Many added courses to support a contingency choice or changed majors to reflect a change in their goal. Some made follow-up appointments with counselors. These students had begun taking charge of their career decision making in an informed and rational way.

A final note on the interviews: They highlight the folly of using "decidedness" as a criterion in judging who should receive career guidance and who has benefited from it. Some students who were undecided did progress toward "decidedness," but others who had made a decision found it useful to reexamine their choice, reopen the decision-making process, and move in another direction. As Newman, Fuqua, and Minger (1990) showed, it is enlightening to take into account the "comfort level" that people have with their state of decidedness or undecidedness. They found that many "decided" people (especially those "uncomfortable" with their decision) can benefit from career guidance. The benefit can take the form of corroboration or change—that is, it can make them more comfortable with the decision they have made (like Marilyn) or identify the source of their discomfort and thereby turn them in a direction that provides greater comfort (like Jason).

The questionnaire results are duller to report than the interviews, but they provide the advantage of quantifying more extensively the benefits gained by SIGI users. Here, the reader may appreciate being spared the long tables of numbers included in the voluminous report; instead, a summary of the major results is listed. Remember that each college was asked to assign about 200 students randomly to an experimental or a control group. The experimental group completed the questionnaire after using SIGI; the control group, before. Data were collected and analyzed for each college separately. Notwithstanding the great differences between colleges in geography (six different regions), setting (dense metropolitan, small city, suburban and rural), size (from more than 20,000 to about 4,000 students), nature of student bodies (age distributions, ratios of males to females, socioeconomic status, proportions of various ethnic and racial groups), and so on, the similarities in the way students at different colleges responded to the questionnaire justified pooling the results for summary purposes.

The main finding was highly significant differences ($p < .01$) between those who had used SIGI and those who were waiting: For example, the former displayed clearer understanding of their values and goals; had a greater knowledge of the rewards and satisfactions they wanted from an occupation; explored more occupations; had more definite career plans; thought they could predict their grades better; were more certain about which program to enroll in for their occupational goals; had greater confidence in their career decision-making ability; were more frequently consulting sources of occupational information; and had more accurate information about the occupations they were considering.

The measurement of this last item involved a unique feature. Other efforts at measuring occupational information ask questions about a sample of occupations. Scores on such tests tend to be misleading: It is likely that a given student may have no need or desire to be well informed about most of the occupations used in the test. Such questions may tap general information, but fail to focus on salient information for CDM – that is, information regarded as important by a particular student. Students often reject occupations from further consideration (quite validly) because of one feature that is objectionable – for example, more education is required than the student wants to invest in, or the activities are of a nature that the student strongly dislikes. A turnoff in one respect deemed very important may make further information superfluous. So students may fail to answer questions about a variety of occupations, and yet be well informed about those occupations that pass muster and are under active consideration.

The questionnaire completed by experimental and control groups, therefore, asked students first to name an occupation they were considering. They then answered a set of questions on the *occupation they had named.* The point was to test students' knowledge on the occupation about which they should be well informed. In other words, this procedure tapped occupational information under the optimum conditions of salience and relevance.

Obviously, a test of this sort is generally avoided because it is difficult to score. Since students respond in respect to an occupation they have themselves specified, a different scoring key is needed for each occupation chosen. It was feasible for us to develop and use keys for such a large number of occupations by drawing on the occupational information stored in SIGI.

Counselors were in a good position to observe the impact of SIGI on the career guidance program, on students, and on their own work. We interviewed some counselors, and all 57 filled out extensive questionnaires on the impact of SIGI at their institutions. Again, despite the differences between colleges, the responses were similar enough to be pooled.

Our aims in respect to counselors were clear. Early in the development of SIGI, I had taken some pains to emphasize that it was designed

> to fit into the regular career guidance programs. . . . It will not supplant counselors. Rather, it will complement the work of the guidance staff. SIGI does superbly some things that human counselors cannot do efficiently, or at all. It stores, retrieves instantly, and manipulates vast amounts of information, putting great resources at the fingertips of each student, tailored to his or her individual needs. It brings together many sets of variables – personal, occupational, and institutional. By combining these sets of variables in distinctive ways for each student, it constructs new and unique information. . . . On the other hand, SIGI does not attempt to do what many counselors do superbly. It does not provide a warm human relationship; it does not purport to solve personal, social, or academic problems; it does not attempt to cope with emotional upsets. There are, however, ways in which the counselor's work may articulate quite closely with SIGI. . . . SIGI may stir up concerns that the student will want to discuss with the counselor. Furthermore, while SIGI deals with occupational decisions, it does not include placement into specific jobs within an occupation. A counselor or placement officer may apply many of the SIGI paradigms in assisting students to choose and seek particular jobs. Thus, working together, the counselor and SIGI can help students much more than either could manage independently. In short, SIGI can increase the productivity of counselors.

This was all very well for me to say. The evaluation aimed to find out whether counselors agreed. In their responses to the questionnaire, the counselors showed a high degree of acceptance of SIGI, did not view it as a threat or a fad, and said that the presence of SIGI had helped students make career decisions and had relieved problems in the career planning program (such as providing accurate and up-to-date occupational information and getting students to read it). They did not perceive SIGI as taking over all responsibility for CDM, but its use improved the quality of counseling sessions: Students arrived for appointments much farther advanced in the CDM process, with a better formulation of what the process consisted of, with a better understanding of themselves, with more occupations in mind, with a more structured approach to CDM. Their observations corroborated what the student questionnaires had shown – SIGI users were rated much higher than others on being able to express the satisfactions they wanted from an occupation, to name alternatives to their primary choices, to state sound reasons for their preferences, to be well informed about the occupations they were considering, to designate suitable programs of study for those occupations, and to evaluate their chances of success in those programs.

Counselors also said that SIGI fit well into the configuration of their career planning program. In some colleges, use of SIGI was scheduled as a laboratory for a course in career development. At the other extreme, use of SIGI was optional, entirely at each student's initiative, with no adjunctive counseling unless the student sought it. Other modes of use fell between these extremes. The results were generally similar at all colleges, and we could only conclude that the "best" way to use SIGI was the way that best suits the circumstances and style at each college. (At all colleges, students said they would prefer to use SIGI for some purposes, counselors for others, and a combination of SIGI and the counselors for still others. In each case, the preference coincided with the kind of division of labor anticipated, as just described.)

In addition to interviews and questionnaires completed by students and counselors, another component of the evaluation was the record of students' interactions with SIGI automatically recorded by the computer. These records took two forms. One collected responses for all users at each computer, without identification of any individual, and provided data for summary descriptions of the people who had used SIGI at each college and of the nature of the use. Thus, we could note the distribution of users at each college by age, sex, and enrollment status, their initial status on CDM variables (such as awareness of values, information about a preferred occupation, ability to predict grades, knowing which program to choose); we could also note the patterns of values weights (including means and standard deviations), interest field selection, specifications used in structured search (dimensions and levels), and the frequencies with which specifications were changed, each occupation was retrieved, each occupation was selected for query in direct access, each question was asked, predictions were sought for each course, programs were planned for each occupation, and each occupation was chosen in the Strategy section. These data on usage contributed, as already indicated, mainly to formative evaluation, showing how all components of the system were being used.

The other form of record was for individuals. Having obtained informed consent from the students, each college could turn on a utility program that recorded individuals' pathways through SIGI. This utility program collected, interpreted, and printed the student's responses and interactions in compressed form to provide data on specified variables in each section. A random sample could be obtained by setting the program to record every nth student (such as 5th, 20th), according to the proportion required.

These observations are not to be confused with responses derived from surveys of people who may or may not be actively engaged in career decision making at the time they are questioned. These data were collected unobtrusively in the course of students' interactions with a career guidance treatment. Thus, data collection neither interrupted the process of CDM nor depended on retrospection or recall of processes. In short, such observations were made through a "window" in the CDM process. The variables are elements in that process, not made-up answers to questions that may or may not have been salient to the respondents.

Perusal of many such individual records showed that students were using SIGI in a consistent, logical way. For example, the values they had weighted as most important tended universally to be used as specifications in structured search. The occupations retrieved in structured search tended to be selected for further examination in direct access and to be considered in Prediction, Planning, and Strategy. The occupations with highest desirability and probability tended to be chosen at the end of Strategy; if no occupation was best in both regards, appropriate decision rules were applied. When we did spot an apparent inconsistency and had a chance to interview the student, there was always a reasonable explanation: looking up an occupation for a friend who didn't have access to the system; browsing; testing the system; playing "What if?" games; and so on.

This student record was particularly useful in the focused interviews described previously. Interviewers could ask probing questions: Why did you make this change in your values weights? Why did you ask about this occupation here but never follow it up later? How did you feel about this prediction? Was it hard to make your choice at the end of Strategy? How confident do you feel about this choice?

The record of individual students' interactions with the system also made possible additional research that bears on one of the questions raised earlier about effects on different subgroups of users. For example, questions have often been asked about the suitability of various inventories and other treatments for people of different ages and for males and females.

The student records enabled us to compare such subgroups in CDM. A descriptive research study employing these records examined the extent to which variations in CDM were associated with age, gender, and "gender-typed" values (Norris et al., 1978). This last term is explained in the account that follows.

COMPARISONS OF MALES AND FEMALES IN CDM

In the interest of brevity, let it be said at the outset that differences between age groups (18 and under, 19 to 24, 25 and over) were infrequent and small. So the data concerning age is omitted here, except to note a slight tendency for the youngest group of females to have values closer than the older females to the values of the male groups. "Perhaps changing beliefs, customs, and opportunities have begun to exert greater effect on the youngest group in breaking down stereotypes and in liberating females from traditional perceptions of sex roles," was the inference I drew in 1978. (It would be interesting to repeat the study in the 1990s.) At that time a number of reviews (e.g., Brief & Aldag, 1975) had summarized scores of studies on gender differences related to variables associated with CDM, such as interests, values, and occupational preferences. Most of the studies contributed to or corroborated certain gender stereotypes—for example, that females tended to be more "social" and altruistic, while males tended to be more concerned with money and power. These characteristics are often said to be functions of child rearing and socialization practices. But countervailing forces had been recognized. Role models with nontraditional characteristics had become highly visible during the previous two decades. Affirmative action had helped open up more options for women. Had sex-stereotyped CDM survived such phenomena?

Part 1: Stereotypes Corroborated

The first part of this study compared the behaviors of male and female college students engaged in the process of CDM. It reported on similarities and differences and set the stage for the second part, which analyzed the behaviors of two subgroups identified for each gender. The study was based on a 5% random sample of individual records, automatically collected, of people who used SIGI during a fixed period in 1976 at six colleges in different regions of the country. The sample comprised 433 complete individual records (176 males and 257 females). No screening procedures were used, nor were special incentives provided for participation. Thus, the sample represents the run of students at these institutions who used the system during a given time. Summary statistics were reported for some 50 variables, including self-appraisal, identifying options, seeking information, predicting success, making plans, and using decision rules to evaluate occupations for choice. Highlights of the findings on similarities and differences between males and females are as follows:

1. Means of values weights show that all values tended to be at least of moderate importance (on the average) to both genders, with no significant differences between means for 4 of the 10 values weighted.

2. The largest gender differences appeared for the values Helping Others, Early Entry, Leadership, and Income. Females weighted the first two higher than males did, while males weighted the latter two higher than females did. These differences are consistent with the stereotype of the striving male and the nurturant female.

3. Smaller but still significant differences appeared in Work in Main Field of Interest, weighted higher by females, and Independence, weighted higher by males.

4. Interest preferences were also in accord with longstanding cultural expectations: The Scientific field was more frequently chosen by males, and the Personal Contact field by females. To a lesser but still significant degree, Technological and Administrative fields were more popular with males, and Verbal and Aesthetic fields with females.

5. Although both genders tended to choose occupations consistent with their values and interests, females whose main interest was Personal Contact were more likely than females whose main interest was Scientific to wind up preferring an occupation consistent with their interest.

6. Both males and females who chose occupations consistent with their interests had attributed greater importance to interests than those whose choices were inconsistent with their interests.

Neither the similarities nor the differences were surprising. The differences particularly seemed to corroborate "conventional expectations." But we were particularly conscious of the high standard deviations on each variable and on the overlaps between the groups. At a time when inroads were being made into gender stereotypes, we wanted to include in our investigation the career decision making of people who departed from the stereotype: what about striving females and nurturant males?

Part 2: Liberation from Stereotypes

In the second part of the study, therefore, we classified the members of each group into two subgroups, designated *typical* and *atypical*, by means of a regression analysis in which gender was the dependent variable and values weights (on Helping Others, Early Entry, Leadership, and High

Income) were the predictors. The distribution of predicted gender scores was then cut to match the actual gender distribution (59% females, 41% males). Scores above the cutoff point were designated *predicted female*, and those below, *predicted male*. Students for whom the predicted and actual gender agreed were classified as gender-typical; those for whom the predicted and actual gender disagreed were classified as gender-atypical. Thus, four subgroups were created out of the interaction between actual gender and values: typical males, atypical males, typical females, and atypical females.

These four subgroups were compared on (a) their interests, (b) the opportunities for distinctive rewards and satisfactions offered by the occupations chosen by members of each subgroup, (c) the consistency between these occupational characteristics and the subgroups' values profiles, and (d) the predominant gender membership of occupations chosen by members of each subgroup. Highlights of the findings follow:

1. Gender differences in interests previously noted were attributable to the typical males and typical females. Parallel to these differences were those between typical and atypical groups of each gender. For example, typical males and atypical females preferred the Scientific field, while typical females and atypical males preferred the Personal Contact and Aesthetic fields.

2. Differences in the degree to which occupations chosen by the four subgroups offer opportunities for various rewards and satisfactions showed the two typical groups at the extremes and the two atypical groups close together, with the progression running consistently in the order typical males, atypical females, atypical males, and typical females. Thus, the choices of atypical females tended to resemble those of typical males more than those of typical females.

3. Occupations chosen by each subgroup tended to be very consistent with the differentiated values of the subgroups. For example, atypical females, like typical males and unlike typical females, planned for occupations that offer good opportunities for high income, prestige, and independence; atypical males resembled typical females, but not typical males, in a tendency to pursue occupations that are oriented toward helping others.

4. In tendencies to choose occupations that were populated predominantly by males, predominantly by females, or equally by the genders, the major differences were between the two typical groups. Distributions for the two atypical groups were quite similar, with each more likely than the typical group to choose occupations well populated by the other gender.

Discussion

A point that might be overlooked warrants mention first. Because some of the findings highlight gender differences, it would be easy to lose sight of the many similarities found between genders in the CDM process. Particularly noteworthy is the finding that all groups tend to make choices of occupations consistent with their values and interests.

CDM is a highly individualistic enterprise, and individual differences are ubiquitous. But these variations are often independent of gender. Even when significant differences are found between genders, there is always considerable overlap. Male and female college students are not making career decisions in grossly different ways. Some members of each gender resemble some members of the other gender in the CDM process.

In some instances, similarities may be attributed to development of understandings and competencies that generally result from use of SIGI. All students have been helped to discover the extent to which each occupation provides the configuration of rewards and satisfactions that best meet their individual values and interests. Consequently, a "ceiling effect" constrains findings of differences in consistency between groups.

It was not surprising, in the first part of the study (Norris et al., 1978), to see the corroborations and supplementations of previous findings of gender differences. But we went a step further to ask about people of either gender who break the stereotype (say, striving females and nurturant males). What are the effects of the interaction between gender and values in CDM? It was to explore this question that we classified the members of each gender into two groups, typical and atypical, according to their scores on the four differentiating values dimensions.

We reasoned that if gender stereotypes are in the process of breaking down, clearly the change would not affect all members of each gender simultaneously. Some males and some females would respond rather quickly to new liberating attitudes, others more slowly, and still others not at all. So the four subgroups formed on the basis of values were compared on other CDM variables. The classification scheme proved to be enlightening not only in respect to interests but also in respect to the characteristics of occupations chosen and consistency between those characteristics and each subgroup's values. So the classification of each gender by "typicality" is not merely academic. Thus, atypical females, like typical males, plan for occupations that offer good opportunities for high income, prestige, and independence. So gender per se does not appear to be a major barrier to selecting occupations that are instrumental in providing the particular configuration of rewards and satisfactions deemed important by each group.

These findings are essentially liberating. Given an appropriate guidance intervention, there is precedent for people of either gender who want to escape from sex-role stereotypes and seek career satisfactions in terms of their own values. Substantial numbers are not locked into gender roles but are capable of entertaining and acting on self-concepts that reflect their own values.

Questions for Further Research

In answering the questions we had raised, this study posed questions for additional research. A prime question is, granted the crucial importance of values that is confirmed in this study, are people equally free to develop value systems that are not gender-bound? Certainly we cannot ignore the statistically significant differences between means of values weights assigned by males and females on 6 of the 10 dimensions. But we should also note the great degree of overlap between distributions and the high standard deviations on every dimension. We know very little about the ways in which values are introcepted, except in general terms. Clearly, an individual's values come from family, from the culture at large, and from specific environments. What are the relative effects of these sources? Have recent changes in the cultural context been breaking down gender differences in occupational values at an accelerating rate?

Another question for research is the extent to which cultural effects on values may diminish in importance with maturation. Without denying impact of the environment on formative years, we can ask how much space a young adult has for conscious, intentional development and even change in values? And what are the stages of that development and the timing of such changes? To what extent is the attainment of autonomy a function of maturation? As one progresses through various stages toward maturity, what are the conditions that are most conducive to taking thought about where one's values have come from and where they are taking one (Katz, 1963)?

On the basis of the study and other evaluation research just reported, it is my judgment that an appropriate guidance intervention can effectively implement young adults' drive for autonomy by helping them examine their own values as a primary step in the process of making informed and rational career decisions. It can also serve as a stimulus and a medium for collecting data to answer the questions for research posed earlier, and many other questions as well. I hope that before too long the kind of research exemplified here can be resumed, by restoring the capability of looking through the "window" of students' records at CDM in process.

THE EVALUATION OF SIGI PLUS

The goals of SIGI PLUS were substantially like those of SIGI, except insofar as it was designed for a broader population. Consequently, as soon as the preliminary version of SIGI PLUS was ready, it was field tested and evaluated by methods similar to those used for SIGI, and the results were similar (Norris et al., 1985). To reflect the larger population for which SIGI PLUS was developed, the sample of users differed in several respects from the SIGI test sample. The sites included four state universities, a state "college without walls," two community colleges, a high school, a "regional learning service" associated with a library, and a corporation. Of these, one state university, the state college, the high school, and the corporation had not used SIGI. The users tended to be older, a majority of them over 31, and a higher proportion (more than 65%) were female. Obviously, these characteristics varied by site: The high school students were younger, with an equal number of males and females.

The main difference in method was the absence of a control group. There were also fewer interviews, which tended to take place while the interviewer observed the user's interactions with the system. This procedure was particularly helpful in capturing users' thoughts and reactions as they went through the system. It may also be noted that while the field test and evaluation were going on, several improvements were made to the original version of SIGI PLUS; a second wave of people used the new version.

Data to answer such questions as clarity, ease of use, comfort with instructions, needs for help, and so on were collected through logs and observations. More objective data were collected automatically by a computer program that recorded such variables as characteristics of users; time spent within each section; number of sections used per session; typical pathways through each section and the system as a whole; importance assigned to each dimension of values, interests, and activities; frequency with which each feature was used in structured search; frequency with which each occupation was listed in Search, and the sizes of lists; frequency with which each question was asked in Information and Coping; number of occupations explored in Preparing and Skills; ratings of skills; kinds of self-estimates made in Deciding; rationales for occupational choices (inferred from reactions to Deciding Squares); consistency of those choices with occupations used in Next Steps; and so on.

A questionnaire similar to the one used for SIGI was completed by 317 users of the first version and 146 users of the second version. Users rated all elements of SIGI PLUS, and also the system as a whole, favorably on such qualities as interest and usefulness. Asked whether they would recommend SIGI PLUS to a friend, 96% said yes. There were few differences in ratings by site and age; some significant differences did appear by gender, with females generally giving higher grades than males. Perhaps this difference reflects the particular concern of the SIGI PLUS developers for the needs of women. The development took place at a time when women were seeking to enter or re-enter the work force at a rapidly accelerating rate. Thus, some of the material, especially in Coping, raised and answered questions of special interest to women.

Questionnaires were also completed by 36 counselors at the educational institutions in the field test. Almost all of them felt that SIGI PLUS helped students and other adults make rational career decisions, did not view it as a threat or fad, and reported favorable reactions by users. Most of them said that users had brought their printouts to interviews. Almost 90% said that SIGI PLUS had an impact on problems they had experienced before the system became available: For example, it enabled more individuals to be helped in CDM and gave clients a "sense of self-help," "motivated clients," and "stimulated their thinking." Of the 36 counselors, 35 believed that the writing style and vocabulary of SIGI PLUS were appropriate for their clients. A high proportion rated it as better than other career guidance resources in general and also rated it better on specific features such as those pertaining to occupational information. All but one of the respondents said they would recommend SIGI PLUS to a colleague. The lone exception would not recommend it to a colleague but would "recommend it to adults as step one of a career transition" (perhaps interpreting the question to bear on use in the colleague's own CDM).

It is fair to say that the major purpose of the SIGI PLUS evaluation was formative. Many open-ended questions were included in the questionnaires, and interviews and observations of use were combined to scout opportunities for improvement. Thus, a revised version during the field test and later revisions took into account suggestions, comments, and reactions of users and counselors. Consequently, computer response time was speeded up at some points, color combinations on the screen were changed for better legibility, and "back up" and exit functions were improved. A number of counselors said they missed the values game from SIGI; a similar game was developed and incorporated in SIGI PLUS.

Notwithstanding the distinction made in this chapter between formative and summative purposes in evaluation, my view is that all evaluations of a viable product or treatment should be formative. An evaluation is summative insofar as it indicates that a product or treatment is worth continuing for a while or is worthless and should be junked. In the former case, a good evaluation identifies what needs to be improved and should, in the best of worlds, lead to corresponding improvements. Then, still in the best of worlds, there should be a continual alternation between development and evaluation to the point of either diminished returns or – because of technological or other changes – obsolescence of the product. Of course, developers do not have to wait for field tests to evaluate what needs to be improved. They are capable of reviewing their own work, observing changes in the world of work and in the needs of the clients they serve, even getting new ideas, and revising their product accordingly. The regular revision of occupational information is an example of developer-initiated improvement.

The catch is that changes cost money, and that some portion of the revenue brought in by a product must be earmarked for evaluation, research, improvement, and new development. Otherwise, there is the risk of stagnation. One would hope that in the long run a discriminating marketplace (still in the best of worlds) would support only sponsors willing to plow back a sufficient portion of their earnings in the cause of continuing evaluation, research, improvement, and development. Cronbach et al. (1980) stated: "To make public a periodic summary [of continual monitoring of a fully operational treatment] maintains trust."

Of course, in the real world money to sustain such a cycle is often difficult to obtain. It saddens me to acknowledge that after the initial field tests and evaluations, funded by The National Science Foundation for SIGI and the W. K. Kellogg Foundation for SIGI PLUS, we have not been able to obtain support for additional studies. It is worth noting, however, that neither SIGI nor SIGI PLUS was evaluated just once. In addition to the field tests and evaluations reported here, many independent evaluations have been conducted by institutions and individual scholars. The tenor of these independent studies is illustrated by reference to evaluations conducted in three California institutions in the 1970s.

INDEPENDENT EVALUATIONS

In California, each component of the higher education system wanted to ensure, by its own independent study, that SIGI was suitable for its use. So separate evaluations were conducted by Pasadena City College (in conjunction with the Chancellor's Office of California Community Colleges), California State Polytechnic University, Pomona (on behalf of the California State Universities and Colleges), and the University of California, Irvine.

Each of these is described briefly to provide what evaluators call "heterogeneous instances" (Cronbach et al., 1980). As noted in the account of our own evaluations, we took care to involve heterogeneity in types of institutions, composition of client populations, degree of staff commitment, and so on. Still, these diverse components were all part of evaluations that were uniform in one respect: They were conducted by the developers of the treatment, who obviously had a vested interest in the outcome. This uniform sponsorship might be seen as a contaminant that could conceivably contribute to the similarity of effects found across all participating institutions. The independent evaluations, however, provide heterogeneity of sponsorship; they should be free of any uniform contaminating element, having been conducted by staff at each institution for decisions to be made by that institution and by similar institutions.

The Pasadena study (Risser & Tully, 1977) used random assignment of students to experimental and control groups, 250 in each group; the former used SIGI, and the latter took a series of "traditional vocational tests," including the Strong–Campbell Interest Inventory, Kuder Occupational Interest Survey, Personality Research Form, and Comprehensive Tests of Basic Skills. The sample turned out to include students from various age, ethnic, gender, and college major groups in proportions similar to their representation in the college enrollment. Students in both groups then received career guidance counseling, and questionnaires were completed by students and counselors. Highly significant differences were found in favor of the experimental group on all of the 20 criteria of competence in CDM, such as (from the student questionnaires) knowledge of factors important in making a career decision, information about chosen occupations, knowledge of college course and other entry requirements for chosen occupations, confidence in succeeding in educational and vocational plans, satisfaction with educational and vocational plans, and (from the counselor questionnaires) ratings on students' probability of obtaining stated vocational goal, realistic changes in career objectives, ability to make career decisions, and ratings of the overall value of the counseling conferences. The authors concluded that students who had used SIGI were better prepared for career decision making than were the students who had the "traditional vocational testing and counseling program."

California State Polytechnic University, Pomona, forwarded the report of its evaluation of SIGI to the office of the Chancellor of State Universities and Colleges with this conclusion: "Our experiences with SIGI were highly positive and our expectation for the program was exceeded." About 1,300 students filled out questionnaires before and after using SIGI, with no control group (Fredericksen & Fullerton, 1978). Highly significant changes ($p < .001$) were found in the responses for all five criteria: current state of occupational or career plans, knowledge of values, ability to make career decisions, ability to make decisions in general, and amount of information about possible career options. The same level of change was found for virtually all subgroups (age, gender, ethnicity, academic year, and division). Students graded SIGI on various aspects: Over 94% gave it an A or B on "How interesting was SIGI to you?" About 96% gave A or B to "Showing you the relationship between values and career decisions," and over 94% to "Overall, how good is SIGI?"

Counselors reported that use of SIGI improved the quality of counseling sessions: Students had learned important concepts and vocabulary, showed greater readiness and motivation to pursue career questions, and generally made counselor time more productive. Fredericksen and Fullerton, (1978) also reported that "Numerous faculty members [spontaneously] incorporated SIGI into their course work."

The University of California, Irvine use of SIGI (Career Planning and Placement Center, 1979) did not leave generation of faculty interest in SIGI to the vagaries of spontaneity. Instead, it started by inviting chief administrators, faculty from all departments, and student leaders to use the system before making it available to all students. Periodic meetings were held between academic deans, program directors, and faculty advisers to ensure cooperation in providing information for the Planning section. Thus, in a carefully orchestrated campaign by the Career Planning and Placement Center (then directed by Cynthia Johnson), all elements of the university were introduced to SIGI.

Here we may note that reports of evaluations are enriched by descriptions of the conditions surrounding a treatment. These too often go unmentioned, even though they may plausibly play a significant role in the use and effects of the treatment. Something is added to the findings of an evaluation if similar effects are noted across a wide variation in conditions of use. For example, many institutions in their focus on completing an evaluation limited publicity about the availability of SIGI. They feared that if they were swamped with applicants to use the system they would have to extend the waiting period between sessions for each client. Then their final collection of data and report would be delayed. Thus, at California Polytechnic State University more users had found out about SIGI from friends than from any other source. University of California at Irvine, on the other hand, publicized SIGI as widely as possible, through letters to new students; brochures; newsletters; orientation programs; announcements in campus publications, on radio, and on local cable television; fliers, posters, banners, and balloons. A "roving terminal" was placed at strategic locations around the campus, with demonstrations by student assistants. All this outreach might be expected to produce a Hawthorne effect, and perhaps it did. The findings could hardly have been more favorable. Yet the same statement holds for California Polytechnic State University and others.

The Career Planning and Placement Center at the University of California, Irvine had listed three major objectives: to improve assistance to students in defining career objectives and plans; to make this improvement at low cost, with no increase in counselor time; to meet more effectively the specialized career planning needs of minorities, women, and nontraditional students. The report concluded that, in addition to meeting successfully the stated objectives, "the benefits [of use of SIGI at the university] have extended well beyond the original goals." Some of the benefits ascribed to SIGI included making the Career Planning and Placement Center more visible and increasing the use of its other resources and services; "providing an important vehicle for staff development and a vital link between career counseling and academic advising";

facilitating work with other student affairs units such as minority student programs; providing "career guidance services that would have required more than 11,500 hours of additional career counseling"; serving as a component in a project (funded by the National Science Foundation) to facilitate and promote "better science career preparation for handicapped students."

Questionnaires on career decision-making skills were administered to about 2,900 clients before and after use of SIGI. Substantial and statistically significant gains ($p < .0001$) were found on all five criteria chosen by the university: knowledge of work-related values; knowledge of occupations or careers; confidence in personal career decision-making skills; certainty of career goals (there we go again!); knowledge of academic requirements and curricula. The data were also analyzed for 28 subgroups, such as sex, ethnicity, school, class, and so forth; gains at the same high level of significance were found on all criteria for all groups except a few with very small numbers (Graduate School of Administration students). In addition, when asked to rate the helpfulness of SIGI, almost all students reported SIGI to be helpful or very helpful: 97% in becoming more aware of their values, 93% in identifying occupations that fit their values, 96% in obtaining occupational information, 93% in learning how to make career decisions, and 96% in providing information about educational requirements and recommended curricula.

Follow-up counseling sessions were mandatory. These sessions enabled counselors to judge that students who had used SIGI were much more advanced than others in their career decision-making skills. Each session concluded with an explanation of Career Planning and Placement Center services and a tour of the facilities. Thus, the use of SIGI helped to extend knowledge about the Center and to integrate SIGI into the total program of the Center.

It is interesting to compare results of this evaluation with those previously reported for California State Polytechnic University. The criteria and instruments were similar, and the findings were also similar. Perhaps any differences between the total effort at outreach characterizing one institution and the cooler approach at the other are canceled out by differences in the populations of the two institutions. But we have seen similar results across many kinds of populations, conditions of use, methods of evaluation, and criteria. In other words, a good case can be made for "heterogeneity of instances." Similar results can be cited for SIGI PLUS.

In short, the results of independent studies, undertaken because the institutions wanted to find out in their own terms how well SIGI was meeting their needs, reiterate several main themes: satisfaction with SIGI by clients and counselors; evidence of effectiveness, however defined, in meeting stated objectives at low cost; saving counselors' time and enhancing their contributions to clients' career decision making; and bringing increased attention to services and resources at career planning and placement centers. The evidence appears not only in questionnaires and tests; it comes also from such unobtrusive observations as long waiting lists to use SIGI, the high proportion of users who have been referred by their friends and who spread the word to other friends, the development of courses built around the SIGI model, and the integration of SIGI into a total career guidance program. Finally, the fact that the presence of SIGI has prompted independent evaluation and research studies on campuses is itself a bonus. It is useful for colleges and other institutions to define their objectives in career guidance, to plan programs, to collect and analyze evidence of effectiveness. Thus, SIGI may serve as a catalyst in the process of informed and rational decision making by the colleges themselves as they strive to meet the career development needs of students.

This treatment of the efficacy of SIGI and SIGI PLUS closes the triangle of evaluation shown in Figure 2. Notwithstanding the universally favorable results under heterogeneous instances, the evaluation effort – as I said before – cannot be laid to rest. The system undergoes continual change, and so do the world of work and the needs of various institutions and populations. It is only through persistent monitoring of a current operating system that a developer can maintain progress and trust. But there must also be an opportunity to try out new ideas for future development. And of course more work is needed on the development of appropriate criteria and worthy measures. Finally, to end where this chapter on evaluation began, the evidence for efficacy must feed back into ongoing evaluations of strength and accuracy. Only then can the evaluation of SIGI and SIGI PLUS, or any other treatment, accomplish that Cronbach et al. (1980) called "the proper mission of evaluation . . . [as] a process by which society learns about itself. . . . An evaluation of a particular program is only an episode in the continuing evolution of thought about a problem area."

6

Conclusion

. . . what's past is prologue.

— The Tempest II, 1

Don't look back; something may be gaining on you.

— Satchel Paige

A conclusion to a book, as to a life (see the Introduction), tends to "concentrate the mind." Like Janus, it faces both backward and forward. Looking backward, a conclusion to a book, as to a life, implies a challenge to the author to stand on one foot and say what the whole enterprise adds up to. This challenge at the end of a life is often slurred, or even evaded, as suggested in e. e. cummings's lines: "it's very easy to be dead, you don't even have to get out of bed, wherever you may be, they bring it to you free." This approach would interpret a conclusion to a life as simply an end.

For a book, the conventions are sometimes more demanding. For example, novices in expository writing have been instructed, "Tell your readers what you're going to say, say it, and then tell them what you've said." This dictum may be a convenience to some readers but an insult to others. Perhaps that is why an author's agent was reported to have told his client, "Cut off the ending and we'll send it to *The New Yorker*." A conclusion that is just a rehash of what has gone before runs the risk of boring both author and readers. If I could boil it all down to a few words at the end, why bother writing all these pages? For a reprise, re-read the book; for an overview, see the Introduction, or the table of contents, or perhaps the recapitulation of topics in chapter 5. As I think back over what

I have written, I have no new revelations to report, no epiphanies, no sudden manifestations, no hot flashes of inspiration.

Of course, there is always the temptation to repeat a few things, just for emphasis. Elderly people, with whom at 76 I began to feel I must associate myself, are notoriously prone to repetition. This tendency is not due exclusively to senility. There is also a desire to emphasize the distilled wisdom of years, the tenets (or parables) that seem urgently worth repeating. But my most familiar juniors have taught me a lesson. When I start one of these gambits, feel a sudden qualm, and interrupt myself– "Have I ever told you this before?"–they may politely reply, "Only a few thousand times." So I have learned, perhaps overlearned, that this is a temptation to be resisted. Even if they haven't paid attention before, or don't remember, a reminder will not help. Janus looks both ways, but the month named for him emphasizes beginnings, not ends. So this conclusion hearkens to Satchel Paige and looks not backward but forward.

PROSPECTS

Looking toward the future of career guidance in the light of the past and present should be congenial to people interested in the process of career decision making or in the practice of career guidance. Career decisions are made in the present and have been partly moulded in the past, but they bear on the future. Guidance helps people engage in excursions through time, bringing past and future into the psychological present; thus it helps them see past, present, and future in a unified field of view. Similarly, having already looked at the past and present of computerized guidance systems, we can extrapolate to their future. In a relatively short time, we have seen computerized career guidance systems progress from a gleam in the eye through conception, gestation, birth, infancy, childhood, adolescence, and now perhaps reach maturity. Still youthful, they have made their way in the world and have achieved widespread recognition and use. What of their future?

All systems have been revised over the years of their existence. It is a truism that they will continue to change. It is also inevitable that change will continue to occur around a core of continuity. Thus, over several decades, there has been no deviation from the principles of career guidance on which SIGI was founded. On the other hand, I hope that no reader of the preceding pages has come away with the impression that SIGI PLUS is seen as a perfected product of those principles. SIGI underwent continual revisions until SIGI PLUS superseded it. SIGI PLUS has also been improved continually, and will also someday be replaced by successors. Although I have explained and even defended some of our decisions and solutions to problems, as developers we have never been content. We have always wanted to do more to reduce the discrepancy between our ideal of a career guidance system and the actual system in use at any moment. Of course, we keep adding to our "wish list." The ideal moves too fast for the reality ever to catch up.

For example, we have always been eager to make advantageous use of the latest improvements or changes in technology. But new technology is often too expensive for our licensees. We have to wait for a period of relative stability and cost reductions.

Change of any kind is also expensive for us. We would never want to skimp on the quality of the annual update of occupational information. But it costs a lot. Too often, financial support is not available for the *additional* research and development we would like to do. SIGI PLUS could serve as a wonderful machine for research (as SIGI did in the study of gender differences in CDM). Well, developers can propose, but others dispose. Frankly, it had been my dream in initiating the development of SIGI that, someday, when it had grown up to earn its way in the world, a fixed proportion of the revenue it brought in would be dedicated to a continuing program of research and development. It saddens me to say that things have not worked out that way. This outcome is not unusual in the real world. In any case, developers' reach must always exceed their grasp. The ideal product is a moving target. Change never attains the ideal but progresses toward it. The glum alternative is entropy.

Getting back to the future – I have no crystal ball, and what I envision may not come to pass. But what follows in this chapter is a small sample of what I expect and would like to see.

New Delivery Systems

Obviously, one driving force will be the opportunities offered by changes in technology that have already edged into view. Just as rapid development of interactive capabilities in computing made SIGI and other early systems feasible, the integration of multimedia delivery systems will lead to a new generation of developments for career guidance – as well as many other applications. An integrated multimedia system can provide not just the text, graphics, and color that people are used to seeing on their personal computer screens but also dynamic graphics, animation, and television-quality moving pictures, accompanied by stereo sound with the quality of compact disks – all articulated in an interactive mode under the client's control at one convenient user-friendly station. It will take a little while for the technology to "shake out" and a longer while for costs to come down within reach of institutions and agencies that provide career guidance. The history of technology, however, suggests that recent trends in these directions will accelerate.

An integrated multimedia station is not just a matter of adding "bells and whistles" to a computer. It can extend the content and processes of career guidance. Consider, for example, the first two functions in my model of guidance: self-assessment and seeking relevant occupational information. A client sitting at such a station can call up vignettes in which competing occupational values are dramatized; the client can intervene in such dramas, or even play a role in them. Indeed, thanks to the powers of audiovisual simulation, a client trying to evaluate alternatives can, as in Robert Frost's poem, "travel both [roads], And be one traveler." Clients can see and hear representative activities and environments for any occupation; can summon interviews with people in occupations that seem of interest; can get different points of view on each occupation; can try to solve problems typically encountered in an occupation: indicating what information they might need first (and getting it), taking steps toward solving the problem (and seeing the consequences of those steps), and responding to cues that lead them to a solution. Clients can then judge whether these activities and problems are of interest to them and whether they have or can develop sufficient skills to enter, succeed in, and derive satisfaction from that occupation. In short, occupational information can become more vivid and intensive.

Information about educational options can be enriched in similar ways. Teachers can be seen and heard, describing and illustrating the content and activities of various courses. Clients can try to solve representative problems encountered in a course and can see how the course will help them learn how to solve such problems. Without leaving their station, clients can "sit in" on a class of their choosing. They can examine textbooks and other instructional materials. They can listen to previous students, some of whom may have taken different paths toward an occupation, explain how a course or program or other experience contributed (or did not contribute) to their careers. Similarly, training programs in schools or on the job can be examined "on line."

It is easy for a developer to be swept away on a wave of euphoria by the capabilities of new technology. But there is an antidote to getting caught up too much in the "gee whiz" response to technology. Anyone with experience in development is aware of difficulties and disadvantages sure to come with multimedia systems. One of the major gains in improving computerized career guidance systems over the years will be lost to the new complexities of multimedia stations. Initially, developers were heavily dependent on computer scientists and programmers to translate their models, scripts, and flow charts first into suitable hardware and software configurations and then into working systems. Over the years, however, computer languages have become more user-friendly. "Prototyping tools" enable authors to develop prototypes that show what the finished system should look like. These tools are not efficient for programming the product to be marketed, but give the programmer a clear pattern to follow. At the next level, "authoring systems" enable developers who are not trained programmers to take over major responsibility for the finished system. These technical enhancements have given authors unprecedented flexibility and control. They can go through iterations of trial and error, revise freely on their own, change an earlier section in the light of a new idea for a later section, and still meet deadlines for the finished product. In the early days, an author trying to meet a deadline for development of a system had to turn over to the programmer a final script and flow chart for one section, then go on to write the next section. As far as the programmer was concerned, each successive section had to be cast in concrete. Any change resulted in inordinate and intolerable delay. Those days have mercifully gone by.

The multimedia technology, however, may restore elements of dependence and rigidity. Those who direct development will no longer be able to exercise so much individual control, will no longer be so free to try something, see immediately how it looks, and revise it on the spot. Formalities in procedures and in relationships between specialists may have to be reintroduced. Development costs will be much higher. Each medium requires specific talents, training, and expertise. Specialists in different fields will have to be brought together, briefed, and coordinated. Control will be diffused, and flexibility diminished. For example, a video may turn out not to have quite the content, style, or emphasis that the director of development wanted. But to go back and reshoot may be too time consuming and expensive. The director may have to make many compromises between the envisioned ideal and the actual product.

Although I do not want to devote too much space to technology, I should mention a concurrent, but different, technical development that may have an impact on career guidance: the use of telephone lines to bring career guidance systems to people in their homes. This projected extension of locale from institutions to homes is not really new. It is just that the delivery mode will be less expensive than any previously available. Initially, computerized career guidance systems resided on mainframes or minicomputers. Each computer could "time-share" a system among a large number of terminals. Over a short distance, say at one college, the terminals could be "hardwired" to the computer. Over longer distances, they would be connected to the computer over telephone lines. Thus, a statewide or regional system could be handled by one or a few computers, depending on the number of terminals a particular computer could accommodate. Theoretically, with permission of the host, a person anywhere with a telephone line, an appropriate terminal, and a modem could connect to the system. In practice, such arrangements were rarely made and were not a viable option for people in general.

Later, most systems were converted to run on microcomputers. This was feasible because computerized guidance systems do not require much computing power; they do not engage in number crunching. What they do need is storage capacity for large data bases, along with speed and flexibility for retrieval and other interactions. The relatively inexpensive microcomputers had always had more than enough power. As soon as microcomputer capacity increased enough to hold and quickly retrieve huge quantities of information, SIGI (with the help of ingenious compression techniques) was shoehorned into one. Now, all systems have been converted to run on personal computers. Because the PC is freestanding, each one has its own copy of the system. So anyone who is licensed by the distributor of the system could run the system over a home PC. For a variety of reasons (such as relatively high investment for limited use), no significant number have ever done so.

Recently, two major developments seem likely to accelerate access to guidance systems, along with many other resources, in almost any home. One is the rapid increase in use of fiber-optic telephone lines and other technical advances that will open over 100 channels into the home; the other is an October 1991 court decision that permits telephone companies to provide substance, such as television programs and information services, as well as communication over their lines. The huge volume generated for all these resources should make costs to each user of a guidance system much lower than any previous method of access from the home.

The feasibility and popularity of information services by telephone have been demonstrated in France. Over a decade ago, the French telephone system initiated "teletele" – linking a home telephone and terminal ("minitel") to a wide range of computer and information services. Minitels started modestly; they were distributed free in some regions to replace telephone directories (updating could be done continuously, and minitels were much less expensive than issuing printed directories every year). Gradually, they came to include access to practical information of many sorts: Subscribers could consult timetables for railroad and air travel; make reservations for such travel and for hotels; conduct business transactions; scan curricula at educational institutions. Eventually, they could also play simple interactive games, and – with a delay of a day or two for human intervention – get answers to questions relevant to CDM (Aubret & Guichard, 1989). Slow response time and an inadequate terminal were drawbacks to extended applications in the first few years. More recently, improved terminals have been distributed, and Aubret and Guichard say that eventually teletele should be capable of supplying access to a fully interactive career guidance system like SIGI.

The main point of this too-long discussion of technology is that career guidance can be brought directly to homes by telephone. Clients will no longer have to seek out an educational institution, community organization, corporation, or private counseling agency as the host for a system.

This prospect is seen by many to have drawbacks in divorcing use of a career guidance system from a milieu in which it is complemented by professional human counselors (Ballantine & Watts, 1989). Previous research has shown that some clients prefer to use a guidance system alone, while others prefer to use it with counseling support. As I said previously in chapter 5 on evaluation, a division of labor, in which system and counselor each make a unique contribution, is desirable. Need the counselor's contribution be lost in a home delivery system? Not necessarily. The system could list local counselors available for consultation, if desired by the client. Such consultation could be over the phone line or face-to-face. Thus, the home-delivered career guidance system might create even more demand for counselors.

In any case, it should be noted that most people make their decisions with little or no consultation with professional counselors. They depend, instead, on informal sources readily available – families, friends, casual others. Access to a coherent, professionally developed system will improve on the quality of CDM even for people who do not choose to consult counselors.

The convenience of an additional resource provided by a home delivery system also deserves mention: easy access to "bulletin boards" (like those on current computer networks). People with interest in an occupation could form an ad hoc network, sharing information and sources; they could post questions for members of that occupation to answer. Communication of this sort can enrich and extend the resources available to them.

International Development

In this discussion of a technical development I have touched on a significant prospect for the future: the rapid growth of an international community of discourse on computerized guidance. Lecturing at international conferences and consulting in various parts of the world, I have been struck by the spread of computerized systems and by the impact of those systems on the practice of career guidance. In many countries, as in the United States, such systems have amplified the power of existing career guidance counselors. This trend is clear in the countries of Europe, as well as in Canada, Israel, and Australia. In Taiwan, development of computerized guidance is following hard on the heels of development of a general career guidance profession (Katz, 1986). Japan, however, is a particularly interesting case. Interest in computerized guidance has grown quickly, with scant previous tradition of practice or profession of guidance. I suspect there is a good chance that in Japan computerized guidance will leapfrog transitional stages of career guidance; it may deploy computerized systems without ever having had a corps of professional counselors.

At any rate, the growth of computerized guidance makes international discourse on guidance much more specific and pointed than it has been. Our dialogues get less nebulous as we refer to reified treatments, and less is lost in translation. The effects of this postulated improvement in international communication on career guidance and information may soon be tested. As the European Community prepares for "free trade" in people as well as in commodities, occupational information will have to cross national boundaries. Interest in extending and sharing data bases, first to cross frontiers and then to cover the continent, is percolating (Plant, 1991; Watts, 1989). National occupational information systems have been developed in several European countries (e.g., Germany, Denmark, the Netherlands, Sweden, Finland, France, and the United Kingdom, which has also recently introduced a guidance system, PROSPECT, patterned in some ways on SIGI). It does not seem unlikely that communications networks may make some of these systems accessible to nationals in other countries who seek to migrate for employment. A European "intelligent gateway" (Newton, 1989) could provide "multihost access," select appropriate resources, make the necessary searches, and display the relevant information.

I hope that any such transcontinental system will not put exclusive emphasis on occupational or job information. It is likely that some adults who know what they are looking for would benefit from information alone. Most people, however, can be overwhelmed by collections of facts about a job or occupation that, for the most part, provide no means for relating the facts to themselves as decision makers, for distinguishing what is relevant (for them) from what is irrelevant, and for making a choice between options. The missing context is career guidance. Guidance serves to help people discover what they want, helps them seek information about rewards and satisfactions that are important to them, helps them determine their chances of meeting qualifications for entry and success, and helps them make informed and rational decisions. Ideally, systems within each country would provide the context of career guidance and would then reach out to bring in transnational information at appropriate points.

Planning for Retirement

We say that we "grow older." We like to think that we do not wither or decline into old age, but *grow* into it. Growth implies not just change but development, progression into new stages of life.

These stages are usually linked to biological changes. They are also often functions of social and cultural arrangements, such as laws and policies governing education, work, and retirement – which in turn may be associated with demographic characteristics, economic conditions, and other circumstances of time and place. Each stage is visible as a distinct discontinuity, a point at which various courses of action are available and decisions are to be made. Career guidance traditionally focused on such points as the onset of adolescence and adulthood, roughly corresponding with the beginnings and ends of secondary and tertiary schooling. More recently, it has extended into the "middle" periods of adulthood, as people have increasingly tended to make mid-career changes.

It has long been known that there is life after these choice-points. What follows mid career, however, was characterized in the last term of the nomenclature frequently used in designating "vocational life stages" (Super et al., 1957): growth, exploration, establishment, maintenance, and *decline*. That concept of maintenance giving way to decline may have been depressing but was generally realistic. In the long run, strive as one might to maintain a given career status, the outcome was inevitable. Of course, it was not a trivial accomplishment to postpone the inevitable, and for some that may still be the name of the game. For most others, the game has changed. They do not have to retreat, willingly or unwillingly, into a state defined merely as nonwork. People are aware of other options, other possibilities for decisions and plans.

The new awareness is attributable in part to people's longer life spans and retention of capacities for activity, and in part to the much greater numbers in successive cohorts approaching traditional retirement age. The fastest growing segment of our population consists of people 65 and older: from 1 in 8 Americans in 1989 to 1 in 5 in 2030. The burgeoning numbers surviving into post-65 vigor have already begun to focus more attention on what all these lively superannuated people are to do – or what society is to do about them. They are beginning to become more assertive about their choices as they seek to "grow" (rather than fade) into retirement, the final phase of their career.

Seeing these demographic patterns in the 1970s, even as SIGI was coming into use, we anticipated a need for retirement planning. Actual development began to materialize in 1977. Henry Chauncey, having twice retired (first after long service as the first president of ETS, then as president of EDUCOM), proposed that we develop a retirement planning system patterned after SIGI. In an extensive series of interviews, he found support for the concept among experts on aging, corporations, educators, and government officials. We designed the system, like SIGI, to help people analyze their values, interests, skills, objectives, and resources, get relevant information about options, and apply their knowledge to decisions. The decision topics, for people over 50, were to include the timing of retirement, work after retirement, financial planning, provisions for health care, choice of living place, leisure activities, and continuing education. Under Chauncey's leadership, considerable progress was made: We drew up the model for the system, and he arranged with expert groups to develop the analytical financial planning and health modules. Within a year, however, the project was abruptly discontinued, for reasons too interesting to go into.

The main point is that recently my colleagues, Lila Norris and Laurence Shatkin, have revived the proposal, which they have tentatively titled Great Expectations, on a more modest scale. In the interval since 1977, useful interactive computer programs for financial planning have appeared on the market. So there is no need for them to repeat what has already been accomplished. They will also leave the health planning for others. To keep the task within bounds of what they can do themselves, they currently plan to focus on issues that relate to how retirees will spend their time: paid work, volunteer work, education, leisure activities, living places, and lifestyles. At this writing, the proposal is still awaiting final decision by others. All signs point to the likelihood that such a system will be built by someone somewhere. The experience of Norris and Shatkin in developing SIGI and SIGI PLUS as well as other interactive computer applications qualifies them preeminently for the task. (Late news flash: Their proposal has not been funded.)

In summary, these glimpses into the future of computerized career guidance – including new technologies and delivery systems, new opportunities for international cooperation, new clienteles, and new research – augur well for those organizations that are venturesome, competent, and prepared.

A FINAL NOTE

In less than three decades, computerized guidance has moved from a gleam in the eye to a state near ubiquity in secondary schools and colleges. It is gathering momentum in other agencies and in corporations. It is spreading around the world. In the face of such successes, I hope that the sponsoring organizations will not be complacent. The developers all have their "futures lists" of research, improvements, and innovations. It would be particularly shortsighted to fail to support them now. They are within sight of the Promised Land of computerized career guidance.

The popularity of computerized guidance systems is emphasized not just in surveys and other formal observations but in everyday encounters – a more vivid and memorable source of many of the notions we hold.

For many years I have been unable to refrain from scratching a professional itch to learn about the careers of people I meet casually. There is no need to worry about exceeding the bounds of civility in trying to satisfy my curiosity. Given just an inkling of an interested listener, most people like to talk about their own careers: their hopes, dreams, plans, problems, difficulties, successes, conditions that may have led to failure, past, present, and future. They talk about their current occupation, prospective changes in their occupation or job, or–if they are students–about their occupational goal. The degree of identification with an occupation is usually strong, even though the expectation of job stability is diminishing for many. (Sometimes, however, it is rueful, with stories of ignorance, misinformation, missed chances, and regret: "If I had only known. . . .") Now particularly in conversations with young people, I feel a special *frisson* when they credit satisfaction with their career decisions to use of a computerized guidance system called SIGI. I knew that millions of people had used SIGI and SIGI PLUS by now, but to meet some of them casually, not as part of a research study, still gives me a bit of a thrill–and a reminder of what a serious responsibility is involved in offering career guidance. I keep rediscovering how important career decisions and guidance (or the lack of it) are. My concern for sustaining and improving the quality of our career guidance system remains unabated.

I also get a kick out of what a research colleague told me of interviews with a sample of college seniors for the National Science Foundation; his mission was to find out why some had changed their majors from science to another field and why others had changed from another field to science. In both groups, they often attributed the change to their interaction with SIGI PLUS. I wonder how the National Science Foundation, which helped support the development of SIGI, will feel about the first group. Perhaps they will share the attitude of the carnival owner: "What I lose on the swings I make on the roundabout." Or perhaps they may take a more optimistic view and agree that the nation's needs for scientists will be met best not by proselytizing but by helping people make informed and rational career decisions. Perhaps they will also agree that scientific education can be fostered by helping people learn a process of informed and rational decision making in the face of uncertainty. (Samuel Butler said that life is the art of drawing sufficient conclusions from insufficient premises.) If SIGI PLUS and its descendants can accomplish these related objectives, I will be satisfied. So, I hope, will NSF.

Before this book is published, I expect to have retired at the age of 76 without benefit of Great Expectations. So I feel an occasional pang of regret that I will not be able to enter the Promised Land of computerized career guidance. But I recall that Moses, who led the way for many years through the wilderness until at last he reached the east bank of the Jordan

River, was allowed to see into the Promised Land. But he was not allowed to enter it.

I remember also that the Promised Land viewed by Moses turned out not to be all milk and honey. It brought new problems and much travail. Still, what more can one ask in a career than opportunities, with a band of dedicated and congenial colleagues, to solve problems, work through difficulties, and create a useful contribution? The fun is in moving *toward* the Promised Land. I would not have missed the years in the wilderness for anything. The Promised Land offers no greater expectations.

References

Allport, G. (1943). The ego in contemporary psychology. *Psychological Review, 50*, 451–478.

American Institute for Research. (1976). *Planning career goals.* Monterey, CA: California Test Bureau/McGraw-Hill.

American Psychological Association, American Educational Research Association, & National Council on Measurement in Education. (1985). *Standards for educational and psychological testing.* Washington, DC: American Psychological Association.

Anastasi, A. (1964). *The fields of applied psychology.* New York: McGraw-Hill.

Arbeiter, S. (1979). Mid-life career change: A concept in search of reality. *AAHE Bulletin, 32*, 1, 11–13, 16.

Arbeiter, S., Schmerbeck, F., Aslanian, C., & Brickell, H. (1976). *40 million Americans in career transition: The need for information.* New York: College Entrance Examination Board.

Aubret, J., & Guichard, J. (1989). Minitel and careers guidance. In A. Watts (Ed.), *Computers in careers guidance* (pp. 13–17). Cambridge, UK: CRAC.

Bachman, J., O'Malley, P., & Johnston, J. (1978). *Adolescence to adulthood: Stability and change in the lives of young men* (Youth in Transition, No. 6). Ann Arbor: Institute for Social Research, University of Michigan.

Baird, L. (1976). *Using self-reports to predict student performance* (Research Monograph Number 7). New York: College Entrance Examination Board.

Ballantine, M., & Watts, A. (1989). Computers and careers guidance services: Integrating the technology into the organization. In A. Watts (Ed.), *Computers in careers guidance* (pp. 18–22). Cambridge, UK: CRAC.

Barton, P. (1978). Adult career guidance: Emergence of need. In R. Campbell & R. Shaltry (Compilers), *Perspectives on adult career development and guidance.* Research and Development No. 181. Columbus: Ohio State University, National Center for Research in Vocational Education. (ERIC Document Reproduction Service No. ED 189 290.)

Barzun, J. (1990). The paradoxes of creativity. In J. Kaplan (Ed.), *The best American essays 1990* (pp. 20–37). New York: Ticknor & Fields.

Bauernfeind, R. (1963). *Building a school testing program.* Boston: Houghton-Mifflin.

Beder, H. (1977). *AAENJ Research Monograph No. 1.* Union, NJ: Association for Adult Education of New Jersey.

Beilin, H. (1955). The application of general development principles to the vocational area. *Journal of Counseling Psychology, 2*, 53–57.

Berg, I. (1970). *Education and jobs: The great training robbery.* New York: Praeger.

Berger, J. (1989, June 18). Study of welfare clients says trade schools fail. *New York Times*, p. 28.

Berger, S., Dertouzos, M., Lester, R., Solow, R., & Thurow, L. (1989). Toward a new industrial America. *Scientific American, 260*, 39–47.

Betz, E. (1969). Need reinforcer correspondence as a predictor of job satisfaction. *Personnel and Guidance Journal, 47*, 878–883.

Beynon, H., & Blackburn, R. (1972). *Perceptions of work: Variations within a factory.* London: Cambridge University Press.

Bisconti, A., & Gomberg, I. (1976). *Where have they gone? Careers in the private sector: A national study of college graduates in business and industry* (Report No. 6). Bethlehem, PA: The CPC Foundation.

Bishop, J., & Carter, S. (1990). *The worsening shortage of college graduates.* Ithaca, NY: Cornell University School of Industrial and Labor Relations, Center for Advanced Human Resource Studies.

Bonynge, E. (1991). No work and all play: An analysis of a response style on the Strong–Campbell Interest Inventory. *Journal of Counseling and Development, 69*, 275–276.

Borgen, F., Weiss, D., Tinsley, H., Dawis, R., & Lofquist, L. (1968). *The measurement of occupational reinforcement patterns.* Minneapolis: Work Adjustment Project, University of Minnesota.

Bowen, W., & Sosa, J. (1989). *Prospects for faculty in the arts and sciences.* Princeton, NJ: Princeton University Press.

Brewer, J. (1942). *History of vocational guidance.* New York: Harper.

Brief, A., & Aldag, R. (1975). Male-female differences in occupational attitudes within minority groups. *Journal of Vocational Behavior, 6*, 305–314.

Brill, A. (1949). *Basic principles of psychoanalysis.* New York: Doubleday.

Brogden, H. (1949). When testing pays off. *Personnel Psychology, 2*, 171–185.

Bruner, J., & Krech, D. (Eds.). (1949). *Perception and personality.* Durham, NC: Duke University Press.

Bruner, J., & Postman, L. (1948). Symbolic values as an organizing factor in perception. *Journal of Social Psychology, 27*, 203–208.

Buehler, C. (1933). *Der menschliche lebenslauf als psychologisches problem* [The course of human life considered as a psychological problem]. Leipzig: Hirzel.

Campbell, D. (1971). *Handbook for the Strong Vocational Interest Blank.* Stanford, CA: Stanford University Press.

Career Planning and Placement Center, University of California Irvine. (1979). *SIGI Project: Student evaluation, first 18 months.* Irvine: University of California.

Carey, M. (1980). Evaluating the 1975 projections of occupational employment. *Monthly Labor Review, 103*, 10–21.

Centers, R. (1949). *The psychology of social classes.* Princeton, NJ: Princeton University Press.

Chapman, W., & Katz, M. (1981). *Survey of career information systems in secondary schools: Final report of study 1.* Princeton, NJ: Educational Testing Service.

Chapman, W., & Katz, M. (1982). *Career information systems in secondary schools. Final report of study 2: Comparative effects of major types of resources.* Princeton, NJ: Educational Testing Service.

Chapman, W., & Katz, M. (1983). Career information systems in secondary schools: A survey and assessment. *Vocational Guidance Quarterly, 31*, 165–177.

Chapman, W., Katz, M., Norris, L., & Pears, L. (1977). *SIGI: Field test and evaluation of a* computer-based system of interactive guidance and information (2 Vols; also 15-page *Summary* of the report). Princeton, NJ: Educational Testing Service.

Cohen, B., (1977). *Career development in industry: A study of selected programs and recommendations for program planning.* Princeton, NJ: Educational Testing Service.

Cooley, W., & Lohnes, P. (1968). *Predicting development of young adults* (Project TALENT Report 5). Palo Alto, CA: American Institutes for Research and University of Pittsburgh.

Cottle, W. (1950). A factorial survey of the Multifasic, Strong, Kuder, and Bell inventories using a population of adult males. *Psychometrika, 15,* 25–47.

Crites, J. (1973). *Career maturity inventory.* Monterey: California Test Bureau/ McGraw-Hill.

Cronbach, L. (1956). Assessment of individual differences. In P. Farnsworth & Q. McNemar (Eds.), *Annual review of psychology* (pp. 173–196). Stanford, CA: Stanford University Press.

Cronbach, L. (1969). Validation of educational measures. In *Proceedings of the 1969 Invitational Conference on Testing Problems* (pp. 35–52). Princeton, NJ: Educational Testing Service.

Cronbach, L., Ambron, S., Dornbusch, S., Hess, R., Hornik, R., Phillips, D., Walker, D., & Weiner, S. (1980). *Toward reform of program evaluation.* San Francisco: Jossey-Bass.

Cronbach, L., & Gleser, G. (1965). *Psychological tests and personnel decisions* (2nd ed.). Urbana: University of Illinois Press.

Cross, K. (1978). *The missing link: Connecting adult learners to learning resources.* New York: College Entrance Examination Board.

Curry, E., & Walling, D. (1984). Occupational prestige: Exploration of a theoretical basis. *Journal of Vocational Behavior, 25,* 124–138.

D'Costa, A., Winefordner, D., Odgers, J., & Koohs, P. (1969). *Ohio Vocational Interest Survey.* New York: Harcourt, Brace, & World.

Dolliver, R. (1969). Strong Vocational Interest Blank versus expressed vocational interests: A review. *Psychological Bulletin, 72,* 95–107.

Donahue, J. (1989). *The privatization decision.* New York: Basic Books.

Drewes, D., & Katz, D. (1975). *Manpower data and vocational education: A national study of availability and use.* Raleigh: Center for Occupational Education, North Carolina State University.

Duncan, O. (1961). A socioeconomic index for all occupations. In A. Reiss, O. Duncan, P. Hatt, & C. North (Eds.), *Occupations and social status* (pp. 109–138). New York: Free Press.

Dyson, F. (1979). *Disturbing the universe.* New York: Basic Books.

Employment and Training Report of the President. (1977). Washington, DC: U.S. Department of Labor.

Erikson, E. (1963). *Childhood and society* (2nd ed.). New York: Norton.

Erikson, E. (1968). *Identity: Youth and crisis.* New York: Norton.

Executive Office of the President, Office of Management and Budget. (1972). *Standard industrial classification manual.* Washington, DC: U.S. Government Printing Office.

Flanagan, J., Tiedeman, D., Willis, M., & McLaughlin, D. (1973). *The career data book: Results from Project TALENT's five-year-follow-up study.* Palo Alto, CA: American Institutes for Research.

Forer, B. (1953). Personality factors in occupational choice. *Educational and Psychological Measurement, 13,* 361–366.

France, M., Jin, Y., Huang, K., Si, F., & Zhang, W. (1991). Career needs of Chinese middle school students and implications for school guidance in the People's Republic of China. *Career Development Quarterly, 40,* 155–167.

Fredericksen, G., & Fullerton, T. (1978). *The report of the pilot project to evaluate the System of Interactive Guidance and Information.* Pomona: California State Polytechnic University.

Freedman, M., & Dutka, A. (1980). *Training information for policy guidance* (Research and Development Monograph 76). Washington, DC: U.S. Department of Labor.

Freeman, R. (1976). *The overeducated American.* New York: Academic Press.

French, J. (1954). *Comparative prediction and other techniques for use with a guidance battery* (Research Bulletin 55-4). Princeton, NJ: Educational Testing Service.

French, J. (1961). *Comparative prediction of success and satisfaction in college major fields* (ETS RB 61-7). Princeton, NJ: Educational Testing Service.

French, J. (1963). Comparative prediction of college major-field grades by pure-factor aptitude, interest, and personality measures. *Educational and Psychological Measurement, 23,* 767–774.

From home to career: A statistical snapshot of high school class of 1989. (1989, November). *College Board News,* p. 8.

Gardner, J. (1961). *Excellence, can we be equal and excellent too?* New York: Harper.

Gati, I. (1982). Testing models for the structure of vocational interests. *Journal of Vocational Behavior, 21,* 164–182.

General Education in a Free Society. (1945). Report of the Harvard Committee. Cambridge, MA: Harvard University Press.

Ghiselli, E. (1966). *The validity of occupational aptitude tests.* New York: Wiley.

Ginzberg, E., Ginsburg, S., Axelrod, S., & Herma, J. (1951). *Occupational choice: An approach to a general theory.* New York: Columbia University Press.

Gleick, J. (1987). *Chaos: Making a new science.* New York: Viking Penguin.

Grant, D. (1985). *Effects of System of Interactive Guidance and Information (SIGI) on career indecision in college students.* Unpublished doctoral dissertation, The University of Toledo, Toledo, OH.

Grasso, J., & Shea, J. (1979). *Vocational education and training: Impact on youth.* New York: Carnegie Foundation for the Advancement of Teaching.

Gribbons, W. (1960). Evaluation of an eighth-grade group guidance program. *Personnel and Guidance Journal, 38,* 740–745.

Gribbons, W., & Lohnes, P. (1968). *Emerging careers.* New York: Teacher's College Press.

Gribbons, W., & Lohnes, P. (1969). *Career Development from age 13 to age 25.* Washington, DC: U.S. Office of Education.

Guilford, J. (1948). Factor analysis in a test development program. *Psychological Review, 55,* 79–94.

Hackman, J., & Lawler, E. (1971). Employee reactions to job characteristics. *Journal of Applied Psychology, 55,* 259–286.

Hafer, A. (1987). *Treatment effects of a computer-assisted career guidance system (SIGI PLUS), the SCII, and SDS for engineering freshmen.* Unpublished doctoral dissertation, Clemson University, Clemson, SC.

Hansen, L. (1970). *Career guidance practices in school and community.* Washington, DC: National Vocational Guidance Association.

Harris, L., & Associates. (1979). *The Playboy report on American men: A study of the values, attitudes, and goals of U.S. males 18-to-49 years old.* Chicago: Playboy.

Havighurst, R. (1953). *Human development and education.* New York: Longmans, Green.

Havighurst, R. (1964). Youth in exploration and man emergent. In H. Borow (Ed.), *Man in a world at work* (pp. 215–236). Boston: Houghton–Mifflin.

Herzberg, F., Mausner, B., & Snyderman, B. (1959). *The motivation to work* (2nd ed.). New York: Wiley.

Hitchcock, A. (1978). Public policy and adult career/occupational services. In R. Campbell & P. Shaltry (Compilers), *Perspectives on adult career development and guidance* (Research and Development No. 181). Columbus: Ohio State University, National Center for Research in Vocational Education. (ERIC Document Reproduction Service No. ED 189 290)

Holland, J. (1973). *Making vocational choices: A theory of careers.* Englewood Cliffs, NJ: Prentice–Hall.

Hoppock, R. (1957). *Occupational information.* New York: McGraw–Hill.

Hoyt, K. (1974). *Career education, what it is and how to do it* (2nd ed.). Salt Lake City, UT: Olympus.

Hull, C. (1928). *Aptitude testing.* Yonkers-on-Hudson, NY: World Book.

Hunter, J., Crosson, J., & Friedman, D. (1985). *The validity of the Armed Services Vocational Aptitude Battery (ASVAB) for civilian and military job performance.* Rockland, MD: Research Applications.

Ironside, D., & Jacobs, D. (1977). *Trends in counseling and information services for the adult learner.* Toronto, Canada: Ontario Institute for Studies in Education.

Jencks, C., Bartlett, S., Corcoran, M., Crouse, J., Eaglesfield, D., Jackson, G., McClelland, K., Mueser, P., Olneck, M., Schwartz, J., Ward, S., & Williams, J. (1979). *Who gets ahead? The determinants of occupational success in America.* New York: Basic Books.

Jepsen, D. (1975). Occupational decision development over the high school years. *Journal of Vocational Behavior, 7,* 225–237.

Jordaan, J., & Heyde, M. (1979). *Vocational maturity during the high school years.* New York: Teachers College (Columbia University) Press.

Kaplan, A. (1964). *The conduct of inquiry.* San Francisco: Chandler.

Katz, M. (1954). *A critical analysis of the literature concerning the process of occupational choice in high school boys.* Harvard Career Studies (No. 6). Cambridge, MA: Harvard University Graduate School of Education.

Katz, M. (1959). *You: Today and tomorrow* (3rd ed.). Princeton, NJ: Educational Testing Service.

Katz, M. (1962). Interpreting Kuder Preference Record–Vocational scores: Ispative or normative? *Vocational Guidance Quarterly, 10,* 96–100.

Katz, M. (1963). *Decisions and values: A rationale for secondary school guidance.* New York: College Entrance Examination Board.

Katz, M. (1965). Review of Kuder Preference Record–Vocational. In O. Buros (Ed.), *The sixth mental measurements yearbook* (pp. 1285–1292). Highland Park, NJ: The Gryphon Press.

Katz, M. (1966a). A model of guidance for career decision-making. *Vocational Guidance Quarterly, 15,* 2–10.

Katz, M. (1966b). Criteria for evaluation of guidance. In R. Hummel (Ed.), *Occupational information and vocational guidance for non-college youth* (pp. 167–182). Pittsburgh: University of Pittsburgh.

Katz, M. (1968). *Learning to make wise decisions* (ETS Research Memorandum 68–14). Princeton, NJ: Educational Testing Service.

Katz, M. (1969a). Interests and values. *Journal of Counseling Psychology, 16,* 460–462.

Katz, M. (1969b). Theoretical foundations of guidance. *Review of Educational Research, 30,* 127–140.

Katz, M. (1973). The name and nature of vocational guidance. In H. Borow (Ed.), *Career guidance for a new age* (pp. 83–133). Boston: Houghton–Mifflin.

Katz, M. (1974). Career decision-making: A computer-based System of Interactive Guidance and Information (SIGI). In *Measurement for self-understanding and personal development. Proceedings of the 1973 Invitational Conference* (pp. 43–69). Princeton, NJ: Educational Testing Service.

Katz, M. (1975). *A computer-based System of Interactive Guidance and Information.* Princeton, NJ: Educational Testing Service.

Katz, M. (1978a). Prepare for making career decisions. In D. Tiedeman, M. Katz, A. Miller-Tiedeman, & S. Osipow (Eds.), *The cross-sectional story of early career development as revealed by the National Assessment of Educational Progress* (pp. 47–90). Washington, DC: American Personnel and Guidance Association.

Katz, M. (1978b). Review of Career Maturity Inventory. In O. Buros (Ed.), *The eighth mental measurements yearbook* (pp. 1558–1567). Highland Park, NJ: The Gryphon Press.

Katz, M. (1979). Assessment of career decision making: Process and outcome. In A. Mitchell, G. Jones, & J. Krumboltz (Eds.), *Social learning and career decision making* (pp. 81–101). Cranston, RI: Carroll Press.

Katz, M. (1980). SIGI: An interactive guide to career decision-making. *Journal of College Student Personnel, 21,* 34–40.

Katz, M. (1986). The Buddha and the computer: Career guidance in Taiwan of China. In W. Bingham (Ed.), *A cross-cultural analysis of transition from school to work* (pp. 29–42). Paris: Unesco.

Katz, M., & Norris, L. (1972). The contribution of academic interest measures to the differential prediction of marks. *Journal of Educational Measurement, 9,* 1–11.

Katz, M., Norris, L., & Halpern, G. (1970). *The measurement of academic interests: Part I. Characteristics of the Academic Interest Measures* (CEEB RDR 70–71, No. 4, and ETS Research Bulletin 70–57). Princeton, NJ: Educational Testing Service.

Katz, M., Norris, L., & Kirsh, E. (1969). *Development of a structured interview to explore vocational decision-making* (ETS Research Memorandum 69–30). Princeton, NJ: Educational Testing Service.

Katz, M. Norris, L., & Pears, L. (1976). *Simulated occupational choice: A measure of competencies in career decision-making.* Princeton, NJ: Educational Testing Service.

Katz, M., Norris, L., & Pears, L. (1978). Simulated occupational choice: A diagnostic measure of competencies in career decision making. *Measurement and Evaluation in Guidance, 10,* 222–239; *11,* 59.

Katz, M., & Shatkin, L. (1980). *Computer-assisted guidance: Concepts and practices* (ETS Research Report 80–1). Princeton, NJ: Educational Testing Service.

Katz, M., & Shatkin, L. (1983). Characteristics of computer-assisted guidance. *Counseling Psychologist, 11,* 15–31.

Kelley, S., Chirikos, T., & Finn, M. (1975). *Manpower forecasting in the U.S.: An evaluation of the state of the art.* Columbus: Ohio State University Center for Human Resources Research.

Kelly, G. (1955). *The psychology of constructs.* New York: Norton.

Kilborn, P. (1990, July 1). Brave new world seen for robots appears stalled by quirks and costs. *New York Times,* p. 16.

Kline, M., & Schneck, J. (1950). An hypnotic experimental approach to the genesis of occupational interests and choice. *British Journal of Medical Hypnotism, 1.*

Koch, J. (1974). Technicians: Need-environment congruity and self-investment in organizational roles. *Sociology of Work and Occupations, I,* 175–196.

Kohen, A., Grasso, J., Myers, S., & Shields, P. (1977). *A longitudinal study of the educational and labor market experience of young men: Career thresholds* (Vol. 6, R & D Monograph 16). Washington, DC: U.S. Department of Labor.

Kohut, A., & DeStefano, L. (1989). Working in America: Modern employees expect more from their careers; job dissatisfaction particularly high among the young. *Gallup Poll News Service, 54,* 17.

Kroll, A., Dinklage, L., Lee, J., Morley, E., & Wilson, E. (1970). *Career development: Growth and crisis.* New York: Wiley.

Krumboltz, J. (1965). Agenda for counseling. *Journal of Counseling Psychology, 12,* 226.

Krumboltz, J. (1966a). Behavioral goals for counseling. *Journal of Counseling Psychology, 13,* 153–159.

Krumboltz, J. (1966b). *Stating the goals of counseling* (Monograph No. 1). Los Angeles: California Counseling and Guidance Association.

Krumboltz, J. (1979). *The effect of alternative career decision-making strategies on the quality of resulting decisions.* Stanford, CA: Stanford University School of Education.

Kuder, G. (1960). *Kuder Preference Record – Vocational*. Chicago: Science Research Associates.

Laing, J., Swaney, K., & Prediger, D. (1984). Integrating vocational interest inventory results and expressed choices. *Journal of Vocational Behavior, 25*, 304–315.

Lancaster, A., & Berne, R. (1981). *Employer-sponsored career development programs* (Information Series No. 231). Columbus: National Center for Research in Vocational Education, Ohio State University.

Last, A. (1978). Computer-assisted guidance in Britain: Will the development be of use to adults? *Journal of Occupational Psychology, 51*, 49–53.

Levin, H. (1977). Review of *Ph.D's. and the American labor market* by A. M. Cartter and *The overeducated American* by R. Freeman. *Harvard Educational Review, 47*, 226–231.

Levy, F. (1989). Paying for college: A new look at family income trends. *College Board Review, 152*, 18.

Lindsay, P., & Knox, W. (1984). Continuity and change in work values among young adults: A longitudinal study. *American Journal of Sociology, 89*, 918–931.

Lipman-Blumen, J. (1976). The implications for family structure of changing sex roles. *Social Casework, 57*, 67–69.

Lipman-Blumen, J., & Tickamyer, A. (1975). Sex-roles in transition: A ten-year perspective. *Annual Review of Sociology, I*, 297–337.

Locke, E. (1976). The nature and causes of job satisfaction. In M. Dunnette (Ed.), *Handbook of industrial and organizational psychology* (pp. 1297–1349). Chicago: Rand McNally.

Lord, F. (1962). Cutting scores and errors of measurement. *Psychometrika, 27*, 19–30.

Louviere, J. (1988). *Analyzing decision making: Metric conjoint analysis*. Beverly Hills, CA: Sage.

Lusterman, S. (1977). *Education in industry*. New York: The Conference Board.

Lynd, R., & Lynd, H. (1937). *Middletown in transition: A study in cultural conflicts*. New York: Harcourt, Brace.

Marland, S. (1974). *Career education: A proposal for reform*. New York: McGraw-Hill.

Marrou, H. (1982). *History of education in antiquity*. Madison: University of Wisconsin Press. (Original French work published 1948)

Maslow, A. (1954). *Motivation of personality*. New York: Harper.

Mason, K., Czajka, J., & Arber, S. (1976). Change in U.S. women's sex-role attitudes, 1964–1974. *American Sociological Review, 41*, 573–596.

Medical Education in the United States, 1987–1988. (1988 p. 1066).

Metfessel, M. (1947). A proposal for quantitative reporting of comparative judgments. *Journal of Psychology, 24*, 229–235.

Mezirow, J., Darkenwold, G., & Knox, A. (1975). *Last gamble on education: Dynamics of adult basic education*. Washington, DC: Adult Education Association.

Miller, D., & Form, W. (1951). *Industrial sociology: The sociology of industrial organizations*. New York: Harper & Row.

Mollenkopf, W. (1950). Predicted differences and differences between predictions. *Psychometrika, 15*, 409–417.

Morgan, M., Hall, D., & Martier, A. (1979). Career development strategies in industry: Where are we and where should we be? *Personnel, 56*, 13–30.

Morse, N., & Weiss, R. (1955). The function and meaning of work and the job. *American Sociological Review, 20*, 191–198.

Mortimer, J. (n.d.). *Changing attitudes toward work: Highlights of the literature*. Scarsdale, NY: Work in America Institute.

Mortimer, J., & Lorence, J. (1979). Work experience and occupational value socialization. *American Journal of Sociology, 84*, 1361–1385.

Mortimer, J., & Lorence, J. (1981). Comment on Samuel and Lewin-Epstein. *American Journal of Sociology, 87*, 708–714.

MOW International Research Team. (1987). *The meaning of working*. London: Academic Press.

Muller, H. (1953). *The uses of the past*. New York: Oxford University Press.

Naipaul, V. (1990, November 5). Our universal civilization. *New York Times* p. 21.

Newman, J., Fuqua, D., & Minger, C. (1990). Further evidence for the use of career subtypes in defining career status. *Career Development Quarterly, 39*, 178-188.

Newton, W. (1989). Towards 2000 via 1992: Implications of likely technical and other developments. In A. Watts (Ed.), *Computers in career guidance*. Cambridge, UK: CRAC.

Norris, L., & Cochran, D. (1977). The SIGI prediction system: Predicting college grades with and without tests. *Measurement and Evaluation in Guidance, 10*, 134-143.

Norris, L., & Katz, M. (1970). *The measurement of academic interests, Part II: The predictive validities of academic interest measures* (College Board Research and Development Report 70-71, No. 5, and ETS Research Bulletin 70-67). Princeton, NJ: Education Testing Service.

Norris, L., Katz, M., & Chapman, J. (1978). Sex differences in the career decision-making process (ETS PR 78-3). Princeton, NJ: Educational Testing Service.

Norris, L., Shatkin, L., Schott, P., & Bennett, M. (1985). *SIGI PLUS: Development and field test of the computer-based System of Interactive Guidance and Information . . . PLUS more*. Princeton, NJ: Educational Testing Service.

Oppenheim, P. (1957). Dimensions of knowledge. *Revue Internationale de Philosophie, 40*, 1-41.

O'Toole, J. (Ed.). (1973). *Work in America*. Cambridge: MIT Press.

Parsons, F. (1909) *Choosing a vocation*. Boston: Houghton–Mifflin.

Paterson, D., & Darley, J. (1936). *Men, women, and jobs*. Minneapolis. University of Minnesota Press.

Paterson, D., Gerken, C., & Hahn, M. (1941). *The Minnesota occupational rating scales*. Chicago: Science Research Associates.

Pears, L., & Weber, A. (1976, 1978, 1980, 1982). *Occupational information in SIGI. A handbook for data collection, interpretation, preparation, and documentation*. Princeton, NJ: Educational Testing Service.

Personick, V., & Sylvester, R. (1976). Evaluation of the BLS 1970 economic and employment projections. *Monthly Labor Review, 99*, 13-26.

Peterson, R. (1979). *Lifelong learning in America*. San Francisco: Jossey–Bass.

Peterson, R., & Hefferlin, J. (1975). *Postsecondary alternatives to meet the educational needs of California's adults* (Final report). Sacramento: Postsecondary Alternatives Study, California Legislature.

Pitz, G., & Harren, V. (1980). An analysis of career decision making from the point of view of information processing and decision theory. *Journal of Vocational Behavior, 16*, 320-346.

Plant, P. (1991). Transnational vocational guidance in the EC. *Educational and Vocational Guidance, 52*, 17-20.

Pool, R. (1990). Who will do science in the 1990s? *Science, 248*, 433-435.

Postman, L., Bruner, J., & McGinnies, E. (1948). Personal values as selective factors in perceptions. *Journal of Abnormal and Social Psychology, 43*, 142-154.

Pyle, K. (1976). *The relationship of group career counseling and computer-assisted career guidance to the career maturity of community college students*. Unpublished doctoral dissertation, University of Florida, Gainsville.

Quinn, R., Staines, G., & McCullough, M. (1974). Job satisfaction: Is there a trend? *Manpower Research Monograph No. 30*. Washington, DC: U.S. Department of Labor.

Raiffa, H. (1968). *Decision analysis*. Reading, MA: Addison-Wesley.

Reinhold, R. (1971, March 3). Recent graduates of Harvard found taking manual jobs. *New York Times*, p. 45.

Richards, I. (1968, February 3). The secret of 'Feedforward.' *Saturday Review*, 14-17.

Risser, J., & Tulley, J. (1977). *Pasadena City College* (SIGI Project Research Study). Pasadena, CA: Author.

Rockwell, P., & Rothney, J. (1961). Some social ideas of pioneers in the guidance movement. *Personnel and Guidance Journal, 40,* 349–354.

Roe, A. (1956). *The psychology of occupations.* New York: Wiley.

Rokeach, M. (1971). Long-range experimental modification of values, attitudes, and behavior. *American Psychologist, 26,* 453–459.

Rokeach, M. (1973). *The nature of human values.* New York: The Free Press.

Rue, L. (1982, September 8). While most of the world prepares for less, a generation of U.S. students wants more. *Chronicle of Higher Education,* p. 25.

Rutkevich, M. (Ed.). (1969). *The career plans of youth* (M. Yanowitch, Trans.). White Plains, NY: International Arts and Sciences Press.

Salters, L. (1984). *SIGI, values-based computer software – its effect on undecided students.* Unpublished doctoral dissertation, University of South Carolina, Columbia.

Schaffer, R. (1953). Job satisfaction as related to need satisfaction in work. *Psychological Monographs,* No. 364.

Schmidt, F., Hunter, J., & Northrop, L. (1983). *Cognitive skill correlates of success in the world of work for non college graduates.* Office of Examination Development Report 87-6, Washington, DC: U.S. Office of Personnel Management.

Schor, J. (1992). *The overworked American.* New York: Basic Books.

Segal, S. (1953). *Role of personality factors in vocational choice: A study of accountants and creative writers.* Unpublished doctoral dissertation, University of Michigan, Ann Arbor.

Shartle, C. (1952). *Occupational information.* New York: Prentice-Hall.

Shepard, R. (1964). On subjectively optimum selection among multivariate alternatives. In M. Shelby & G. Bryan (Eds.), *Human judgments and optimality* (pp. 257–281). New York: Wiley.

Shimberg, B., & Katz, M. (1962). Evaluation of a guidance text. *Personnel and Guidance Journal, 41,* 126–132.

Shoben, E. (1965). The counseling experience as personal development. *Personnel and Guidance Journal, 44,* 224–230.

Siegel, P., Hodge, R., & Rossi, P. (1974). *Occupational prestige in the United States.* New York: Academic Press.

Small, L. (1953). Personality determinants of vocational choice. *Psychological Monographs* (No. 351).

Smith, D. (1979). *Social stratification, perceived rewards and job satisfaction.* Unpublished doctoral dissertation, Princeton University, Princeton, NJ.

Spilerman, S. (1977). Careers, labor market structure, and socioeconomic achievement. *American Journal of Sociology, 83,* 551–593.

Sproat, K. (1979). Using longitudinal surveys to track young workers. *Monthly Labor Review, 102,* 28–33.

Stephens, W. (1970). *Social reforms and the origins of vocational guidance.* Washington, DC: National Vocational Guidance Association, Division of the American Personnel and Guidance Association.

Sternberg, R. (Ed.). (1988). *The nature of creativity: Contemporary psychological perspectives.* New York: Cambridge University Press.

Stewart, N. (1947). AGCT scores of army personnel grouped by occupation. *Occupations, 26,* 5–41.

Strong, E. (1943). *Vocational interests of men and women.* Stanford, CA: Stanford University Press.

Strong, E. (1948). *Vocational interests of men and women.* Stanford, CA: Stanford University Press.

Strong, E. (1958). Satisfactions and interests. *American Psychologist, 13,* 449–456.

Strong, E. (1966). *Strong Vocational Interest Blanks* (Revised by D. Campbell). Stanford, CA: Stanford University Press.

Super, D. (1953). A theory of vocational development. *The American Psychologist, 8,* 185–190.

Super, D. (1976). *Career education and the meanings of work* (U.S. Office of Education). Washington, DC: U.S. Government Printing Office.

Super, D. (n.d.). *The use of multifactor tests in guidance* (Reprint series from *Personnel and Guidance Journal*). Washington, DC: American Personnel and Guidance Association.

Super, D., Crites, J., Hummel, R., Moser, H., Overstreet, P., & Warnath, C. (1957). *Vocational development: A framework for research.* New York: Teachers College, Columbia University.

Super, D., Kowalski, R., & Gotkin, E. (1967). *Floundering and trial after high school.* New York: Teachers College, Columbia University.

Super, D., & Overstreet, P. (1960). *The vocational maturity of ninth-grade boys.* New York: Teachers College, Columbia University.

Swerdloff, S. (1969). How good were manpower projections for the 1960's? *Monthly Labor Review, 92,* 17–22.

Tatsuoka, M. (1956). *Joint probability of membership and success in a group: An index which combines the information from discriminant and regression analyses as applied to the guidance problem.* Unpublished doctoral dissertation, Harvard University, Cambridge, MA.

Temme, L. (1975). *Occupation: Meanings and measures.* Washington, DC: Bureau of Social Science Research.

Thomas, L. (1979). Causes of mid-career changes from high status careers. *Vocational Guidance Quarterly, 27,* 202–208.

Thorndike, R. (1985). The central role of general ability in prediction. *Multivariate Behavioral Research, 20,* 241–254.

Thorndike, R., & Hagen, E. (1959). *10,000 careers.* New York: Wiley.

Thorndike, R., Weiss, D., & Dawis, R. (1968). Canonical correlations of vocational interests and vocational needs. *Journal of Counseling Psychology, 15,* 101–106.

Tiedeman, D. (1958). *The Harvard studies in career development in current perspective.* Cambridge, MA: Harvard Graduate School of Education.

Tiedeman, D., Katz, M., Miller-Tiedeman, A., & Osipow, S. (1978). *The cross-sectional story of early career development as revealed by the National Assessment of Educational Progress.* Washington, DC: American Personnel and Guidance Association.

Tittle, C. (1981). *Careers and family: Sex roles and adolescent life plans.* Beverly Hills, CA: Sage.

Tumin, M. (1970). Evaluation of effectiveness of education: Some problems and prospects. *Interchange, 1,* 3.

Tyler, L. (1978). *Individuality: Human possibilities and personal choice in the psychological development of men and women.* San Francisco: Jossey-Bass.

U.S. Bureau of the Census. *1970 Census of population: Classified index of industries and occupations.* Washington, DC: Bureau of the Census.

U.S. Department of Commerce, Office of Federal Statistical Policy and Standards (1977). *Standard occupational classification manual.* Washington, DC: U.S. Government Printing Office.

U.S. Department of Health, Education, and Welfare/Office of Education, Bureau of Adult, Vocational, and Technical Education. (n.d.). *Working papers on career education.* Washington, DC: Office of Education.

U.S. Department of Labor. (1965). *Dictionary of occupational titles* (3rd ed., Vol. 2). Washington, DC: U.S. Government Printing Office.

U.S. Department of Labor. (1970). *Manual for the USES General Aptitude Test Battery: Section III, development.* Washington, DC: U.S. Government Printing Office.

U.S. Department of Labor. (1972). *Handbook for analyzing jobs*. Washington, DC: Author.

U.S. Department of Labor. (1974). *Occupational supply* (Bulletin 1816). Washington, DC: Author.

U.S. Department of Labor. (1977). *Dictionary of occupational titles* (4th ed.). Washington, DC: U.S. Government Printing Office.

U.S. Department of Labor. (1979). *Guide for occupational exploration*. Washington, DC: U.S. Government Printing Office.

U.S. Department of Labor. (1986). *Dictionary of occupational titles* (4th ed. supplement). Washington, DC: U.S. Government Printing Office.

U.S. Department of Labor. (1989). *Working capital*. Washington, DC: Author.

U.S. Department of Labor, Bureau of Labor Statistics. (1988). *Occupational outlook handbook*. Washington, DC: U.S. Government Printing Office.

U.S. Department of Labor, Bureau of Labor Statistics. (1990, January) *Employment and earnings*. Washington, DC: authors.

U.S. Employment Service. (1958). *Guide to the use of the General Aptitude Test Battery*. Washington, DC: U.S. Government Printing Office.

Vetter, L., Winkfield, P., Lowry, C., & Ranson, R. (1977). *Career planning programs for women employees: A national survey* (Research & Development Series No. 135). Columbus: National Center for Research in Vocational Education, Ohio State University.

Walker, J., & Gutteridge, T. (1979). *Career planning practices. An AMA survey report*. New York: AMACOM (a division of American Management Associations).

Watts, A. (Ed.). (1989). *Computers in careers guidance*. Cambridge, UK: CRAC.

Weber, M. (1930). *The Protestant ethic and the spirit of capitalism*. New York: Scribner.

Weiss, D. (1972). Review of General Aptitude Test Battery. In O. Buros (Ed.), *The seventh mental measurements yearbook* (pp. 1055–1061). Highland Park, NJ: The Gryphon Press.

Westbrook, B., Sanford, E., & Donnelly, M. (1989). The relationship between career maturity test scores and appropriateness of career choices: A replication. *Journal of Vocational Behavior, 38*, 20–32.

Whitney, D. (1969). Predicting from expressed vocational choice: A review. *Personnel and Guidance Journal, 48*, 279–286.

Wilensky, H. (1964). Varieties of work experience. In H. Borow (Ed.), *Man in a world at work* (pp. 125–154). Boston: Houghton–Mifflin.

Witkin, H., Moore, C., Oltman, P., Goodenough, D., Friedman, F., Owen, D., & Raskin, E. (1977). Role of the field-dependent and field-independent cognitive styles in academic evolution: A longitudinal study. *Journal of Educational Psychology, 69*, 197–211.

Yaeger, J., & Leider, R. (1975). Career planning: Personnel in the third party role. *Human Resource Management, 14*, 31–36.

Zytowski, D., & Hay, R. (1984). Do birds of a feather flock together? A test of the similarities within and the differences between five occupations. *Journal of Vocational Behavior, 24*, 242–248.

Author Index

Subject Index

A

Accuracy, 210–213
Adolescence and work, 1
Adult(s), 191
  and design of SIGI/SIGI PLUS,
    202–203
  needs and situations of regarding career
    guidance, 40–42, 48–53
  and planning for retirement, 261–263
  in transition, 192–193
Apprentice training, 28–29
Aptitude, 111–112, 139–144
  sources of concern over, 111
Armed Services Vocational Aptitude
  Battery, 175
Authoring system, 258
Autonomy, 121
  and career decision making (CDM),
    56–58

B

Batch-processing system, 197
Behaviorism
  and self-understanding, 115–117
Bulletin boards, 260
Bureau of Labor Statistics (BLS), 33, 167,
  169–170, 171
Business. *See Corporations*

C

Career, *see also Employment; Job(s);
    Labor market; Occupation(s); Infor-
    mation, occupational; Projection,
    occupational; Vocation; Work*
  advancement, 51
  choice, U.S. vs. other countries, 54
  definition of, 6
  means-end chain regarding, 2–3
  development
    negative consequences of program, 66
    universal stages of, 40
  prospective vs. retrospective perspec-
    tives regarding, 26–27, 35
    self-appraisal vs. self-concept con-
    cerning, 3 transition, 40–41
Career decision making (CDM), 1–36,
  42–43, 79–81
  about occupations and jobs, 17–26
  components of, 3–6
  decisions into actions in, 190–196
    coping, 192–195
    next steps, 195–196
    preparing, 190–192
  democracy and autonomy concerning,
    56–58
  and developmental stages, 44–46
  formal decision analysis in, 177–178
  gender differences in, 242–246

G

Gender, *see also Women*
   differences in career decision making,
      242–246
   feminist movement, 194
   and SIGI PLUS' Coping section, 194–195
   and work, 17, 41
General Aptitude Test Battery (GATB), 93,
      111,
      139–141, 143, 175
   criticism of, 140–141
   predictive validity of, 140
GIS system, 69–70, 141–143
Goal seeking
   long- vs. short-range, 43–44
Goal selection, 219–220
Government
   funding for guidance, 54–55
Growth projections, 170–176
   supply and demand concerning, 172–176
   unreliability of, 171
Guidance. *See Career guidance*
Guidance Inquiry project, 72–73
Guidance models, 54–56, 77, 107, 215
Guidance system. *See Career guidance
      system*
Guide for Occupational Exploration (GOE),
      21–22
   interest areas in, 130–131

H

Hardware
   for computerized guidance system,
      198–200

I

Income. *See Earnings*
Independence, 121
Information acquisition
   structured search vs. direct access,
      83–84, 158–162, 167
Information, occupational, 153–176, 219,
      257, *see also Career; Career decision
      making (CDM); Employment;
      Job(s); Labor market; Projection,
      occupational; Vocation; Work*
   local, in SIGI PLUS' Coping section,
      193–194
   menu of topics in, 159, 160–161

occupational titles, 154–158
occupational topics, 158–163
quality of, 163–176
regarding income, 167
sources of, 164–166
Information services, 259–260
Interactive systems, *see also Computerized
      guidance (CG) system*
   historical progression of, 197–198
Interests
   and occupational activities, 129
   and occupational choice, 20–24
   occupational vs. homogeneous scales to
      measure, 125–128
   structure of, 125–135
   and values regarding self-understanding,
      105–109, 112
ISVD system, 69, 88

J

Job(s), *see also Career; Career decision
      making (CDM); Employment; Labor
      market; Occupation(s); Information,
      occupational; Projection, occupa-
      tional; Vocation; Work*
analysis, 80
attributes, 25–26
changing, 51
decisions about, 4–5
definition of, 6
Job market
   supply and demand regarding, 168–169,
      171–176
Job satisfaction, 13, 14–17, 50, 107, 121
   and values, 113
Job Training Partnership Act (JTPA),
      29–30, 54

K

Kuder Occupational Interest Survey
      (KOIS), 127
Kuder Preference Record-Vocational, 127

L

Labor market, *see also Career; Career deci-
      sion making (CDM); Employment;
      Job(s); Occupation(s); Information,
      occupational; Projection, occupa-
      tional; Vocation; Work*

W

Women, 65, 161, *see also Gender*
  entry or re-entry of into occupations,
    194
  and work, 41
Work, *see also Career; Career decision
    making (CDM); Employment;
    Job(s); Labor market; Occupation(s);
    Information, occupational; Projec-
    tion, occupational; Vocation*
  adolescence vs. adulthood, 1
  alternatives to, 11–12
  commitment to, 11–13
  concept of self-fulfillment in, 9

  decisions about, 4, 7–17
  definition of, 6
  and enhancement of self-esteem, 9
  extrinsic vs. intrinsic values regarding,
    14–17, 18
  gender differences regarding, 17, 41
  historic overview of, 7–10
  importance of choice of, 9
  as a means of upward mobility, 9
  reasons for wanting to, 10–17
  in relation to occupation, 1–2
  religious ideas about, 8–9
  views on of U.S. vs. other countries, 11
  as a vocation, 7
  white-collar vs. blue-collar, 16

$$120$$
$$\underline{12}$$
$$240$$
$$120$$
$$\underline{}$$
$$1,440$$
$$1$$